Sparks

3-9-65

(64-10319)

ALBERT SIDNEY JOHNSTON

Soldier of Three Republics

Shiloh was hallowed ground to Dr. Roland as he was growing up in West Tennessee, only an hour's drive from the famed battlefield. Its historic spots—the Hornets' Nest, the Peach Orchard, the Bloody Pond—were branded into his memory. So were Shiloh's great characters—Johnston and Beauregard, Grant and Sherman. When, as professor at Tulane University, Dr. Roland found there a store of Johnston's private papers, he felt "compelled" to write this account of a distinguished citizen and soldier of three republics. His research is thorough, extending to widely scattered and little-known manuscripts, and his accounts of battles are clear and precise. The description of the Battle of Shiloh, in particular, leaves the reader with the feeling of having participated in that tragic event.

Dr. Roland, author of two books on Civil War subjects, is now Head of the Department of History, College of Arts and Sciences, Tulane University.

ALBERT SIDNEY JOHNSTON

Soldier of Three Republics

By Charles P. Roland

UNIVERSITY OF TEXAS PRESS, AUSTIN

Published with the assistance of a grant
from the Ford Foundation
under its program for the support of publications
in the humanities and social sciences

Manufactured in the United States of America

TO

KAREN, CLIFF, AND CHARLES

PREFACE

Shiloh was hallowed ground to me in my childhood. Born and bred in West Tennessee, only an hour's drive from the famed Civil War battlefield, I visited there often. I went there on family occasions, on school excursions, to religious revival meetings. Shiloh's historic sites—the Hornets' Nest, the Sunken Road, the Peach Orchard, the Bloody Pond—were forever branded into my memory. So were Shiloh's historic figures—Johnston and Beauregard, Grant and Sherman. I listened to the saga of valor at Shiloh; I looked upon the spot where Albert Sidney Johnston fell at the head of the Confederate Army; I pondered the effect of his death upon the outcome of the battle. His presence seemed to abide at Shiloh.

Years later I came to Tulane University to teach history. In the University library, I discovered, were Johnston's private papers. I felt compelled to write the story of his life.

CHARLES P. ROLAND

New Orleans, Louisiana

ACKNOWLEDGMENTS

I wish to acknowledge my gratitude to the many persons and institutions whose assistance has made it possible for me to write this book. I especially wish to thank William R. Hogan, chairman of the Department of History, Tulane University, for calling to my attention the presence of Albert Sidney Johnston's private papers in the Howard–Tilton Memorial Library, Tulane University; Connie G. Griffith, head of the Manuscripts Division of the Howard–Tilton Memorial Library, for service "above and beyond the call of duty" in placing these papers at my convenience; and Dorothy J. Whittemore and Betty A. Mailhes of the Reference Department, Howard–Tilton Memorial Library, for their diligence in procuring for my use many of the books, articles, and maps required for the writing of this work.

I am indebted to the following persons who have read all or portions of the manuscript and have made invaluable suggestions for improving it: Bell I. Wiley, William C. Binkley, William R. Hogan, Ellen Whitney, Norman F. Furniss, Otis A. Singletary, Grady McWhiney, Hugh F. Rankin, Edison B. Allen, and Allie Lee Roland.

I wish to express my appreciation to the staff members of the following libraries and repositories who have assisted in providing me with information for this book: the Archives, University of Texas Library; the Southern Historical Collection, University of North Carolina Library; the Duke University Library; the University of Utah Library; the Manuscripts Division, Brigham Young University Library; the Collection of Western Americana, Yale University Library; the Bancroft Library, University of California; the United States Military Academy Archives; the National Archives; the Library of Congress; the manuscripts departments of the Historical Society of Pennsylvania; the Texas State Archives; the Texas State Library; the Tennessee State Archives; the Utah Historical Society;

the California Historical Society; the Illinois State Historical Library; the New York Public Library; the Rosenberg Library, Galveston, Texas; the Huntington Library; the Church Historian's Office, Church of Jesus Christ of Latter-Day Saints; the Shiloh National Military Park; and the Jefferson Davis Shrine.

I am thankful to the following institutions for the generous financial support that has enabled me to accomplish this work: the American Philosophical Society for supporting my research for one summer; the John T. Monroe Scholarship of Tulane University for supporting my research for two summers; the Tulane University Council on Research for granting me a year's compensated leave of absence in order to complete my research; and the John Simon Guggenheim Memorial Foundation for a fellowship grant during my year of research leave.

I wish to acknowledge the careful work of the cartographers for this book—Frances Jean Hansen, who made nine of the sixteen maps, and Ethel S. Vernon, who made seven of them.

I acknowledge permission to quote from the following published works:

The Utah War: Journal of Albert Tracy, 1858–1860. Edited by J. Cecil Alter. Published by the Utah State Historical Society, Salt Lake City, Utah. Copyright, 1945.

The Rise of U. S. Grant. By Arthur L. Conger. Copyright, 1931, by the Century Company, all rights reserved, including the right to reproduce this book, or portions thereof, in any form.

Samuel Maverick, Texan, 1803–1870. Edited by Rena Maverick Green. Privately printed, 1952. Used with the permission of George M. Green, independent executor of the estate of Mrs. Rena Maverick Green.

The Utah Expedition, 1857–1858: Letters of Captain Jesse A. Gove. Edited by Otis G. Hammond. Published by New Hampshire Historical Society, Concord, New Hampshire. Copyright, 1928.

Black Hawk: An Autobiography. Edited by Donald Jackson. Published by University of Illinois Press, Urbana, Illinois. Copyright, 1955.

On War. By Karl von Clausewitz. Translated by J. J. Graham. Published by E. P. Dutton & Company, Inc. Copyright, 1940.

Texas Indian Papers, 1825–1843. Edited by Dorman H. Winfrey and others. Published by Texas State Library, Austin, Texas. Copyright, 1959–1961.

"Union Discipline and Leadership in the Civil War," *Marine Corps Gazette* (January, 1956). By Bruce Catton. Used with the permission of the editor and publisher.

"Albert Sidney Johnston and the Loss of Forts Henry and Donelson," *Journal of Southern History,* XXIII (February, 1957). By Charles P. Roland. Used with the permission of the managing editor.

"Albert Sidney Johnston and the Shiloh Campaign," *Civil War History,* IV (December, 1958). By Charles P. Roland. Used with the permission of the State University of Iowa, publisher of *Civil War History.*

P.G.T. Beauregard: Napoleon in Gray. By T. Harry Williams. Published by the Louisiana State University Press, Baton Rouge. Copyright, 1954.

Acknowledgment is made of permission from the Church Historian's Office, Church of Jesus Christ of Latter-Day Saints, to quote from the "Journal History of the Church of Jesus Christ of Latter-Day Saints"; from the New York Public Library to quote from the J. W. Phelps Journal and Papers; from the Huntington Library to quote from manuscripts by Henry W. Bigler, Orville S. Cox, Silas Haris, Edwin Harley, John Langston, Hannah H. H. Romney, Azariah Smith, Elias Smith, and Allen Joseph Stout; from the University of North Carolina Library to quote from the Jeremy F. Gilmer Papers; from the Western Reserve Historical Association to quote from the Braxton Bragg Papers; from the Howard–Tilton Memorial Library, Tulane University, to quote from the Mrs. Mason Barret Collection; from Duke University Library to quote from the Alfred Cumming Papers; from the Historical Society of Pennsylvania to quote from the Josiah Stoddard Johnston Papers; from the Western Americana Collection, Yale University Library, to quote from the Brigham Young Papers; and from the University of the South to quote from the Bishop Leonidas Polk Papers.

C.P.R.

CONTENTS

ILLUSTRATIONS

Following page 192

Albert Sidney Johnston

Mrs. Albert Sidney Johnston and
a Pen-and-ink Sketch by Eliza Johnston

*Paintings of Bluebonnet, Gaillardia, Cactus Bloom,
and Turk's Cap by Mrs. Albert Sidney Johnston*

United States Military Academy in the 1820's

Battle of the Bad Axe

View of Monterrey in the Mexican War and
Review of Texas Troops in the Mexican War

The March to Fort Bridger and
Fort Bridger in the Winter of 1857–1858

Battle of Shiloh

MAPS

ALBERT SIDNEY JOHNSTON
Soldier of Three Republics

Prologue

~~~~~~

ALBERT SIDNEY JOHNSTON must have been touched to the heart. Before him was the letter of a Texas mother petitioning that her son, a young Confederate officer, be transferred from Virginia to Johnston's Confederate Army in the west. "I wish him," she said, "to be near the moulding influence of such a Texan, such a soldier, and such a gentleman." [1] In a single poignant line she gave Johnston the three titles most befitting his career.

Johnston was a Texan. Almost three decades before the Civil War, he went to Texas from his native Kentucky to help the young republic in her fight to preserve independence. His love for Texas grew with the passing years. He led her army; he labored with his hands in her soil; he defended her frontiers against the Indians. When on one occasion he stood to gain financially by giving up his Texas citizenship, he scorned the suggestion. "This [gain] I would regard as a mere mess of pottage in comparison with my citizenship," he exclaimed.[2] When Texas left the Union, Johnston gave his sword

[1] Mary A. Maverick to Albert Sidney Johnston, February 17, 1862, in the Mrs. Mason Barret Collection of Albert Sidney and William Preston Johnston Papers (hereinafter cited as Johnston Papers, Barret Collection).

[2] Johnston to William Preston Johnston, August 27, 1859, *ibid.*

to his adopted state; he did it in sorrow, for his heart was cruelly torn between conflicting allegiances. "Texas has made me a rebel twice," he said. Near life's end he told a kinsman, "When I die, I want a handful of Texas earth on my breast." [3] Of all her sons, Texas had none more loyal than Albert Sidney Johnston.

Johnston was a soldier. Whether he had the talents of a great general, or wanted them, can never positively be known; he was killed in his one battle as a combat commander, where he made decisions both wise and unwise. He did not fulfill the exaggerated estimates of his ability that preceded the Civil War or followed it; yet he showed himself worthy of colleague and opponent alike. One thing is certain: as a leader of men, Johnston was superb. He considered the welfare of the troops under him an inviolable trust. When hardship or hazard was their lot, he shared it without hesitation. Johnston's last words to his embattled soldiers were, "I will lead you." Small wonder that his associates looked upon him with deference. They "not only respected him but loved him," wrote one who years before had served under him in the United States Army. [4]

Johnston was a gentleman. He was also a devoted husband and kind father; reared in the chivalric tradition of the Old South, he exalted womanhood as above reproach. He strove always to spare the feelings of others. "In bringing one's duties before them," said an acquaintance, "it was done in such a way as to make them feel it was suggested by their own sense of right & not his." He commanded subordinates not as a martinet, but through "high-bred courtesy, which gained him the affection of all who came near him." He veiled his military authority under the "politeness of the gentleman." [5] "He was one of the most unselfish men I ever knew," recalled a former comrade, "and one of the most just and considerate to those under his command." [6] To loyalty and valor, Johnston added grace.

Character was his sustaining force. He was mortal; his conduct

[3] Eliza Johnston to Colonel Stevenson, December 16, 1884; and M. D. Hancock to William Preston Johnston, n.d., 1873, both in *ibid.* William Preston Johnston, *The Life of General Albert Sidney Johnston*, p. 699 (hereinafter cited as Johnston, *Life of Johnston*).

[4] Richard W. Johnson, *A Soldier's Reminiscences in Peace and War*, p. 107.

[5] Thomas C. Reynolds to William Preston Johnston, November 13, 1875, Johnston Papers, Barret Collection.

[6] Johnson, *A Soldier's Reminiscences in Peace and War*, p. 107.

sometimes fell short of the high code of life that he espoused; but his faith in the code never dimmed; his efforts to fulfill it never abated. Reverence for God and respect for man were his guiding principles. Johnston's associates, whether eulogists or critics, felt the effect of his character. Testimony to this quality in him survived the hottest passions of the age—those of the Civil War; many of his admirers were men who fought for the Union.

Johnston regarded the fulfillment of duty as man's noblest ambition. "Fealty to duty was the prevailing and absorbing characteristic of General Johnston," wrote a Unionist friend. "He may have been mistaken, for he was not infallible, but he followed his mental and moral instincts and conclusions with unwavering fidelity." [7] General Grant, an associate of Johnston in the United States Army before the Civil War and Johnston's supreme adversary in the war, disparaged Johnston's generalship but called him "a man of high character." [8] General Beauregard, who shared Johnston's one Civil War campaign, and who, like Grant, looked with disdain upon Johnston as a general, said of him, "[General Johnston] was a great & good man . . . and was a brave soldier & an unselfish patriot. I am one of the *many* . . . who believe that, if he had been at the head of our Confederate Government during the late war, the latter might have ended very differently, if not with success to us, certainly with less disastrous consequences." [9]

Albert Sidney Johnston served the United States of America, the Republic of Texas, and the Confederacy; he was a distinguished citizen and gallant soldier of three commonwealths.

[7] N. J. Eaton to William Preston Johnston, January 24, 1856, Johnston Papers, Barret Collection.

[8] Ulysses S. Grant, *Personal Memoirs of U. S. Grant*, p. 187.

[9] P. G. T. Beauregard, "Extract of a Letter to Marrin, March 30, 1887," P. G. T. Beauregard Papers.

Origins of a Soldier

~~~~~~

ALBERT SIDNEY JOHNSTON was born on February 2, 1803, in Washington, Kentucky. He came of a blending of two powerful, conflicting strains in American culture: he was a New Englander by ancestry and a Southerner by birth and association. New England left its trace on Johnston's life; of his Puritan antecedents he once said, "Notwithstanding their follies, their fantastic & ludicrous mental constitution, we no doubt owe [to them] nearly all that is valuable in our glorious form of government. . . . There is not much in them to love, but a good deal to laugh at & pity & much to admire." [1] Nevertheless, environment prevailed over blood in the shaping of Johnston's character; he died defending the South against the land of his fathers.

Johnston's forebears in New England were respectable, if not distinguished. His grandfather, Archibald Johnston, was a captain in the American Revolution and later was half-owner of an iron works at Salisbury, Connecticut. Though Archibald Johnston accumulated a measure of property, his family remembered him as a mechanic.

[1] Johnston to William Preston Johnston, January 19, 1851, Johnston Papers, Barret Collection.

"Your ancestors have risen from the same level on both sides," Albert Sidney Johnston told his son, "if those who really constitute the greatness of our country, that is the working men, may be said to be on a level from which others not so worthy may be said to rise." [2] Archibald Johnston sent one of his five sons, John Johnston, to the nearby medical school of Litchfield. In 1788, after practising medicine briefly in Salisbury, John Johnston departed from New England and took his wife and three sons to settle at Washington in Mason County, Kentucky.[3] He left no record of his reason for the move; perhaps he simply shared the prevailing American urge to go west.

They found Mason County a frontier. Bordered on the north by the Ohio River, the county embraced much of the northeastern portion of the District of Kentucky. Settled only twenty years before, the vast county yet held fewer than three thousand inhabitants. Washington was a village of mud-daubed log huts set about a rude stockade; hunting rivaled planting as a source of food for the people. The war whoop still sounded in the settlements; indomitable Indian fighter Simon Kenton still led his bands of Kentucky riflemen across the Ohio to chastise the audacity of the tribes. Only strong men could thrive in such a country.[4]

John Johnston was a strong man, bold of address, sound of body, and keen of mind. One of the earliest physicians in the county, he soon had a large medical practice and was diligent and capable in his profession. Other practitioners were said to have called in Dr. Johnston in desperate or difficult cases.[5] He became a leader in the community; by 1793 he was a member of the Board of Trustees of Washington.[6]

That year John Johnston's first wife died. A year later he married Abigail Harris, who was to become the mother of Albert Sidney. Abigail was the daughter of another New Englander settled in frontier Kentucky. Her father, Edward Harris, a veteran of the American Revolution, was postmaster at Washington and a member of the town Board of Trustees, along with John Johnston. Harris was a sturdy patriot, a vigorous thinker, and an implacable Presbyterian.

[2] *Ibid.*

[3] Deed, Daniel Johnston to James Johnston, October 30, 1792, in Records of Town Clerk, Salisbury, Connecticut; *Historical Addresses Delivered at the Centennial Celebration in Salisbury, Connecticut*, pp. 36, 53–54.

[4] G. Glenn Clift, *History of Maysville and Mason County*, I, 33, 55, 60.

[5] Johnston, *Life of Johnston*, p. 2.

[6] Clift, *History of Maysville and Mason County*, I, 119.

When instructed to tend office on Sunday, Harris wrote the Postmaster General that he would resign his position rather than violate the day of "divine appointment." [7] Harris's tongue was quick to defend the faith, and his pen turned to lines of religious zeal. "My greatest concern is that I might enjoy the light of God's countenance," he wrote to a friend. "I hope we shall meet where Sin & Sorrow will be at an end: & where Singing Worthy is the Lamb will never have an end." [8] Abigail Harris Johnston was a woman of handsome appearance, strong intellect, and a quiet and gentle nature. Albert Sidney Johnston was heir to the fiber of his New England progenitors.

But Kentucky moulded his character in his youth. Mason County had outgrown its rude beginnings and was now a thriving community, favored with rich soil, a pleasing landscape, and an energetic population, where were united the vitality of the persisting frontier with the grace of mature society. Washington was a county seat. The town lay four miles south of the Ohio River on the stage route from the river port of Maysville to the city of Lexington. Plantations flourished on the labor of Negro slaves or white tenants. Elegant houses in the Federal style of architecture adorned town and countryside: Federal Hill, home of Captain Thomas Marshall (brother of Chief Justice John Marshall), overlooked Washington from the east; Cedar Hill, home of Governor John Chambers, faced the town from the west. Taverns abounded along the way.[9]

Lawyer-politicians of keen sense and compelling oratory led the public mind and served the area in local and national affairs. Henry Clay of Lexington was the rising star of the entire state; John Chambers, Colonel Marshall Key, Judge Adam Beatty, and the Marshall brothers were leaders of Washington. In a day before the coming of public schools, private academies trained the children of those who aspired to education and could afford it. The mansions of society resounded with balls and banquets, and thoroughbreds ran on the track of the Maysville Jockey Club. New England Puritanism lost edge in these surroundings.[10]

---

[7] William Preston Johnston, *The Johnstons of Salisbury,* pp. 56–58.

[8] Edna H. Best, *The Historic Past of Washington, Mason County, Kentucky,* pp. 72–73.

[9] Clift, *History of Maysville and Mason County,* I, 144–149.

[10] Best, *The Historic Past of Washington, Mason County, Kentucky,* pp. 93–98.

The Johnstons shared moderately in the prosperity of the community. In a society that paid highest tribute to landed proprietors and men of the forum, the Johnstons were of the middle class. Dr. Johnston's earnings were spread thin to support a numerous family. He had three children by his first wife; Abigail bore him six others, and after her death, he married a widow with nine of her own. The Johnston home was ample but not pretentious; the fare and apparel adequate but not sumptuous. Albert Sidney's birth could claim neither the distinction of the mansion nor the virtue of the cabin.

Albert Sidney Johnston was the fifth child born to John and Abigail Johnston. Out of esteem for the English Whig martyr, Dr. Johnston proposed the name of Algernon Sidney for his new son. When an elder son protested that so famous a name would be too much of a burden for the infant, family compromise produced the name of Albert Sidney. The character of Albert Sidney Johnston as a man sheds light on the sparse information concerning his early years. His mother died when he was three, leaving him to the care of elder sisters, and presently of a stepmother said to have been "of a sad gloomy, tearful, character, drawing prognostications of evil from every sign in the heavens & earth." [11] Yet the child's wants were not neglected, and neither the loss of his mother nor the melancholy of his stepmother clouded his nature; his childhood was healthy and cheerful, and he became a man of buoyant spirit.

The boy's early education was sound, both at home and in school. He imitated the ways of his father (acquaintances said that he inherited Dr. Johnston's "frank, manly nature"), and attended a variety of private preparatory schools, most of them in or near Washington. On one occasion he persuaded his father to permit him to study in western Virginia under Dr. Louis Marshall, brother of the Chief Justice, but he soon returned home, disillusioned with the experience.

One of Albert Sidney's first teachers was Mann Butler, a competent scholar and later a writer of Kentucky history. Nothing of Johnston's tutelage under Butler remains for the historian's perusal, but his later attitudes and scholarship suggest that he learned much from this association. Butler was a stanch nationalist of aristocratic sympathies, and an admirer of Henry Clay; [12] perhaps he was one

[11] William Preston Johnston, "My Father's Family," Johnston Papers, Barret Collection.

[12] Mann Butler, *A History of the Commonwealth of Kentucky*, pp. 294–295.

source of his pupil's similar convictions. Beyond question, Johnston's early schooling grounded him well in the three R's and gave him a lifelong respect for learning.

As a youth he knew the vicissitudes of the young. Favored by nature in body and mind, he learned all subjects easily and excelled in mathematics. He was born to the saddle, and loved horse and dog as true companions. He enjoyed hunting and athletic contests, in which he earned a reputation for extraordinary strength and courage.

Some episodes of his childhood had a flavor of Tom Sawyer about them. Johnston was a keen shot in the game of marbles, which he played "for keeps." Aspiring at one time to hoard all the marbles in the world, he buried his winnings in a jar in the earth, only to discover that a competitor was stealing them out to stake against him in the next match. The experience taught him the futility of avarice, he later said.[13] He attended school in plain clothing, and, in season, went barefoot. Fear of Johnston's ridicule caused a classmate to hide his own shoes and ruffled collar on the road to school. In a boy's society where the fist prevailed, Johnston was at ease; an associate testified that local bullies gave him wide berth. Indeed, he was himself something of a playground tyrant, but a benevolent one, according to the later bias of his son.[14]

Young Johnston was generally well behaved, but when he was a child he acted as a child. He sometimes gave way to severe outbursts of temper: once when his elder brothers offended him over some trifle, he threw himself under their horses' feet in an apparent infantile attempt at suicide. At another time, unable to pull on a tight boot, he angrily threw it out the window. At times he lied to his parents; years later he told his son that his first lie had required so many others to conceal it that he had seen the folly of lying and had never done it again, but this declaration may perhaps be discounted as a parental lesson in morality. Yet such occasions of youthful impatience, wrath, and deceit seem rather to have been the exception than the rule, for his family and acquaintances credited his early years with uncommon honesty, poise, and self-control.[15]

In 1818 Johnston entered Transylvania University at Lexington,

---

[13] Johnston, *Life of Johnston*, pp. 3–5.
[14] Johnston, "My Father's Family," Johnston Papers, Barret Collection.
[15] *Ibid.*

Kentucky, but his college education was soon interrupted because of outside influences that weighed heavily with a stalwart boy in the midst of adolescence. Stirred by accounts of heroism in the War of 1812, and by the example of companions entering the United States Navy, he yearned for the life of the sea. His family, fearing he might enlist in the Navy at the close of his first year at Transylvania, persuaded him to spend a season in the company of two elder half-brothers in Louisiana. Josiah Stoddard Johnston, eldest of the Johnston sons, had settled in Louisiana in 1805; John Harris Johnston had soon followed, and both were now prominent lawyers and citizens of the state. For a year Albert Sidney lived with the Josiah Stoddard Johnstons in Alexandria, Louisiana.

The stay in Louisiana failed in the end to turn Albert Sidney Johnston from a military career, but his character was strengthened and refined under the touch of the Josiah Stoddard Johnstons. Polished in manner, judicious in counsel, and skilled in the practice of law, Josiah Stoddard was to have a distinguished political future. In 1821 he would be elected to the United States House of Representatives, in 1825 to the United States Senate, and would become a friend, supporter, and adviser of Henry Clay. Johnston's wife, formerly Eliza Sibley of Natchitoches, Louisiana, was of renowned beauty and culture. The Johnstons lived the gracious life: dinners, balls, horsemanship, and theatricals gave release from the duties of a responsible public career.[16] Albert Sidney profited much from this association; to the end of his life he would say, "I am more indebted to my brother Stoddard for whatever I am, than to any other man." [17]

In the fall of 1821, supported by the counsel and funds of his brother, Albert Sidney returned to Transylvania. Now aspiring to make his father's profession of medicine his own, he studied there for two more years.[18] Transylvania, under the direction of the brilliant Unitarian minister Horace Holley, was the outstanding college west of the Appalachians. Two of Johnston's brothers, including Josiah Stoddard, had been educated there. Numerous men destined

---

[16] John Harris Johnston to Eliza [Sibley] Johnston, October 11, 1822, Josiah Stoddard Johnston Papers.

[17] Johnston, *Life of Johnston*, p. 8.

[18] Johnston to Josiah Stoddard Johnston, November 10, 1821, Josiah Stoddard Johnston Papers.

to become public leaders were trained at Transylvania; there Albert Sidney Johnston met and became a companion of a fellow student who one day would command the destiny of Johnston and of the South. This was Jefferson Davis.

Johnston was a thorough student in college. A classmate reported that he was conspicuous for always knowing his lessons. He received high marks in mathematics, for which he was said to possess both "genius and fondness," and was diligent enough to keep up the study of Latin and geometry during summer vacation, becoming sufficiently competent in Latin to translate Sallust with moderate fluency twenty-five years later.[19]

In the midst of his education at Transylvania, Johnston suddenly changed his mind and abandoned the goal of a medical career. As late as the fall of 1821 he had written his brother that he preferred medicine to any other study, but now he unexpectedly chose instead to seek admission to the United States Military Academy. Perhaps the urge for martial life had lain dormant within him ever since he had been dissuaded by his family from enlisting in the Navy. Now he had an opportunity to go into service under more favorable circumstances: he could be nominated to the Military Academy by his brother, Congressman Josiah Stoddard Johnston, and thus enter the elite officer corps of the Army.[20]

In 1822 Josiah Stoddard Johnston nominated Albert Sidney Johnston to the Academy from the state of Louisiana.[21] Technically, young Johnston may have been a resident of Louisiana, since he had lived there for several months before returning to college; actually his nomination from this state seems to have been a matter of expediency. Whatever the case, authorities of the Military Academy raised no question when Albert Sidney, still a minor, gave Kentucky as the state of his parents' abode. His father signed approval of the nomination, though he secretly hoped that after graduation his son would give up his soldierly aspirations and enter the practice of law.[22] Albert Sidney Johnston arrived at West Point in June, passed

[19] W. T. Barry to Josiah Stoddard Johnston, March 14, 1822, *ibid.;* Johnston, *Life of Johnston,* p. 8.

[20] Johnston to Josiah Stoddard Johnston, November 10, 1821, Josiah Stoddard Johnston Papers.

[21] Johnston to John C. Calhoun, May 15, 1822, Letters Received, Adjutant General's Office, Records of the War Department.

[22] John Johnston to Josiah Stoddard Johnston, October 19, 1826, Josiah Stoddard Johnston Papers.

the entrance examination, and was admitted to the Corps of Cadets.[23] The making of a soldier had begun.

Approaching manhood, Johnston was prime metal for a soldier. An inch above six feet in height and built in true proportion, he was superb of frame and feature. Family and college training had given him poise and a measure of cultivation. A young companion who joined Johnston on his way to the Academy admired his unfeigned kindness and his striking presence.[24]

His first morning at West Point was auspicious; the sun shone fair on the broad water and forested hills of the Rhinelike Hudson. Martial music filled the Plain as the Corps of Cadets paraded smartly for inspection. The new cadet looked upon the scene and felt the spell of it.

Johnston was a cadet during the Academy's golden age. The superintendent was Colonel Sylvanus Thayer, who had brought order and discipline out of confusion and fractiousness at the Academy, and insisted upon excellence in curriculum and instruction.[25] Major William J. Worth was commandant of cadets. Of gallant bearing and sonorous voice, Worth was an ideal instructor. He taught the cadets those little flourishes of arms and execution that gave spirit to the drill and made the Corps a model of precision. But he taught them more than fancy exercises: he helped instill in the fledgling soldiers a will and courage that one day would lead American troops with distinction in the conquest of Mexico and in the Civil War. During Johnston's last two years of training, Dennis Hart Mahan was on the staff of the Academy, stressing Napoleon's maxims of warfare. Johnston was of the West Point era that produced many of the most illustrious names in American military history.[26]

His training began. He purchased the required Spartan items of equipment—looking glass, basin, pitcher, pail, broom, and brush— and the regulation gray uniform, visor cap, and fatigue clothing. During July and August there was no academic instruction while the new cadets were introduced to military life in the summer encampment. They lived in tents on the West Point Plain where

---

[23] Post Orders, United States Military Academy, 1822–1823.

[24] N. J. Eaton to William Preston Johnston, January 1, 1873, Johnston Papers, Barret Collection.

[25] Edward C. Boynton, *History of West Point and of the United States Military Academy*, pp. 217–223.

[26] Oliver E. Wood (ed.), *The West Point Scrap Book*, pp. 35–36.

under the eye of Commandant Worth they learned the rudiments of drill, of soldiering, and of Academy regulations. The regulations were strict. They tediously set forth duties and studies for every hour of the day, and were equally explicit in saying what the cadets could not do. Among many other things, they could not drink alcohol, use tobacco, play cards, visit taverns in the vicinity of the post, participate in duels, or fight with fists. Even Sundays were largely filled with required activities: cadets were to attend divine worship twice on that day; for a brief period during Sunday afternoons they were permitted to walk on the Plain. Life was thoroughly accounted for in the Corps of Cadets.

Military organization and discipline were rigorously impressed, and the duties of an army in the field prevailed. Fife and drum awakened the cadets at five o'clock in the morning. Their days were filled with drill, instruction in arms, and standing guard. They were marched and drummed to the performance of every duty: to and from guard mount, to and from meals, even to and from periodic bathing in the Hudson. They pitched and dropped tents in prescribed sequence, making each movement in unison at the tap of a drum. At summer's end, marching in battalion formation to the music of a full band, the Corps returned to the barracks, and academic studies began.

Routine became even more exacting. Reveille sounded at dawn and lights went out at ten in the evening; virtually every minute between was filled with scheduled instruction, preparation, or drill. Johnston set himself to the task. In the beginning he was adequate but not distinguished in his studies. In January of 1823, in a class of ninety-four, he ranked eighteenth in French and seventeenth in mathematics, his strongest field. As he became accustomed to Academy life, and doubtless as he worked more diligently, he advanced in class standing; at the end of his first year he was ninth in his class in general average.[27] By that time the number in the class had dropped to sixty-six, but most of those who had departed were from the bottom layer. Among the few who excelled Johnston in their studies, six would be kept as instructors at the Academy after graduation. The top student, William H. C. Bartlett, would become one of West Point's most respected figures as professor of natural and experimental philosophy (physical science). Johnston had found his true

[27] Post Orders, United States Military Academy, 1823–1824; June 21, 1823.

academic level among his associates, and would vary but little from ninth place throughout the remainder of his cadet career.

Bonds of friendship never broken were formed at West Point. Johnston's closest friend was said to have been Bennett H. Henderson of North Carolina—a roommate and just above Johnston in class standing. Another fond companion was William P. Bainbridge of Kentucky, a highly ranked cadet of two classes above. Aboard the steamboat that carried Johnston to West Point he met N. J. Eaton, also on his way to enter the Academy. Their acquaintance soon ripened into an affection that one day would withstand the severest stress of their lives—opposing loyalties in the Civil War—and would outlive Johnston himself. A decade after Johnston's death Eaton wrote, "When he [died] I felt as if I had lost a brother." [28]

Johnston also renewed a friendship begun at Transylvania with Jefferson Davis, who entered the Academy two years after Johnston. With Robert E. Lee, also in the class two years behind Johnston, he was cordial but not close. During his second summer encampment, Johnston occupied a tent with a new cadet who later, as a roommate in the barracks, would become a friend for life.[29] Nearly forty years afterward, he and Leonidas Polk of North Carolina would share in combat the climax of their careers.

Duties claimed most of the cadets' time at the Academy. Any visits that Albert Sidney made to his home were brief, and though cadets were required to attend only two summer encampments, he spent all four summers on the post. Nevertheless, family joys and sorrows touched him. In a gay moment he once wrote, "Give my love to sister . . . & my *respects* to the young ladies." Somber events at home stirred a darker mood within him. He must have known of a brother's derangement, and of his father's financial embarrassment and occasional resort to alcohol.[30] When in the spring of 1826 a sister died, he wrote, "The death of one so young so pure & innocent and so necessary to the happiness of our parents, tends still more, if possible, to heighten the affliction." [31]

Johnston shared a common campus trait: he was more likely to

[28] Eaton to William Preston Johnston, January 1, 1873, Johnston Papers, Barret Collection.

[29] Post Orders, United States Military Academy, July 5, 1822; August 22, 1823; June 29, 1824; June 17, 1825.

[30] James Byers to Josiah Stoddard Johnston, August 12, November 23, 1823, Josiah Stoddard Johnston Papers.

[31] Johnston to Josiah Stoddard Johnston, March 24, 1826, *ibid.*

write to his family when he needed money than when he had plenty
of it. Once after asking his eldest brother for a small sum, he said
lamely, "Some apology may be necessary for my neglecting so long to
write, but I have been so often a delinquent in this that my corre-
spondents have become more negligent than myself." [32] He got the
money, but he did not become a more faithful correspondent.

As a cadet, he continued to turn to his elder brother, Josiah
Stoddard, for cash, favors, and advice. On one occasion he went so
far as to ask the Congressman to intercede in the interest of a cadet
who had been dismissed from the Academy; the offense had been
trivial and not habitual, said Albert Sidney. [33] In the summer of 1824
Congressman Johnston visited the Academy as a member of the
Board of Examiners and was gratified by Albert Sidney's progress
there. Though the knowledge that Cadet Johnston's brother was a
United States congressman (and later a senator) may well have disposed the staff to regard Albert Sidney kindly, he neither sought nor
received his brother's influence in his behalf. [34] He needed no such
support.

Albert Sidney was a competent student, but never a punctilious
one. He was strongest in tactics and in his old favorite, mathematics,
and weakest in drawing. Try as he might, he was never able to
perfect this skill; in the middle of his senior year he wrote with
resignation to his brother, "Have devoted 2 hours every day to
pencil drawing, apropos I thot my crayon drawing not worth sending. Perhaps I may have a better one after the examinations." [35] But
he never had a better. Jefferson Davis said that Johnston valued
mastery of subject rather than high class standing, and Davis was
right. Once after a series of examinations, Johnston said:

This places me sixth in general merit & I cannot be higher without making
greater exertion than I am willing to do. Whoever acquires a good standing
here the first year can almost always maintain it, that is, if his recitations
are even tolerable; to rise then under these circumstances requires patience
and constant study & good fortune. [36]

His secure grades encouraged indifference to scholarly competition.
Fortune's caprice united with a bit of indifference to bring him to

[32] *Ibid.,* October 26, December 29, 1825.
[33] *Ibid.,* October 26, 1825.
[34] John Harris Johnston to Josiah Stoddard Johnston, July 29, 1824, *ibid.*
[35] Johnston to Josiah Stoddard Johnston, December 29, 1825, *ibid.*
[36] *Ibid.,* January 30, 1825.

a single crisis in his studies at the Academy. In January of 1825, when he was being questioned on natural philosophy by the Board of Examiners, to his consternation, he was given the only two problems that he had not reviewed in preparing for the test and was forced to admit that he could solve neither. A third problem he worked satisfactorily, but he feared that he might be failed in the course. Manfully he told the Board that he knew the rest of the subject well; if a doubt remained, he said, he must demand a complete examination. Superintendent Thayer replied that his performance had been sufficient, and Johnston was ranked seventh in the course.[37]

Whatever the foibles of his youth, Johnston was a splendid cadet. Once accustomed to Academy routine, he bore it with ease. His striking figure, sound judgment, and fine bearing quickly marked him as a leader, and he was respected by fellow cadets. During the summer and fall of 1823 Leonidas Polk repeatedly wrote his family of his good fortune in having such roommates as Bainbridge, Henderson, and Johnston—all of high rank in class and military conduct.[38] Cadet Johnston was "popular among the officers of the staff on account of his strict attention to duty and steadiness of character," Polk asserted.[39] "Johnston was esteemed by all," [40] one classmate later wrote, and another said, "He was remarkable for great firmness and decision of character. He decided quickly and executed promptly." [41] Still another recalled, "His nature was truly noble, and untouched by anything small or contracted." [42] His behavior seems to have been exemplary; he apparently stayed away from Benny Havens', a popular but forbidden nearby tavern, and was never reprimanded by the staff. A rumor that he once fought a duel with his friend Bennett Henderson is unconfirmed by official report or testimony of acquaintances.[43] Johnston was a young man of purpose; he hewed to the line.

Instructors as well as classmates held him in high regard. In

[37] *Ibid.*
[38] Leonidas Polk to "My Dear Mother," July 17, August 29, September 13, 1823, Leonidas Polk Papers, University of the South Library, Sewanee, Tennessee.
[39] Joseph H. Parks, *General Leonidas Polk, C.S.A.*, p. 24.
[40] N. C. Macrae to "My Dear Sir," January 11, 1873, Johnston Papers, Barret Collection.
[41] George Woodbridge to William Preston Johnston, January 1, 1873, *ibid.*
[42] W. H. C. Bartlett to William Preston Johnston, January 11, 1873, *ibid.*
[43] Edward B. White to William Preston Johnston, March 3, 1873, *ibid.*

his second summer encampment he was appointed a color corporal on the staff of the Corps of Cadets; a year later he became a sergeant in the first company of the Corps; the next summer he rose to be sergeant major of the Corps; and, finally, at the beginning of his senior year, he was made adjutant, the most coveted position in the Corps.[44] This honor was not reserved for the cadet of highest academic rank (Johnston stood eighth at the close of his training); Superintendent Thayer and Commandant Worth selected the adjutant on the basis of leadership and general soldierly qualities as well as on classroom grades. Johnston served well as adjutant; except for six weeks in the fall, when he was incapacitated by illness, he prepared every order issued from the commandant's office.[45] Major Worth looked upon his adjutant as a young man of superior talent; years later he would support the appointment of Johnston for heavy responsibility. All who knew Cadet Johnston predicted for him a distinguished career.

Johnston and his comrades were ardent young Americans alive to an ardent young America. Their spirits quickened to the eloquence of Henry Clay and his congressional colleagues and to stories of valor from the War for Independence and the recent War of 1812. West Point offered them testimony of the nation's past glory and glimpses of her future greatness. Heroes of earlier conflicts visited the Academy from time to time: in the fall of 1824 the Corps of Cadets passed in review for the aged General LaFayette; [46] the next fall they greeted with a parade and a cheer the first boat through the Erie Canal.[47] To these youths, liberty seemed on the march as the Greeks rose against Turkish oppression and new governments sprang up in Latin America. The cadets were tempted by offers of foreign commissions. In Johnston the urge to assist in the birth of a nation remained strong, and within a decade he would cast his lot with the infant Republic of Texas as it struggled for survival.

When Johnston graduated from the Military Academy in June of 1826 the spirit of West Point was strong within him, rooted in soil prepared by family and early school. In addition to receiving technical training, he had been deeply impressed by certain courses and

---

[44] Post Orders, United States Military Academy, August 22, 1823; August 20, 1824; June 25, August 25, 1825.
[45] *Ibid.*, October 31–December 14, 1825.
[46] *Ibid.*, September 14, 1824.
[47] *Ibid.*, November 3, 1825.

instructors. From his studies in American constitutional law he had gained esteem for the federal union and the Constitution, but, significantly, the textbook in the course sanctioned state secession in an extremity.[48] From Chaplain Charles P. McIlvaine he had acquired a strengthened respect for man and reverence for God. From Superintendent Thayer, Commandant Worth, and others of the staff he had learned that personal honor and the pursuit of duty to country were the noblest of earthly virtues. Weakness of the flesh would at times in his life cause Johnston to waver; sectional passions ultimately would force him to a bitter choice of loyalties; but in his heart he would carry the ideals of West Point to the grave.

[48] In American Constitutional Law, Johnston studied William Rawle, *A View of the Constitution of the United States of America.* See Johnston to Josiah Stoddard Johnston, March 24, 1826, Josiah Stoddard Johnston Papers.

Garrison and Fireside

～～～～～～～～～～～～～～～～～～～～～～～～～～～～

A^{s} ^{A} ^{CADET,} Johnston sometimes dreamed of a career in the west. He had once hoped to join a proposed American expedition to the Oregon country. Even if fortune should place him in the top five of his class, he said, and thereby in line for the elite Corps of Engineers, he would choose artillery or infantry, as the duties of these combat arms would permit him to lead a more active life but at the same time give opportunity for reading and improvement.[1] Finally he turned to infantry, for he preferred service in the field to the sedentary existence of Old Point Comfort, Virginia, where he would have been ordered for the first two years if an artilleryman. Upon his request, Superintendent Thayer recommended him for infantry, and presently he was assigned to the Second Infantry Regiment as brevet second lieutenant.[2]

After a few weeks on furlough in Kentucky with his family, Lieutenant Johnston traveled to Washington, D.C., to visit the Josiah

---

[1] Johnston to Josiah Stoddard Johnston, January 30, December 29, 1825; June 12, 1826, Josiah Stoddard Johnston Papers.

[2] Johnston to "Sir," August 11, 1826, Letters Received, Adjutant General's Office, Records of the War Department.

Stoddard Johnstons for a gay interlude in his life. The young lieutenant was the picture of an ideal soldier—stalwart, handsome, and alert. Senator Johnston's position and congeniality united with his wife's charm to admit Albert Sidney into the most favored circles of the nation's capital. He was introduced to President John Quincy Adams and was a guest in the home of Secretary of State Henry Clay.[3] He met the highest officers of the Army and Navy and the fairest young ladies of Washington society.

He met General Winfield Scott, ranking officer of the United States Army. Pleased with the young man's intelligence and bearing, Scott asked him to become his aide-de-camp—a high honor, as well as an opportunity for gentle living and quick promotion. To the surprise of all, Johnston turned the offer down, saying that he preferred field duty to the inactivity of a city assignment. Senator Johnston would not importune him to change his mind; Mrs. Johnston's tears and scolding could not move him. Albert Sidney later came to believe that General Scott remembered this incident against him, but, undisturbed at the time, he left the ease and glamor of Washington for active service in camp and field.[4]

Lieutenant Johnston's first duty was at Madison Barracks, Sacket's Harbor, on Lake Ontario, where he arrived in early November, 1826. Inactive since the close of the War of 1812, the post was lightly manned, its garrison virtually idle. Johnston admired the beauty of water and shore, and enjoyed the company of his associates, a "nice, genteel, sort of folks," he said, "though not very refined." Drill and practice in arms took some of his time, but he was left with much leisure. He was the only unmarried officer of the command and lived alone in a block of eight rooms in the quarters. To fill his empty hours he began to read books—a habit that would last his lifetime. As a cadet he had prepared his lessons well, but had not read for pleasure. According to the remaining records of the Military Academy, Johnston did not borrow a single volume from the library during his last two years at West Point, but now he turned to "the Store Houses of literature" for companionship and culture.[5] To his

[3] Mr. and Mrs. [Henry] Clay to Lieutenant Johnston, October 25, 1826, Johnston Papers, Barret Collection.

[4] Eliza Gilpin to William Preston Johnston, April 4, 1870, *ibid.*; Johnston, *Life of Johnston,* p. 17.

[5] Johnston to Mrs. Josiah Stoddard Johnston, December 15, 1826, Josiah Stoddard Johnston Papers.

former roommate Leonidas Polk he wrote that his time was largely spent in reading. Duty at Sacket's Harbor was not demanding.

He must soon have wearied of idleness at this obscure post. To help occupy his mind he wrote letters to friends and relatives— letters that sometimes rambled in reminiscence, or again, were almost without theme. Once he made a near-maudlin apology to his sister-in-law for having asked her to write to him before he had written to her; ". . . a thing so contrary to etiquette and even good manners, would scarcely be forgiven by anyone less forgiving than yourself," he said.[6] Perhaps boredom moved him to an act of dangerous irresponsibility, which he later described to his son. One day as he and other officers were practising artillery on frozen Lake Ontario, a party of sleighers dashed impudently to and fro near the target. Thinking to frighten them away with a close shot, Johnston waited until they were near the mark, then fired. For a moment they disappeared in a spray of ice and snow. He was sure he had killed them, but to his deep relief, they emerged shaken but unharmed. He recounted the experience as a rebuke to his own youthful recklessness.[7]

Johnston did not long languish at Sacket's Harbor. On April 4, 1827, he was ordered to join the Sixth Infantry Regiment at Jefferson Barracks near St. Louis, Missouri—an assignment more to his taste. Commanded by General Henry Atkinson, the Sixth Infantry was considered an elite organization, and St. Louis, though a town of but 5,000 inhabitants, was the most cosmopolitan center west of the Mississippi. The barracks were unfinished and the troops lived in tents. Johnston was "agreeably disappointed" in the location and site of the post, which overlooked the Mississippi River and was covered with groves of oak and hickory. But the land was excellent for horsemanship, he said. More important, Jefferson Barracks commanded the frontier; from there troops could with great facility be transported throughout the west. This post was to be Johnston's home for the remainder of his initial career in the United States Army.

Soon he was on his first expedition. In August a detachment of the Sixth Regiment, along with two companies of the Fifth, was ordered to the Wisconsin River country to "chastise" the Winnebago Indians

---

[6] *Ibid.*
[7] Johnston, *Life of Johnston*, p. 18.

for the murder of white settlers. At the portage of the Wisconsin the force from Jefferson Barracks was joined by another sent from Green Bay. Together these troops brought the Winnebagoes to council without bloodshed, and the Indians agreed to set a boundary on their tribal lands, to leave the white settlers in peace, and to surrender for trial certain of their own members accused of the recent atrocities.

Johnston shared the hostility and contempt of his comrades for Indian character; yet he admired the courage and bearing of one of the captives, Red Bird.

I must confess that I consider Red Bird one of the noblest and most dignified men I ever saw [he wrote]. When he gave himself up, he was dressed, after the manner of the Sioux of the Missouri, in a perfectly white hunting-shirt of deerskin, and leggins and moccasins of the same, with an elegant head-dress of birds' feathers; he held a white flag in his right hand, and a beautifully-ornamented pipe in the other. He said, "I have offended. I sacrifice myself to save my country." He displayed all of that stoic indifference which is wrongfully attributed to the Indian character alone.

Johnston himself would one day be known for his great composure under adversity; possibly he remembered the example of Red Bird.

The campaigners were back at Jefferson Barracks in late September; the expedition had been hardly more than an outing for them. Johnston was undisturbed that permanent quarters were still unfinished and that he still lived under canvas. On a crisp October night, while serving as officer of the guard, he wrote to a West Point classmate, "I am almost converted into bacon . . . by the smoke from a big log-fire before my tent. . . . [We have] plenty of sport. I am in excellent health and fine spirits." These were the words of a man in the green of life.[8]

One of the happiest periods of his career ensued. Rich in the social graces, General Atkinson and his wife made the post congenial to the temper of young officers. Dinners and cotillions refreshed their leisure, the fairest of young ladies graced their entertainments, and Jefferson Barracks gave welcome relief from the ennui of Sackett's Harbor.[9]

[8] Johnston to William Bickley, October 10, 1827, Johnston Papers, Barret Collection.

[9] Johnston to Josiah Stoddard Johnston, December 28, 1828, Josiah Stoddard Johnston Papers; George H. Kennerly to Johnston, August 21, 1829, Johnston Papers, Barret Collection; Johnston, *Life of Johnston,* p. 20.

Associations in St. Louis sharpened the pleasure of service at Jefferson Barracks. The town was growing rapidly from American migration and because it was a trading center for furs and general merchandise; yet it retained the flavor of its French colonial heritage. Families of French descent—the Chouteaus, Gratiots, Bertholds, and Cabannes—shared distinction with those of American lineage—the Clarks, Bentons, O'Fallons, Lucases, and Darbys. An aristocracy of trade and politics prevailed. Men were quick to defend family or personal honor; duels were as frequent as in the plantation South, which St. Louis resembled in many ways.[10] The social pace was lively; there was said to be "a fiddle in every house and a dance somewhere every night."[11] The spirit of the place suited Johnston's mood, and as an officer and a gentleman, he was at home among the town's best.

These years were rich also in masculine companionship. Johnston was usually reticent and undemonstrative, but he was a man of strong affection. Once in saying goodbye to a classmate and regimental comrade he betrayed his feeling with a "God bless you."[12] He was pleased by the successes of friends of former days and smiled at their whims and minor vicissitudes. Still a footloose bachelor himself, he playfully urged marriage upon an acquaintance. "You told me the next time I saw you you would have a wife to pour tea out for me. You are well established; take the step at once, don't be *thinking* about it all your life time," he wrote.[13] From Lieutenant Bennett Henderson, now an instructor at West Point, he learned, "The Corps of Cadets have the same principles of motion as when you and I were parts of the machine." Then this choice gossip: "Our old friend Polk is married to a rich, ugly, and (I believe) skeptical young lady in N.C.—I say young lady out of civility—for she is in fact an old maid of disagreeable person—I always thought Polk was a man of taste, didn't you?"[14] If Johnston made any reply, it is lost. Much of his leisure was spent in riding, reading, playing chess—in

[10] Frederic L. Billon, *Annals of St. Louis in Its Territorial Days*, pp. 105–107; James Cox, *Old and New St. Louis*, p. 133; Elihu H. Shepard, *The Early History of St. Louis and Missouri*, p. 59.

[11] John F. Darby, *Personal Recollections*, pp. 5–12.

[12] N. J. Eaton to William Preston Johnston, January 1, 1873, Johnston Papers, Barret Collection.

[13] Johnston to Bickley, October 10, 1827, *ibid.*

[14] Bennett Henderson to Johnston, September 15, n.d., *ibid.*

which he both delighted and excelled—and talking over pipe and brandy. He was most at ease among men.

That he had not altogether mastered the hot temper of his youth was illustrated in a story of Jefferson Barracks that he later told his son. To occupy some of his leisure, he took up the flute, but the jests of comrades made him both doubtful and touchy about his skill. One day while practising, he heard a tapping from the room above. When he stopped playing, the tapping stopped; when he began again, the tapping began. In quick anger he rushed to the upper room, only to discover a colleague cracking walnuts on the hearth, apparently indifferent to the sound of the flute. Shamed by his own outburst, Johnston quietly withdrew. He quit the flute. "I did not think that a man so sensitive about his skill was fit for a flute-player," he said.[15]

He held lofty views about womanhood. According to a friend, Johnston once overheard a man say that he did not believe in the existence of feminine virtue. "Sir," Johnston is recorded to have said, drawing himself up to full height, "You have a mother, & I believe you have a sister." Enough said! The base fellow hung his head in shame.[16] The story may be apocryphal—it has been told of others—yet it fits the nature of the man. Never an admirer of Andrew Jackson as a politician, Johnston wrote, upon hearing of Rachel Jackson's death:

I do most sincerely sympathise with him for his loss; had she lived her conduct would have been a triumphant refutation of the foul slanders that have been uttered against her character; how unmanly & malignant must that spirit be that can prompt a *man* to attack female character." [17]

The suicide of a colleague stirred his compassion and moved him to reveal a strong fatalistic philosophy:

Our friend and fellow-soldier has destroyed himself. Notwithstanding the manner of his death, let us mourn the loss of a chivalric companion; let us not in the vigor of health and intellect reproach his memory for committing an act which the paramount control of reason alone can prevent. Our fate is the result of a combination of circumstances; if we cannot destroy the

---

[15] Johnston, *Life of Johnston*, p. 21.

[16] Eaton to William Preston Johnston, January 1, 1873, Johnston Papers, Barret Collection.

[17] Johnston to Josiah Stoddard Johnston, December 28, 1828, Josiah Stoddard Johnston Papers.

combination, we must submit to it. The *ups* and *downs* of human life make up these combinations. No philosophy can distinctly foresee them. . . . As a general rule we might as well attempt to govern the changes in a Kaleidoscope, as to alter our fate.[18]

These were charitable words in a society that looked upon suicide as being both sinful and cowardly.

Interests of barracks and ballroom inevitably drew him farther away from his family. Visits home were infrequent, and, reluctant in all personal correspondence, he shamefully neglected to write to his brothers and aged father. Dr. Johnston scolded, "I have Recd no letter from Albert since he left here nor has he written to any of the Family since his return from [the Wisconsin River expedition]." [19] A sojourn at home in December, 1828, soothed his parent's feelings; at the end of his stay, Albert Sidney said that he left his father in peace and plenty. Serenity had come to the elder Johnston through more than the presence of his son, for he had recently quit alcohol and embraced religion. Never a communicant, Albert Sidney remarked curtly, "I found my father a member of the church, a very exemplary one & liberal enough to belong to a less rigid sect than the *presbyterians.*" [20]

Like the rest of his family, Johnston was of conservative social and political preference. He admired Henry Clay and supported the National Republican Party. "Does your original fondness for Mr. Clay continue, or has a military life inclined you to the Hero?" one of his brothers asked him.[21] Military life had not changed Johnston's views, but he refused to despair over the administration of Democratic President Andrew Jackson. "We are disposed to regard the excitement produced by elections as a mere struggle for power among individuals," he said with a sagacity beyond his years. "So long as the Constitution which we consider the strong federal bond remains unviolated, we esteem the republic *in no danger.*" He went so far as to chide Senator Josiah Stoddard Johnston for lamenting Jackson's intention to divide the United States Treasury surplus

[18] Johnston to Eaton, October 3, 1830 (copy), Johnston-Eaton Letter Book, Johnston Papers, Barret Collection.
[19] John Johnston to Josiah Stoddard Johnston, January 14, November 26, 1828, Josiah Stoddard Johnston Papers.
[20] James Byers to Josiah Stoddard Johnston, August 25, 1828; and Johnston to Josiah Stoddard Johnston, December 28, 1828, *ibid.*
[21] John Harris Johnston to Johnston, August 21, 1828, Johnston Papers, Barret Collection.

among the states according to population rather than by the amount each had paid in taxes. "You made this remark hastily," Albert Sidney officiously wrote his brother, "for you know perfectly well, that it is a matter of indifference where the revenue is paid at first; finally the consumer pays it & therefore in the ratio of the population." [22]

Soon after arriving at Jefferson Barracks, Johnston met the young woman who was to become his first wife, and ultimately to cause his career to take an unforeseen turn of great consequence. At a ball in the Chouteau mansion in St. Louis, Lieutenant Johnston was introduced to Miss Henrietta Preston of Louisville. Henrietta was the daughter of Captain William Preston, a veteran of the Revolution and one of Louisville's most respected citizens.[23] She was also a relative of the wife of Missouri Senator Thomas Hart Benton and was a guest of the Bentons at the time Albert Sidney Johnston met her.

The spark of interest struck by this meeting flared into love during the next year (1828), when for several months Johnston was in Louisville on recruiting service,[24] and shortly Albert Sidney and Henrietta were engaged to be married. For some undisclosed reason, Johnston anticipated opposition from the one person whose approval he most desired—Josiah Stoddard Johnston. In late December he wrote to his beloved elder brother that he was then on his way to Louisville for his wedding:

In any other matter I would have sought your advice & made it my rule of conduct, but in this, I have purposely defered informing [you] until now, lest your opinion should be unfavorable to my views; this would have been a source of *pain* to me, inasmuch as being resolved *I* always execute.[25]

On January 20, 1829, Albert Sidney Johnston and Henrietta Preston were married in the Preston home in Louisville.

Mrs. Johnston's nature was suited to that of her husband. Though

[22] Johnston to Josiah Stoddard Johnston, January 21, 1830, Josiah Stoddard Johnston Papers.

[23] Captain Preston was in General Anthony Wayne's army during the Revolution. See John Mason Brown, *Memoranda of the Preston Family*, p. 38.

[24] Johnston to "Sir," May 1, 1828, Letters Sent, Adjutant General's Office, Records of the War Department.

[25] Johnston to Josiah Stoddard Johnston, December 28, 1828, Josiah Stoddard Johnston Papers.

not beautiful, she was a striking young woman who came of a family known for their character, intelligence, and comeliness—traits that she shared.[26] Henrietta was described as being about five feet six inches in height, of full form, rich color, hazel eyes, dark hair, and somewhat irregular but pleasing features. Well schooled by private tutors, including an accomplished aunt, Henrietta possessed uncommon literary taste and talent. She was a woman of poise and dignity, and she brought to her husband a full measure of love and devotion.[27] A year after his wedding, Johnston said, "I married after long deliberation & now . . . I have every reason to rejoice in the affection . . . of the object of my choice." [28] Later he told his son, "It was impossible to have felt [your mother's] influence, and afterward to cherish low views. . . . To her [I owe] the wish to be truly great. . . . If I am anything, I owe it to your mother." [29]

In a nation at peace, the garrison of Jefferson Barracks followed an easy routine of drill and instruction, and for three years the Johnstons knew a life of gladness and simple graciousness on the post. The modesty of their wants equalled the modesty of their income; Johnston took pride in his young wife's good sense and economy, which he said was a cardinal virtue for people of their small means. They enjoyed the warm social life and camaraderie of Jefferson Barracks and their frequent visits and entertainment among friends and Henrietta's relatives in St. Louis.[30]

Whatever doubts Johnston's own family may have had about Henrietta soon disappeared. After a year of married life, Albert Sidney wrote candidly to Josiah Stoddard on this point, "I knew you were misinformed touching some particulars. . . . I trusted that time would do justice to my judgment & it has done it; this I infer from your last letter." [31] Family ties with the Prestons were kept strong by

---

[26] Mrs. Johnston's younger brother, William Preston, was an extraordinarily handsome man. See Edward Younger (ed.), *Inside the Confederate Government: The Diary of Robert Garlic Hill Kean,* p. 131.

[27] Family descriptions of Mrs. Johnston are the only ones that remain. Without flamboyance or obvious exaggeration, they seem authentic. See Johnston, *The Johnstons of Salisbury,* p. 101; Brown, *Memoranda of the Preston Family,* pp. 30, 38.

[28] Johnston to Josiah Stoddard Johnston, January 21, 1830, Josiah Stoddard Johnston Papers.

[29] Johnston, *The Johnstons of Salisbury,* p. 101.

[30] Johnston to Josiah Stoddard Johnston, January 21, 1830, Josiah Stoddard Johnston Papers.

[31] *Ibid.*

occasional visits to Kentucky. In the fall of 1830 Johnston wrote from the home of his wife's mother near Louisville to a fellow officer at Jefferson Barracks, "The last two months I have passed pleasantly and quietly in the country, reading, shooting the rifle, etc. Have your augur Nick ready for a trial of skill." The same letter bore tidings of a more important prospect. "I shall be ready to return at the expiration of my furlough," said Johnston, "if *fortunate* with a larger family." [32] On January 5, 1831, their first child, William Preston, was born at Louisville. Johnston returned immediately to duty, to be followed by his wife and son in the spring.

As Johnston had been a splendid cadet, so he became a splendid officer, admired by colleagues of all ranks. Ironically, he chafed over the want of opportunity to exercise his martial skill and thus advance in his profession and complained to Senator Johnston:

I confess I have no hopes of rapid promotion unless you who conduct the political ark would give us something to do. Then, I would show that I am not unambitious, that I am not unqualified for my station appertaining to my profession. The position of the country and the attitude of affairs do not admit of a well grounded expectation that anything very favorable could arise. [33]

Within a year General Atkinson appointed Johnston adjutant of the Sixth Regiment, and in this position he earned the confidence of commanding officer and subordinates. His support was sought and his frown avoided.

I never knew a man who could say a keen, cutting word with more effect than Albert Sidney Johnston [wrote a comrade later]. His commanding presence, added to the dry & withering sarcasm that he could throw into a rebuke, gave a crushing effect. . . . And yet . . . his modesty was only exceeded by his bravery. . . . While no man was more approachable, no one could remain unimpressed by his dignity. [34]

To another, Johnston was the "beau ideal" of a soldier, one who possessed to an extraordinary degree the esteem of the entire regi-

---

[32] Johnston to Eaton, October 3, 1830 (copy), Johnston-Eaton Letter Book, Johnston Papers, Barret Collection.

[33] Johnston to Josiah Stoddard Johnston, January 21, 1830, Josiah Stoddard Johnston Papers.

[34] Eaton to William Preston Johnston, January 1, 1873, Johnston Papers, Barret Collection.

ment. "He was the soul of Honor, his judgement accurate, his decision firm & uncompromising, his courage no man who ever knew him, could doubt." [35] He seemed destined for high command.

[35] T. L. Alexander to William Preston Johnston, January 25, 1873, *ibid.;* Johnston, *Life of Johnston,* p. 21.

Chastisement of Black Hawk

~~~~~~

I N THE SPRING OF 1832 a call to arms
broke the placid rhythm of barracks life. Black Hawk and his
faction of the Sauk and Fox Indian warriors invaded the northwestern frontier, and panic was upon the settlements. For the nation
this was the most serious Indian outbreak since the overthrow of
Tecumseh's Confederacy during the War of 1812. For Johnston it
was a test of personal fortitude and professional skill and his apprenticeship in warcraft.

Ancient hatred among the northwestern tribes had struck the
spark of conflict; during the preceding summer some of the Sauk
and Fox had made a vengeance raid against the Menominee on the
upper Mississippi. When the United States Indian agent at Fort
Crawford, in the present state of Wisconsin, demanded that the
guilty Sauk and Fox be delivered for trial, the tribal councils refused.
The Menominee prepared for a war of retaliation. To preserve the
peace, General Atkinson was ordered to punish the Sauk and Fox
marauders and arrest the movement of the Menominee.

Had the matter stopped there, General Atkinson probably could
have exacted punishment without resort to war, as he had done with

the Winnebago five years before. But the frontier was now tinder for
the spark. Resentment against the whites was strong within Black
Hawk. By a treaty of 1804 the Sauk and Fox had sold their land in
Illinois to the United States, and agreed to move west of the Mississippi in due time. They were permitted by the treaty to live where
they were as long as the area remained public land. In the 1820's,
ignoring this government promise, white squatters moved upon the
Indians' fields and hunting grounds and upon the graves of their
fathers.[1]

Black Hawk was belligerent. But he was not the chief of his
nation; he was only a war leader. Keokuk, spokesman of the Sauk
council, was conciliatory toward the whites and willing to abandon
the tribal lands in Illinois. Black Hawk and Neapope were the
leaders of a hostile party within the tribe—a group known as the
British Band because they were in communication with British
agents in Canada. Though he had "touched the quill" on numerous
treaties affirming that of 1804, Black Hawk now affected to believe
that his tribal village in Illinois had never been sold to the whites.
"My reason teaches me that land cannot be sold," said Black Hawk.
"The Great Spirit gave it to his children to live upon, and cultivate.
. . . Nothing can be sold but such things as can be carried away."[2]
But when in the summer of 1831 a force of Illinois volunteers
approached Black Hawk's village, he was awed into submission, and
on a June night his sullen little band crossed to the western side of
the Mississippi.

By the next spring Black Hawk was desperate. His people were
hungry; they had crossed the Mississippi too late the year before to
plant corn. His evil genius, White Cloud the Prophet, beckoned to
him to return to the cornlands of Illinois. White Cloud was a crafty

---

[1] My account of the Black Hawk War is derived from a number of sources,
among them Donald Jackson (ed.), *Black Hawk: An Autobiography,* pp. 18–31;
Reuben Gold Thwaites, "The Black Hawk War," *How George Rogers Clark Won
the Northwest and Other Essays in Western History,* pp. 115–200 (hereinafter
cited as Thwaites, *George Rogers Clark and Other Essays*); and *Before the Indian
Claims Commission,* pp. 78, 82–84. The narrative is indebted throughout to Mrs.
Ellen Whitney's "Chronology of the Black Hawk War," Black Hawk War
Collection. The preceding paragraphs also contain background material drawn
from letters as follows: Joseph M. Street to Thomas P. Burnett, February 1, 1832;
George Davenport to Joseph Duncan, February 11, 1832; Henry Atkinson to
Alexander Macomb, April 3, 1832; and Atkinson to Edmund P. Gaines, April 7,
1832, all in the Black Hawk War Collection.
[2] Jackson (ed.), *Black Hawk: An Autobiography,* p. 114.

medicine man, half Sauk and half Winnebago, who lived with his followers at Prophet's Village on the Rock River about forty-five miles above its mouth. Black Hawk later reported how White Cloud had tempted him:

Follow us [back to Illinois] and act like braves, and we had nothing to fear, but much to gain. That the American war chief might come, but would not, nor dare not, interfere with us so long as we acted peaceably! That we were not yet ready to act otherwise. We must wait until we ascend Rock river and receive our reinforcements, and we will then be able to withstand any army! [3]

Stirred by false hopes, brought by Neapope, of British support and hoping for alliance with the Winnebago and Potawatomi Indians, Black Hawk determined to recross the Mississippi River. On April 5 he led his small group of warriors, with their wives and children and belongings, back across the Mississippi just below the mouth of the Iowa. Thus was the state of Illinois invaded.[4]

Three days later General Atkinson and his regiment were on the move up the Mississippi by steamboat, with Lieutenant Johnston as aide-de-camp and assistant adjutant general.[5] Lieutenants seldom make strategy for generals, and Johnston did not set the course for General Atkinson. Yet, he was close to his commander; his opinions may have had some influence on the campaign. Certainly he made the movements and shared the hardships and frustrations of the entire expedition. His personal diaries of the Black Hawk War are among the most accurate and lucid accounts of the conflict.[6]

[3] *Ibid.*, pp. 136 n, 137.

[4] Thwaites, *George Rogers Clark and Other Essays,* pp. 127, 139. Most of Black Hawk's followers were of the Sauk tribe.

[5] Lewis Cass to John Reynolds, June 15, 1832, Illinois Militia Documents, 1833; and Order No. 19, Henry Atkinson Order Book (April 5–August 29, 1832), April 5, 1832, both in Black Hawk War Collection.

[6] Johnston left two diaries of the Black Hawk War. During the war he kept a hastily written diary, dated June 12 to August 2, 1832. Shortly after the war he wrote another, enlarging and emending the original, apparently from memory. The second one, dated April 3 to August 2, 1832 (hereinafter cited as Second Johnston Diary), is the one usually referred to in these notes. The second diary may have been made in response to a request by General Atkinson, who wrote that he desired a copy for the use of a scholar who was writing a history of the Black Hawk War. The second one is, in a few places, more favorable to General Atkinson than is the first. Both diaries are in the Johnston Papers, Barret Collection. A copy of the original is in the Stevens Collection, Illinois State Historical Library, Springfield, Illinois.

On April 12 the United States expedition reached the Yellow Banks and here learned beyond a doubt what they had already heard from afar: Black Hawk was east of the Mississippi with a band of between 400 and 500 horsemen, besides women and old men and boys capable of rowing canoes, foraging, and bearing arms in an emergency. Counting women and children, Black Hawk had perhaps 1,500 Indians in his party. On the night of the twelfth, Atkinson and his troops arrived at Fort Armstrong, Rock Island, just above the mouth of the Rock River. Having outdistanced the Indians with this swift movement, Atkinson could have stopped Black Hawk's advance at this point.

Instead, fearing battle before he was reinforced by Illinois volunteers and by regulars from other posts, he and his staff sought to keep the peace through council. They spent much of the thirteenth in talk with Keokuk and his associates, friendly chieftains of the Sauk and Fox. Atkinson warned Keokuk to have nothing to do with Black Hawk. If he and his band would not recross the Mississippi, said the commander, "I will treat them like dogs." Keokuk replied honestly that he could not control the hostile faction under Black Hawk; but to appease Atkinson, Keokuk agreed to surrender some members of his own tribe as hostages.[7] Meantime, scouts brought word that Black Hawk's horsemen were passing up the east bank of the Rock River and that his canoes were on its surface. General Atkinson and his staff sat and talked while Black Hawk moved unmolested into the interior of Illinois.[8]

Schism within the Sauk and Fox took the military unawares. "The recent movement of the British-band is . . . a new affair not anticipated by the Government . . . and not comprehended in the instruc-

---

[7] For a description of troop movement and councils, see Second Johnston Diary, April 13, 1832; and Johnston, "Minutes of Council at Rock Island between Atkinson and Keokuk, April 13, 1832," both in Johnston Papers, Barret Collection. See also "Minutes of Fort Armstrong Council, April 19, 1832"; Macomb to Atkinson, March 17, April 10, 13, 1832; Atkinson to Reynolds, April 13, 1832, all in Reynolds Order and Letter Book, Black Hawk War Collection; and Atkinson to General Edmund P. Gaines, April 3, 1832; Atkinson to General Macomb, April 3, 1832; Atkinson to Reynolds, April 13, 1832, all in Atkinson Letter Book (April 3–May 27, 1832), in the Black Hawk War Collection.

[8] Colonel Zachary Taylor criticized Atkinson sharply for permitting Black Hawk to get away in this fashion. See Holman Hamilton, "Zachary Taylor and the Black Hawk War," *Wisconsin Magazine of History*, XXIV (March, 1941), 309. Atkinson testily denied that he could have stopped Black Hawk on the Rock River with the troops on hand. See Atkinson to "Sir," November 19, 1832, Josiah Stoddard Johnston Papers.

tions received by Gen. A[tkinson]," wrote Johnston.[9] Nevertheless, Atkinson now set about trying to induce Black Hawk to return west of the Mississippi.[10] He sent messengers to Black Hawk ordering him to do so, and threatening to pursue and coerce him if he refused. Atkinson's emissaries brought no sure word of the Indians' intentions, but shortly Atkinson heard from an Indian agent that Black Hawk was defiant, that Black Hawk had replied "that his heart is bad—that he intends to go further up Rock River—and that if you send your officers to him he will fight them." [11] Atkinson prepared his campaign.

Three additional companies of regulars under Colonel Zachary Taylor were brought down from Fort Crawford, Governor Reynolds of Illinois was instructed to come up with his force of militia, and steamboats were sent to St. Louis for ammunition and provisions. Atkinson planned to strike from a base at Dixon's Ferry about sixty-five miles up the Rock River from its mouth, and to Dixon's Ferry he ordered the bulk of the troops and supplies.

On May 9 the troops began to ascend the Rock River. Atkinson and his staff moved by boat, taking with them the 400 regulars, 300 volunteer infantry, and the cannon and supplies. They proceeded at a snail's pace. Fierce storms of wind and rain fell upon them; the river was high; frequently the troops waded waist-deep for hours pushing heavy-laden keelboats against an angry current. "The soldiers strain every nerve," wrote Johnston. Led by Brigadier General Samuel Whiteside, and moving overland, the 1,300 volunteer cavalry outdistanced the commanding general and reached Dixon's Ferry on the twelfth. Events soon were to show that Atkinson had erred in permitting the volunteers to go ahead of him.

Meantime Black Hawk pressed on. He now knew that talk of British support was idle, and at Prophet's Village he had learned that he would receive few reinforcements from the Winnebago. Hope of an alliance with the Potawatomi was dim, as one of their

[9] Second Johnston Diary, April 19, 1832, Johnston Papers, Barret Collection.
[10] Jackson (ed.), *Black Hawk: An Autobiography*, p. 138; Atkinson to Reynolds, n.d., Illinois Militia Documents, 1833; Atkinson to Reynolds, April 27, 1832, in Reynolds Order and Letter Book; and Atkinson to General Macomb, April 13, 1832, in Atkinson Letter Book (April 3–May 27, 1832), all in Black Hawk War Collection.
[11] Atkinson to Black Hawk, April 24, 1832; Black Hawk to Atkinson, April 26, 1832; Henry Gratiot to Atkinson, April 27, 1832, all in Black Hawk War Collection.

principal chiefs, Shaubena, had induced the majority to remain at peace. Even now Shaubena was alerting the white settlers to Black Hawk's advance. Sensing disaster, Black Hawk was almost ready to obey Atkinson's demand that he recross the Mississippi, but before doing so, the Indian leader resolved to keep a rendezvous on the upper Rock River with the Potawatomi, some of whom still wished to join him. This was Black Hawk's tragic mistake.[12]

At Dixon's Ferry, General Whiteside found a group of about 350 volunteer rangers under Majors Isaiah Stillman and David Bailey. Impatient over the tardiness of the regulars, these frontiersmen chafed to close with Black Hawk at once. Apparently without Whiteside's permission they left Dixon's Ferry on the thirteenth, with Stillman in command. The next afternoon they pitched camp in a grove on the north side of a small creek that flowed into the Rock River.

Black Hawk was but three miles beyond. The Indian leader was preparing a dog feast for the Potawatomi dignitaries when he learned of the rangers' presence. Thinking them to be General Atkinson and an advance party, Black Hawk sent out messengers to sue for council; seemingly, he now intended to obey Atkinson's order to leave Illinois. When the Indian emissaries approached Stillman's site bearing a white flag, the rangers set upon them pellmell and hustled them into camp. Other Indian horsemen sent by the wary leader as observers were pursued and some of them killed. Those escaping rode in haste to tell Black Hawk of the fate of their comrades. Filled with wrath, the aged warrior bade his men prepare to avenge the blood of their brothers.[13]

Black Hawk had with him only a small escort of horsemen, probably not more than fifty. Yet so dauntless was the Indian attack that the entire body of rangers fled in panic. Black Hawk later said, "I never was so surprised in all the fighting I have seen—knowing, too, that the Americans, generally, shoot well—as I was to see this army

---

[12] Second Johnston Diary, April 13–29, 1832, Johnston Papers, Barret Collection; Atkinson to "Sir," November 19, 1832, Josiah Stoddard Johnston Papers; Thwaites, *George Rogers Clark and Other Essays*, pp. 143–145.

[13] Jackson (ed.), *Black Hawk: An Autobiography*, p. 142; Second Johnston Diary, May 9–15, 1832, Johnston Papers, Barret Collection; Order No. 12, May 9, 1832, in Atkinson Order Book (April 5–August 29, 1832), Black Hawk War Collection.

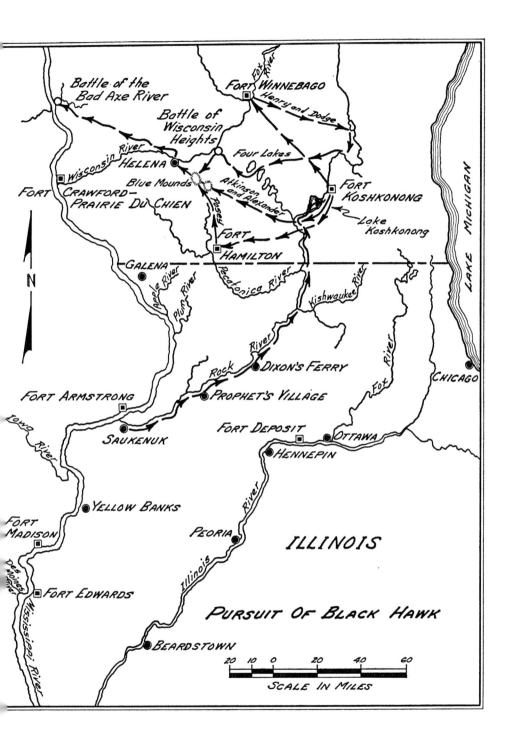

Battle of the
Bad Axe River
Battle of
Wisconsin
Heights
FORT WINNEBAGO
Fox River
Henry and Dodge
Four Lakes
Wisconsin River
HELENA
Blue Mounds
Atkinson
and Alexander
FORT
KOSHKONONG
Lake
Koshkonong
FORT
CRAWFORD-
PRAIRIE DU CHIEN
Pecatonica River
FORT
HAMILTON
Pasey
GALENA
N
Apple River
Plum River
Kishwaukee River
LAKE MICHIGAN
Rock
River
DIXON'S FERRY
FORT ARMSTRONG
PROPHET'S VILLAGE
Fox River
CHICAGO
Iowa River
SAUKENUK
FORT DEPOSIT
OTTAWA
HENNEPIN
YELLOW BANKS
River
FORT
MADISON
PEORIA
Illinois
ILLINOIS
Des Moines River
FORT EDWARDS
Mississippi River
PURSUIT OF BLACK HAWK
BEARDSTOWN

20 10 0   20   40   60

SCALE IN MILES

of several hundreds, retreating without showing fight." [14] Johnston wrote in contempt:

They were said to have been overpowered by a superior force, but the truth is, there was no action or engagement between the troops of Gen. Stillman and the indians, from the incapacity of their leader, the total absence of discipline in his battallion and consequently a want of confidence in each other. These troops that might under different circumstances have contended successfully against any enemy had not the courage to face the indians. . . . Only one man was killed near the ground where they met the indians. The remainder [of the dead, eleven in number,] were killed in flight . . . at or below a small deep creek (now called par excellence Stillman's *Run*) .[15]

Black Hawk had drawn first blood.

Stillman's rout was complete. The frightened rangers fled to Dixon's Ferry thirty miles away. Some of them did not stop running until they had reached their own firesides. Others sought refuge with General Atkinson, still on his way up Rock River. With wild tales of ambush by a force of as many as 2,000 Indians, the rangers pleaded with Atkinson to rush the regulars ahead at once.[16] Knowing that General Whiteside with his volunteers was marching toward the enemy, Atkinson remained calm and kept his troops and supplies together. "The pleasure of giving tranquillity to the slumbers of this valiant leader [Stillman] was not considered of sufficient importance to make a disposition of that kind at all necessary," commented Johnston.[17]

Tragedy and farce alike came of the encounter. On the eve of it, Black Hawk seemed to be at the point of returning west of the Mississippi without further coercion. Now Atkinson would not permit it. Grossly exaggerating the strength and cruelty of the Indians, word of Stillman's defeat spread terror throughout the frontier. It raised the blood lust among the whites: Black Hawk and his followers must be put to the sword. Despairing of a council with American leaders, and perhaps emboldened by initial success, Black Hawk withdrew into the wild lake and swamp country of southern

---

[14] Jackson (ed.) , *Black Hawk: An Autobiography,* p. 144.

[15] Second Johnston Diary, May 15, 1832, Johnston Papers, Barret Collection.

[16] I. Stillman to "Dear Sir," May 21, 1832, Illinois Militia Documents, 1833; Atkinson to Stillman, May 15, 1832, in Atkinson Letter Book (April 3–May 27, 1832) , Black Hawk War Collection.

[17] Second Johnston Diary, May 15, 1832, Johnston Papers, Barret Collection.

Wisconsin, and from there he loosed his raiding parties upon the settlements.[18]

To trap the crafty old warrior was not simple, and fragmentation of American forces complicated the task. Just when General Atkinson prepared to invade Black Hawk's retreat, the Illinois volunteers declared their enlistments ended and clamored for release. The Indians could never be caught in their impenetrable swamps, said the weary militiamen. At the end of May, Governor Reynolds was obliged to disband the entire force, except for about 300 who agreed to remain an additional twenty days to defend the area until new companies could be formed.[19]

Meantime, the Indians scourged the land. Parties from other tribes, the Potawatomi and Winnebago, took advantage of the prevailing disorder to fall upon isolated settlers. Black Hawk seemed more interested in seizing horses than in taking scalps; yet he was blamed for all atrocities. The settlers defended themselves as best they could. Here they repelled the marauders; there they were overwhelmed and massacred. In a hot fight on the Pecatonica River in southwestern Wisconsin, Militia Colonel Henry Dodge and a small band of citizens defeated and wiped out a party of eleven savages who the day before had slain five whites.

Fearing to be lured on a fruitless chase, and perhaps reluctant to risk his diminished command in a bold stroke, General Atkinson withdrew his base to Ottawa, above the rapids of the Illinois River, and placed garrisons at the more vulnerable settlements along the border.[20]

[The Indians'] mode of warfare is such [wrote Johnston] that while you keep a sufficient force in motion against them to contend with their main body you must necessarily keep troops at every available point on the frontier to hold in check small parties which it is their custom to detach to a great distance.[21]

General Atkinson awaited a fresh levy of volunteers before resuming search.

[18] Benjamin Drake, *The Life and Adventures of Black Hawk*, pp. 147–149; Thwaites, *George Rogers Clark and Other Essays*, pp. 153–155.

[19] Second Johnston Diary, May 28, 1832, Johnston Papers, Barret Collection.

[20] Atkinson to General Macomb, May 30, 1832, in Atkinson Letter Book (May 26–September 23, 1832) ; and Order No. 27, June 5, 1832, in Atkinson Order Book (April 5–August 29, 1832) , both in Black Hawk War Collection; John Reynolds, *My Own Times*, pp. 375–376.

[21] Second Johnston Diary, May 29, 1832, Johnston Papers, Barret Collection.

During the lull in campaigning Johnston was ordered to return briefly to Jefferson Barracks to supervise the shipment of fresh supplies to the expedition. Perhaps General Atkinson's purpose was also to give Johnston a visit with his family, for in his absence his wife had borne him a daughter, Henrietta Preston. Mingling domestic affairs with collecting provisions for the army, Johnston authorized an agent to sell certain Louisville property belonging to Mrs. Johnston, to make payment on a note owed by the Johnstons, and to purchase slaves to be used as house servants by them.[22] After ten days at home he left Jefferson Barracks to rejoin the expedition.

Meantime, unhappy over Atkinson's failure to take Black Hawk at once, and alarmed by pleas from the citizens of Illinois, Secretary of War Lewis Cass ordered General Winfield Scott with 1,000 additional regulars to the scene of action to take command. This force was stricken by cholera on the way and reached Rock Island by way of Detroit after the Black Hawk War was over.[23]

Immediately after disbanding the Illinois militia in May, Governor Reynolds recruited a new body of volunteers, and within three weeks three brigades were collected at the foot of the rapids on the Illinois River. They were assigned to Generals Alexander Posey, M. K. Alexander, and James D. Henry. As the brigades formed, General Atkinson sent them forward to Dixon's Ferry on the Rock River, and on June 25 he and his staff arrived there. The next day, hearing that the Indians were on the move toward the Mississippi River, Atkinson ordered General Alexander's brigade to the Plum River in an effort to cut off their retreat. Alexander was to return to Dixon's Ferry without further instructions if he should fail to meet the foe. But Black Hawk had not made for the Mississippi; he was still hiding in the lake country of Wisconsin, and on June 28 Atkinson moved his main force out of Dixon's Ferry and pressed north toward Black Hawk's lair.[24]

[22] Johnston to Edward D. Hobbs, June 4, 1832, *ibid.*

[23] Jackson (ed.) , *Black Hawk: An Autobiography*, p. 28.

[24] For General Atkinson's orders pertaining to these movements, see Order No. 39, June 19, 1832; Order No. 40, June 20, 1832; Order No. 41, June 20, 1832; Order No. 42, June 21, 1832; Order No. 43, June 25, 1832, in Atkinson Order Book (April 5–August 29, 1832) , Black Hawk War Collection. For his reports on the movements, see Atkinson to Secretary of War, June 23, 1832; Atkinson to General Macomb, June 26, 1832; Johnston to General Alexander Posey, June 30, 1832, in Atkinson Letter Book (May 26–September 23, 1832) , Black Hawk War Collection.

Three weeks of exhausting marches and fruitless search followed. On July 3 the army discovered an abandoned camp near Lake Koshkonong; the Indians had fled three days before.[25] Johnston explained the difficulties of the chase: "The facility of conveying information in this open country is so great, especially to those perfectly acquainted with it, that we almost despair of bringing the indians to battle unless they choose to do so with great advantage." [26]

Dispatching scouting parties to seek Black Hawk's trail, Atkinson halted on the Koshkonong until Alexander's brigade and Dodge's rangers joined him. Then for three days they combed the swamps in vain for their elusive quarry. On July 9, virtually out of provisions, Atkinson was forced to disperse his troops in order to feed them. The brigades of Alexander and Henry, plus Dodge's ranger battalion, were sent across fifty miles to Fort Winnebago on the Wisconsin River; General Posey led his brigade a like distance to Fort Hamilton near the Pecatonica; and General Atkinson and the regulars remained in a fortified camp, Fort Koshkonong (now Fort Atkinson, Wisconsin), on the Rock River a short distance above Lake Koshkonong. The army was to concentrate again at this place as soon as possible.

Within a week Atkinson received supplies and began to regather his troops at Fort Koshkonong. In returning by way of the upper Rock River, General Henry and Colonel Dodge discovered Black Hawk's track. Fear and hunger had done their work; the Indian leader was now striking for the Mississippi.[27]

We were forced to dig roots and bark trees, to obtain something to . . . keep us alive [he later explained]. Several of our old people became so much reduced, as actually to die with hunger! And, finding that the army had commenced moving, and fearing that they might come upon and

[25] Johnston Diaries, July 3, 1832, Johnston Papers, Barret Collection. General Atkinson wrote, apparently in mistake, that the abandoned camp was discovered on July 2. See Atkinson to Secretary of War, July 6, 1832, in Atkinson Letter Book (May 26–September 23, 1832), Black Hawk War Collection.

[26] Second Johnston Diary, July 3, 1832, Johnston Papers, Barret Collection.

[27] Johnston Diaries, July 9–21, 1832, *ibid.;* Frank E. Stevens, *The Black Hawk War,* pp. 214–215; and Atkinson to General Winfield Scott, July 9, 21, 1832; Atkinson to Generals James D. Henry and Henry Dodge, July 20, 1832, in Atkinson Letter Book (May 26–September 23, 1832) ; and Orders No. 51, 52, July 9, 1832, in Atkinson Order Book (April 5–August 29, 1832) , all in Black Hawk War Collection.

surround our encampment, I concluded to remove my women and children across the Mississippi, that they might return to the Sac nation again.[28]

The volunteers were jubilant. Sending word of their discovery to General Atkinson, they at once took up the pursuit, and Atkinson marched promptly to join them.

From the upper Rock River the trail led west through a country of swamps and sinkholes; with prodigious effort but rekindled zeal the troops pressed after Black Hawk. Between the upper two of the Four Lakes (Monona and Mendota) they followed his trace, passing the site of present Madison, and continued northwest toward the Wisconsin River. Exhaustion took heavy toll among the horses, but the volunteers went forward afoot when their mounts fell. Slowed by hunger and fatigue, the Indians lost ground in their race for life; on the afternoon of July 21, as they began crossing the Wisconsin, their rear guard was overtaken.

Resolved to destroy the Indians before they could cross the Wisconsin, Henry and Dodge attacked immediately. From late afternoon until nightfall the Battle of Wisconsin Heights was fought. Deserted by Neapope, Black Hawk commanded alone. Placing himself on a hill overlooking his line, he skilfully directed his men by voice, and they fought courageously and yielded ground sparingly. Black Hawk's strategy was successful; while he occupied the attackers, the women and children and belongings passed over the river in bark canoes hastily built. Fatigued by the long march, and perhaps sobered by the Indians' fierce resistance, Henry and Dodge halted their assault at dark, and during the night the braves gained the opposite bank of the river. Black Hawk had again demonstrated his cunning.[29]

While the Battle of Wisconsin Heights was being waged, the remainder of the army marched to join Henry and Dodge. Atkinson, with the regulars and Alexander's militia brigade, proceeded from Fort Koshkonong; Posey and his brigade moved from Fort Hamilton. Three days after the Battle of Wisconsin Heights the entire expedition was concentrated at Blue Mounds a few miles from the Wisconsin. The pursued were now spent and the pursuers almost so, for

[28] Jackson (ed.), *Black Hawk: An Autobiography,* pp. 153–154.
[29] *Ibid.,* pp. 157–160; Cyrenus Cole, *I Am a Man: The Indian Black Hawk,* pp. 199–204; William T. Hagan, *Black Hawk's Route through Wisconsin,* pp. 29, 31–32.

many of the army's mounts were worn beyond further service. Yet, wrote President Andrew Jackson, Black Hawk must not be permitted to cross the Mississippi; he must be severely chastised so that the frontier might live in peace. Atkinson prepared the final chase.[30]

From the militia organizations he selected a number of men equal to the number of serviceable horses—a total of about 900; the remainder he sent back to Fort Hamilton. With these choice volunteers plus the regulars, some 1,300 troops in all, Atkinson, on July 27 and 28, crossed the Wisconsin at Helena. For four days the army marched through a rugged country of hill and forest. In spite of the delay caused by reorganizing, they pressed close upon the Indians.[31]

From the Wisconsin, Black Hawk fled in desperation toward the Mississippi. Starvation slowed his pace and littered his track with the dead and dying of his people; only bark and roots and the flesh of scrawny ponies sustained them on the bitter trek. On August 1, famished to skin and bone, the depleted column reached the Mississippi at a point two miles below the mouth of the Bad Axe River, and passage of the Mississippi began at once. The river flowed in numerous channels between narrow, wooded islands that strewed its bed; by canoe and raft Black Hawk attempted to shuttle his women and children to the opposite shore. Hardly had the move begun when the steamer *Warrior* of Fort Crawford came upon the scene, for Black Hawk's appearance had been expected. Armed with a cannon at the bow, and with troops aboard, the *Warrior* blocked the route of escape.

Again Black Hawk sought to surrender; again his effort was in vain. He waved a white flag from the shore and asked for a small boat to bring him aboard the *Warrior*. Fearing ambush, or affecting to fear it, Captain Joseph Throckmorton ordered Black Hawk to come out in a canoe. When the Indian answered that he could not do so, that all canoes were filled with women and children and were beyond hail, Throckmorton opened fire on him with canister. A few braves fell; the others returned the fire. Shooting continued until dark, when the *Warrior* left to refuel. Black Hawk's courage now

[30] Henry Smith, "The Indian Campaign of 1832," *Report and Collections of the State Historical Society of Wisconsin*, X (1888), 150–166; Jackson (ed.), *Black Hawk: An Autobiography*, p. 157 n.

[31] Atkinson to General Scott, July 27, 1832, in Atkinson Letter Book (May 26–September 23, 1832); and Order No. 64, July 26, 1832; Order No. 65, July 27, 1832, in Atkinson Order Book (April 5–August 29, 1832), all in Black Hawk War Collection.

failed him, and during the night he and the Prophet abandoned their people.[32]

Meantime, the Army closed upon its prey. Atkinson's men were well fed, for he had brought provisions by pack horse and also some beeves on the hoof, but the horses had become so weak from hunger that infantry kept pace with cavalry. At dark, as the *Warrior* was breaking off the engagement, the troops camped near a spring a few miles from the river. "The appearance of the trail indicated our near approach to the main body of the enemy," wrote Johnston. "General Atkinson directed the commanders of Brigades to hold their troops in readiness to march at 2 A.M. tomorrow morning." [33]

At that early hour on August 2 the troops broke camp and marched toward the Mississippi. Skirmishing began an hour after sunrise when Atkinson's scouts encountered the Indian rear guard of twenty braves four or five miles from the river. Scattered in the timber, this party purposely gave the impression of being the main body, and Atkinson deployed his force to assault. Alexander and Posey were on the right, Dodge and the regulars in the center, and Henry on the left. Black Hawk was now gone, but his tactics prevailed. Retreating under attack, the rear guard fell back some distance upstream from the crossing, and, deceived by this stratagem, Atkinson and most of the army followed. Henry's brigade alone was left to cover the rear.

Many historians believe that jealousy moved Atkinson to leave Henry, in the hope of preventing the bold militia general from earning still more glory out of the campaign. If so, Atkinson was to be disappointed. Shortly after sunrise, with the bulk of the army decoyed two miles off course, Henry's scouts discovered the main body of the fugitives still attempting to cross the Mississippi. He at once descended the bluff overhanging the river and engaged the Indians in mortal combat in the Battle of the Bad Axe.[34] "We here had to charge for some considerable distance, over the worst kind of ground; the logs, and weeds being in some places as high as a man's

[32] Jackson (ed.), *Black Hawk: An Autobiography*, pp. 158–160; Second Johnston Diary, August 1, 1832, Johnston Papers, Barret Collection; "Minutes of Examination of Indian Prisoners" (typescript), Black Hawk War Collection of Manuscripts in Secretary of War Files, National Archives.

[33] Frank E. Stevens (ed.), *Wakefield's History of the Black Hawk War*, pp. 125–126; Johnston Diaries, July 27, August 1, 1832, Johnston Papers, Barret Collection.

[34] Johnston Diaries, August 2, 1832, *ibid.*

head," wrote a participant.[35] Drawn by the din of battle, Atkinson and the rest of the army hastened to the scene, and at about the same time the *Warrior* reappeared on the river. The chastisement of the Indians was at hand.

Chastisement was massacre, with no quarter shown.

The Ruler of the Universe, He who takes vengeance on the guilty, did not design those guilty wretches to escape His vengeance for the horrid deeds they had done [said one of Henry's volunteers]. He here took just retribution for the many innocent lives those cruel savages had taken on our northern frontiers.[36]

Driven from cover to cover, hundreds of the Indian band finally attempted to swim the river. Many drowned. When a small party of fugitives gathered on an offshore willow island, the *Warrior* promptly raked it with canister; then a body of regulars and volunteers were ferried out and cleared it with ball and bayonet. Unable to distinguish sex or age, if not indifferent to these distinctions, marksmen shot swimmers without compassion. "Unfortunately some women and children [were killed] which was much deplored by the soldiers," Johnston wrote laconically. About two hundred Indians were dead of wounds or drowning when the Battle of the Bad Axe ended. Six or seven whites died.[37]

The Indians who reached the opposite bank of the Mississippi found no safety, as they had hoped, for General Atkinson had permitted the Sioux to enter the war against their old enemies, the Sauk and Fox, and a Sioux war party now fell upon the forlorn survivors of the Bad Axe and slaughtered many of them. Of Black Hawk's band, once some 1,500 strong, less than one third came out of the tragic anabasis, and the Indian menace was gone from the Northwest.[38]

Black Hawk was not in the Battle of the Bad Axe. From a nearby bluff he witnessed the destruction of his people. In horror and rage he fled, only to be captured a few days later by the Winnebago and delivered to the Indian agent at Fort Crawford. He was placed in irons and sent down the Mississippi, guarded by two officers who

[35] Stevens, (ed.) , *Wakefield's History of the Black Hawk War,* p. 130.

[36] *Ibid.,* pp. 130–133.

[37] Jackson (ed.) , *Black Hawk: An Autobiography,* pp. 160–162.

[38] Stevens, *The Black Hawk War,* p. 223; Atkinson to General Scott, August 5, 9, 1832, in Atkinson Letter Book (May 26–September 23, 1832) ; and Order No. 66, August 3, 1832, in Atkinson Order Book (April 5–August 29, 1832) , both in Black Hawk War Collection.

would one day become deadly foes of each other—Lieutenants Jefferson Davis and Robert Anderson. After a short time in prison Black Hawk would be returned to his tribe, where, bereft of authority, he would live out his days under the guardianship of a hated rival, Keokuk. The hawk was clipped in wing and talon.

The Black Hawk War was Johnston's baptism of fire. From General Atkinson he learned the importance of careful planning for supply and logistics, especially in operations across a country void of roads and provender, but in other aspects of command his education profited more from the boldness of General Henry and Colonels Dodge and Taylor than from the cautiousness of General Atkinson, for Atkinson tended to exaggerate the prowess of the enemy and to minimize that of his own army.[39] The remorseless pursuit and destruction of Black Hawk's followers hardened Johnston to stern treatment of the Indian; he would forever share the frontiersman's view that the red man's time had come.

The Black Hawk War was not a big war. But it had the evils of all wars; it was an affair of fatigue, filth, hunger, disease, petty jealousy, bickering, frustration, loneliness, boredom and finally a measure of hazard in action. All of these Johnston endured manfully. He entered the campaign a garrison soldier; he emerged a field soldier.

Johnston impressed all who knew him with his courage and judgment: "He has talents of the first order, a gallant soldier by profession and education," wrote General Atkinson.[40] "He was a cool, clear-headed man, and an excellent officer," said a comrade.[41] "He acquired a very high reputation for his wise and successful conduct during the Black Hawk War," attested another.[42] Johnston met officers, such as Zachary Taylor, who later would influence his career; he renewed friendship with others, such as Jefferson Davis and Robert Anderson, who one day would shape his fate. It is possible that he came in touch with Abraham Lincoln, who served for a time as a volunteer in the campaign. The Black Hawk War was vital in developing the character and career of Albert Sidney Johnston.

---

[39] Atkinson maintained that he lacked the strength for boldness, since other tribes might have reinforced Black Hawk. See Atkinson to "Sir," November 19, 1832, Josiah Stoddard Johnston Papers.

[40] Atkinson to Carson, June 25, 1836, Johnston Papers, Barret Collection.

[41] G. H. Crossman to William Preston Johnston, March 12, 1873, *ibid.*

[42] Robert Anderson, "Reminiscences of the Black Hawk War," *Report and Collections of the State Historical Society of Wisconsin,* X (1888), 170.

Family Tragedy

WITH THE SUCCESSFUL ENDING of the Black Hawk War, Johnston looked forward to a period of sunshine in his own life. His conduct in the struggle had earned the praise of superior and subordinate alike, and he had weathered the campaign without a wound. Afterward, at Fort Crawford, according to his son's narrative, he survived both an onset of cholera and the barbarous drenchings and dosings prescribed to cure it.[1]

A joyous family awaited his return from the field; his wife felt grateful relief that he had been spared in the lottery of war; his young son was growing rapidly in mind and stature; an infant daughter increased the gladness of his home. When he returned to Jefferson Barracks in mid-autumn rich years seemed ahead.

But the seeds of tragedy had fallen unawares into the Johnston circle within the brief months of the Black Hawk War. His father

---

[1] Johnston, *Life of Johnston,* pp. 45–48. Johnston may have been among a group of soldiers who, according to General Atkinson, suffered light attacks of cholera during the early days of September, 1832. Atkinson did not, however, mention Johnston's name among them, which would have been a strange omission, considering the close relationship between the two. Henry Atkinson to General Winfield Scott, September 16, 1832, Atkinson Letter Book (May 26–September 23, 1832), Black Hawk War Papers.

died in October; during the war his wife had undergone physical and emotional trials from which she never recovered. In the summer she and both of her children had become seriously ill of what was probably influenza, and in July the baby daughter of three months weakened and, to all appearances, died. Mrs. Johnston wrote, "Supposed to be dead, [she] was, by God's mercy, restored to us." According to family account, the infant was actually in her coffin when an aunt, Mrs. Thomas Hart Benton, detected signs of life and revived her with hot baths and other stimulation. The effects of such an experience for a young wife, unsupported by the presence and consolation of her husband, are beyond telling.

Sickness continued to afflict the entire household.

Between physical fatigue and mental anxiety for my children, for you, and for my good husband, I am scarcely myself [Henrietta wrote to her mother in despair]. I try to be cheerful. God alone knows how it will all terminate. . . . I have so bad a cold that I can't be heard when I speak, and I am often fatigued and sick.

She had tuberculosis.[2]

Johnston's safe return from the Indian campaign seemed to restore the felicity of his fireside. The children mended quickly, and Mrs. Johnston appeared to grow stronger. Yet she was not content. Shaken by her trials during her husband's absence, yearning for permanent tranquillity, and possibly sensing the nature of her malady, she began to urge Johnston to resign his commission and take up life in a country home. It was much to ask of a young officer who appeared headed for an illustrious career in the service. His son records the struggle that went on within Johnston as he groped for the wise decision. To resign would be to cast aside the training, experience, and associations of a decade, to reject the obligation for his West Point education, to deny his own sense of personal destiny. On the other hand, he was financially pressed because of expenses incurred during the Black Hawk campaign and believed that he could earn more as a civilian than as a soldier; he enjoyed the out-of-doors and admired plantation life. Finally, a husband's love and his anxiety over his wife's health and happiness weighed heavily upon him. At year's end he reached his choice: he would leave the Army.[3]

[2] Johnston, *Life of Johnston,* pp. 45–48.
[3] Johnston to Edward D. Hobbs, January 13, 1833, Johnston Papers, Barret Collection.

As he had so often done in the past, Johnston asked for advice from his brother, Senator Josiah Stoddard Johnston.[4] Josiah Stoddard replied with optimism, saying that Albert Sidney could retire at that time under the most favorable and flattering circumstances, and that if he should aspire to political life, his military reputation would greatly aid him. "Wherever you go and whatever you do," wrote Josiah Stoddard, "you will find that it will exert a favorable influence in your intercourse with society." The elder brother declined to urge a particular occupation, but pointed out the advantages and disadvantages of many. If Albert Sidney should choose to become a planter, he ought to move to Louisiana, where profits were highest and where the Johnston family influence would support him. This was the last advice that Albert Sidney ever received from Josiah Stoddard. On May 19, 1833, Senator Johnston was killed in the explosion of the steamer *Lioness* on the Red River in Louisiana.[5]

Notwithstanding the favorable advice of his brother, Albert Sidney did not at once resign from the Army. Josiah Stoddard's death may have caused him to pause; certainly it chilled his interest in Louisiana as a place of abode. Want of funds also deterred him. He had intended selling some of his wife's property in Louisville to raise capital for whatever new venture he might make; now he learned that, at the moment, money was dear and real estate cheap. Since Mrs. Johnston's health seemed improved, they made no move during the spring or summer of 1833.[6]

In mid-September Henrietta suddenly fell ill again. She was expecting another child in a month, and when she failed to recover promptly from the illness, Johnston took furlough and returned with her to her mother's home in Louisville. There, for the first time, physicians accurately diagnosed her ailment and began treatment according to the practice of the times. She was freely bled and her diet restricted to goat's milk and Iceland moss. Years later her son truly said that no more certain means could have been devised to destroy her waning strength. On October 28 a second daughter was born to the Johnstons; she was named Maria Preston.[7]

---

[4] Johnston to Josiah Stoddard Johnston, February 7, 1833, Josiah Stoddard Johnston Papers.

[5] Johnston, *Life of Johnston*, pp. 48–50.

[6] Hobbs to Johnston, January 5, 1833, Johnston Papers, Barret Collection.

[7] Johnston, *Life of Johnston*, pp. 51–52.

Seeing his wife continue to weaken, Johnston journeyed with her to New Orleans the following spring for medical advice and the supposed benefits of Southern climate. They were guests of Dr. J. P. Davidson and his family, relatives of the Johnstons.

In New Orleans Johnston took the step which he had so long debated; on April 22, 1834, he resigned his commission in the Army.[8] Shortly afterward he wrote his friend N. J. Eaton that he had felt "some little pain" over the resignation. "I quit my profession and my regiment with lively interest for the welfare of *all,* and the recollection of strong friendship for very many of the officers of the regiment," he said, in a mild account of the turmoil within him over leaving the Army.[9] Dr. Davidson later told Johnston's son that Johnston gave the letter of resignation to him, with instructions to mail it at noon if Johnston had not by that time reclaimed it. "How anxiously your mother watched the dial of the clock, until the hands marked the hour of 12, when she bade me hurry to mail it," recalled Davidson. "The letter could hardly have reached its destination before both regretted the step, particularly your father." [10]

From New Orleans the Johnstons returned to Louisville. Upon the recommendation of physicians, they unwittingly dealt the last blow to Mrs. Johnston's flagging vitality. In the hope that travel and vacation would strengthen her, they embarked by boat and carriage upon an exhausting journey that covered most of the eastern United States. No wonder that Johnston would later advise a friend whose wife was ill, "Do not depend upon Medicine. While I entertain the highest respect for medical science I cannot conceal from myself that there are diseases which cannot be reached by it." [11] Beginning in mid-July, they visited the Red Sulphur Springs and other Virginia watering places esteemed as of value to the restoration of health. From near Fairfield, Virginia, Johnston wrote in September:

Mrs. J[ohnston's] health has improved rapidly since we left the Red Sulphur springs and although the symptoms of her disease were so much aggravated as to keep her confined a great part of her time to her bed, we

[8] Johnston to "Sir," April 22, 1834, Miscellaneous Manuscripts Collection, Jefferson Davis Shrine [Beauvoir], Biloxi, Mississippi.
[9] Johnston to N. J. Eaton, April 24, 1834 (copy), Johnston-Eaton Letter Book, Johnston Papers, Barret Collection.
[10] J. P. Davidson to William Preston Johnston, January 16, 1873, *ibid.*
[11] Johnston to Hobbs, October 14, 1835, *ibid.*

accord the merit of her increased strength now to the use of the Red Sulphur waters.[12]

Hope of recovery had bred the illusion of recovery.

After stopping with relatives in Lexington, Virginia, and elsewhere, the Johnstons moved on to Baltimore, then to Philadelphia for further medical consultation, and from there to New York City. On October 21, "after much traveling and fatigue," they came back to Louisville and to sorrow; while they were gone their infant daughter had died and been buried. "My babe is in her place of rest," said Mrs. Johnston with a weary poignancy. "The Lord gave and the Lord hath taken away. Blessed be the name of the Lord." [13]

Disease, fatigue, and grief had done their work. Her own time was fast approaching. The futile visits of physicians became more and more frequent; the despair of husband and kin became increasingly acute.[14] For nearly a year she lingered an invalid in the home of her mother in Louisville, and later in the nearby country abode of her uncle George Hancock. Johnston remained at her bedside; his tenderness and devotion to his stricken wife became a legend among relatives and acquaintances. On August 12, 1835, Henrietta Preston Johnston died.[15]

Johnston reeled under fortune's blows. Within three years of the ending of the Black Hawk War he had lost four persons dear to him—his father, his eldest brother, his infant child, and now the wife of his first love. Distraught with grief and the shattering of his plan of life, he withdrew to a farm near St. Louis which he had acquired a year before in the hope that he and his family might find well-being there. He left his small son and daughter with their grandmother in Louisville.

For a few months he went through the motions of improving the land and preparing it for the plow. Actually, he seems to have used the farm as a retreat to recover serenity. But he remained restless of spirit. He wrote an acquaintance that he preferred selling the Missouri property and moving farther west, and the following spring he journeyed to Washington, D.C., to ask in vain for government permission to settle a colony of whites in the country of the Sioux

[12] Johnston to "Dear Sir," September 7, 1834, *ibid.*
[13] Johnston, *Life of Johnston*, pp. 51, 53.
[14] L. Powell to Johnston, January 1, 1834, Johnston Papers, Barret Collection.
[15] Mrs. M. D. Hancock to William Preston Johnston, n.d., 1873, *ibid.;* Johnston, *Life of Johnston*, p. 53.

Indians.[16] Friends attempted to cheer him and besought him to come back to Louisville. "How much cause you have to feel flattered in your [children]," wrote one sympathizer. "Had I just such children my dear friend, I should not feel myself the same desolate being that I do now." [17]

When he did quit the Missouri residence and return to Louisville he chafed under inactivity. He was a man without a family and a soldier without a uniform. Latent urges stirred him to seek the frontier and to share in great undertakings. He was ripe for the call of an infant republic striking for independence.[18]

[16] Johnston to William Preston, April 20, 1836, Johnston Papers, Barret Collection.
[17] Hobbs to Johnston, December 31, 1835, *ibid.*
[18] Johnston, *Life of Johnston*, pp. 54–55.

Texas Command

~~~~~~

O N MARCH 3, 1836, in Louisville, Johnston first heard the summons that was to give new purpose to his life—the appeal of Stephen F. Austin, Commissioner from Texas, in behalf of his embattled people. The day before Austin spoke in Louisville a Texas convention had declared the land independent of Mexico; Mexican dictator Santa Anna was at that moment besieging the Alamo with six thousand troops to coerce the Texans into submission. Austin asked for men and money for the support of Texas and found the entire Mississippi Valley ablaze with sympathy. Residents of Louisville shared this emotion; Austin wrote from there: "Every thing is cheering in this part of the world for Texas The hearts of this people are with us." [1] One of the hearts touched by Stephen F. Austin was that of Albert Sidney Johnston.

Yet Johnston did not go at once to the defense of Texas. At the time of Austin's visit to Louisville, Johnston still contemplated settling a colony in the land of the Sioux. Only after he had been to

---

[1] Stephen F. Austin to James F. Perry, March 4, 1836, in Eugene C. Barker (ed.) , *The Austin Papers,* III, 317.

Washington and found the administration cool to his proposal of such a colony did he seriously consider moving to Texas. Tidings both tragic and stirring came from the beleaguered republic. In early March the Texas border garrisons at the Alamo and at Goliad were overwhelmed and put to sword and torch; a month later, after desperate flight by both soldiers and civilians, the Texas Army, led by Sam Houston, turned and destroyed Santa Anna's Mexican force at the Battle of San Jacinto. Captured in the rout, the Mexican leader made a treaty pledging to stop the invasion and acceding to Texas independence. Shortly the Mexican congress repudiated this agreement and prepared a fresh campaign against the rebellious province.[2] As the people of Texas braced for the blow, another of their agents, William H. Daingerfield, approached Johnston for support.[3]

The Texas Revolution attracted Johnston irresistibly. It appealed to his hunger for adventure on a new frontier; it awakened his instinct to render a stroke for freedom from despotism. It relit in him an old family vision of American expansion in the southwest; twenty-four years earlier two of Johnston's brothers had participated in the Magee filibustering expedition intended to add Spanish territory to the United States.[4] Johnston later told his son that he initially supported the independence of Texas in the hope that she soon would be annexed to the Union. At a moment when his career was in shambles and his life without meaning, service in Texas gave opportunity for personal fame and fortune. That Johnston would say goodbye to his small son and daughter to embrace the perils of war in a faraway country was a measure of the urge within him, for he loved his children deeply. But when summer came he left for Texas.

From Louisville he traveled by steamer to New Orleans, and then on to the plantation home of his brother, Judge John Harris Johnston, near Alexandria, Louisiana. After a few days' visit he rode west with a small party of horsemen bound for Texas. On July 13 they crossed the Sabine River, and two days later arrived in Nacogdoches, the chief community of eastern Texas. There Johnston met Sam

[2] Eugene C. Barker, *The Life of Stephen F. Austin: Founder of Texas, 1793–1836,* pp. 499–502; William C. Binkley, *The Texas Revolution,* pp. 94, 103–104, 108–109, 116.

[3] Johnston, *Life of Johnston,* p. 55.

[4] *Ibid.,* p. 68.

Houston, hero of San Jacinto and Commander in Chief of the Texas Army.[5] Wounded in the battle, Houston had spent nearly a month in New Orleans under medical care. Now he was back in Texas keeping his eye on the many pots boiling there—on the ominous gathering of Mexican troops at Matamoros just across the Rio Grande, on the turbulent Texas Army posted at the Coleto River near Goliad, and on the coming first presidential election in Texas. Sam Houston was ready to become the George Washington of the Lone Star Republic.

Houston wisely did not rejoin the Army in the field; instead, he left General Thomas J. Rusk at its head. Commanding the Texas Army at this time was a grievous chore. Most of the Texans who fought at San Jacinto had now gone home, convinced that the war was over. In their places were nearly two thousand volunteers recently arrived from the United States, most of them from the South—a bold and impetuous band moved by emotions at once noble and sordid. In its ranks true soldiers of liberty mingled with adventurers seeking only the spoils and glory of conquest. Frustrated by inactivity and incensed over the refusal of the Provisional Government to execute Prisoner Santa Anna, the Army threatened the Republic with military rule.

In early June the military took Santa Anna away from the civil authorities and placed him in irons. A month later, when General Mirabeau B. Lamar was ordered to take over Rusk's command, the troops rejected Lamar's appointment as "an unceremonious interference by the cabinet with the affairs of the army." [6] Pressing their advantage, some of the officers then sought to arrest Provisional President David G. Burnet and his Cabinet and arraign them before a military court. Foiled in this effort, the Army then voted Rusk out of command and replaced him with General Felix Huston of Mississippi. The Provisional Government repudiated this action, and, since Felix Huston was not at the moment present with the main body of the Army, Rusk retained his position. Thus stood affairs at the time of Johnston's arrival in Texas.[7]

Sam Houston doubtless welcomed to the new republic a man of Johnston's training and experience. Johnston brought with him

[5] Johnston to George Hancock, July 16, 1836, Johnston Papers, Barret Collection.
[6] Binkley, *The Texas Revolution*, pp. 115–116.
[7] Johnston, *Life of Johnston*, p. 71.

many letters of introduction extolling his skill as an officer and his virtue as a citizen.

You could not in an individual receive a greater acquisition [wrote General Atkinson]. Johnston has talents of the first order, a gallant soldier by profession and education and a gentleman of high standing & integrity. I commend him to you as qualified for any situation in the army, or civil duties, and one to be fully and entirely confided in.[8]

After a few days in Nacogdoches discussing with Houston and others the present needs and future possibilities of Texas, Johnston left to join the Army.

Upon arriving at General Rusk's headquarters, he was assigned to the cavalry because he owned a mount. At first he served as an enlisted man; according to his son's later account, he refused to use the flattering letters of recommendation to gain rank. But a man of his presence and skills could not long be overlooked in a small band as wanting in training as was the Texas Army. Johnston was now in the prime of manhood, six feet and an inch in height, 180 pounds in weight, and straight as a Comanche arrow. His handsome features had acquired the stamp of maturity sometimes known as character lines; his hair was brown, his complexion ruddy, his eyes blue and penetrating under heavy brows. His appearance betokened great physical strength and mental alertness; lithe and supple, he sat his horse with conspicuous ease. Johnston wore the look of command.[9]

Presently the Army moved to Lavaca Bay, a place considered more healthful than the previous location on the Coleto River. Johnston enjoyed the Gulf breezes and admired the fertility of the soil. Texas impressed him with her immense agricultural promise; he wrote that he was encamped on the richest cotton and sugar lands in the world. But the landscape of vast grassy plains broken by patches of oak did not strike him as being beautiful.

We are too apt to attribute superior beauty to things of conspicuous utility. I think on this account so many persons concur in describing Texas as a most lovely and charming country—Whatever may be said in praise of its delightful climate fertile soil and great capacity . . . may be relied upon, but in point of beauty Illinois, Missouri and the country on the upper Mississippi is far superior.

[8] Henry Atkinson to Mr. Carson, June 25, 1836, Johnston Papers, Barret Collection.
[9] Johnston, *Life of Johnston*, pp. 71–72.

Pangs of homesickness made him lament his absence from his "dear little boy and girl" and from friends and relatives in Kentucky. Johnston did not fall in love with Texas at first sight.[10]

He quickly caught the eye of General Rusk, who on August 5 named him adjutant general of his force; [11] but hardly were his duties begun when Johnston was stricken with a fever for many days. Not until September could he write his sister-in-law, "Thanks to a good constitution I have entirely recovered . . . and can now congratulate myself that I am acclimated altho' I suffered much and am quite as gaunt a figure as the most fastidious dandy could desire to be." [12] Once his strength returned, he worked with a will.

Fearing an early invasion by Mexican forces, Johnston strove diligently to bring order to the army of volunteers. "There is but little organisation or discipline in our army at this time," he confessed, "but we hope much from the future." He had little faith in the constancy of volunteers; his memory of the Black Hawk War was still fresh. But he trusted that the newly elected Texas Congress would strengthen and make permanent the fledgling "Regular Army" that had just been created by statute. "Should this be the case," he said, "my most ardent hopes for the cause will be entirely realised." [13]

Johnston did not long remain in the field. Upon learning of his qualifications, Provisional President Burnet appointed him adjutant general of the Republic with the rank of colonel in the Regular Army. Impressed by Johnston's efforts with the troops, and sorely needing a man of purpose to give system to the newly formed War Department, Secretary of War John Wharton called Johnston to the capital. Johnston doubtless would have preferred a command in the Army; an onerous task awaited him as adjutant general. In summoning him, Wharton complained that the previous adjutant general had neglected his job, that all records were in complete confusion, and that applicants came daily claiming compensation for services unknown to the Secretary. In early October Johnston arrived at the

---

[10] Johnston to Caroline H. Preston, September 10, 1836, Johnston Papers, Barret Collection.

[11] Thomas J. Rusk to Johnston, August 5, 1836, Albert Sidney Johnston Papers, Manuscript Division, Library of Congress.

[12] Johnston to Caroline H. Preston, September 10, 1836, Johnston Papers, Barret Collection.

[13] *Ibid.*

capital, which was then Columbia, and at once tackled the chaos of his new office.[14]

He discharged his duties well. But he was soon on the move again; in mid-November President Houston sent him to New Orleans on business "connected with the public interest." Among other duties, he was to recruit men for the Texas Army and obtain forms for keeping its records,[15] but he had not been in New Orleans long when the President wrote him to return to Texas without delay. "It is highly important both to your own and the interests of Texas," said Houston, "that you . . . assume your military duties as you are in nomination and doubtless will be commissioned to the office of Brigadier General soon." [16] Two weeks later the Secretary of War wrote, "You have been appointed Senior Brigadier General of the army of Texas. . . . It is vital[ly] important to the interests of the country that you should hasten immediately." [17] Johnston's feelings as he hurried to join the Army must have mingled gratification with apprehension. Heavy responsibilities awaited him.

On February 4, 1837, Johnston reached Army headquarters at Camp Independence on the Lavaca River. He found officers and men in a mood of ominous suspense, with General Felix Huston at the center of the unrest. Huston was the Hotspur of the Texas Army. A native of Kentucky, he was a lawyer in Natchez, Mississippi, at the outbreak of the Texas Revolution. Boundless zeal for the Texas cause moved him to raise and equip a body of volunteers for service in its behalf; so great was his ardor that he borrowed $40,000 to do this. He arrived in Texas in early July, burning to smite the Mexican force at Matamoros and to establish a military colony along the Rio Grande, with himself at its head. He saw himself as a veritable baron of the border. Rejected by the Provisional Government when he was elected commander in the field, Huston later was appointed junior brigadier general to serve under Johnston. Since

---

[14] John Wharton to Johnston, September 17, 1836, *ibid.*

[15] Sam Houston to "T. Toby & Brother," November 19, 1836, in Amelia W. Williams and Eugene C. Barker (eds.), *The Writings of Sam Houston, 1813–1863,* I, 486–487.

[16] Houston to Johnston, December 22, 1836, Johnston Papers, Barret Collection; Houston to "All Who Shall See These Presents," December 22, 1836, Albert Sidney Johnston Papers, Library of Congress.

[17] William S. Fisher to Johnston, January 11, 1837, Johnston Papers, Barret Collection.

Huston was already present with the Army, he was temporarily in command when Johnston arrived to assume the position.

Johnston's appointment as senior general was a blow to Huston's ambition and pride; he felt it a blow to his honor. Huston was a caricature of an ante-bellum Southerner, a man of reckless courage, fiery eloquence, and renowned skill with the duelling pistol. His impetuosity appealed to that of the Texas volunteers, among whom he was affectionately called "Old Long-Shanks" or "Old Leather-Britches," and a majority of them preferred him to be their commander. Unable to strike at the author of his frustration—President Sam Houston, who made the appointments—Felix Huston resolved to strike at the object of his frustration—Albert Sidney Johnston. Huston would satisfy honor in the one way that he knew to do it: he would challenge Johnston to a duel.[18]

On the day of Johnston's arrival the two generals greeted each other with courtesy; one account has it that Huston entertained Johnston and his staff at dinner that evening.[19] Huston seems to have respected Johnston as a gentleman and a soldier. But etiquette concealed passion; that night Johnston received from Huston a letter expressing the man's true emotions.

Your assuming the command of the army would have excited in me no feelings but those of respect and obedience . . . were it not for the fact that your appointment was connected with a tissue of treachery and misreputation, which was intended to degrade me, and blast my prospects in the Texan army. You in assuming the command under an appointment connected with the attempt to ruin my reputation, and inflict stigma on my character, of course stand in an attitude of opposition to myself. . . . I therefore propose a meeting between us at as short a period as you can make convenient.[20]

Thus was the gauntlet flung down.

Johnston was not given to the duel as an arbiter of honor. Later in life he would ignore such a challenge, but now he was pressed by circumstance. Should he refuse to fight, the unruly volunteers doubtless would believe him afraid to fight; and without conspicuous

[18] Williams and Barker (eds.), *The Writings of Sam Houston,* I, 515–517.
[19] James M. Morgan, "Extracts from the Reminiscences of General George W. Morgan," *Southwestern Historical Quarterly,* XXX (January, 1927), 191.
[20] Felix Huston to Johnston, February 4, 1837, Johnston Papers, Barret Collection.

physical courage he could not hope to command them a day. His personal career and the authority of the government appeared at stake. He afterward said that he fought as a public duty, that he considered the dignity of the Republic assailed in his person.[21] The evening that he received Huston's note, Johnston replied in the stilted phrases customary to the occasion:

After reciprocating the sentiments of respect and esteem which you have been pleased to express toward me, it only remains to accord to you the meeting proposed. I have designated 7 o'clock A.M. tomorrow My friend Col Morehouse is authorized to make the necessary arrangements.[22]

Thus was the gauntlet taken up.

Details of the duel have been blurred in legend and conflicting accounts by witnesses.[23] Johnston and Huston rode with their escorts across the Lavaca, through the skirting timber, and to the edge of the prairie, where they prepared for a drama at once comic and somber. Since Johnston was the party challenged, he had the privilege of selecting the kind of weapons to be used. To the surprise of all, he chose pistols. Just why he did so is not clear. Huston was known to be a keen shot with this arm; Johnston was reputed to be skilled with rifle and rapier, but unsure with the pistol (he afterward told a friend that he had not fired one since leaving Jefferson Barracks).[24] Johnston's son later speculated that his father elected to fight at such disadvantage and risk in order to gain the greater moral ascendancy over the troops—if he should come out alive. Whatever Johnston's reasons, at 7 o'clock on the morning of February 5 the two men faced each other with Huston's long horse pistols at the ready.

Shooting began upon signal. Tradition says that Johnston used a stratagem to flaw his opponent's reputed deadly aim: without taking the time to sight, he fired instantly. Startled by the quick report, Huston shot prematurely with a nervous touch on the hair trigger. Neither man was hit. Both loaded and fired again; still both were

[21] N. J. Eaton to William Preston Johnston, January 1, 1873, *ibid.*

[22] Johnston to Felix Huston, February 4, 1837, *ibid.*

[23] For accounts of the duel, see William L. Norvell to William Preston Johnston, March 11, 1877, *ibid;* Morgan, "Extracts from the Reminiscences of General George W. Morgan," *Southwestern Historical Quarterly,* XXX (January, 1927), 192–193.

[24] Eaton to William Preston Johnston, January 1, 1873, Johnston Papers, Barret Collection.

untouched. Their marksmanship was abominable; repeatedly they loaded and fired; again and again their bullets flew wide of the mark. Only on the fifth or sixth exchange was blood drawn; then at last Johnston fell with a ball through his right hip.

Friends and the attending surgeon rushed to him. He appeared to be wounded mortally. His second, Colonel Morehouse, is said to have promised vengeance upon Huston; the stricken Johnston gently rebuked this threat as insubordination and counselled obedience to Huston as second-in-command of the Army. Approaching the fallen man, Huston expressed regret and pledged himself to obey Johnston, should the commander's life and faculties be spared. Chivalry thus carried the day.

Though not fatal, Johnston's wound was severe. The ball had struck him on the front of the right side, passed through the orifice of the pelvis, and come out at the back of the hip. Friends lifted him on a litter and carried him to a private home in the nearby village of Texana. There he lay prostrate for weeks.

Notwithstanding his loss of the duel, Johnston gained what he had hoped to gain in fighting it—moral pre-eminence over Huston and the troops. Turbulence prevailed in the camp on the morning of the fight. Word of the affair had circulated beforehand, and many of the troops rushed toward the scene of conflict as the sound of pistol shots reached camp. Huston was the favorite of a majority; they doubtless hoped for Johnston's death and the elevation of Huston to top command. Excitement over this prospect was heightened by the drinking of much whiskey that unaccountably appeared on the morning of the encounter. Some said later that a general mutiny would have occurred if Huston had been killed, but the wounding of Johnston, followed by his chivalrous conduct toward his opponent, took the triumph out of victory. Filled with remorse, Huston waved aside the congratulations of admiring soldiers and was seen afterward pacing to and fro in deep agitation before his quarters. Sobered by near tragedy, he and the troops now accepted Johnston as commanding general.[25]

President Sam Houston was thunderstruck when he heard of the duel. In all his Texas career Houston never accepted a challenge, though he received many of them; San Jacinto had made him secure

---

[25] Morgan, "Extracts from the Reminiscences of General George W. Morgan," *Southwestern Historical Quarterly*, XXX (January, 1927), 192–193.

enough in the hearts of his compatriots that he could ignore these invitations without losing face.

To my boundless mortification and regret, I learn that an unfortunate meeting took place between Genl. Huston and yourself [he wrote to Johnston]. It is done and must be so. At this time when the enemy are expected it is strange to me that such things should happen. The field of battle may require the prowess of all the best men in our land. . . . Let harmony in Camp be inculcated and by all means prevent *Duelling* in future! [26]

Secretary of War William S. Fisher reprimanded Johnston in like manner.[27] Certainly the President and the Secretary were right in counselling harmony in the Army command. That in this instance harmony would have been possible without a duel is problematical. Sam Houston's letter of disapproval may have been simply a tap on the wrist; he must have realized that rude problems sometimes require rude solutions.

Johnston's recovery was slow. Although the wounded tissue mended quickly and the attending physician predicted that he would soon be well, he continued to suffer grievously from an injured sciatic nerve that had lain in the track of the bullet. More than a month after the duel he was still bedridden, with much pain in the heel and side of his right foot. Even after he was able to walk, he remained for a long time unable to mount his horse. Thus incapacitated, Johnston for two weeks was commander in name only, and Felix Huston largely ran the Army.[28] But good will now prevailed among officers and men, including the two generals.[29] A week after the duel, Sam Houston wrote Johnston that he had learned with great pleasure of the splendid condition of the Army. "I confidently rely on every thing possible being done for the country that can be accomplished by the army," Houston said, and he told Johnston that prospects were bright for recognition by the United States. But the President warned Johnston to remain alert for further Mexican invasion as scouts along the border and sources in New Orleans had reported 5,000 Mexican troops concentrated at Matamoros and Saltillo. "[The Army] is the salvation of the country," said President Houston.[30]

[26] Houston to Johnston, February 7, 1837, Johnston Papers, Barret Collection.
[27] Fisher to Johnston, February 7, 1837, *ibid.*
[28] Johnston to Caroline H. Preston, March 9, 1837, *ibid.*
[29] Fisher to Johnston, February 11, 1837, *ibid.*
[30] Houston to Johnston, February 11, 13, 1837, *ibid.*

Despite a lingering infirmity, Johnston soon regained physical strength and before the end of February was in true command of the Army. Felix Huston continued popular with many of the troops, but his influence was on the wane. Possibly at Huston's request, Johnston posted him with a small command at Victoria on the Guadalupe River, but shortly afterward, when, for want of cavalry, these troops seemed in danger of being cut off and destroyed, Johnston ordered them back to the main body of the Army.[31] Huston protested that he desired to remain where he was in order to observe movements of the enemy and to obtain beef.[32] Johnston nevertheless recalled the detachment.

Within a month he dispatched Huston to New Orleans to procure ammunition and supplies. Huston's letters back to Johnston were filled with friendly advice and small talk of a personal nature. "I have been most charmingly regaled with the ague & fever and am just at this time in rapture and ec[s]tasy with the effects of 30 gns calomel and near a gill of oil," Huston once wrote while on this mission.[33] Apparently the two erstwhile rivals were now cordial to each other.

Johnston found himself beset with burdens. Most of the problems arising out of the recent revolution and the immaturity of the Republic were yet unsolved, while threat of Mexican invasion seemed ever more acute. In early March Johnston heard from a cavalry detachment on the Nueces that 6,000 enemy soldiers were then at Matamoros, with about 3,000 others nearby.[34] Unrest persisted among the Texas soldiers as the President failed to press for a counteroffensive; moreover, the Administration was unable to provide the Army adequately with weapons, horses, or supplies.[35] Still in constant pain from his wound, Johnston strove diligently to shape his impetuous troops into an effective defensive force.

He expected action at any moment and shared the hope of his followers that it would come. Santa Anna was now free, released on the promise that he would persuade his own statesmen to accept the treaty of Texas independence. President Sam Houston calmly awaited the outcome of Santa Anna's efforts. Misjudging the Mexi-

---

[31] Johnston to Felix Huston, February 28, 1837 (copy), *ibid.*
[32] Felix Huston to Johnston, March 1, 28, 1837, *ibid.*
[33] *Ibid.*, March 28, 1837.
[34] Juan N. Seguin to Johnston, March 9, 1837, *ibid.*
[35] Houston to Johnston, March 1, 1837, *ibid.*

can leader's devious ways, both President Houston and Johnston believed him to be sincere; but Johnston doubted Santa Anna's ability to change the minds of his people.[36]

The Texas Army at this time amounted to 1,700 regulars and long-term volunteers. Except for 400 new recruits without arms, the men were well drilled and trained. Johnston felt them capable of repelling any invasion that the Mexicans could launch. "I have never seen a finer body of men—or troops I would lead to the charge with more confidence," he said.[37]

But Johnston was not content to watch and wait for a Mexican attack. He aspired to increase his force and himself take the offensive at the earliest moment, and he chafed at a Fabian yielding of the initiative to the foe. He seconded Felix Huston's desire to rekindle the quiescent war.

I hope little from the war policy of the administration [Felix Huston said to Johnston]. As to our waging active war [President Houston] will not hear of it. . . . Not expecting to be attacked and not intending to attack, there is but little energy shown. I am in very low spirits as to our prospect and deem Texas in a most critical situation. . . . By prudence and activity we must remedy the evil as much as we can. . . . Your next chance is that the enemy may come on and that settles the matter—there can be no delay then.[38]

Johnston hopefully anticipated that Santa Anna would fail to pacify the Mexican people and thus hostilities would be resumed. "In [this] most favorable event," Johnston said, "Texas may yet be called to act an important part in the establishment of [Santa Anna's] power and authority by which [Texas'] own Independence is to be secured." Only by carrying war to the enemy and dictating peace on Mexican soil could Texas assure the recognition of her nationhood and the security of her frontier, thought Johnston.[39] An even deeper and less rational urge probably moved him to favor renewing the war—an instinct of which he may have been only dimly aware. Perhaps he yearned to fight the Mexicans out of a sheer hunger for combat.

Johnston's hope of striking the foe was not to be fulfilled. Forbidden to attack, and with forces too weak to do so with assurance even

36 Johnston to Houston, March 13, 1837 (copy), *ibid.*
37 Johnston to Caroline H. Preston, March 9, 1837, *ibid.*
38 Felix Huston to Johnston, March 28, 1837, *ibid.*
39 Johnston to Houston, March 13, 1837 (copy), *ibid.*

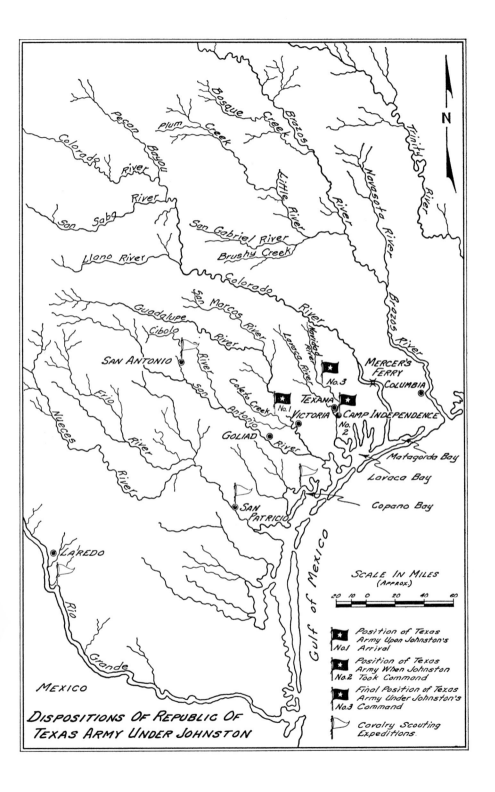

N

Pecos Bayou
Colorado
River
San Saba River
Llano River

Bosque Creek
Plum Creek
Little River
San Gabriel River
Brushy Creek
Colorado
River

Brazos
River
Navasota River
Trinity River

Guadalupe
Cibolo
San Marcos River
San Antonio River

SAN ANTONIO

Frio River
Nueces River

Colete Creek
San Antonio River
GOLIAD

Lavaca River
Navidad River

★ No.3

★ No.1 TEXANA
VICTORIA ★ CAMP INDEPENDENCE
No.2

MERCER'S
FERRY
COLUMBIA

Brazos River

Matagorda Bay
Lavaca Bay
Copano Bay

SAN
PATRICIO

Gulf of Mexico

LAREDO

Rio Grande

MEXICO

SCALE IN MILES
(Approx.)
20 10 0 20 40 60

★ Position of Texas
No.1 Army Upon Johnston's
Arrival

★ Position of Texas
No.2 Army When Johnston
Took Command

★ Final Position of Texas
No.3 Army Under Johnston's
Command

⚑ Cavalry Scouting
Expeditions

DISPOSITIONS OF REPUBLIC OF
TEXAS ARMY UNDER JOHNSTON

if given the opportunity, he retired the main body of the Army behind the Navidad River, where he stayed on the move to deceive the enemy and to keep his own troops occupied and fit. Should Texas be heavily invaded, he would withdraw behind the Colorado River at Mercer's Ferry and make his stand there.[40] Meantime, he posted cavalry parties along the frontier to observe and report all enemy movements: Lysander Wells to San Patricio on the lower Nueces, James W. Tinsley to Copano Bay on the coast, Erastus (Deaf) Smith toward Laredo, and Juan Seguin to San Antonio.[41] From Seguin, on March 13, he received an account of a scene of supreme pathos in Texas history. Three weeks before, said Seguin, he had buried with military honors the ashes of the defenders of the Alamo—whose bodies Santa Anna had ordered cremated in a giant pyre in front of the Alamo after the little fort had fallen the year before.[42]

By early spring, through the arrival of additional recruits from New Orleans, Johnston's force had grown to 2,000 men. All the while, he drilled and instructed his troops with the greatest energy he could muster. Inspecting the Army in late March, Secretary of War Fisher found it in top condition.[43]

Food and equipment grew shorter as time went by. During the months of March and April the troops were without sufficient bread or vegetables; Johnston conserved these meager supplies by increasing the ration of beef and issuing flour and beans on alternate days only.[44] He could secure meat by sending mounted parties to round up beeves along the Nueces River, and he called upon citizens of neighboring communities to provide food, arms, and ammunition against the day of hostile invasion.[45] Yet his men were in want. Regimental commanders reported that many had not "even an apology for shoes"; one cavalry leader wrote that his troopers were "naked, barefoot, and without horses."[46] Times were austere for Johnston and the Texas Army.

Johnston gradually lost faith in President Sam Houston's capacity

---

[40] Johnston to Fisher, April 4, 14, 22, May 4, 1837 (copies), *ibid.*

[41] For reports from two of these reconnaissance parties, see Seguin to Johnston, March 13, 1837; Lysander Wells to Johnston, May 10, 1837, *ibid.*

[42] Seguin to Johnston, March 13, 1837, *ibid.*

[43] Fisher to Johnston, March 28, 1837, *ibid.*

[44] Johnston to Fisher, March 12, April 28, 1837 (copies), *ibid.*

[45] Ira Ingram [and others] to Johnston, April 17, 1837; H. R. Wigginton to Johnston, n.d., 1837, *ibid.*

[46] Seguin to Johnston, March 13, 1837, *ibid.*

to defend the Republic. Houston probably accomplished what could be accomplished with the resources at hand, for Texas was weak with the weakness of infancy. Yet Johnston could reasonably feel that he wanted valid information and effective support from the Administration. President Houston offered gratuitous advice on elementary military tactics: he warned Johnston to hold his army concentrated, to beware of Mexican feints and ambuscades, to keep in touch with his cavalry scouts, and so to dispose his troops in battle that he could defend against enemy cavalry and not come within range of enemy artillery. He scolded Johnston for failing to inform him of the strength and needs of the Army.[47] To these messages Johnston replied courteously. He acknowledged Houston's military advice and wrote the President that complete reports and requisitions had already been submitted to the War Department.[48]

As the weeks went by, the Army's prospects worsened. Johnston sorely needed additional cavalry to patrol the frontier; President Houston promised to fill the need. On March 1, the President wrote Johnston that he had raised part of one company of horsemen and had ordered them to the Army. "I will continue my exertions and God alone can give success," said Houston. But a month later he owned that he had failed. "All my efforts to get you cavalry appear in vain," he wrote, and in an afterthought, revealed the hazards of life on the Texas frontier: "Were they there, I have no hope that they wou'd be retained, but wou'd be taken by the Indians." [49]

Messages from the Texas War Department confounded Johnston's estimate of enemy capabilities and revealed doubt and conflict of judgment within the Administration itself. On April 1 Secretary Fisher informed Johnston that a "rather doubtful" source had reported strenuous Mexican preparations for the immediate invasion of Texas.[50] But on the same day, Fisher secretly wrote to Johnston, "My Individual opinion is that more importance is to be attached to the information . . . than you would infer from my official communication." [51] Ten days later a Mexican fleet blockaded the Texas coast, captured arms and provisions intended for Johnston's troops, and caused a rumor that an army of 16,000 was marching upon the new

47 Houston to Johnston, February 7, March 1, 1837, *ibid.*
48 Johnston to Houston, March 13, 1837 (copy), *ibid.*
49 Houston to Johnston, March 1, 31, 1837, *ibid.*
50 Fisher to Johnston, April 1, 1837 [official], *ibid.*
51 *Ibid.* [unofficial].

republic.[52] In panic the Secretary wrote Johnston to call in all detachments and be ready to retreat behind the Colorado. "For Gods sake have every thing prepared," [53] Fisher pleaded.

Johnston calmly awaited the blow, which was not to fall. President Houston judged more sagely than did his colleagues the temper and capacity of the enemy. Felix Huston, who itched for action, railed:

Tell [Houston] that the Mexicans are marching troops on the Rio Grande and letters from Vera Cruz, Tampico & Matamoros all say that they will invade Texas, he replies that such is the character of the Mexicans they always make a great fuss and do nothing, and they never again will invade Texas.[54]

The President was right. The readiness of Johnston's troops, together with domestic upheaval in Mexico, prevented a fresh offensive against Texas.

On March 21 President Houston wrote joyfully to Johnston, saying that word had arrived of the recognition of Texas independence by the United States. "The recognition was the last official act of General Jackson," said Houston. "The next thing to be hoped for is annexation & peace." [55]

An uneasy quiet prevailed along the Nueces, but, ironically, peace for Texas caused unrest in the Texas Army and made Johnston's job immeasurably harder. Without a live campaign, soldiers grew unruly; the sound discipline established by Johnston during his early weeks of command began to disappear.[56] The soldiers bristled over rumors that veterans' bounty lands were falling into the hands of speculators; volunteers resented a War Department order prohibiting the election of officers.[57] Inactivity and want of pay and provisions were the true sources of the Army's malaise, Johnston perceptively wrote to the Secretary of War, but Johnston was powerless to remove the sources.[58] "Above all," said a Texas soldier afterward, "the troops needed an enemy to fight." [59]

---

[52] *Ibid.*, April 10, 1837 [unofficial].
[53] *Ibid.*, April 14, 1837 [unofficial].
[54] Felix Huston to Johnston, March 28, 1837, *ibid.*
[55] Houston to Johnston, March 21, 1837, *ibid.*
[56] Fisher to Johnston, April 14, 1837, *ibid.*
[57] F. S. Gray to Johnston, May 12, 1837, *ibid.*
[58] Johnston to Fisher, April 22, 1837 (copy), *ibid.*
[59] Morgan, "Extracts from the Reminiscences of General George W. Morgan," *Southwestern Historical Quarterly*, XXX (January, 1927), 194.

Increasingly the men turned to whiskey for relief from the boredom, frustration, and austerity of life in service. Particularly schooled in the dangers of drink, President Houston repeatedly instructed Johnston to permit no alcohol in camp; and Johnston, equally aware of the menace, banned whiskey within his lines. He considered liquor peddlers to be destroyers of military organization and enemies of the country. "Should any of [them] fall into my hands you need not be surprised if they should be treated with but little delicacy," he wrote to the President. Yet to keep out whiskey altogether was impossible, and a secret and lucrative traffic in spirits throve about the outskirts of the post.[60]

Unrest in the Army came to a head in early April when Johnston imprisoned some soldiers caught bringing whiskey into camp.[61] Led by a few disgruntled junior officers who were described by the Secretary of War as "military demagogues," a group of about one hundred troops overpowered the stockade guards in the night and freed the prisoners. Johnston promptly arrested the leaders of the uprising and created a main guard to restore discipline. Johnston permitted the officers engaged in the affair to resign, saying he believed this course to be more conducive to the good of the service than a trial would be.[62] The soldiers involved addressed a letter to Johnston, justifying their behavior as a defense against the brutality of a certain officer, and denying any intention toward insubordination. For the moment, tumult subsided into sullen obedience.[63]

But the affair was not ended. A few weeks afterward, one of the regimental commanders, Colonel Henry Teal, was murdered in his sleep. Again many of the troops rioted. Suspicion pointed to a rival officer who had recently been relieved of command and bitterly tongue-lashed by President Houston,[64] but Johnston and his staff thought that Teal, an exacting officer, had been assassinated in a conspiracy against discipline and adherence to duty. Once more Johnston imposed order with the main guard.[65]

The events of this spring chilled Johnston's spirit for his command. All hope of an offensive against Mexico was gone; his con-

---

[60] Johnston to Fisher, April 4, 1837 (copy), Johnston Papers, Barret Collection.
[61] E. Morehouse to Johnston, April 5, 1837, *ibid.*
[62] Johnston to Fisher, April 17, 1837 (copy), *ibid.*
[63] "Soldiers of the Army of Texas" to Johnston, April 8, 1837, *ibid.*
[64] Fisher to Johnston, May 11, 1837, *ibid.*
[65] Morgan, "Extracts from the Reminiscences of General George W. Morgan," *Southwestern Historical Quarterly*, XXX (January, 1927), 193–194.

fidence in the Administration had vanished; his troops were in
tatters and on reduced rations; he could keep discipline only with an
iron hand. Moreover, he suffered constantly from his wound, which
still kept him out of the saddle and robbed him of the energy that
his job required. By late April he could endure no more. He wrote
to the Secretary of War, asking to be relieved of command, and
saying:

I should be wanting in honor were I to conceal from you that I am unable
to discharge all my duties, and have been restrained until this time from
reporting it by the hope of recovery, which I do not now believe will be
soon. . . . I have recommended the appointment of a major-general. Should
any other arrangement be deemed more conducive to the public interest,
let no motive of consideration for me interfere.[66]

The Administration would not at once relieve Johnston of his
command. Secretary of War Fisher acknowledged that Johnston's
infirmity justified his request, that he served under grievous circumstances, and that the Texas government was much obligated to him
for having filled so disagreeable a post. "Should you leave the army
at the present time," said Fisher, "I know of no one who could
supply your place." [67] Presently the Secretary wrote again, asking
Johnston to bear his situation as patiently as possible, and promising
to replace him within the next few days.[68]

Secretary Fisher did not reckon with the depth of Johnston's
despondency. In writing a kinsman that his wound compelled quitting the service of Texas, Johnston said further,

I find that in a state of inaction it is impossible to impose the most
necessary regulations for the government of troops without producing
discontent. I do not believe you will like the service. I therefore withdraw
my recommendation to you to come over for the purpose of joining.[69]

On May 7, before receiving the Secretary of War's reply to his
resignation, Johnston turned over the Army to his second-in-
command, a Colonel Rogers.[70]

[66] Johnston to Fisher, April 22, 1837 (copy), Johnston Papers, Barret Collection.
[67] Fisher to Johnston, May 6, 1837, *ibid.*
[68] *Ibid.*, May 11, 1837.
[69] Johnston to "Dear Griffin," May 6, 1837, Johnston Papers, Barret Collection.
[70] Johnston to "Army of Texas," May 7, 1837, *ibid.*

This precipitate action was a grave mistake. Johnston's retirement was signal for fresh insubordination among many of the troops. "Huzza for Rogers, and down with the main guard," they cried as soon as Johnston left camp.[71] Rogers supinely abolished the guard, and discipline all but vanished from the Army.[72] Two weeks later, President Houston restored order through a stroke that has been called true statecraft: he disbanded the bulk of the Army by granting indefinite furloughs to all volunteers.[73] The disbanding would have occurred if Johnston had remained in command, for the President neither felt the need for so large an army, nor could he provide for it. And even had Johnston been in sound health, he probably soon would have resigned from the service, for he could not long abide inactivity. Nevertheless, his premature yielding of command ill became one of his position and training. Perhaps his deep sense of duty would have prevented it if he had been himself; torment from the injured nerve seems temporarily to have swayed him.

In retiring from command, Johnston retained the confidence of Administration and subordinates. Still refusing to accept Johnston's resignation, the Secretary of War granted him a furlough to return to the United States for medical treatment and to be absent until his health should be restored.[74] Officers of the Army extolled Johnston's virtues without stint. Lamenting the need of his retirement, they nevertheless felt it necessary, that he might preserve himself for future usefulness and distinction.

Since his first appearance amongst us [they said], we have viewed in the conduct of Genl Johnston the characteristics of the high minded chivalrous soldier, accomplishing his designs by a firm and honorable course of policy, never deigning to stoop for favor to the petty artifices of the demagogue. . . . He has not exerted himself merely for the good of the army or of a portion of it, or of the citizens or a portion of them, but . . . he has had ever at heart the prosperity of the whole country. In his skill as a commander we have the most implicit confidence; and from our knowledge of his character, hesitate not to pronounce him unsurpassed in coolness of courage and firmness of purpose in the hour of danger. . . . Acknowledging a preference for no other man, [we] convey to him our high appre-

[71] T. J. Morgan to Johnston, May 16, 1837, *ibid.*
[72] Morgan, "Extracts from the Reminiscences of General George W. Morgan," *Southwestern Historical Quarterly,* XXX (January, 1927), 194.
[73] Llerena Friend, *Sam Houston: The Great Designer,* p. 82.
[74] Fisher to "All Whom It Concerns," May 17, 1837, Johnston Papers, Barret Collection.

ciation of his character both private and publick, and our aspiration warm
as the heart can give it for his future prosperity.[75]

Few commanders have left their posts with greater tribute ringing in
their ears.

Johnston immediately went to New Orleans for treatment of his
wound. Confirming that the intense pain in his right foot was caused
by injury to the sciatic nerve, physicians there subjected him to a
harrowing round of cupping, leeching, suppuration, friction, electri-
cal currents, hot baths, iodine, and ointments.[76] Plagued by continued infirmity, and gloomy over the disbanding of most of the
Texas Army, Johnston again offered his resignation to the Texas
government.[77] Again it was refused. He was instructed to remain
absent as long as necessary, but to return to command when he could
do so.

After a month in New Orleans he went to Louisville, and there he
stayed through summer and fall, gladdened over being again with
his children and with relatives and friends. Because of his experience
in Texas, he found himself a celebrity among former acquaintances
and men of affairs. United States Attorney General Henry D. Gilpin,
now married to the widow of Josiah Stoddard Johnston, wrote from
Washington to recommend the waters of the Virginia springs for
Johnston's still painful wound.

You must allow me to congratulate you on a safe return and escape from
the dangers of your knight-errantry, [Gilpin said]. When we saw you at
the head of the army, we began to think of Cortes and DeSoto . . . and
conjectured that . . . [you would be] putting a new flag on the same walls as
[did Cortes].

The Attorney General went on to expound the importance of
the annexation of Texas to the United States. Inviting Johnston to
come to Washington, Gilpin said, "I am sure your presence and
information might often, very often, be of service." [78] From Nashville
Colonel George W. Hockley, formerly of the Texas Army, wrote to
Johnston that he had just spent a week with Andrew Jackson at
Jackson's abode, The Hermitage. "He will be pleased to see you, if

[75] Resolutions of H. R. A. Wigginton and others, n.d., 1837, *ibid.*

[76] J. P. Davidson to R. Davidson, June 20, 1837; [Charles] Luzenburg to "Dear
General," n.d., *ibid.*

[77] Johnston to Fisher, June 27, 1837 (copy) , *ibid.*

[78] Henry D. Gilpin to Johnston, August 13, 1837, *ibid.*

you can make it convenient to pass this way." Johnston was looked upon as something of an oracle on Texas.[79]

Time and rest eased the injured nerve, and with the return of strength came the urge to go back to Texas. Disregarding the pleas of friends that he remain in the United States and the hints of some that by staying he might expect political preferment, in late autumn Johnston took passage for Texas. He sailed from New Orleans with renewed confidence in the vigor of the Texas government. "The news from Texas is very favorable," he said. "The new Congress has more ability than the last & more honesty, gained by the loss of some members." Distance had softened his views toward the Administration of President Sam Houston.[80]

Arriving in Houston in late December, Johnston found the people of Texas in alarm over reports that San Antonio had been retaken by the Mexicans. Public meetings throughout the land rekindled the spirit of resistance and pledged full aid to the government in repelling the invaders. Although the commander of the garrison at San Antonio presently reported the city safe and explained that rumor of its fall had grown out of nothing more than the nearby appearance of a band of Mexican horse thieves, the government nevertheless ordered Johnston to resume active command of the Army of Texas.

Again he yearned for hostilities with Mexico. "The alarm, I hope, will act as a solemn admonition to the Government to commence preparations for the renewal of the war in the most energetic manner," he wrote.[81] Believing reports from the border that Texas was about to be invaded, and that one Mexican column was indeed already north of the Rio Grande, Johnston at once left Houston for San Antonio. He would pick up a body of two hundred horsemen at the Colorado River, he said, then reconnoiter the frontier for information necessary for an energetic defense of the nation.[82]

From Houston, Johnston hastened to Mercer's Ferry on the Colorado River; there he found but forty horsemen to accompany him on his reconnaissance.[83] In vain he called upon the government for

[79] George W. Hockley to Johnston, November 5, 1837, *ibid.*
[80] Johnston to "My Dear Sir," November 26 [1837], *ibid.*
[81] Johnston to Edward D. Hobbs, December 31, 1837, *ibid.*
[82] Johnston to Edward Burleson, January 13, 1838, *ibid.*
[83] Special Order No. 1, January 13, 1838, Order Book of A. S. Johnston, *ibid.*

more troops; instead of soldiers, he received word of insubordination in the small garrison at San Bernard. Secretly he was sympathetic with the unpaid and ill-provided troops. Quieting them with a lofty appeal to honor and a stern warning of dishonorable discharge, he recommended to the new Secretary of War, Barnard Bee, that their petition be granted for back pay and prompt release from service.[84] Bee agreed with Johnston. "Poor devils," Bee wrote. "They have suffered so much I do not wonder they were refractory." But mustering of additional troops would be impossible, said the Secretary, with the scant provisions at hand. "The nakedness of the land you are by this time struck with." Johnston must be content with an escort of forty men.[85]

Again he grew restive under inactivity. To a friend in Kentucky he wrote that he had but a handful of men to scout the frontier but that he would not give up the reconnaissance even if all the powers of Mexico were in full array against him. "Our Government wants energy and the prudent foresight, which those intrusted with the liberties of a people should possess," [86] he confided, and a curt note to the Secretary of War acknowledged the government's failure to collect adequate troops and supplies.[87] That day he and his party left for San Antonio.

Perhaps fearing some rash act by Johnston, the President explicitly forbade him to go beyond San Antonio. There Johnston found the Texas garrison destitute and demoralized. "They have only a few broken down sorry jades which serve to drive in cattle," he informed the War Department. If not at once paid and equipped, he said, these troops had as well be discharged.[88] Again President Houston cannily weighed the probabilities of a Mexican invasion of Texas; again disharmony in Mexico removed such a threat. Traders reported that the Mexicans had no more than five hundred troops along the entire frontier, and that these were without supplies, horses, or spirit. "Fortunately our Enemy are not disposed to humble us," Secretary Bee wrote to Johnston.[89]

With his meager forces he did what he could to make the border

[84] Johnston to Barnard Bee, January 14, 1838 (copy), *ibid.*
[85] Bee to Johnston, January 20, 1838, *ibid.*
[86] Johnston to Hobbs, January 17, 1838, *ibid.*
[87] Johnston to Bee, January 26, 1838 (copy), *ibid.*
[88] *Ibid.*, February 6, 1838 (copy).
[89] Bee to Johnston, January 20, 1838, Johnston Papers, Barret Collection.

secure against raids. His presence in San Antonio inspired confidence among the citizens. One admiring Texan wrote:

How fortunate we are in having such a man [as Johnston] at the head of our military establishment & located in this place. He is . . . a man whom I admire for his firmness, his modesty, his gentlemanly deportment & good sense. I would not give him for any other 100 men out of the army, for the security of this frontier and further . . . as a great secret I have to say that Johnston intends in a few days to visit the Rio Grande, for the purpose of planting the star banner at our farthest western town on the Rio Grande (on East Bank) the name of which is Laredo.[90]

Johnston posted scouting parties to observe the roads and river crossings leading from Mexico into Texas and forbade trading with the Mexicans across the Rio Grande. He pleaded with the government for additional soldiers; with the few troops in his present command he could not even keep out enemy scouts and spies, he said, and supplies for a larger Texas Army could easily be obtained from the country west of San Antonio, he told the Secretary of War.[91] But President Houston was adamant against any advance to the west. Johnston must languish in San Antonio.

Vexation grew with lengthening idleness. Another opportunity was slipping away, Johnston felt, to exact from Mexico an acknowledgment of Texas independence and a satisfactory boundary settlement. Many other Texans were of this persuasion. "I am in hopes the enemy will soon releive [sic] us from this embarrassment, and enable us to 'go it alone,' " wrote Hugh McLeod.[92] "I hope that the Mexicans have ere this given you an opportunity of breaking a lance with them," wrote J. Pinckney Henderson, Texas emissary to England.[93]

Other Texans encouraged Johnston to seize the initiative and "carry the war to Africa." Former Secretary of War William S. Fisher wrote that he had raised a company of men to support Johnston, but had disbanded them upon word that operations were confined to the line of the San Antonio River. The people had lost faith in the Houston Administration, said Fisher, and cried aloud

[90] Samuel A. Maverick to "Dearest," March 13, 1838, in Rena Maverick Green (ed.) , *Samuel Maverick, Texan: 1803–1870*, p. 66.

[91] Johnston to Bee, February 27, 1838 (copy) , Johnston Papers, Barret Collection.

[92] H. McLeod to Johnston, February 26, 1838, *ibid.*

[93] J. Pinckney Henderson to Johnston, March 1, 1838, *ibid.*

for action to end the harassment of their frontier and the uncertainty of their nationhood. Since many of the Mexican states chafed against their central government, Fisher believed that Texas troops would be welcomed by them as liberators. Mexico might now be easily crippled and dismembered, he thought. Said Fisher:

Should your anxiety to carry on offensive operations against the enemy impel you to pass the [President's] proscribed limits, you will be sustained in the course you pursue by the universal approbation of the sovereign people.... My candid and sincere conviction is that any officer who shall at this time meet the views of the people, and anticipate that of the next administration, will wear for himself a chaplet forever green.[94]

Thus was Johnston tempted almost beyond forbearance.

He had not the means to renew the war. Nor would he probably have done so in defiance of the government had he possessed the means; his sense of honor required strict obedience to the civilian authorities, however distasteful their policies. Meantime, the impotence of the Texas government became ever clearer. "The Treasury has allowed itself to be drained," wrote Secretary Bee to Johnston in early February, "so that notwithstanding provision was made for this Department—not a dollar can be had." [95] Soon the Secretary informed him that no additional troops could be sent to San Antonio and that Johnston was free to return to Houston if he chose to do so. Said Bee, "We must be satisfied for the present to fold our arms." [96] To a Kentucky friend, Johnston then wrote, "If all this matter ends in smoke Othello's occupation is gone & you will see me early in the summer prepared with a mind sobered by some experiences & a heart devoted to business to enter upon a more profitable career & mingle in calmer scenes." [97]

Though Johnston abandoned the prospect of immediate action, he did not at once leave San Antonio, for he hoped still to induce the government to strengthen its border defenses. Admitting that Mexico would be unable to attack within the year, he warned his superiors of other dangers to the security of the Republic:

If the expense of protecting the frontier were an entire loss to the treasury I would not consider the obligation of the government to provide the

---

[94] Fisher to Johnston, February 6, 1838, *ibid.*
[95] Bee to Johnston, February 8, 1838, *ibid.*
[96] *Ibid.*, February 21, 1838.
[97] Johnston to Hobbs, February 17, 1838, Johnston Papers, Barret Collection.

means [of protection] diminished in the least, but it will occur to you that nothing could contribute more to the rapid increase of population & prosperity of the country & the consequent increase of the revenue of the government, than the provision of ample & effectual means for the security of the inhabitants of the frontier whose situation is always one of great privation & entitled especially to the fostering care of the government.[98]

Johnston spoke from his own experience in guarding the western reaches of the United States. He recommended to the Texas government that a regiment of cavalry be raised to protect the frontier against hostile Indians. A portion of the regiment ought to be posted on the Rio Frio so as to command the western mountain passes and thus restrain the Comanches, he said; the remainder of the regiment ought to be placed on the Brazos River to hold in check the Indians of the north. These were words of wisdom, but they called for measures beyond the resources of the Houston Administration.[99]

President Houston hoped to remain at peace with the Indians of Texas. Upon arriving in San Antonio, Johnston had accordingly begun preliminary talks with the fiercest of the Texas tribes—the Comanches. From time to time during the following weeks he entertained groups of their leaders at his headquarters.[100] He reported that the two principal Comanche chiefs, Essowakkenny and Essomanny, first approached him with the haughtiness they customarily showed Mexican officials, and ordered him to take care of their horses. To teach them that he was not a "Mexican hostler in uniform," Johnston replied, "You ride good ponies. I advise you to watch them well. All white men are not honest. I take good care of my own horses. Take care of yours." With a grim smile, one of the chiefs dispatched Indians to guard the grazing mounts. Once this contest of wills was ended, Johnston and the chiefs sat down to friendly discourse.[101]

The Comanche chiefs impressed Johnston favorably. He advised President Houston to court them with gifts and to make a treaty of amity with them, as he thought such a treaty would at once end the threat of their depredations and favorably influence the Mexicans

---

[98] Johnston to Bee, March 13, 1838 (copy), *ibid.*
[99] *Ibid.*
[100] *Ibid.*, February 6, 1838 (copy).
[101] Johnston, *Life of Johnston*, pp. 88–89.

toward Texas. Concerning the Comanches' most urgent anxiety—the question of what territory belonged to them—Johnston had no authority to negotiate. The Mexicans had told them that the Texans would take their land from them, said the chiefs. Johnston advised the Administration that if Texas would recognize the Indians' rights to the mountainous district to the west, a treaty of peace could promptly be signed. Otherwise, he warned, the Republic should prepare for Indian war.[102] On this point, President Houston equivocated. The Comanches might continue hunting where they were accustomed to hunt, instructed Secretary Bee, and in this area both Texans and Comanches were to treat each other kindly. But since Texas was still at war, she could not now set aside territory for the Indians.[103] For the moment, Johnston and the Comanches remained friends; but the Republic of Texas was to achieve no permanent peace with this warlike tribe.

On April 8 Johnston received a startling message from the Secretary of War: information out of New Orleans and Matamoros indicated a strong Mexican force was on the move to San Antonio. President Houston instructed Johnston to avail himself of every possible means of defense; if necessary, he was to call upon the Comanches for assistance. "Your force is so inadequate," wrote the Secretary of War, "that I can scarcely do more than say, I know all that bravery can achieve will be accomplished." [104] To which Johnston at once replied, "You are aware of the very limited means of defence at my disposal but such as they are you may rely upon their being employed to the best advantage." [105] His hope of combat seemed at last to be upon the point of fulfillment.

As he prepared to receive the blow he was willing to employ Indians as allies. Only two months earlier he had written to Secretary Bee, "I think the occasion a favorable one . . . to make available [the Comanches'] powerful aid in the prosicution [sic] of the war with Mexico." [106] But if Johnston now called upon the Indians, they did not heed the call. His entire force was about two hundred men, equally divided between Texans of American origin and Texans of

[102] Johnston to Bee, February 6, March 31, April 21, 1838 (copies) ; Johnston to Houston, March 5, 1838 (copy) , all in Johnston Papers, Barret Collection.

[103] Bee to Johnston, April, n.d., 1838, *ibid.*

[104] *Ibid.*, April 8, 1838.

[105] Johnston to Bee, April 15, 1838 (copy) , Johnston Papers, Barret Collection.

[106] *Ibid.*, February 6, 1838 (copy) .

Mexican birth, and he was short of ammunition for even so small a body. But he doubled his vigilance on the routes leading to San Antonio and combed the Mexican newspapers for indications of an armed advance.[107]

Johnston later told his son that he now sallied forth with his small band, resolved, if possible, with boldness to awe the enemy into retreat. Should this have failed, Johnston said, he was prepared to contest the way, even to repeating the scenes of the Alamo.[108] Such a sacrifice was not required; no Mexican force appeared. Again internal discord in Mexico, this time combined with hostilities between Mexico and France, extinguished any threat against Texas. Late in April Secretary Bee informed Johnston that all apprehension of invasion was over. The Secretary further said that he had recommended to Congress either the establishment of an adequate force of regulars on the frontier or the disbanding of the entire Army so that the country might learn to look to the militia for protection.[109]

Johnston's old impatience returned as the promise of combat faded and he again lapsed into idleness. Mexico was unable to invade Texas; President Houston was unable and unwilling to invade Mexico; stalemate must be the result. Without an army to command, Johnston felt himself a man without purpose and sought anew to resign from the service of Texas. His friends implored him to remain, predicting that the next administration would fulfill the wishes of the people to strike at Mexico. "Nothing you know is so captivating as military renown and no way so sure a road to the favor of this sovereign [the public]," wrote one of Johnston's companions. "Therefore I think every exertion will be used to assume the offensive." [110] The Secretary of War begged Johnston to take furlough but not to quit his command. Yielding to these entreaties, Johnston in the early summer again took a leave of absence and returned to Kentucky to visit his children, relatives, and friends. When in August a brief insurrection of Mexicans and Indians (the Cordova Rebellion) flared in Texas against the government, the Secretary of War, now Colonel George W. Hockley, wrote to Johnston, "You hold your rank—and are wanted." [111] But the Cordova

---

[107] *Ibid.*, April 21, 1838 (copy).
[108] Johnston, *Life of Johnston*, p. 91.
[109] Bee to Johnston, April 26, 1838, Johnston Papers, Barret Collection.
[110] James Love to Johnston, April 28, 1838, *ibid.*
[111] Hockley to Johnston, August 21, 1838, *ibid.*

Rebellion collapsed before Johnston could return to Texas. He would serve no more as active commander of the Texas Army.

Johnston's career as commanding general of the Army of the Republic of Texas was brief and trying. He was able to take command only after fighting a duel which almost cost his life and left him incapacitated for months. Without money, provisions, or clear mission, he strove diligently to shape a trained army out of an unruly band of adventurers. All the while, he labored under the frustration of disagreement with President Houston's policy of inactivity. Measured by Johnston's own hope of achievement, his role as commander was one of disappointment and failure. Yet out of this experience he acquired an abiding sense of identity with the fate of Texas, and the people of Texas acquired an enduring admiration for the qualities of Albert Sidney Johnston.

Scourge of the Red Man

~~~~~~

JOHNSTON and his supporters believed their impatience with the passivity of the Houston Administration to be common to the people of Texas. The Constitution prohibited Houston from succeeding himself in office, and as the Texas presidential election of 1838 approached, the anti-Houston forces resolved to appeal to the popular urge for action. Johnston himself was the choice of some for the Presidency, with General Thomas J. Rusk for the Vice Presidency,[1] but Johnston did not respond to overtures that he become a candidate. If he felt political aspiration at this time, it quickly vanished when his friends Mirabeau B. Lamar and Peter W. Grayson became rival contenders for the Republic's top honor. Strangely, two of the candidates for the Presidency, Grayson and Judge James Collinsworth, committed suicide during the campaign. On September 3 Lamar was overwhelmingly elected President of Texas, with David G. Burnet as Vice President.

Johnston had favored the election of Lamar. The new President

---

[1] Charles Harrison to Johnston, April 9, 1838; Thurston to Johnston, April 9, 1838, Johnston Papers, Barret Collection.

embodied the spirit of Texas nationalism. Gallant soldier in the Texas war for independence, Lamar now opposed annexation to the United States; instead, he dreamed of a Texas empire spreading one day to the Pacific and promised to establish at once the boundary of Texas along the Rio Grande. He would strengthen the economy and currency of Texas through a national bank, he said; he would develop the intellect of Texas through a system of public schools; he would protect the independence of Texas through vigorous diplomacy supported by an efficient regular army and navy. To assist in the fulfillment of this grand design, Lamar appointed Cabinet members who shared his vision: Barnard Bee as Secretary of State; Richard G. Dunlap, Secretary of the Treasury; Memucan Hunt, Secretary of the Navy; and Charles Watrous, Attorney General. To the office of Secretary of War, Lamar named Albert Sidney Johnston.[2]

Fortune at last seemed to smile upon Johnston. Less than three years before, he had ridden into Texas unheralded and adrift in life. Now he was in the topmost circle of Texas politics and society, surrounded by influential friends and apparently on the path to fame, if not also to fortune. His health was once again sound and his mood buoyant; to a friend he said, "I live for the future—Who can lift the veil?" [3] He charmed French diplomat Admiral Baudin, who, after leaving Texas, sent his compliments with a box of cigars, and expressed the hope of returning soon. An acquaintance, inviting Johnston to the races at Velasco, appealed to what he must have deemed two of Johnston's strongest fancies, saying, "Many fine horses & fine ladies are in attendance." [4] From New Orleans a gay Texas agent wrote, "I delivered your message which her ladyship [a Miss Bullette] received most graciously and bid me send you a thousand compliments and congratulations." [5] Johnston had become both warrior and gallant.

As long as Houston was President of Texas, Johnston had been reticent in advising friends to join him there. He lacked confidence in Houston's ability to make Texas live. His brother-in-law once wrote:

[2] For accounts of the election of Lamar and of his ambitions for Texas, see Asa K. Christian, *Mirabeau Buonaparte Lamar,* pp. 18–19, 20–25; Louis J. Wortham, *A History of Texas: From Wilderness to Commonwealth,* IV, 56, 61.

[3] Johnston to Edward D. Hobbs, January 12, 1839, Johnston Papers, Barret Collection.

[4] Thomas J. Green to Johnston, February 17, 1839, *ibid.*

[5] William H. Daingerfield to Johnston, n.d., *ibid.*

You never have opened yr lips which seem to have had the seal of Solomon spoken of in the Arabian nights, placed upon them, in regard to yr intentions of permanent residence in Texas, the country, the chances of advancement for me and yrself, and all of those topics which selfishness and friendship render interesting to me.[6]

Lamar's vigor—Houston and the more conservative among the population thought it Lamar's frenzy—changed Johnston's mind; in the spring he wrote that he had lost all doubt as to the stability of Texan institutions.[7] He now sought a position in the Texas government for his brother-in-law, William Preston, of Kentucky.[8] Preston hoped to become the Texas minister to France, or the secretary of the Texas legation at Washington. He wrote, perhaps humorously, to Johnston, yet doubtless expressing the mood of many Americans who came to Texas, "If it be necessary I am willing to become a citizen of yr country. In this life I never intend if I have an opportunity, to let an unvalued adherence to my own country interfere with my prosperity in another." [9] Despite Johnston's assistance, however, Preston did not receive an appointment—or did not accept one, if it was offered.

Perhaps Johnston shared the hope of the Texas diplomat J. Pinckney Henderson that King Cotton diplomacy would come to the support of Texas independence. Henderson wrote to Johnston at a moment when war between the United States and England seemed probable over the Maine–New Brunswick boundary dispute.

[England] must see how very important our cotton trade must be to her manufactures in the event of a war between her and the United States. Without exulting in the misfortunes of any country and especially my native land . . . I cannot forbear to contemplate the very great advantage such an event would give to Texas. She would immediately become the most important country in America to England. . . . When England recollects that she has a population of two millions . . . whose very subsistence depend upon their daily employment in the cotton manufactories . . . she will not delay cultivating the friendship of the only other country which can relieve the difficulty.[10]

---

[6] William Preston to Johnston, January 14, 1839, *ibid.*
[7] Johnston to George Hancock, April 21, 1839, *ibid.*
[8] A. T. Burnley to Johnston, April 1, 1839, *ibid.*
[9] Preston to Johnston, April 19, 1839, *ibid.*
[10] J. Pinckney Henderson to Johnston, June 23, 1839, *ibid.*

Johnston believed that the policies of the Lamar Administration were sound because they were of the people. The bitter opposition of Houston and his supporters to the new government was "prostrate," said Johnston. "They are forced to vent their spleen in petty abuse which will every day bring them more & more into contempt." [11] "Sell out," he implored a Kentucky relative, "and come to this land of promise. The unclouded dawning of our prosperity should make even the wavering resolute." [12] His faith in the future of Texas was at full tide.

Johnston was part of a dynamic—or, as some thought, foolhardy—administration. Lamar's resolute diplomacy persuaded many leading nations of Europe (England, France, Belgium, and Holland) to recognize the independence of Texas; his eloquence moved the Texas Congress to set aside public land for the support of common schools and a university; his vigilance brought to an end a commerce in fraudulent land certificates that had sprung up during the Republic's early months. As a measure of his faith in the future greatness of Texas, and as a challenge to her people to fulfill this faith, Lamar pitched the nation's new capital at Austin, near the western edge of settled territory. Upon Secretary of War Johnston fell the task of providing force of arms suited to Lamar's vaulting national ambitions. [13]

Johnston weighed the goals of the Administration against its resources for achieving them. Texas was still at war with Mexico, he reasoned, however dilatory may have been the Mexican operations. Concert between Mexico and the Indian tribes on the western and northern frontiers of Texas would imperil the life of the infant republic. Johnston urged the creation of a force of regulars, as already authorized by a statute that the Houston Administration had largely ignored. This law called for the establishment of one regiment of cavalry, one of artillery, and four of infantry, with a suitable number of engineers and ordnance troops. Supported by the militia, such a body would guarantee the security of Texas, thought Johnston. [14]

Johnston applauded Lamar's apparent intention of renewing the

[11] Johnston to Daingerfield, April 12, 1839, Miscellaneous Documents Collection, Texas State Archives.

[12] Johnston to Hancock, April 21, 1839, Johnston Papers, Barret Collection.

[13] Christian, *Mirabeau Buonaparte Lamar*, p. 43.

[14] Johnston to M. B. Lamar, December 18, 1838 (copy), Johnston Papers, Barret Collection.

war with Mexico, having long advocated taking the offensive as the surest means of attaining Texas independence and security. "If peace can only be obtained by the sword," said President Lamar in his inaugural address, "let the sword do its work." [15] Many who voted for Lamar believed that he would reopen the conflict, and looked to Johnston to lead an avenging Texas army into Mexico. "Oh my dear General if we are to invade Mexico do not forget yr absent friends," a Texas agent wrote from Baltimore. "Under your leading we will do what we will not say untill it be done. . . . Do give me a chance if we have a war of being near you." [16] Such a prospect pleased Johnston.

Lamar asked Congress to establish a standing army and navy to support his policies. The lawmakers complied; but, to Johnston's disappointment, they created only one regiment of 840 troops to guard the long frontier. Even more disheartening to Johnston was the response of the people of Texas; the commander of the new regiment, Colonel Edward Burleson, failed to fill its ranks for want of enlistments. Texans shunned professional military service; they would come to the colors only when invasion was upon them or when a campaign against the enemy was under way. Once the threat had vanished or the fighting had ended, they returned to civilian pursuits.[17] Disregarding American laws against foreign recruiting, Johnston permitted Texas officers to solicit soldiers in New Orleans; still he could not fill the new organization.[18]

Fortunately, Texas then had little need for a strong standing army. Mexico lay impotent as the French navy blockaded her coast and revolution flamed within. Notwithstanding his defiant inaugural oration, President Lamar welcomed peace with Mexico; in the summer of 1839 he sent Secretary of State Bee to Vera Cruz in the hope of negotiating the recognition of Texas independence. Though Bee's mission failed, the Lamar Administration still did not resort to arms; Lamar aspired to expansion above the Rio Grande rather than to conquest south of it.[19]

Johnston at first had hoped to attack Mexico, but, lacking the

[15] Christian, *Mirabeau Buonaparte Lamar*, p. 44.

[16] Daingerfield to Johnston, June 11, 1839, Johnston Papers, Barret Collection.

[17] Christian, *Mirabeau Buonaparte Lamar*, p. 44.

[18] Samuel Plummer to Johnston, April 9, 1839, Johnston Papers, Barret Collection.

[19] William C. Binkley, *The Expansionist Movement in Texas, 1836–1859*, pp. 46–47; Christian, *Mirabeau Buonaparte Lamar*, p. 145.

army for a successful invasion, he recognized the folly of precipitate action and concurred in the opinion of colleagues. Secretary Bee foretold prompt French diplomatic recognition and advised Johnston, "Prepare moderately for defence, but with the certainty that you will never have a Mexican force to contend with." [20] In the fall of 1839 the Mexican Federalist General Anaya came to Texas seeking assistance in the revolt against the Centralist Mexican government. Some of Johnston's friends thought this a golden moment to strike at the old enemy. Johnston demurred. The Federalist envoy urged an alliance on the ground that all republics ought to be federal in design.[21] But Johnston contended, "Every nation ought to choose its own form of government, and be a good neighbor. Texas could exist alongside a monarchy if it treated her well." [22] The war with Mexico remained quiescent.

From unwritten truce with Mexico, the Lamar Administration turned to relentless warfare upon the Texas Indians. As an adopted Cherokee, President Sam Houston had sought to live at peace with all the tribes, and, to a measure, had succeeded. Except for occasional depredations and minor affrays on the frontier, Houston kept Texas free of Indian uprising during the precarious early months of her independence. But his sympathy for the Indians ran counter to two of the deepest of American urges, now transplanted into Texas— land hunger and the resolve to make the continent "white man's country."

Lamar and Johnston had none of Houston's compassion for the red man. Only a few years before, Lamar had been associated with Governor George M. Troup of Georgia in driving the Creeks and Cherokees from that state; fresh in Johnston's experience was the pursuit and destruction of Black Hawk's band.

As long as we continue to exhibit our mercy without showing our strength, so long will the Indians continue to bloody the tomahawk [Lamar said to Congress]. . . . The time has come for the prosecution of an exterminating war upon their warriors; which will admit of no compromise and have no termination except in their total extinction or total expulsion.[23]

---

[20] Barnard Bee to Johnston, July 1, 1839, Johnston Papers, Barret Collection.
[21] C. Vann Ness to Johnston, September 3, 1839, *ibid.*
[22] Johnston, *Life of Johnston*, p. 97.
[23] Anna Muckleroy, "The Indian Policy of the Republic of Texas," *Southwestern Historical Quarterly*, XXVI (July, 1922) , 129.

Johnston at once ordered volunteer cavalry groups to chastise the depredations of the frontier tribes.[24]

The Cherokee War came on inevitably. Since 1822 a small body of Cherokees had inhabited the northeastern portion of the Mexican state of Texas; a decade later this band was swelled by additional thousands of Indians expelled from Georgia and elsewhere by state and federal authorities. Among these exiles were numbers of Cherokees, Choctaws, Shawnees, Kickapoos, Delawares, Quapaws, and other branches. Cherokee Chief Bowles (or The Bowl), who was spokesman for the entire Indian colony of northeastern Texas, had petitioned the Mexican government for title to the land occupied by his people; but, though they were permitted to remain in Texas, their request for title was not fulfilled.[25]

During the Texas Revolution, the Provisional Government had courted the friendship of the Cherokees. To assure their neutrality, a Texas commission, including Sam Houston, in February of 1836 had made a treaty with them granting title to their lands and acknowledging self-government to the tribes. But the treaty was never ratified by the Texas Senate. The Provisional Government was too busy waging war with Mexico to spend effort on Indian affairs, and after repulsing the Mexican invasion, the Texas authorities no longer deigned to bargain with the Cherokees.

As President, Sam Houston conciliated the Indians. In spite of Cherokee depredations against white settlers on their border, and even when the Cherokees were suspected of being accomplices in the Cordova Rebellion in the summer of 1838, Houston would not wage war against his former people, and resisted a growing demand among the citizens of Texas for the expulsion of the Cherokees. Yet, holding their lands at the sufferance of Texas authorities, the Cherokees should have realized that their days were numbered.

Johnston saw eye to eye with President Lamar in regarding the Cherokees with suspicion. Self-government made the Indians a nation within a nation and a menace to the Republic; tribal possession of land denied the area to white settlement. To a group of admirers

---

[24] Johnston to Lamar, January 9, 1839, in Charles A. Gulick, Jr., and Katherine Elliott (eds.), *The Papers of Mirabeau Buonaparte Lamar*, II, 404–405.

[25] For the background to the Cherokee War, see Muckleroy, "The Indian Policy of the Republic of Texas," *Southwestern Historical Quarterly*, XXV (April, 1922), 255–257; *ibid.*, XXVI (July, 1922), 1–29.

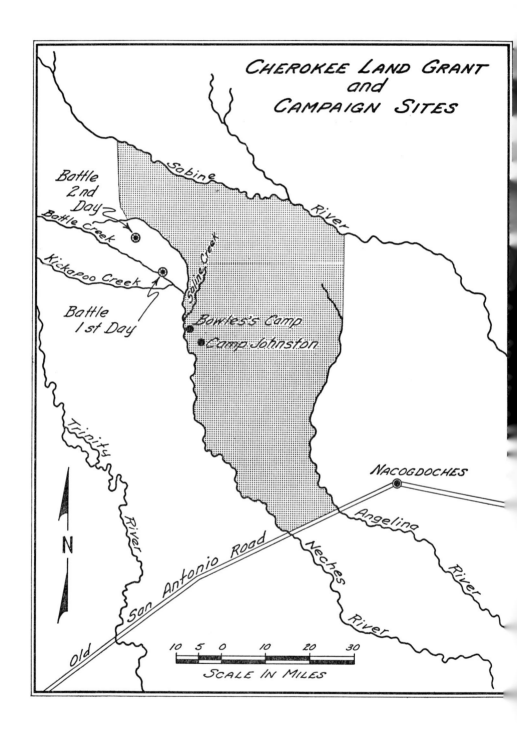

CHEROKEE LAND GRANT and CAMPAIGN SITES

in Nacogdoches, Johnston later candidly explained the necessity for expelling or breaking up the tribe:

The position occupied by the Cherokees & their associate bands had the effect to estrange the east from the west & the north from the south [and] to prevent the attainment of those great results which flow from union & sympathy and to encourage Mexico to meditate tho' vainly, yet imperiously to us, the subjugation of the Republic.[26]

President Lamar offered to individual Indian families the privilege of remaining on their farms, subject to the laws of Texas; but he denied tribal right to any part of Texas. Should the Cherokees accept his policy, Lamar would send agents among them to put it into effect; should the Indians reject it, he would send troops to drive them from the soil of Texas. Johnston shared these intentions.

Public outcry rose against the Cherokees at the moment some Texans began to turn cool toward the Lamar Administration. The Houston faction had been critical from the first; others now charged Lamar with favoritism in appointments to office. Certain of Lamar's supporters thought war upon the Indians would restore the loyalty of wavering citizens. As a friend wrote Johnston:

In case of a genl. war with our red brothers you will find that every other feeling will be absorbed in and give way before one general burst of indignation against the savages. If the war must break out this summer, do let me see either his Excely or yourself on the frontier. The effect of such a move would be electric on our Eastern people.[27]

Political expediency was not the cause of the Administration's resolve to expel the Cherokees; but political expediency may have been a spur to action.

Quite likely the Cherokees would have been ousted from Texas in any event. As their presence in the United States had offended the American sense of destiny, so their presence in Texas offended the Texan sense of destiny. But the Cherokees invited expulsion from Texas by conniving with the Mexicans against the security of the new republic. In March, 1839, Vincente Cordova, leader of the futile rebellion of a year before, was discovered encamped near the Colorado hills with a party of about seventy Mexicans, Indians, and Negroes. Colonel Edward Burleson and a company of volunteers

---

[26] Johnston to J. F. Graham [and others], July 31, 1839, Johnston Papers, Barret Collection.

[27] J. W. Burton to Johnston, May 14, 1839, *ibid.*

pursued and overtook them at the Guadalupe River, where, in a hot skirmish, the outlaw band was defeated and dispersed.

Texas authorities believed that Cordova had been on his way to Matamoros to obtain arms for the Cherokees and their fellow tribes. Cherokee Chief Bowles denied the accusation, saying that Cordova had sought such an alliance but had been rejected by the Indians. In a sharp note to Bowles, Johnston branded the Chief's explanation false—a stratagem to deceive the Texans and gain time for Cordova to complete his mission. "This design has been happily prevented by the destruction of Cordova's party & perhaps of Cordova himself," said Johnston.

He sternly warned Bowles against making common cause with the enemies of Texas.

The President grants peace to [the Indians], but is not deceived—They will be permitted to cultivate [their land] undisturbed as long as they manifest by their forbearance from all aggressive acts and their friendly conduct the sincerity of their profession or until Congress shall adopt such measures in reference to them as in their wisdom they may deem proper, with a clear view of all matters connected with their feelings and interests—It should not surprise the Cherokees to learn that such measures are in progress under the orders of the President as will render abortive any attempt to again disturb the quiet of the frontier nor need it be any cause of alarm to those who intend to act in good faith—All intercourse between the friendly indians & those at War with Texas must cease—The President directs that you will cause the contents of this communication to be made known to all the chiefs who were present at the council.[28]

Measures against the Indians were indeed in progress. Following President Lamar's policy, Johnston appointed Martin Lacy agent to the Cherokees and their associates, with instructions to keep them peaceful until Congress should decide what was to be done with them, and in late April he sent Major B. C. Waters to eastern Texas with two companies of volunteers to occupy a point on the Saline Creek within Cherokee territory. This movement would separate the Cherokees from the Plains Indians of the west, said Johnston; it would prevent military concert between the two groups and would deprive the Cherokees of the pretense that their own depredations upon white settlers were the work of western tribes. In speaking of

---

[28] Johnston to Bowles, April 10, 1839, in Gulick and Elliott (eds.), *The Papers of Mirabeau Buonaparte Lamar*, II, 522–523.

"the west" and "western tribes" in 1839, Johnston meant the area beyond the upper Trinity River.

Chief Bowles ordered Waters off the Cherokee land, threatening force if he failed to leave. Too weak to withstand a determined Indian attack, Waters retreated to the opposite bank of the nearby Neches River and established his post there.[29] Johnston anticipated war with the Cherokees as the result of Waters's action. Dispatching additional troops to a point near the Cherokee line, he wrote, "In about 20 days Burleson will sweep the frontier towards the northeast with an ample force." [30] The stage was set for the expulsion of the Cherokees.

Final evidence of Cherokee treachery soon came to light. In mid-May a detachment of Texas troops overtook and defeated a small party of Mexican marauders near Austin.[31] Among the slain was Manuel Flores, erstwhile member of the Cordova Rebellion, and on Flores's body were papers linking the Cherokees and other tribes with Mexican designs against Texas. Since Mexico was prevented by its war with France from invading Texas, wrote Mexican General Canalizo, Mexico must strike at the infant nation in other ways: she must induce Mexicans and Indians living in Texas to set fire to houses, to lay waste the fields of the settlers, and thus to prevent the Texans from assembling in great numbers to make war upon Mexico. Wrote Cordova to Flores:

I have already entered upon my duties, by uniting a meeting of the neighboring tribes. . . . The Cherokee and other tribes . . . have promised me to unite as soon as possible for action, and . . . have also agreed that in case our plans should be discovered in the meantime, they then will commence operations with the force we may have at command.[32]

Letters from General Canalizo to Bowles and other Indian leaders promised them permanent possession of their lands in return for assistance against the Texans.

President Lamar now wrote Bowles a stern rebuke and an ultimatum. The Texas government knew of the scheming between

---

[29] Johnston, *Life of Johnston*, pp. 108–109.

[30] Johnston to Hancock, April 21, 1839, Johnston Papers, Barret Collection.

[31] Muckleroy, "The Indian Policy of the Republic of Texas," *Southwestern Historical Quarterly*, XXVI (July, 1922), 27–28; Christian, *Mirabeau Buonaparte Lamar*, pp. 97–98.

[32] Vincente Cordova to Manuel Flores, July 19, 1838, in Dorman H. Winfrey *et al.* (eds.), *Texas Indian Papers, 1825–1843*, I, 8.

Indians and Mexicans, said Lamar. "Professing friendship yet in constant collusion with our foes, you cry peace, peace, when every action betrays a secret disposition to hostility." Major Waters must not be molested in the building of his post among the Cherokees, warned Lamar; the authorities and people of Texas would never tolerate an independent Indian nation in their midst.

[The Indians] are permitted, at present, to remain where they are, only because this Government is looking forward to the time, when some peaceable arrangements can be made for their removal, without the necessity of shedding blood, but that their final removal is contemplated, is certain; and that it will be effected, is equally so. Whether it be done by friendly negociation, or by the violence of war, must depend upon the Cherokees themselves.[33]

This remorseless but forthright letter moved Bowles to reply that the Cherokees would leave Texas if the government would pay them for the improvements on their farms. Lamar at once appointed a commission of five men, including Vice President Burnet and Secretary of War Johnston, to negotiate a treaty of removal and a just settlement of claims.[34] The commissioners were to determine by "fair and liberal" appraisal the value of all crops and improvements and to pay the Indians for them in silver and merchandise.[35]

In early July Johnston and his associates proceeded to a point near Bowles's council grounds. They established a camp—Camp Johnston—and opened negotiations with the Indian leaders. Many days of fruitless talk occurred. Bowles and his colleagues agreed to leave Texas but asked for a delay of three moons to have time to harvest their growing corn. The commissioners denied this request but promised ample compensation for all improvements and for the corn that must be abandoned. Bowles and his war chief, Big Mush, demurred and refused to sign a treaty. Johnston and the other commissioners feared that the Indians were delaying a settlement to give time to mobilize their warriors for battle. At noon of July 15 the

[33] Lamar to "Colonel Bowl and other head men of the Cherokees," May 26, 1839, in Gulick and Elliott (eds.), *The Papers of Mirabeau Buonaparte Lamar,* II, 590–592.

[34] Muckleroy, "The Indian Policy of the Republic of Texas," *Southwestern Historical Quarterly,* XXVI (October, 1922), 135–136; Christian, *Mirabeau Buonaparte Lamar,* pp. 96–99.

[35] Lamar to David G. Burnet, A. Sidney Johnston [and others], June 27, 1839, in Winfrey *et al.* (eds.), *Texas Indian Papers,* I, 67–70.

commissioners quit the meeting in exasperation. The Cherokee War was ready to begin.[36]

Even as Johnston sat in conference with the Cherokees, he prepared to smite them should they reject the President's terms. He put in motion three columns of volunteers to converge upon the Cherokee site: Edward Burleson with a regiment from the west, Willis H. Landrum with a body of troops from the south, and Thomas J. Rusk with a regiment from Nacogdoches to the east. Altogether, Johnston assembled about nine hundred fighting men and placed the entire force under command of General Kelsey H. Douglass. When at noon of July 15 the meeting with the chiefs broke up, Johnston immediately ordered an attack upon the nearby Cherokee camp.[37]

The Texas Army advanced, Johnston with it. Finding the Indian camp empty, the Texans pressed along fresh trail that crossed to the west side of the Neches. Ten miles above the camp site, they came upon the Cherokees in defensive position on the point of a hill. Combat began at once and continued sharply for half an hour, when darkness fell. Unable to withstand the Texans, the Cherokees withdrew during the night, leaving behind eighteen of their dead, along with powder, lead, horses, cattle, corn, and other possessions. The Texans pursued on the following morning and at noon overtook and again attacked the weakened Cherokees. Again the Indians were beaten and put to flight. Among the slain lay Chief Bowles. The broken tribe retreated from a swamp on the Neches where they had taken refuge; the Army followed killing stragglers and destroying villages and fields. With their chief dead, their homes and farms laid waste, and their members hopelessly scattered, the Texas Cherokees fled to a precarious existence in Arkansas. Once the Cherokees had fallen, the smaller tribes were quickly awed into submission. Some were placed on reservations; the Shawnees sold their improvements to the government and returned to the United States. The Indian lands in eastern Texas now belonged to the white man.[38]

---

[36] Commissioners to Lamar, January 29, 1840 (copy), Johnston Papers, Barret Collection; Report of Commissioners (Private Memorandum), n.d.; Johnston, Rusk [and others] to "Colonel Bolles," July 9, 1839, Thomas J. Rusk Papers; Johnston, *Life of Johnston*, pp. 108–110.

[37] Johnston, "Memoranda upon Recent History and Present Status of Indian Relations," in Gulick and Elliott (eds.), *The Papers of Mirabeau Buonaparte Lamar*, III, 230–232; Johnston, *Life of Johnston*, pp. 109–110.

[38] K. H. Douglass to Johnston, July 16, 1839, in Winfrey *et al.* (eds.), *Texas Indian Papers*, I, 76–77.

The Cherokee War enhanced both Johnston's reputation and the popularity of the Lamar Administration. President Lamar warmly commended Johnston for his vigor in pressing the war,[39] and testimonial dinners and words of praise greeted him throughout the Republic.[40] "I rejoice you were present [in the combat]," wrote a friend who hoped to see Johnston become President of Texas. "I am almost malicious enough to wish you were among the wounded, not the slain. . . . Give me the benefit of a good honest fight, and all the stump orators in the universe could not resist me." [41] Texas society and beauty also favored him. A Houston belle sent her good wishes to him,[42] and the young ladies of that city playfully proposed a subscription to buy him a shirt because he had complained of having none suitable for a recent ball there.[43] From the United States came information that victory over the Indians had brightened the prospect of American loans to Texas. "Since the affair with the Cherokees people here [New York] laugh and say that the govt of the U S had better let out the Florida [Seminole] war to you & yr department," a jubilant Texas agent wrote.[44]

But the Cherokee War deeply offended Sam Houston and his supporters, and Johnston's prominent role in the conflict alienated him from Houston's favor. When a report came that the former President had maligned him, Johnston sent Houston a note promising to hold him accountable for his words.[45] Through an intermediary Houston promptly denied having spoken disparagingly of Johnston. "Nor has anything transpired within my knowledge," said Houston, "which could change the estimation, which I have always entertained, of the high and honorable bearing of Genl. Johnson [sic], and his character." [46] Outwardly Johnston and Houston remained cordial; inwardly they smouldered with distaste for each other.

Johnston had little time either to savor eulogies or to resent censure. Expulsion of the Cherokees left him still the baffling task of securing the frontiers against Indian depredation. From every quar-

[39] Lamar to Johnston, July 30, 1839, Johnston Papers, Barret Collection.
[40] J. B. Ransom to Johnston, July 25, 1839; Graham [and others] to Johnston, July 29, 1839, *ibid.*
[41] James Love to Johnston, July 24, December 29, 1839, *ibid.*
[42] James Reily to Johnston, November 14, 1839, *ibid.*
[43] Love to Johnston, December 29, 1839, *ibid.*
[44] Daingerfield to Johnston, August 29, 1839, *ibid.*
[45] Johnston to Sam Houston, January 5, 1840 (copy) , *ibid.*
[46] Houston to Sam M. Williams, January 7, 1840, *ibid.*

ter arose cries of the torch and scalping knife as bands of vengeful Cherokees stole back into their old lands in the east to kill white settlers and burn their cabins.[47] Meantime, Johnston pressed bitter war against the Comanches on the western border.

The Comanches were the most formidable of Texas Indians; they would not be finally conquered for almost half a century, and then only after the white man had perfected the revolver. President Houston had sought through treaty to keep the peace with this fierce tribe. In May, 1838, at the town of Houston, his commissioners signed an agreement with the Comanche chiefs pledging amity between white man and red.[48] Admirable as it was, Houston's hope of peace between the Texans and the Comanches was doomed to disappointment: on their way home from signing the treaty, the Indians slew two white men and seized a young white girl. In keeping with his policy of avoiding general Indian wars, Houston refused to attack the Comanches, and occasional depredations by them kept the western frontier astir during the remainder of his term.[49]

Johnston fully supported Lamar's aim to break the predatory spirit of the Comanches and make the western frontier safe for settlement.[50] The moment Johnston took office as Secretary of War he dispatched additional soldiers to San Antonio and Gonzales to protect these districts against attack, and at the same time recommended mustering eight new volunteer companies for use against the Indians.[51] Throughout the winter and spring of 1839, he energetically sent troops to chastise Comanche marauding parties wherever they appeared. In February Captain John H. Moore, with three companies, fell upon a Comanche village on the upper Colorado and killed many warriors before withdrawing in face of superior numbers;[52] a short time afterward, Colonel Edward Burleson, with a small body of troops, defeated a party of Comanches near Bastrop; in May Captain John Bird, with about thirty-five men, beat

[47] James S. Mayfield to Johnston, October 4, 1839; Thomas J. Rusk to Johnston, September 29, 1839, *ibid.*

[48] "Treaty between Texas and the Comanche Indians," May 29, 1838, in Winfrey *et al.* (eds.), *Texas Indian Papers*, I, 50–52.

[49] Muckleroy, "The Indian Policy of the Republic of Texas," *Southwestern Historical Quarterly*, XXVI (October, 1922), 140.

[50] Henderson K. Yoakum, *History of Texas*, II, 261–263.

[51] Johnston to Douglass, January 1, 1839, Army Papers, Republic of Texas.

[52] J. H. Moore to Johnston, March 10, 1839, in Winfrey *et al.* (eds.), *Texas Indian Papers*, I, 57–59.

off a numerous Comanche assault on Little River, north of Austin, with heavy toll of the Indians.[53] Johnston planned stronger blows against the redoubtable tribe; as soon as adequate forces could be mobilized and the Cherokees dealt with, he would order his officers to "apply the scourge to the Comanches."[54]

The scourge was indeed required along the western border. From the regions of the upper Colorado and Brazos came word that the country was "literally swarming with the redskins." The Lamar Administration was losing friends there, an observer wrote to Johnston, because of its failure to tame the Comanches. "I am convinced that speedy relief must be had, or depopulation will necessarily soon ensue."[55] During the summer the Cherokee War had claimed most of Johnston's energies and the bulk of Texas military strength, but to the western frontier he had given what protection he could afford. When he sent Burleson's regiment east, he ordered Colonel William S. Fisher to raise a company of thirty-day volunteers and engage the Indians of the west.[56] At mid-summer Colonel Henry W. Karnes, commander of the San Antonio garrison, gave a "deplorable account" of the west. Around San Antonio, marauding parties of white Texas outlaws added to the havoc of Indians and Mexicans. Of the three, Colonel Karnes thought the Texans the basest.[57]

When the Cherokee War ended, Johnston immediately turned his attention to a comprehensive plan of national defense. Through Texas agents in the United States, he ordered cannon and equipment from American foundries and firms;[58] though woefully short of facilities, his ordnance department repaired and reissued hundreds of muskets and sabers.[59] Johnston proposed the building of nine frontier military posts along a line beginning near Coffee's trading house on the Red River, curving south through the Cross

[53] Johnston, "Memoranda," in Gulick and Elliott (eds.), *The Papers of Mirabeau Buonaparte Lamar*, III, 230–232.

[54] Johnston to Hancock, April 21, 1839, Johnston Papers, Barret Collection.

[55] L. P. Cooke to Johnston, March 12, 1839, *ibid.*

[56] Johnston to William S. Fisher, June 4, 1839, Army Papers, Republic of Texas.

[57] Charles Mason to Johnston, July 11, 1839, Johnston Papers, Barret Collection; J. Browne to Johnston, September 13, 1839, in Gulick and Elliott (eds.), *The Papers of Mirabeau Buonaparte Lamar*, III, 106–107.

[58] Daingerfield to Johnston, September 11, October 17, 1839, Johnston Papers, Barret Collection.

[59] G. W. Hockley to Johnston, October 18, 1839, in Gulick and Elliott (eds.), *The Papers of Mirabeau Buonaparte Lamar*, III, 136–138.

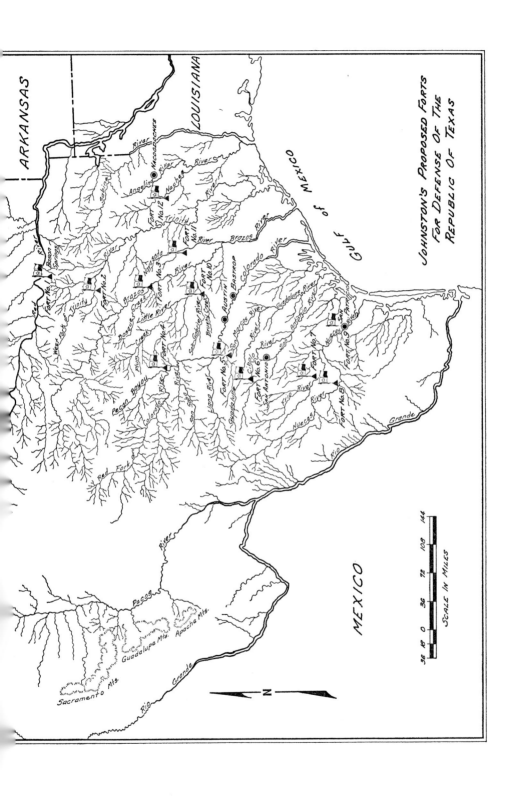

JOHNSTON'S PROPOSED FORTS
FOR DEFENSE OF THE
REPUBLIC OF TEXAS

Timbers near the west fork of the Trinity River, and ending at San
Patricio near the mouth of the Nueces River. At strategic points
behind the forward line were to be three supporting posts. Two
regiments, one each of infantry and cavalry, ought to be created to
garrison the posts, he said. He would not merely supinely defend
these posts; rather, he would use them as bases for striking at concentrations of Indian strength, wherever they might occur.[60]

Meanwhile, he shifted all available troops to the west in an effort
to bring the Comanches to terms.[61] Whether defeat of the Cherokees
and the threat to themselves moved Comanche leaders to seek peace
cannot be certainly known; possibly they merely sought fresh gifts.
Whatever the motive, in early January, 1840, three Comanche chiefs
appeared at the headquarters of Colonel Karnes in San Antonio.
Sensible of their inability to resist further the forces of Texas, they
said, their tribe would now accept peace at any price. They had
rejected overtures of alliance from both the Cherokees and the
Mexicans, said the Comanche emissaries; instead, they desired a
council of Texan and Comanche leaders to draw a treaty ending
hostilities between the two peoples. In return for such a treaty, the
Comanches promised to surrender all white captives and stolen
property in their possession.[62]

The Lamar Administration was willing to make a treaty, but
suspected the sincerity of the Comanches. Lamar appointed commissioners to a council in San Antonio while Johnston prepared troops
to deal with anticipated treachery. He ordered Colonel William S.
Fisher, commander of the First Infantry Regiment, to march three
companies to San Antonio for the security of the council. Fisher was
to make clear to the Indians that the government of Texas had sole
right to set the limits of Indian habitation, that the Indians must
remain within these limits and cease to harm or annoy white settlers
along the border, and that citizens of Texas were free to occupy,
without molestation, any vacant land belonging to the government
of Texas.

If, by giving up all captives and stolen property, the Comanches

---

[60] Johnston to Senate of the Republic of Texas, December 18, 1839, Army
Papers, Republic of Texas.

[61] Johnston to Rusk, August 16, 1839, in Gulick and Elliott (eds.), *The Papers
of Mirabeau Buonaparte Lamar*, III, 67–68.

[62] H. W. Karnes to Johnston, January 10, 1840, in Winfrey *et al.* (eds.), *Texas
Indian Papers*, I, 101–102.

should demonstrate good faith, Fisher was to treat them kindly and permit them to depart without hindrance. If, however, the Comanches should appear without all captives and stolen property, Fisher was to hold the chiefs in hostage against the fulfillment of their promise. Johnston's final word to Fisher gave evidence of the Administration's resolve to settle the issue with the Comanches. "It has been usual heretofore to give presents," said Johnston. "For the future, such custom will be dispenced with." [63]

Johnston was not to remain Secretary of War for consummation of the measures which he helped inaugurate to deal with the Comanches. He resigned office in March of 1840. In late March two Texas commissioners, Acting Secretary of War William G. Cooke and Adjutant General Hugh McLeod, met in San Antonio with twelve Comanche chiefs to draw a treaty. Bloody fighting occurred instead. The Indians brought with them but a single captive white child and replied insolently when asked about other prisoners. When, following Johnston's previous instructions, Colonel Fisher's soldiers attempted to seize the chiefs, they sprang to arms and fought until all of the Comanches inside the council house were killed and more than a score of Indians had died in combat outside the hall. Seven Texans were killed and eight wounded in the melee. One of the Texas commissioners wrote in awe of the Indians' prowess, "Their arrows, when they struck, were driven to the feather." [64]

Comanche savagery and duplicity aroused savagery and duplicity within Texans, and strife continued throughout summer and autumn between Texans and Comanches. In August, General Felix Huston and Colonel Edward Burleson, with two hundred volunteers, surprised and defeated a large force of Indians on Plum Creek; two months later Colonel J. H. Moore, with ninety Texans and a handful of Lipan Indian allies, inflicted heavy casualties upon a Comanche village on the Red Fork of the Colorado River. Temporarily crippled by these blows, the Comanches sought cover, and the western frontier had a respite from their fury. [65] But neither Texas nor Albert Sidney Johnston had seen the last of this bold tribe.

[63] Johnston to Fisher, January 30, 1840, *ibid.*, I, 105–106.
[64] Muckleroy, "The Indian Policy of the Republic of Texas," *Southwestern Historical Quarterly*, XXVI (October, 1922), 142–144; see also Rupert Norval Richardson, *The Comanche Barrier to South Plains Settlement*, pp. 108–115.
[65] Muckleroy, "The Indian Policy of the Republic of Texas," *Southwestern Historical Quarterly*, XXVI (October, 1922), 144–145.

Before leaving the office of Secretary of War, Johnston knew the gratification of living and doing his duties in the Republic's new capital, the town of Austin. He supported President Lamar's cherished purpose of establishing the seat of government on the western frontier. And on the western frontier it was established; the preceding spring Johnston had sent troops there to keep the Comanches away from workmen building houses for the government. In October, 1839, the Administration moved to Austin, where Secretary of War Johnston shared a log cabin with Secretary of the Treasury Dr. James H. Starr. Johnston fell in love with Austin at first sight. The village lay on the Colorado River in a setting of hills, live oak, and wild flowers. To Johnston, it was "in the finest climate, and most beautiful & lovely country that the 'blazing eye' of the sun looks upon in his journey from the east to the west." [66] He would see and admire many places in his varied career, but always he would return to Austin.

In spite of the excitement of Indian wars and the sense of accomplishment in helping to establish a new capital on the frontier, Johnston wearied of his position. Possibly he became disillusioned with the government under Lamar, though he left no record of such mood. The Administration failed to prosper; its goals were visionary—beyond the reach of a fledgling nation. Expense of military campaigns and other ambitious projects led Lamar into the quicksands of excessive paper currency and inflation. Faltering of its own weakness and under relentless attack from its opponents, the Administration lost favor among the people; ultimately, it sank into bankruptcy.[67] A close friend who wished Johnston to become a candidate for the Presidency wrote to him, "Abide your time, and the reason I now have for saying you ought not to retire just now is that your position is better than any one in the country, and ought not to be abandoned hastily." [68] But Johnston kept his own counsel and made his own decision.

According to his son and biographer, Johnston desired to withdraw from the Texas government primarily because of his distaste for the routine of civil office, and secondarily in the hope of regaining his own prosperity. In accepting the Cabinet post, he, perhaps

[66] Johnston to Hancock, October 24, 1839, Johnston Papers, Barret Collection.
[67] Christian, *Mirabeau Buonaparte Lamar*, pp. 34–35.
[68] Love to Johnston, January 12, 1840, Johnston Papers, Barret Collection.

foolhardily, had hoped to march soon into Mexico at the head of a Texas army; once this vision was gone, he chafed under the tedium of bureaucracy. He had quickly used up the modest capital at his disposal when he came to Texas,[69] and his income in the service of Texas had been spare; as Secretary of War he received $3,500 a year in inflated Texas Treasury notes.[70] Friends testified that he was generous, if not prodigal, with his money and possessions. Once he commented with rare impatience on a message from a defaulting debtor, "I loaned this Rascal money . . . twice to assist him after I found out his villainy [as] a forger." [71] Fame and fortune had eluded Johnston in the service of the Republic of Texas.

His weariness in office may have come too of a deep unrest in his personal life.[72] Much as he loved Texas, he was lonely there; more and more he yearned for the presence of his children and kin. In trying to persuade a kinsman to join him in Texas, he wrote, "I feel like an exile. . . . I am not contented, I sometimes fancy myself most miserable, I stand alone without a relative and of course these are feelings not satisfied." [73] His kindling interest in a young lady of Kentucky may also have added to his loneliness in Texas.

Whatever the reasons, by autumn, 1839, Johnston was resolved to quit the Cabinet as soon as possible and to retire from public life altogether. "I do not know when I shall be able to go out of office," he said. "I hope soon, tho' I cannot calculate on it with certainty—I am anxious to see the roof of my cedar cabin peering among the live oaks. When shall it be?" [74] In March of 1840 he resigned.

Like most of the prominent figures of early Texas history, Johnston sought wealth through land speculation. He sold much of his remaining property in Louisville and Missouri and invested the proceeds in Texas land. His most ambitious venture of this sort was the purchase shortly after he arrived in Texas of a league (4,428 acres) of land—the Blossom League—in Harrison County, in northeast Texas.[75] Unfortunately, the title of prior ownership was not

[69] Johnston, *Life of Johnston,* pp. 120–121.

[70] Chief Clerk of War Department, Republic of Texas, to Johnston, December 9, 1839, Civil Service File, Republic of Texas.

[71] L. A. Adler to Johnston, February 14, 1839, Johnston Papers, Barret Collection.

[72] Johnston, *Life of Johnston,* pp. 120–121.

[73] Johnston to Hancock, October 24, 1839, Johnston Papers, Barret Collection.

[74] *Ibid.*

[75] Unsigned statement, October 11, 1838, Johnston Papers, Barret Collection.

clear, and settlers promptly moved onto the land.[76] For the remainder of his life, Johnston attempted to validate his title but was never able to do so.[77]

He purchased real estate in Austin, Galveston, and elsewhere in Texas. "I have waded up to my chin in Galveston lots," he once wrote to a kinsman.[78] After the expulsion of the Cherokees, he acquired a tract of 1,280 acres of land in Van Zandt County, and also assisted friends in the United States in their Texas land speculations. In addition to the Blossom League, he purchased for associates three adjoining leagues in Harrison County. Johnston was to hold title to the land, but was bound to pay the proceeds to his colleagues.[79] This arrangement may have been a device for getting around a Texas law that prohibited aliens from owning land in Texas except by titles obtained directly from the government of the Republic.[80]

Johnston was associated in some way with his kinsman George Hancock in the purchase of land from the notorious speculator John T. Mason.[81] While he was Secretary of War, Johnston wrote to Hancock advising that he dispose at once of all land acquired from Mason, that the Texas government would not confirm title to any of it.

Would you not do well to rid yourself of [the land] on any terms [?] This I have advised before, I then spoke from conjecture, *I now tell you what I know,* no patents will be issued to any person claiming under Mason—State the compensation to be allowed Watrous, Jones & myself, say an equal share with the original holders.[82]

[76] Notation, "Supreme Court of Texas," n.d.; Statement of Clerk of Superior Court [Texas], October 17, 1851, *ibid.*

[77] Eliza Johnston to "Dear Will," July 9, 1875, *ibid.*

[78] Johnston to Hancock, April 21, 1839, *ibid.*

[79] Tax receipts of Johnston, September 10, 1839; C. R. Andrews, Certificate, October 4, 1840, *ibid.*

[80] In writing to Johnston about land claims in Texas, a Kentucky business associate admonished him, "Have the titles so fixed that the non Resident law will not prejudice us—It is very strict I discover." Hobbs to Johnston, March 10, 1838, *ibid.*

[81] As agent of the Galveston Bay and Texas Land Company, Mason had obtained a personal grant of about 300 leagues of land under an act passed by the Legislature of Coahuila and Texas before the Texas Revolution. The government of the Republic of Texas repudiated this grant. William R. Hogan, *The Texas Republic: A Social and Economic History,* p. 83.

[82] Johnston to Hancock, April 21, 1839, Johnston Papers, Barret Collection.

The precise nature of this transaction cannot be determined. Johnston made no money out of his Texas land speculations.

Retirement from the Cabinet ended Johnston's public career in the Republic of Texas. For almost four years he had given unstintingly of his energies in serving the new nation, with disappointment often rewarding his efforts. He shared the grand dreams of President Lamar, only to have them vanish in the daylight of reality. He left office with his strongest ambition unfulfilled; he had failed to exact of Mexico her recognition of the independence of Texas. In spite of Johnston's urging, Texas was still without an effectual regular army, and he now knew that the Texans could be mobilized against Mexico only if Texas were actually invaded. His greatest service as Secretary of War was his vigorous prosecution of the Cherokee and Comanche campaigns. Texans would not forget Albert Sidney Johnston, scourge of the red man.

Invasions, Politics, and Romance

~~~~~~

JOHNSTON LEFT the Texas War Department, but he could not free himself of anxiety over the security of the Republic. For years after quitting office he clung to the vain hope of striking a blow at Mexico. Relations between Texas and her foes remained unsettled as invasions and rumors of invasion by Mexicans and Indians continued to disturb the tranquillity of Texas officials and private citizens. For the next three years Johnston was torn between his desire to be with loved ones in Kentucky and his urge to assist Texas in establishing security against Mexico.

In April of 1840 he heard of a new Mexican threat against San Antonio and of Comanche concentrations near Austin; the people of Texas began to mobilize for the defense of their frontiers. Johnston was then in Galveston preparing for a visit to his family in Kentucky. Friends implored him to stay and defend Texas. From Austin, Inspector General Hugh McLeod wrote of deplorable conditions in the west. The government was without information about the Mexicans; the capitol was barricaded against the Comanches; and General Felix Huston was on his way to take over the Army. "I wish Genl, you had not left us," McLeod said plaintively. "You must be here, to throttle him [Huston]—We are all willing to attack the demagogue, but we cant destroy him—he's too slippery for us."[1] Johnston replied that he would not leave Texas until her security was assured; he would lead a Galveston volunteer company in the war, if no higher command should open to him, he said.[2] But soon the immediate dangers to San Antonio and Austin disappeared, and Johnston went on his trip.

Hardly had he reached Kentucky before his Texas friends were begging him to return. Again the Mexican Federalists had sought the aid of Texas against the Centralist government; this time President Lamar had indicated he was willing to support such a venture. "The war is at hand," wrote one influential Texan to Johnston.[3] Johnston rushed west from Kentucky, hoping to see his dream of the invasion of Mexico at last come true. By early August he was in Galveston, where he wrote to President Lamar:

I infer . . . that yr Exclly contemplates a movement against Mexico, under certain contingencies, as soon as the requisite arrangements can be made. Should such be yr. design I will be much gratified to contribute to its success and with much pleasure place myself at your disposition for that purpose.[4]

But after a season of confusion and patriotic rhetoric the prospect of war again abated, no campaign occurred, and Johnston returned to Kentucky, this time to remain away from Texas for an entire year.

During this period he was adrift, his next move undecided, but relishing being once more with his children and kin in Kentucky. Doubtless he enjoyed the relaxation that came with freedom from responsibility; part of the summer of 1841 he spent at Newport, Rhode Island, and other fashionable eastern resorts, escorting a party of his young relatives on vacation. But he never lost his interest in Texas, nor changed his intention of returning there as soon as personal affairs permitted or the situation in Texas demanded. Texas was now his true home.[5]

[1] Hugh McLeod to Johnston, April 17, 1840, Johnston Papers, Barret Collection.

[2] James Love to M. B. Lamar, April 14, 1840, in Gulick and Elliott (eds.), *The Papers of Mirabeau Buonaparte Lamar*, III, 371–372.

[3] Love to Johnston, June 27, 1840, Johnston Papers, Barret Collection.

[4] Johnston to Lamar, August 6, 1840, in Gulick and Elliott (eds.), *The Papers of Mirabeau Buonaparte Lamar*, III, 427.

[5] Johnston, *Life of Johnston*, p. 123.

Meantime he kept in touch with political and military developments in Texas. For years a group of friends there had looked upon him as the best candidate to oppose Sam Houston for the Presidency upon the expiration of Lamar's term. Foremost of these supporters was James Love of Galveston, onetime United States congressman from Kentucky, and recently a Texas agent to the United States. Sharing Love's views were Albert T. Burnley, James S. Mayfield, Thomas F. McKinney, Judge B. C. Franklin, and Generals Kelsey Douglass and James Hamilton—all men of influence in the civil and political affairs of Texas. In the spring of 1840, Love wrote to Johnston, "If you are ambitious and desire so distinguished a station as President of this great nation, your chance of success is good." [6] Many Texans believed that Johnston, and he alone, could defeat Houston for the Republic's highest office.[7]

As the Texas presidential election came on in September of 1841, Johnston's friends besought him to return to Texas. Even if in the end he should choose not to be a candidate, they said, he ought at least to be on the ground in making such an important decision.[8] When Vice President Burnet entered the contest against Sam Houston, Johnston's backers accurately forecast Burnet's defeat, and continued to urge Johnston to make himself available. "Come home so soon as you can," wrote Love. "The race for President is not yet certainly fixed. A great many are dissatisfied with both Burnet & Houston." [9] "Are you aware that you have lost the Presidency [by being absent from Texas]?" asked another companion, who reported the "universal impression" that, were Johnston in the race, he would take the election.[10]

Why Johnston refused to enter the Texas presidential campaign cannot be known with certainty. His silence toward political ambition might have meant that at the time he had no desire for the office. Or he might have declined to run out of deference for Burnet, for the Vice President was his personal friend. Or Johnston may have read the political omens with surer eye than did his supporters; he may have sensed the futility of opposing the hero of San Jacinto before the voters of Texas. Johnston's behavior alienated, at

[6] Love to Johnston, May 20, June 4, 1840, Johnston Papers, Barret Collection.
[7] Tod Robinson to Johnston, June 4, 1840, *ibid.*
[8] S. A. Roberts to Johnston, April 1, 1841, *ibid.*
[9] Love to Johnston, January 31, April 1, 1841, *ibid.*
[10] A. P. Crittenden to Johnston, June 21, 1841, *ibid.*

least temporarily, some of his former admirers.[11] He was following a course of silence and equivocation, they charged, in the hope of seizing the first available opportunity for himself. "[Johnston] has in truth committed himself to both [parties]," said one critic.[12] Whatever the reasons, Johnston remained in Kentucky. Sam Houston easily won the Presidency of Texas again, and General Edward Burleson was elected Vice President.

Personal interests also helped to keep Johnston in Kentucky during the Texas presidential campaign of 1841. In the spring he had become involved in an affair of honor between a friend, Robert Wickliffe, Jr., and the later famous Kentucky Unionist, Cassius M. Clay. An anxious letter from Wickliffe's sister, who was the wife of Johnston's brother-in-law, William Preston, first brought Johnston into the matter. Against her wishes, Mrs. Preston wrote, her husband had associated himself with Wickliffe in the dispute.

You know my unbounded confidence in your courage and discretion and my mind would be greatly relieved if you were here to act as my brother's friend and adviser. I write to you without consulting any one but I know my family hold you in the same estimation I do.[13]

If Johnston sought to prevent conflict, he failed. The duel occurred near Louisville on May 13, with Johnston apparently acting as second to Wickliffe.[14] Elaborate terms prevailed: weapons were pistols not exceeding ten inches in the barrel nor carrying less than thirty balls to the pound; firing distance was twenty-nine feet; shooting began on prearranged signal. The duellists exchanged one shot without effect; the seconds then agreed that the challenger ought to be satisfied on the point of honor. Clay replied that he was satisfied on the issue involving himself but not on the manner in which he said Wickliffe had referred to Mrs. Clay in public speech. Wickliffe disavowed any intention of maligning Mrs. Clay. Both principals then agreed to drop the affair.[15] Privately, Wickliffe took a

[11] Ashbel Smith to M. Hunt, August 21, 1839; Smith to General Baker, December 30, 1839; Smith to Thurston, January 18, 1840; Smith to General Hunt, January 25, 1840; Smith to "Dear Colonel," July 27, 1840, all in Ashbel Smith Papers.

[12] Smith to Barnard Bee, May 22, 1840, *ibid.*

[13] M. Preston to Johnston, April 30, 1841, Johnston Papers, Barret Collection.

[14] Johnston, "Memoranda of Terms," n.d., *ibid.*

[15] Johnston, "Statement on Wickliffe-Clay Duel," n.d., *ibid.*

final dig at Clay, writing Johnston that a certain lady had called Clay most ungallant for not thinking of his wife until after the first shot. "If Clay had been hit," she said, "Mrs. Clay's honor would have gone unavenged." [16]

Johnston was held in Kentucky also by feelings deeper than his willingness to serve in a relative's duel. He was in love.[17] The lady was Eliza Griffin of Louisville, cousin of his first wife. Johnston's affection for her was strong a year before he quit the Texas Cabinet. "You must not infer any disparagement to Texan Belles," he once said in explaining his want of interest. "Their wit, beauty & accomplishments are unsurpassed—but sympathies are not created in a day nor are they easily forgotten or destroyed, 'hence my griefs.' " [18]

Friends and kinsmen quickened his memory of Eliza with every letter: Eliza did this, Eliza did that, Eliza was the life of the parties.[19] They tempted him with every mention of her name.

Eliza Griffin is still unattached [wrote one] although Jno. J. has been doing his utmost to storm the citadel of her heart.[20]

Eliza Griffin went to St. Louis . . . 5 weeks since with the intention of staying three weeks [wrote another], but I suppose has found it so agreeable that she does not know how time passes. I understand she is very much a Belle and report says she & George Clark are engaged but that is all say so.[21]

"Say so" powerfully attracted Johnston to Kentucky.

Johnston left little record of his courtship with Eliza. Doubtless all of the proprieties of a chivalric and sentimental society prevailed. Eliza was in the bloom of young womanhood—but eighteen years old when Johnston first began to pay suit to her.[22] One of their close friends later described her as the most charming woman in Louisville:

---

[16] Robert Wickliffe to Johnston, June 4, 1841, *ibid.*

[17] A. T. Burnley to Johnston, February 25, April 1, 1839, *ibid.*

[18] Johnston to W. H. Daingerfield, April 12, 1839, Miscellaneous Documents Collection, Texas State Archives.

[19] George Hancock to Johnston, January 29, 1839; William Preston to Johnston, February 22, 1839; Burnley to Johnston, February 25, 1839, all in Johnston Papers, Barret Collection.

[20] "Sue" to Johnston, October 24, 1840, *ibid.*

[21] Josephine Rogers to Johnston, July 21, 1839, *ibid.*

[22] Johnston, *The Johnstons of Salisbury,* pp. 102, 207.

[She] was a dazzling beauty of the Spanish type. Her stature was slightly above the middle size and her form admirably proportioned. She was a brilliant brunette and sang and played with great taste and skill, and drew and painted admirably.[23]

A photograph taken forty years after Eliza's marriage supports the unanimous testimony of acquaintances that she was a beautiful woman. Training in an eastern school for girls had given her poise and grace of social accomplishment, and her character and intelligence were the equal of her comeliness.[24]

Though nearly twice Eliza's age when he began to woo her, Johnston was yet a man of striking form and feature. He was a person of real stature in the Republic of Texas, and of wide reputation in the United States, and stories of his exploits in Texas had cast something of a romantic aura about him among his old acquaintances. Perhaps his winning of Eliza confirmed a certain truth in the rumor that Texans were irresistible. "You have no Idea what vast favorites with the ladies all Texans are," a jaunty Texas agent once wrote to Johnston from Baltimore. "You know the sex all like something devilish and corsair-like—a handsome cutthroat to charm a pretty girl—Again they think us all quite wealthy." [25] For years Eliza knew Johnston as cousin by marriage, and, unquestionably she shared her family's admiration for him all along. Certainly she came to love him, or she would have married someone else, for among her suitors were the wealthiest and most gifted young men of Louisville and other places.

Johnston's feeling for Eliza had been no secret among his Texas acquaintances. Visiting Louisville in the winter of 1839, one of them sent word to Johnston, "Your children are well [and] *she* is well." [26] Another associate wrote:

Report says that you are rendering [attention] to a certain lady who shall be nameless. General! I did not think you could be so rash. What! a Texian, & in the midst of these hard times. & do you still believe that you will be successful? Tis a wilful tempting of providence.[27]

[23] Dudley M. Haydon in unidentified newspaper clipping, Scrapbook, Johnston Papers, Barret Collection.
[24] Johnston to William Preston, July 21, 1847, Johnston Papers, Barret Collection.
[25] Daingerfield to Johnston, June 11, 1839, *ibid.*
[26] Burnley to Johnston, February 25, April 1, 1839, *ibid.*
[27] R. Morris to Johnston, July 23, 1840, *ibid.*

In the summer of 1841, when the Texas presidential campaign was at its height, a bachelor companion playfully wrote to Johnston, who was then in Kentucky:

Rumors of the most alarming kind have been current in this country respecting your movements and intentions. It is said you are about concluding certain arrangements incompatible with a residence in so barbarous a region [as Texas]—that your political notions are changed—that you are determined henceforth to eschew republics and live under an absolute monarchy. . . . If [these] rumors are true, your departure from Texas last year will have had a most remarkable effect upon your condition in life—will have made you the governed instead of the governor which you would have been had you remained.[28]

Romance may have dulled political ambition in Johnston's heart at the very moment when his supporters most desired him as a standard bearer.

Alarms from Texas united with the uncertainty of his financial affairs to delay marriage to Eliza. President Sam Houston had reversed most of the policies of the Lamar Administration. He had reduced the currency, suspended the redemption of Treasury notes, sought peace with the Indians, and adopted a strict defensive policy against Mexico, which did not, however, free Texas from violation of her frontiers. In early March, 1842, a Mexican force of six or seven hundred under General Rafael Vasquez suddenly took San Antonio, which was then guarded by a single company of Texans, and when, two days later, Vasquez withdrew, it was with all the booty he could transport. Instantly the Texas Republic rose to arms. President Houston ordered out the militia and sent agents to the United States to enlist volunteers and to purchase weapons and supplies. Two thousand Texas volunteers rushed to San Antonio, where Vice President Burleson took command, and the long-awaited hour of vengeance upon Mexico seemed at hand.[29]

For a season before the Mexican incursion, Johnston had been in Galveston on business. Always alert to threats against the security of Texas, he and his associates tried in vain to arouse the government to the need for stronger military preparation. At word of the seizure of San Antonio, Johnston hurried there for the volunteers' rendez-

[28] Crittenden to Johnston, June 21, 1841, *ibid.*
[29] Wortham, *A History of Texas,* IV, 93–94.

vous. His feelings on this occasion are not recorded, but his past views on military policy, his present eagerness to take up arms, and the correspondence of his most intimate friends all make clear that he still favored invading Mexico at once. He hoped to command the expedition.[30] However, as in the past, Houston issued stirring proclamations, but shunned decisive warfare, wisely reasoning that Texas wanted the strength for the venture.

As Johnston made his way west toward San Antonio, his friends in Houston (now capital of the Republic, by action of the Houston Administration) did everything within their power to induce the President to authorize an invasion. They planned to present Houston with resolutions calling for an offensive against Mexico; should he reject it, they then would demand his resignation. Public opinion would force Houston either to fight or to retire, believed these Texas war hawks. "The wish of the whole people so far as I have heard, is in favor of prosecuting this matter to a close now," wrote James Love to Johnston. "Is it not awful that the country should be cursed with such a man [as Houston] at such a time?" [31] Johnston probably agreed heartily.

But he and his associates again underestimated Sam Houston's sagacity, his skill in turning public opinion, and his insight into the Texas will. Whether the people of Texas would have fully supported an invasion of Mexico is indeterminable. Johnston and his friends thought that they would; President Houston thought that they would not. The war spirit burned high, said Houston, only as long as the people fought for the defense of Texas. "But," he said, "we are invading Mexico and not defending ourselves against invasion." [32] Houston appeased the demand for action by feigning support of an offensive. He ordered General Alexander Somervell to lead into Mexico any volunteers who wished to go; the expedition was to seize a number of Mexican towns, including Matamoros, if possible.

But Houston had no intention of involving Texas in a full invasion. Scoffing at what he considered foolish and illegal troop move-

[30] For expressions of these sentiments, see Johnston to A. C. Bullit, May 3, 1842; Leslie Combs to Johnston, February 12, 1842; J. S. Mayfield to Johnston, March 22, April 20, 1842; Love to Johnston, April 9, 1842, all in Johnston Papers, Barret Collection.

[31] Love to Johnston, March 31, 1842, *ibid.*

[32] Sam Houston to Daingerfield, in Williams and Barker (eds.), *The Writings of Sam Houston*, III, 14–15.

ments by various Texans, including Johnston, Houston said to a companion:

> You would be amused and miserably provoked at some of our "Heroes." It has been reported . . . that Burleson, [Johnston, and others] are burning with revenge to cross the Rio Grande and "damning the President" that he would not let them go on. Oh, they were snorting. . . . Well, the last news is that Burleson has at San Antonio about 600, and about 100 are under the immortal Genl Johnson [sic] of the Cherokee War. All as I suppose are "on their own hook.". . . Somebody will be taken down a button hole or two! [33]

Johnston and his friends soon realized that without the President's firm support, war against Mexico must fail.[34] In early April, Burleson issued a proclamation saying that he could have raised 5,000 troops, if permitted to cross the Rio Grande at once, but that Houston had refused to let him advance before popular enthusiasm waned. Upon arriving in San Antonio, Johnston seems to have taken temporary command of a small body of volunteers. But he did this expecting to incorporate them soon into an authorized national army, which he hoped to lead. He refused to participate in a filibustering expedition against Mexico, or in an invasion not fully supported by the Texas government. When he learned that Houston would not order a true offensive, and would not retire to make way for a President given to such course, Johnston wisely withdrew from the affair and returned to Galveston.[35] He considered obedience to civil authority one of a soldier's primary duties to the republic.

Johnston and Sam Houston now brushed angrily together again. Ill will between the two had endured since their hot words over the Cherokee War two years before; on a later occasion when Houston drove his carriage up to a hotel in Galveston, Johnston deliberately turned his back and entered into a conversation with someone else.[36] Disagreement over the wisdom of invading Mexico brought their latent hostility to the surface. On April 25 Houston made a proclamation against unauthorized recruiting by Texans in the United States. One sentence of the statement read: "Said agents have offered

[33] *Ibid.*

[34] Burnley to Johnston, April 9, 1842; Love to Johnston, April 9, 1842, Johnston Papers, Barret Collection.

[35] Johnston, *Life of Johnston*, p. 124.

[36] Love to Lamar, April 25, 1840, in Gulick and Elliott (eds.), *The Papers of Mirabeau Buonaparte Lamar*, III, 380.

commissions to gentlemen about to emigrate, as they say, by the authority of General A. Sidney Johnston, whom they represent as in command of the army of Texas." [37]

Johnston claimed innocence of any such recruiting; and there is no evidence that he was guilty. Furious at what he felt was a smear upon his name, he resolved to demand satisfaction of the President.[38] Since Houston was said to have made his statement as a result of information received from a Dr. Turner, Johnston first called upon Turner. In the presence of witnesses, Turner denied having linked Johnston with illegal activities in the United States. Johnston then went in person to Houston and asked that the President publicly clear his name. Houston refused to make a statement, saying that his proclamation did not implicate Johnston; in a later exchange of letters between the two, the President reaffirmed his view that no apology was required since no offense had been committed.[39]

Not satisfied with this reply, Johnston published the full correspondence on the affair, along with his own proclamation denying any part in the enlistment of volunteers in the United States and censuring Houston for having made improper use of his name.

My highest aspiration in times perilous like these is to be useful to my country [he said with a patriotic flourish]. Whether I occupy a high or an inferior station is a matter of no consequence to me, so that our united efforts shall accomplish the great work of obtaining a recognition of our independence.[40]

The fire between the two abated, but it would not die.

At the very time Johnston was threatening Sam Houston with a challenge, he cooperated with others in averting a duel between two of his Texas friends—former President Lamar and General Memucan Hunt. Ignoring his own inconsistency, Johnston joined the arbiters of the Lamar-Hunt controversy in saying: "We remark that in times like the present, two gentlemen whose services are required for their country should not permit personal differences between themselves to interfere with the public good." [41]

[37] Johnston, *Life of Johnston*, p. 125.

[38] Johnston to Bullit, May 3, 1842, Johnston Papers, Barret Collection.

[39] Johnston to Houston, May 1, 1842 (copy) ; Houston to Johnston, May 2, 1842, *ibid.*

[40] Johnston to "The People of Texas," n.d., 1842 (copy), *ibid.*

[41] Johnston [and others] to Mayfield, May 8, 1842, in Gulick and Elliott (eds.), *The Papers of Mirabeau Buonaparte Lamar*, IV, 17–18.

Johnston now again returned to Kentucky, gloomy over affairs in Texas; again he rushed back to Texas, believing that war with Mexico was imminent. Soon after reaching Louisville he had received an account by James Love of another seizure of San Antonio. In early September the city had fallen to a force of about one thousand under General Adrian Woll, a French soldier in the service of Mexico. Only a handful of Texas volunteers had remained at San Antonio after the invasion fever of the preceding spring had cooled, and Woll defeated or scattered these defenders and took the city, capturing in it a Texas District Court then in session there. After a week's occupation, and before a counterattack could be mounted against him, he withdrew. His primary object seems to have been to confound those who, claiming that peace existed between Texas and Mexico, urged the annexation of Texas by the United States.

This time Love did not importune Johnston to come to Texas; Love knew only too well of the many past fiascos in attempting to rekindle the war. "I offer no suggestions as to your course," he said. But he painted a picture of impending doom that he must have known would rally Johnston to the defense of Texas.

There seems to be great apathy in the people. They have been cheated and deluded by a fool or Knave, and have no confidence in him. . . . If the next arrival confirms the opinion that we are invaded, I join the army at once, and fight to the last.[42]

With these words in his ears, Johnston took passage for his adopted land in early November.[43]

Before he reached Texas, President Houston had at last authorized an invasion of Mexico. On November 18 General Somervell started a Texas army southward from San Antonio. Failure was inevitable. Somervell's command was but a corporal's guard of seven hundred men, and after a month of marching and hardship the force split. General Somervell led part of the troops back to Texas; Colonel William S. Fisher, former Secretary of War, led the remainder to battle and to surrender at Mier a week later.[44] Possibly Johnston would have joined this invasion had he reached Texas in time to do so. Headed for Galveston, he ate breakfast at the St. Charles

---

[42] Love to Johnston, September 22, 1842, Johnston Papers, Barret Collection.
[43] Johnston to Edward D. Hobbs, November 1, 1842, *ibid.*
[44] Wortham, *A History of Texas*, IV, 95–100.

Hotel in New Orleans on the morning that General Somervell's advance unit marched for Mexico.[45]

Johnston and his impetuous circle damned President Houston for the failure of the Somervell expedition; they trusted that it would wreck the Administration, and for a time their hopes seemed justified. They heard that the President's friends were advising him to call Johnston, Rusk, and Burnet into his Cabinet, to seek Vice President Burleson's counsel, and to ask Congress for the adoption of measures recommended by these men.[46]

Johnston denounced Houston bitterly for all the ills of Texas:

This is the result of the miserable mismanagement, if not poltroony, of our wretched government. A bold & energetic movement in the month of March last would have spared us this disastrous condition of things and our national humiliation and disgrace. The spirit of the people however is not yet broken and if peace cannot be obtained in any other way equally honorable I am assured that they are quite willing to undertake a warlike movement on a scale of sufficient magnitude to attain their object. The *profound* policy of our executive is now fully appreciated and we are beginning to handle him without gloves.[47]

Again Johnston was urged to seek the Presidency of Texas in the next election, and, influenced by the embarrassment of the Houston Administration, he, for the first time, seriously contemplated becoming a candidate. "If I make a false move my political fate is sealed," he said, explaining his delay in returning to Kentucky. "If the country should be invaded during my absence it would be fatal to my prospects." [48] But Texas was not invaded, the war spirit cooled, and soon Johnston departed for Louisville.

Faith in his political strength remained alive among his Texas acquaintances; but, they emphasized, he must be in Texas to bring his weight to bear. James Love wrote:

It is a thing to be remembered by you that if a campaign [against Mexico] is organized . . . and you not here to go with the forces, that you are a gone man. And also if your mind is fully made up that your destiny is to be . . . here, that it is indispensable to your future ambitious hopes, that you be on the spot, and always on it. . . . Altho you act wisely in your views about

[45] St. Charles Exchange Hotel to Johnston, November 18, 1842, Johnston Papers, Barret Collection.
[46] Mayfield to Johnston, January 23, 1842, *ibid.*
[47] Johnston to Hancock, February 20, 1842, *ibid.*
[48] *Ibid.*

politics, still your friends do regret that you have not been here. Rusk out of the field, you would have doubled any man in Texas but Burleson who would have supported you warmly & so would Rusk.[49]

Johnston's interests, however, were now turned to personal affairs. He would not again dream of becoming President of Texas, but time and circumstance strengthened the many bonds of friendship between him and his Texas associates. Though not given to immoderate self-praise, Johnston took great pride in his Texas citizenship; he must have agreed silently with the views of a comrade who wrote from afar:

I am frequently gratified by a proud consciousness that in the assemblages which we Texans sometimes have been in in the city of New York there is gathered together as much of chivalric honour directed by correct judgement and active intelligence as could be met with in the same number of individuals taken at random from any one of the United States.[50]

Johnston's love for Eliza Griffin did not extinguish his deep pleasure in male companionship or its accompanying conversation, dining, chess, brandy, and tobacco. "You are not forgotten by any of [us]," wrote a friend. "Our standing toast at our suppers, which by the bye, we get up in a style that an Epicurean might envy, is 'our absent friend Genl Johnston.' "[51] From another Texan came the complaint of a want of competition in chess since Johnston's departure for Kentucky. "No one in this region has any science and my victories are followed by no profits and entitled to no honor," wrote this correspondent. "I long for a right good fight with you."[52] Reputedly skilled at the game, Johnston sometimes engaged his opponents by mail, setting up hypothetical situations and moves in the manner of bridge hands in a modern newspaper.[53] To Diplomat J. Pinckney Henderson, he lost a suit of clothes in a wager on the outcome of the 1840 presidential election.[54] He was pleased to learn that Judge Benjamin C. Franklin had named his infant son "Sidney" in Johnston's honor.[55]

[49] Love to Johnston, April 10, August 20, 1843, Johnston Papers, Barret Collection.

[50] Daingerfield to Johnston, August 29, 1839, *ibid.*

[51] Roberts to Johnston, January 17, 1841, *ibid.*

[52] Crittenden to Johnston, June 21, 1841, *ibid.*

[53] William P. Ballinger to Johnston, September 17, 1845, *ibid.*

[54] Johnston to J. Pinckney Henderson, February 11, 1844, *ibid.*

[55] Benjamin C. Franklin to Johnston, July 2, 1841, *ibid.*

Serious conversation was one of Johnston's most cherished pastimes; he was said to talk in a calm and reflective fashion, with a "natural Turkish gravity." [56] Contemplative reading united with keen intelligence to give him a philosophical bent.

What wonderful things have you accomplished during your stay [in Kentucky]? [asked a Texas companion]. Have you erected a pyramid or an obelisk? Or have you made yourself famous by publishing any of those speculations which used to occupy our time last summer? The existence of a natural sense of right and wrong for instance? [57]

Johnston also enjoyed quiet humor. Knowing of his contemplated remarrying and settling on a plantation, a bachelor friend bantered him over the prospect. Johnston must provide him with a cabin on the place, he said; the cabin must be supplied with brandy and cigars "if they be not proscribed by the Supreme Power"; the cabin must have a rifle, a billiard table, a piano, and a library containing the works of Bacon, Burke, and Hooker. "And a noble set of chess men. None of your fantastical womanish red and white ivory toys, but solid, substantial sedate masses of carved oak. With me at your elbow to suggest wants to you I think you will soon be right comfortably fixed." [58]

For several years after leaving the Texas Cabinet, Johnston was without employment, living off income from the sale of his property in Missouri and Kentucky. Though the primary urge of his life seems to have been toward some great public accomplishment, such as leading the Army of Texas to victory over her foes, he yearned also to become a planter. Among his associates, planting was looked upon as an exalted way of life and a lucrative occupation. Perhaps Johnston sought through planting to compensate for his want of true fame in public affairs; or he may simply have decided upon it as a livelihood. In any event, he now wished to acquire a plantation; his frequent visits to Texas were divided between brandishing the sword and seeking a place to settle.

In January of 1843 Johnston and his friend Albert T. Burnley agreed to purchase together China Grove Plantation on Oyster Creek forty miles from Galveston. Johnston was to live on the place

---

[56] Haydon in unidentified newspaper clipping, Scrapbook, *ibid.*
[57] Crittenden to Johnston, February 5, 1842, Johnston Papers, Barret Collection.
[58] *Ibid.*

and plant it.[59] The original owner, W. D. C. Hall, was about to lose the plantation through inability to pay off a judgment against it; [60] in buying the place, Johnston and Burnley contracted to pay the owner's creditors a sum of almost $16,000 plus interest at 10 per cent. Payment was to be completed in five years. China Grove Plantation embraced 5,856 acres, but most of the land was still in unbroken prairie. A friend cautioned against closing the transaction; the place would not pay itself out, he said, and if sold at auction, it would not bring more than $5,000, leaving Johnston and his partner liable for the remainder of the heavy notes against it.[61] Thus warned, Johnston sought to annul the agreement but was unable to do so.[62] In August he signed the deed.[63]

Matrimony doubtless hastened Johnston in his purchase of the plantation, for he needed a home to receive Eliza as his wife. She was often in his thoughts when he was away in Texas; he was upset when her letters failed to reach him promptly.[64] Always his friends and relatives in Kentucky called her to his mind. Possibly unaware that Eliza was about to become his stepmother, Johnston's thirteen-year-old son wrote from Louisville, "Bustles have been increasing of late tremendously and Uncle William [Preston] says that Cousin Eliza out-Bustles all of them." [65] Immediately after closing the purchase of China Grove Plantation, Johnston returned to Kentucky. According to a later account, he was one day visiting a friend in Louisville when he saw a curio representing Cupid riding on the shoulders of the Devil and bearing the inscription, "Le Diable emporte l'Amour." Borrowing the object for a short time, he later returned it with the remark that it had helped to end his courtship successfully. He then announced his approaching marriage to Eliza.[66] In early

[59] William Preston Johnston, "History of China Grove Plantation," [1840–1841], Johnston Papers, Barret Collection.

[60] Judgment in Favor of *Nathl. Townsend* vs. *W. D. C. Hall*, January 22, 1845 (copy) , *ibid.*

[61] Crittenden to Johnston, July 3, 1843, *ibid.*

[62] Johnston to Hancock, February 20, 1843, *ibid.*

[63] Bill of Sale, January 20, 1843; Assignment of Contract, W. D. C. Hall to Pease and R. J. Townes, January 21, 1843, Book B, pp. 209–210; Mortgage, Johnston and Burnley to Hall, August 12, 1843, Book B, pp. 286–287; all in Records of the Clerk of Court, Brazoria County, Angleton, Texas.

[64] Johnston to Hancock, February 20, 1843, Johnston Papers, Barret Collection.

[65] William Preston Johnston to Johnston, postscript on letter from William Preston to Johnston, February 25, 1843, *ibid.*

[66] Haydon in unidentified newspaper clipping, Scrapbook, *ibid.*

October they were married at the home of Eliza's uncle and guardian, George Hancock, near Shelbyville, Kentucky.[67]

Johnston's Texas friends showered the couple with letters of well-
wishing and invitations to come to Texas as soon as possible. "If any
lady has been indiscreet enough to marry you give her our best
regards," wrote Thomas F. McKinney, famed financier of the Texas
Revolution.[68] James Love, after congratulating Johnston warmly on
his marriage, turned to affairs less happy. Johnston's interest in
China Grove Plantation fared badly, said Love; the season's crop of
cotton was greatly reduced by storms, and, moreover, Love questioned the intention of the present tenant, W. D. C. Hall, to pay his
rent, even should the crop be plentiful. Johnston was urged to come
to Texas at once to decide what could be done with the place.[69] His
partner, Burnley, wrote in gloom of crop failure and financial distress. "Under these circumstances we must compromise the infernal
contract or I shall be broke up," [70] he said.

In mid-November Johnston and Eliza left for Galveston, where
friends greeted them with unfeigned pleasure and hospitality. It was
Eliza's first trip to Texas. She enjoyed the country and climate, and
especially the many kindnesses shown by her husband's associates,
but Johnston was disappointed in his hopes of regaining financial
equilibrium. He was unable to release himself and his partner from
the notes signed in buying the plantation, though he was willing to
forfeit a considerable sum to do so. In early spring the Johnstons
returned to Kentucky, still undecided on an occupation.[71]

For more than two years he and Eliza divided their time between
Kentucky and Texas. Johnston tried in vain to sell the Texas plantation to advantage, while continuing to rent it out in the hope of
making it pay for itself. This attempt also failed, because Johnston
and Burnley were unable to stock the plantation with slaves and
equipment or to bring more of its prairie land under the plow.
Apparently, Johnston blamed himself for involving Burnley in the
unprofitable partnership, for in the fall of 1845 he agreed to take
over Burnley's portion of the place and of the indebtedness.[72] Mean-

[67] Johnston, *Life of Johnston*, p. 129.
[68] Thomas F. McKinney to Johnston, October 5, 1843, Johnston Papers, Barret
Collection.
[69] Love to Johnston, November 6, 1843, *ibid.*
[70] Burnley to Johnston, November 26, 1843, *ibid.*
[71] Johnston to Hancock, April 4, 1844, *ibid.*
[72] Agreement of Johnston and Burnley, September 25, 1845, *ibid.*

time, family expense and payments on the plantation notes bore heavily upon Johnston.[73]

His interest in the public affairs of Texas remained keen while he was in Kentucky, but he no longer gave heed to the call of politics or to rumors of impending war with Mexico. From Texas came persistent word that Johnston still was favored for the next presidential election.[74] After traveling through the west a friend wrote that Johnston could take nine tenths of the ballots there, if he only would enter the contest. "A great many of [the people] say if you are not a candidate they do not intend to vote at all." [75]

When Johnston pleaded family responsibility as a hindrance to political activity, a former colleague in the Cabinet, Dr. James H. Starr, chided him sternly:

Your excuse for not running for the presidency . . . "that you have married a wife and cannot come" ought not in this instance to avail you, for when a country finds itself quite destitute of men suited for such a station, save one individual, that man should not under any circumstances be suffered to withhold his services.[76]

But Johnston would not reconsider. At last he wrote James Love that he was determined to stay in Kentucky for the present, unless Texas needed her men for actual defense against invasion. "In that event, I will not, if alive, fail to be with you." [77]

Johnston now turned his thoughts of Texas to the supreme issue before the Republic—annexation by the United States. He had first joined the cause of Texas in the hope that she would become a part of the parent nation. He later shared President Lamar's enthusiasm for permanent Texan independence, but the vicissitudes of the past eight years had moved him, along with most Texas leaders, again to favor union. Hungry for new land, and fearing that Texas was about to become a protectorate of Great Britain, a majority of the American people also approved of annexation. The presence of slavery in Texas caused American political leaders to split in their attitude toward annexation: the Democratic Party generally favored

---

[73] Johnston, *Life of Johnston*, p. 130.

[74] S. H. Walker to Johnston, January 3, 1844, Johnston Papers, Barret Collection.

[75] H. Clay Davis to Johnston, March 26, 1844, *ibid.*

[76] J. H. Starr to Johnston, July 16, 1844, *ibid.*

[77] Johnston, *Life of Johnston*, p. 128.

it; the Northern Whigs generally opposed it. In 1843 the Houston Administration in Texas and the John Tyler Administration in the United States made a treaty of annexation, only to have it defeated in the United States Senate by the efforts of the Whigs. Lifelong admirer of Henry Clay, Johnston now turned cool toward the great Whig because of his role in killing the treaty.[78]

Annexation became the chief question of the presidential election of 1844 in the United States, and Democrat James K. Polk, strong advocate of annexation, was elected President. That same year, Dr. Anson Jones, Texas Secretary of State, was elected President of Texas. Jones remained silent on annexation; he sought instead a treaty of recognition with Mexico. Urged by England and France, Mexico at last agreed to such a treaty. Meantime, rightly regarding Polk's election as a popular mandate for annexation, the outgoing President of the United States, John Tyler, prevailed upon Congress to approve annexation through a joint resolution of the two houses of Congress.[79]

Many Texans, including Johnston's coterie of friends, felt that Jones opposed annexation, and that he would do all in his power to prevent it.[80] "If [Jones] . . . refuses to call congress and take the necessary steps to ascertain the will of the people," James Love wrote Johnston, "we will take the matter in our own hands, have a convention unseat him, or hang him if necessary to carry our purposes, and all that may abide by him." [81] In the summer of 1845 Jones presented the Texas Congress with the alternatives of continued independence with Mexican recognition, or annexation to the United States. To Johnston's gratification, the Texas Congress rejected the treaty with Mexico, censured Jones for his coolness toward annexation, and authorized a convention to consider the offer of the United States Congress.

On July 4, 1845, the Texas convention assembled in Austin to ratify the terms of annexation to the United States, and to draft the first constitution of the state of Texas. Among this body were many of Johnston's closest friends. Unanimously chosen president of the

---

[78] For reflections of Johnston's sentiments, see Preston to Johnston, March 7, 1844; and Love to Johnston, October 29, 1844, Johnston Papers, Barret Collection.

[79] Justin H. Smith, *The Annexation of Texas*, pp. 414–469.

[80] Mayfield to Johnston, March 8, 1845, Johnston Papers, Barret Collection.

[81] Love to Johnston, March 30, 1845, *ibid.*

convention was General Thomas J. Rusk, soldier of San Jacinto and Johnston's comrade in camp and in Indian campaign. Also present were James S. Mayfield and Johnston's most intimate Texas companion, James Love. Johnston was urged to come to Austin for the meeting. "Bring Mrs. Johnston with you & remain until the drama is over," wrote a delegate, "if you stand only as a looker on & note the current of events as it rises & passes." [82] Many members inquired for him, said James Love. "Almost every one expressed for you sincere friendship, there is scarcely anything Texas would not do for you, if you would place yourself in the situation to permit it." [83] These words must have cost Johnston a pang of regret over not being there to share in the historic moment. The convention approved annexation with but a single dissenting vote, and on December 29, 1845, Texas became a state of the United States.

For three years Johnston sought in vain to free himself from the burden of the unwisely purchased China Grove Plantation. He refused to pity himself over his misfortune, or to blame others for it. When a kinsman later suggested that Johnston might have been the victim of a shady transaction, he sternly rejected the idea and commented philosophically:

The policy of society condemns those who fail of success in their undertakings as either deficient in wit or honesty. This may be right because men are stimulated thereby to strive the more to avoid this penalty . . . and society in the main is benefited.[84]

At last he resigned himself to a single honorable course: he would settle on the place and cultivate it with his own hands in an effort to pay off the debts against it and against his name.

Had circumstances not forced this expedient upon him, he doubtless would have returned to Texas anyway. Friends there besought him to return, one saying, "You had better come back soon, and bring that gude wife of yours, destiny is against her, for here her fortune whether for good or ill, will be fixed at some time it cannot be helped, the sooner she comes the better." [85] Presently he and his "gude wife" were not alone; on April 8, 1845, their first child, Albert Sidney, was born at the Hancock home in Kentucky. Welcomes from

[82] Mayfield to Johnston, March 8, 1845, *ibid.*
[83] Love to Johnston, February 1, 1845, *ibid.*
[84] Johnston to Hancock, March 3, 1846, *ibid.*
[85] Love to Johnston, February 1, 1845, *ibid.*

Texas now stirred Johnston to action. Borrowing money, he prepared to equip the plantation for himself and his family. Soon he took them back to Texas; they were at the home of James Love in Galveston when Johnston learned that the United States was at war with Mexico.

Valor at Monterrey

~~~~~~

FEW MEN WELCOMED the coming of war with Mexico as heartily as did Albert Sidney Johnston. For years he had yearned to smite the Mexicans over what he deemed their perfidy and brutality toward Texas. Perhaps his only regret now was that a Democratic President would reap the glory of the conquest, for Johnston still clung to the Whiggish bias of his youth. Yet as it seemed that retribution was about to be visited upon Mexico, the prospect of marching upon the long-sworn enemy stirred his blood.

War was probably fated to occur between the United States and Mexico as the heritage of an ancient enmity between the English and Spanish forms of civilization and to appease a land hunger among the American people that was strong enough to convince them of their "manifest destiny" to reach the Pacific.[1] Many Americans, including President Polk, coveted the Mexican territory of California. More narrowly, the war grew out of the annexation of Texas. For years Mexico had threatened war if Texas should be

[1] For a discussion of the causes of the Mexican War and the events leading up to it, see Otis A. Singletary, *The Mexican War*, pp. 8–20; Justin H. Smith, *The War with Mexico*, I, 58–150.

added to the United States. National tempers rose as provocations accumulated. A multitude of Americans, especially those of the South and Southwest, burned to punish Mexico for past irritations and outrages against Texas and the United States. On the other side, Mexican politicians felt that war with the United States offered opportunity to gain favor among their followers; and Mexico refused to honor the claims of American citizens for lives and property lost in the civil wars of Mexico.

Bloodshed began in dispute over the boundary of Texas. Mexico held that the Nueces River was the boundary; President Polk pressed the Texas claim for the Rio Grande. When in the fall of 1845 Polk sent Emissary John Slidell to offer gold in return for a favorable boundary settlement, including the cession of California to the United States, the authorities of Mexico refused to talk with Slidell. Regarding this as an insult to the nation's honor, Polk ordered General Zachary Taylor, with a small body of regulars, to move to the Rio Grande and at the same time resolved to ask Congress for a declaration of war if Mexico should resist Taylor's movement. In March, Taylor advanced. Ignoring Mexican orders to withdraw, he occupied Point Isabel, commanding the mouth of the Rio Grande, threw up a field fortification (Fort Brown) opposite the city of Matamoros, and called upon the states for volunteers to strengthen him. Mexican troops moved against Taylor, and on April 25 attacked and captured a small body of American dragoons on reconnaissance. The war with Mexico was on.

Outbreak of war found Johnston without military position. His commission in the Army of the Republic of Texas had expired upon the annexation of Texas; for all practical purposes, the commission had been dead since the second election of Sam Houston as President of Texas. Johnston at one time had held the hope of being appointed colonel of a new United States regiment to be formed for duty in Texas. While the Texas state constitutional convention was sitting, James Love had written that Johnston was the choice of all there to head the regiment.[2]

Other influential friends and kinsmen had also urged his appointment. Upon the solicitation of George Hancock, General Zachary Taylor wrote the Secretary of War in the fall of 1845, recommending

---

[2] James Love to Johnston, September 28, 1845, Johnston Papers, Barret Collection.

Johnston in the most favorable language. Remembering him from the Black Hawk campaign, Taylor said that he supported Johnston with clear conscience and hearty good will. "As I know but few as well & none better qualified for the position," said the General, "I can truly say no one desires his success more than myself." Taylor warned, however, that the opposition of Sam Houston, now United States senator from Texas, probably would deprive Johnston of the command.[3] Johnston did not get the regiment.

At the home of the James Loves in Galveston he restlessly listened to reports of military activities on the Rio Grande and watched the departure of troops for Taylor's army. Governor J. Pinckney Henderson of Texas wrote that he was on his way to take command of the Texas volunteers. After asking Johnston to do him the favor of purchasing some articles of personal use for the field, Henderson invited Johnston to meet him in Corpus Christi, where appointments to command the volunteer regiments would be made.[4] On the same day, Thomas F. McKinney wrote at the Governor's request to say confidentially that Johnston would have the highest rank in the volunteers, second only to that of the Governor.[5]

Johnston chafed to be on the march. But Eliza reasonably looked with alarm upon the signs of war; she begged him to remain at home with her and their infant son. Torn between loyalties, he took no move for more than a month. Then, according to family account, in late April a messenger arrived from Army headquarters, saying that General Taylor would welcome Johnston in his force. Promising his anxious wife that without her consent he would not re-enlist at the end of one six-month period of service, Johnston left Galveston, along with a group of other volunteers, bound for Point Isabel and the Halls of Montezuma.[6]

Unable to get immediate passage by sea, he and his associates impatiently set forth by horse on the 300-mile journey. Johnston rode a splendid animal given him for the occasion by an admirer since early Texas days. Camping under the stars at night, and killing wild cattle of the prairies for sustenance, the group made their way toward the Rio Grande. They were joined en route by other bodies

[3] Zachary Taylor to George Hancock, February 8, 1846, *ibid.*
[4] J. Pinckney Henderson to Johnston, May 8, 1846, *ibid.*
[5] Thomas F. McKinney to Johnston, May 8, 1846, *ibid.*
[6] Johnston, *Life of Johnston*, pp. 133, 146.

having the same destination, for a scarcity of shipping obliged hundreds of eager volunteers from Texas and elsewhere to go to the scene of action by land. A month out from Galveston, Johnston's party merged with a larger one under command of Major Jack Hays of Texas; in it was the prominent newspaper proprietor and reporter, George Wilkins Kendall, of the New Orleans *Daily Picayune*. On June 6 the entire company, three hundred strong, rode into Taylor's lines.[7]

At Point Isabel, on the Gulf of Mexico, they found an abundance of sand, heat, and confusion. Center of activities was Fort Polk, a hastily erected earthwork located on a thirty-foot bluff overlooking the sea. A few score tents and a half dozen sutler's huts stood in the midst of a wide array of army supplies and booty of war. Captured guns, lances, drums, saddles, and assorted curiously wrought leatherware gave the appearance of a Mexican museum. Encamped in the open about the fort were the volunteers. Those from Texas were still arriving daily in parties similar to the one that had accompanied Johnston.[8] Governor Henderson, commander of the Texas contingent, was not yet on the scene, and the Texans were without military organization. Contrary to the Governor's wishes, the Legislature required that officers be elected by the troops, not appointed by him. Not until mid-June did the Governor arrive and the regimental organization occur. Then, to Johnston's gratification, he was chosen by the men of the First Texas Infantry Regiment to be their colonel. He set about with a will to shape them into a fighting unit.[9]

For more than a month Johnston and his men remained at Point Isabel. The battles of Palo Alto and Resaca de la Palma had occurred before his arrival there; defeated "bayonet to bayonet and sword to sword," the Mexican army had fled beyond the Rio Grande. Occupying Matamoros, Taylor prepared to strike into the interior of Mexico as soon as he could collect troops, equipment, and transportation for such a campaign. Meantime, the army must be trained.

Making soldiers quickly out of volunteers was as difficult then as ever; Johnston's experience at Point Isabel must have brought back to mind the vexations of commanding the Army of the Republic of

---

[7] *Daily Picayune* (New Orleans), June 14, 1846.

[8] For descriptions of Fort Polk, see *ibid.*, May 30, June 14, 20, July 7, 8, August 2, 1846.

[9] Johnston to Hancock, July 10, 1846, Johnston Papers, Barret Collection.

Texas. Supplies were low and mail arrived weeks late. Most of the volunteers lived exposed to burning sun and drenching rain. Inactivity bred discontent. Yet Johnston was not dismayed.

We are losing no time by waiting [he wrote]. They [the troops] are daily undergoing instruction, which will make them the more efficient. . . . My regiment [is] a fine body of riflemen, capable, from the instruction received here, of manoeuvring with great rapidity and precision; and I do not doubt that they will acquire distinction.[10]

Others also sent back to Texas favorable reports on Johnston's regiment, and promise of early action kept his spirits high.[11]

Eager as Johnston was to close with the enemy, he scoffed at the manner in which the war was then being waged and to a kinsman revealed his own concept of how it ought to be done. His plan was sound, if not brilliant; it anticipated the victorious strategy later employed against the Mexicans by General Winfield Scott. Let the American troops on the Rio Grande offer a mere demonstration to occupy the enemy, said Johnston; concentrate the main American force at some point on the coast below Vera Cruz and strike directly at the capital, where the decisive battle would be fought. He reasoned:

Mexico [City] is to that Republic as Paris is to France. If Mexico [City] falls, her dependencies fall with her. Why then waste a cartridge . . . or throw away the public treasure in a war of marches against a country without population (comparatively) as Santa Fe, Chihauhua or Calafornia [sic]?[12]

In late July, Taylor began to move up the Rio Grande for a blow at the Mexican army concentrating at Monterrey. Taylor's army of above six thousand troops comprised three divisions, two of regulars and one of volunteers. Commanding the regulars were Brigadier General David Twiggs and Johnston's onetime commandant at West Point, Brigadier General William J. Worth; Brigadier General William O. Butler was in command of the volunteers. Unwise as John-

---

[10] *Ibid.,* July 30, 1846. See also *American Flag* (Matamoros) , July 7, 1846.
[11] Ephraim McLean, "My Connexion with the Mexican War," Manuscripts Division, Rosenberg Library; Muster Roll of Field and Staff Officers, 1st Regiment, 1st Brigade, Texas Foot Volunteer Riflemen, July 8, 1846, in Betty Ballinger Papers.
[12] Johnston to Hancock, July 30, 1846, Johnston Papers, Barret Collection.

ston deemed Taylor's strategy to be, he nevertheless welcomed the prospect of battle.[13]

On August 5 Johnston and a portion of his regiment embarked on a steamboat up the Rio Grande for Camargo, the site of Taylor's advance base, which lay about midway between the Gulf and Monterrey. More than three hundred miles the transport wound its way up the river, and Johnston had ample time to observe and reflect upon the country that he traversed. He had opportunity also to write to friends and relatives, and to comment on military operations with a freedom that would subject him to court-martial in a modern army. It ought to have done so in Taylor's, except that everyone else in the expedition wrote with the same abandon. "General Taylor is rapidly concentrating his force at Camargo," Johnston said. "The next movement I suppose in 15 or 20 days will be for Monterrey." [14]

Johnston's admiration for the fertility of the Mexican soil was equalled by his contempt for the people who tilled it. "As a race the inhabitants . . . are inferior," he wrote, "resembling in color the indians of the U. States & not much superior to some of them in civilization." He found himself in a land of thatched huts, broadbrimmed hats, and scanty dress. He observed:

The women usually wear a chemise with very short sleeves & very low before, neither a petticoat. I have seen some at work with out the former garment, its place being supplied with a cotton Handkerchief over the bosom leaving the body bare to the waist; they seemed to suffer no embarrassment, & I presume felt that there was no want of modesty. . . . ce va le monde.[15]

Johnston was an authentic representative of the proud Anglo-Saxon society that now prepared to relieve Mexico of a large measure of her national domain.

Disappointment awaited them in Camargo. Arriving there in mid-August, they found a scene of sickness, death, and demoralization. The town lay on the San Juan River a few miles above the point where this stream flows into the Rio Grande. Sweltering in 112 degrees of heat, plagued with myriads of insects, and supplied with impure water, the army dwindled alarmingly; the camp resounded

---

[13] M. Preston to Johnston, April 30, 1841, Johnston Papers, Barret Collection.
[14] Johnston to Hancock, August 11, 1846, Johnston Papers, Barret Collection.
[15] *Ibid.*

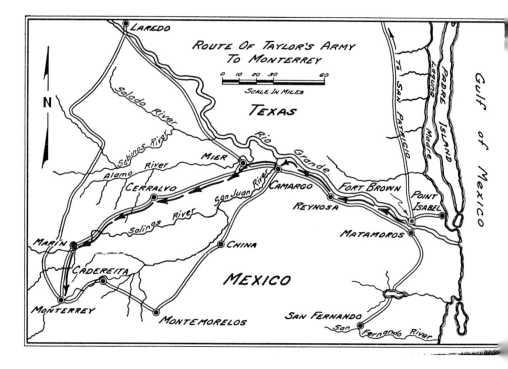

ROUTE OF TAYLOR'S ARMY TO MONTERREY

with the "dead march" and with graveside volleys of musketry as the unseasoned troops fell prey to the ills of climate and circumstance. Camargo is "a Yawning Grave Yard," said one soldier.[16] Johnston was doubtless recalling Camargo when later he wrote:

Few comprehend the ravages & perils of war. They are not to be found in the reports of the battle field; [these] account for but a small portion of the waste of life. . . . Privations without number, hard marches, under a vertical sun or in the chilly hours of the night . . . make up a bill of mortality, treble that of the fiercest warfare. . . . [This] has been particularly so with our [army] in this war.[17]

Camargo offered no glory to Johnston and his men.

At this moment of inactivity and misery, Johnston's regiment encountered that bane of all early American armies: the enlistment period of most of the Texas volunteers drew to an end.[18] According

[16] Smith, *The War with Mexico*, I, 211.
[17] Johnston to Hancock, November 1, 1847, Johnston Papers, Barret Collection.
[18] *Daily Picayune*, September 6, 1846; *American Flag*, October 14, 1846; McLean, "My Connexion with the Mexican War," Manuscripts Division, Rosenberg Library.

to Johnston's later account, a group of dissident soldiers called upon General Taylor to determine the truth of a rumor that they must re-enlist for six additional months or be discharged at once. Taylor was shaving himself in front of his tent when the delegation arrived. Before they could speak, the rough-hewn old soldier said, "I suppose you want to go home. Well, I don't want anybody about me who don't want to stay. I wouldn't give one willing man for a dozen that wanted to go home." Offended by Taylor's bluntness, the volunteers stalked away to urge the immediate disbandment of the regiment. In vain Johnston pleaded with his men to remain: 318 volunteers, including an entire company of German-Americans who had suffered much sickness, left for home. The remaining 224 were thereupon assigned to other commands, and Johnston was left a colonel without a regiment.[19]

Chagrined over this loss of his command, he looked about for a suitable assignment for the duration of his enlistment. General Taylor quickly eased his embarrassment by appointing him inspector general on the staff of Major General William O. Butler, commander of the division of volunteers. In this new capacity, Johnston rode out of Camargo with the army as it marched for Monterrey in late August.

The force moved up the Rio Grande valley to Mier—a place of bitter associations for Johnston and other Texans. Four years before, a remnant of invading Texas troops under Johnston's friend William S. Fisher had surrendered to the Mexicans there, and every tenth man had later been executed. At Mier the route left the Rio Grande and turned southwest toward the pale blue heights of the distant Sierra Madre. After two weeks of marching in heat, rocks, thorns, and thirst, the column reached Cerralvo, a welcome oasis at the foot of the cordillera, supplied with abundant fresh water from mountain sources and surrounded by fertile groves and pastures.

They did not tarry at Cerralvo but, refreshed by their brief halt and animated over the prospect of now pleasant marching, pressed on across a picturesque plateau toward Monterrey. Five days out of Cerralvo, the army closed into Marín, a day's march from their objective. On the morning of September 19, General Taylor and his escort rode to the rim of the plain and looked across fields of corn and sugar cane upon the white cathedral city of Monterrey. Greeted

[19] Johnston, *Life of Johnston*, p. 135.

with cannon shots from one of the defending forts, Taylor withdrew three miles to the wood of San Domingo, a luxuriant growth of oak and pecan watered with numerous fresh springs. This wood, renamed Walnut Grove by the Americans, became Taylor's base of operations in the forthcoming attack.[20]

The Mexican commander of the north, General Pedro Ampudia, was resolved to fight for Monterrey. Protected by mountain spurs and by the Santa Catarina River on west and south, Monterrey occupied favorable defensive terrain, and Mexican ingenuity had augmented natural defenses to give the city genuine strength. Western approaches were guarded by Fort El Soldado on Federation Ridge (across the Santa Catarina) and by the Bishop's Palace (a massive stone building converted into a fortress) on Independence Hill. Fortified walls and parapets crowned the high and virtually inaccessible river bank along the southern border of the city. Commanding the plain north of Monterrey stood the Citadel, a powerful fort constructed upon the masonry of an unfinished cathedral. On the crest of a slope at the southeastern tip of the city lay Fort El Diablo, a strong earthwork armed with cannon. Four hundred yards north of El Diablo was a stone tannery building protected by an earthen redoubt and cannon. This was called Tenería Fort. A small stream ran east and west through the city. At the northern end of this stream's main bridge (Purísima Bridge) was a *tête de pont*, or bridgehead, supported by cannon. Streets were barricaded and the city's stone houses converted into strongholds; the cathedral in the heart of Monterrey served as general magazine. Ampudia's army outnumbered the Americans by perhaps one thousand men. Monterrey would test the mettle of the invaders.[21]

After studying the defenses throughout the nineteenth, Taylor that night held council with subordinate commanders and ordered the assault. Worth, with his division of regulars, was to march across the plain north of the city and seize the Saltillo road on the west; he was then to attack Monterrey from that direction. If successful, this movement would sever Ampudia's line of communications with Saltillo and southern Mexico, and would divert much of his strength to a defense of the city on the west. Meantime, Taylor, with the

---

[20] For accounts of this movement, see Johnston to William Preston Johnston, September 28, 1846, Johnston Papers, Barret Collection; and Hamilton, *Zachary Taylor: Soldier of the Republic*, pp. 200–204.

[21] Smith, *The War with Mexico*, I, 232–234, 249–250.

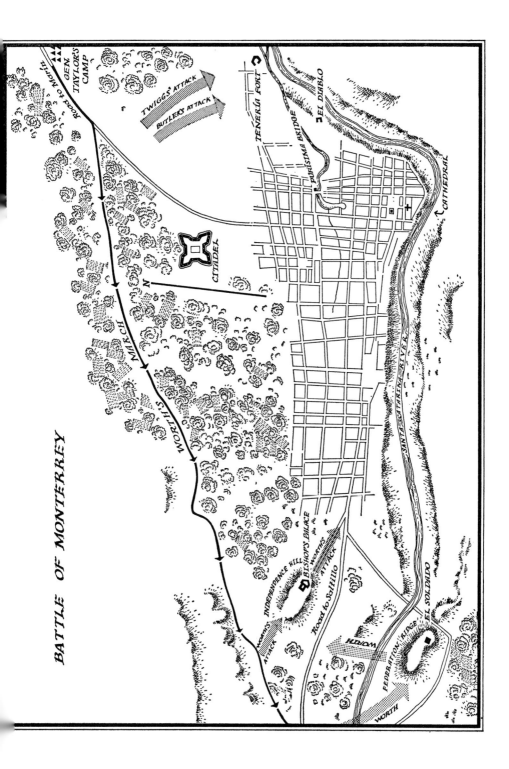

BATTLE OF MONTERREY

remainder of his force, was to assault from the east. The plan was bold to excess. It called for a wide separation of the wings of Taylor's army in the presence of a stronger opponent, and it exposed both segments to counterattack beyond reinforcement by the other. Worth's isolated command would be especially vulnerable while on the march. Sublimely contemptuous of Mexican prowess, Taylor and Worth refused to stoop to a reckoning of chances.

Worth moved out on the afternoon of the twentieth. He led with inflexible purpose. His prestige was under a cloud for having earlier withdrawn from the service, and he now flaunted the significant motto: "A grade or a grave." Fighting in a drizzle of rain, he beat off an attack by enemy lancers and gained the Saltillo road on the morning of the twenty-first; then he moved promptly against Mexican defenses on the western side of the city—the fortress El Soldado on Federation Ridge and the Bishop's Palace on Independence Hill. By mid-afternoon El Soldado was in American hands; Worth prepared to attack the Bishop's Palace before dawn.

All this time Taylor contrived to prevent a concentration of Mexican troops against Worth by firing artillery and making feints with his infantry against the eastern defenses of the city. On the morning of the twenty-first, while Worth was fighting for El Soldado, Taylor ordered the remainder of the army to attack from the east. Twiggs's division of regulars moved first. It engaged the Tenería redoubt and Fort El Diablo, only to be stopped by heavy enemy fire. Seeing this assault momentarily halted, Taylor sent Butler's division of volunteers to its support.[22]

The volunteers advanced under severe bombardment from the Citadel. Johnston rode forward with General Butler and the other members of the staff. Accompanied by General Taylor himself, this group joined Brigadier General Thomas L. Hamer at the head of one of his regiments, the First Ohio Volunteers, on the extreme right of the assault. Resistance there, as elsewhere, was fierce. Every street was barricaded and swept by artillery and musketry; concealed on the flat roofs of the stone houses, enemy troops shot pointblank into the advancing American skirmishers. Taylor and his subordinates contemplated breaking through the walls from house to house in

---

[22] For descriptions of Taylor's tactics, see Smith, *The War with Mexico*, I, 236–246, 248–254; Hamilton, *Zachary Taylor, Soldier of the Republic*, pp. 208–210; Singletary, *The Mexican War*, pp. 33–39; Johnston, *Life of Johnston*, pp. 136–139.

order to escape the galling fire in the streets but abandoned the plan for want of axes or crowbars, and the attackers, rank and file, braced themselves into the iron sleet. Shortly before noon a combined attack by regulars and Mississippi volunteers under Colonel Jefferson Davis routed the Mexicans defending Tenería Fort and occupied that position.[23]

A hundred yards from El Diablo, Taylor's attack faltered. Men fell fast under converging fires from El Diablo, from the Purísima bridgehead, and from a masked battery across the ravine. The heaviest American losses of the battle occurred here; in two hours the volunteer division lost one fourth of its numbers in killed and wounded. General Butler was hit and borne to the rear; Hamer became division commander.

Johnston remained with Hamer. All was noise, smoke, dust, confusion, and courage. Remaining in the saddle, Johnston was a perfect target for enemy marksmen, but, though his horse was lightly struck three times, he was unscathed. Eliza later gratefully attributed his survival to the "kind care of a merciful Providence." [24] Taylor, Hamer, Johnston, and other officers moved from position to position, shouting orders amid the uproar in a gallant effort to keep the assault moving. All was in vain. At about five o'clock Taylor reluctantly ordered a withdrawal of the attackers at the eastern end of the city, except for a small force to hold the captured Tenería Fort.

Johnston's finest moment of the battle came then. As the weary and disorganized Americans drew away from the edge of the city, a column of Mexican mounted lancers counterattacked the Ohio regiment. The lancers were deemed the most formidable of Mexican fighting men. Sweeping across the plain and killing stragglers as they came, they spread panic among the retreating volunteers. Many of the Americans threw aside their arms and fled through a nearby cornfield. Separated from his commander during the confusion, Johnston rode calmly among the frightened troops, urging them to turn and form line against their pursuers. His courage and air of command prevailed; taking position behind a chaparral fence, the

[23] Butler's attack is described in these official reports: Thomas L. Hamer to "Sir," September 25, 1846; William O. Butler to "Sir," September 25, 1846; Jefferson Davis to General John A. Quitman, September 26, 1846, all in Letters Received, Adjutant General's Office, Records of the War Department.
[24] Eliza Johnston to Hancock, November 20, 1846, Johnston Papers, Barret Collection.

volunteers opened a fire that emptied a number of Mexican saddles and sent the lancers galloping in retreat.

Captain Joseph Hooker, who one day would command the Army of the Potomac in the Civil War, was with Johnston throughout much of the day at Monterrey. Hooker was later quoted as saying that Johnston was the outstanding officer of the entire division, that after Butler was wounded, Johnston in fact commanded the division.[25] Of the brush with the lancers, Hooker wrote, "It was through [Johnston's] agency, mainly, that our division was saved from a cruel slaughter. . . . The coolness and magnificent presence [that he] displayed on this field . . . left an impression on my mind that I have never forgotten." [26] Johnston had proved himself equal to crisis on the battlefield.[27]

Throughout the night of September 21, Johnston and General Hamer remained with the isolated garrison in Tenería Fort. A counterattack by Ampudia probably could have retaken the position, but the Mexican leader was in no mood to mount an offensive; instead, he proposed to abandon El Diablo and other outer works and concentrate for desperate resistance in the heart of the city. Johnston and his comrades spent a night of anxiety and misery in the fort, exposed to torrential rain and continuous artillery fire. In the morning the weary garrison was relieved by Quitman's brigade.[28]

Taylor's men were idle on Tuesday, the twenty-second, except for exchanging cannon fire with the enemy and moving into position for renewed attack. Not so Worth's division. At three o'clock that morning this intrepid commander awakened his soldiers and sent them up the near-vertical slope of Independence Hill to seize the Bishop's Palace. After a sharp exchange of fire the Americans gained the crest of the hill, and at dawn Taylor's men in the valley cheered the sight of the Stars and Stripes floating from the top of Independence Hill. Fighting for the Palace continued throughout most of the day, but by four o'clock in the afternoon this stronghold was in Worth's hands.

---

[25] William Preston Journal, May 23, 1848 (copy), *ibid.*

[26] Joseph Hooker to William Preston Johnston, June 3, 1875, *ibid.*

[27] In describing the battle to his son, Johnston did not even mention his own role in this crisis. Johnston to William Preston Johnston, September 28, 1846, *ibid.*

[28] Hamer to "Sir," September 25, 1846, Letters Received, Adjutant General's Office, Records of the War Department.

On the morning of the twenty-third Taylor renewed his attack from the east. He found El Diablo abandoned, but every yard of advance beyond this fort was hotly contested. Fighting in the streets, on the rooftops, and breaking through the walls from house to house, the Americans laboriously made their way forward toward the cathedral, last stronghold of the enemy. Apprised of Taylor's attack by the clamor of combat from the city below, Worth assaulted afresh from the west, and gradually the two American columns closed the gap between them. But when night fell, Taylor, curiously, again withdrew most of his troops from the eastern portion of the city. Again, despondency and indecision prevented Ampudia from counterattacking with profit.

Taylor seems to have attempted little coordination between the two groups of his army. By repeatedly disengaging his troops on the east from battle, he time and again exposed one or the other of the two segments to concentrated enemy attack. In the end this mattered not at all. Cut off from reinforcements and supplies, pounded by American artillery, and pressed by the dauntless American infantry, the Mexicans had little fight left in them. On the morning of September 24, Ampudia sent out a flag of truce to seek terms of capitulation.[29]

Taylor at first demanded unconditional surrender, but when Ampudia demurred, the American commander agreed to negotiate through a joint commission. General Worth and Colonels Jefferson Davis and J. Pinckney Henderson were appointed to sit with three Mexican officers to consider terms. Lengthy discussions followed; convinced finally of equivocation and calculated delay on the part of the Mexican commissioners, the Americans brought them to account with a threat to resume hostilities. According to terms then agreed upon, Monterrey was to be surrendered to the Americans, all Mexican troops were to retire beyond the Rinconada Pass of the Saltillo road, and an armistice of eight weeks was to be observed by both sides. Ampudia and his army were permitted to escape. Considering the weakened and exhausted condition of the American army, and the near depletion of its ammunition and supplies, Taylor made perhaps the wise decision in accepting such an arrangement. Victory at Monterrey made heroes of Worth and Taylor. Worth was now the

---

[29] Smith, *The War with Mexico,* I, 258–261; Hamilton, *Zachary Taylor, Soldier of the Republic,* pp. 214–215.

"high-comb cock" of the Army; Taylor was on his way to the White House.[30]

In the aftermath of the negotiations for capitulation, Johnston and Jefferson Davis shared a tense and hazardous experience, according to a later account by Davis. Deliberations of the commission were finished and copies of the terms were in Ampudia's hands, but were yet unsigned by the Mexican commander. Davis was to call at Ampudia's headquarters the following morning to pick up the signed articles. Johnston voluntarily joined his longtime friend for the ride from Walnut Grove into the city. Approaching the Mexican lines about the plaza, Johnston and Davis, with apprehension, observed Mexican musketeers stationed on the roofs and cannon trained from behind the barricades. Johnston's garb had already excited the wrath of Mexican civilians along the way, who recognized it as that of a hated Texan. (Because of having shrunk his uniform by an accidental soaking in sea water while at Point Isabel, he was clad in red flannel shirt, blue jeans, and low-crowned felt hat.)

Just when the two Americans had begun to fear violence at the hands of troops or mob, Ampudia's adjutant general appeared, but attempted to ride away without relieving the plight of the two Americans. Johnston suggested to Davis that they keep the Mexican officer with them. Quickly squaring their horses across his path, they demanded to be escorted to Ampudia. Boldness had the desired effect, said Davis. Under the implied threat of the Americans, the Mexican turned about with apparent pleasure and conducted them to his commander, who received them graciously and gave them the signed copies of the order of surrender. Davis was of the opinion that he and Johnston escaped harm through Johnston's instant decision to take the Mexican officer hostage. The episode may have had its influence on Johnston's subsequent career, for it increased Davis's admiration for Johnston's qualities of leadership. He said, "[Johnston] exhibited that quick perception and decision which characterize the military genius." Davis held this opinion until his death.[31]

Johnston's enlistment ended shortly after the Battle of Monterrey. He unquestionably expected now to be offered a command. Whether

[30] Singletary, *The Mexican War*, pp. 41–42.
[31] Johnston, *Life of Johnston*, pp. 142–144.

he would have remained with the Army if he had received a command cannot be known, for he had promised Eliza that he would not do so without her approval. He was saved this difficult choice, for no command was tendered him. His failure to receive an offer is puzzling, since all of his superiors, including General Taylor, praised his conduct in the Monterrey campaign.[32] Generals Butler and Hamer paid especial tribute to his courage and skill as a soldier.[33] Johnston suspected that political partisanship deprived him of the offer of a command.[34] In early October he left Monterrey to rejoin his family in Galveston.

[32] Certificate by Taylor on United States Army Pay Voucher, September 30, 1846, Johnston Papers, Barret Collection.

[33] Butler to "Sir," September 30, 1846; Hamer to "Sir," September 25, 1846, Letters Received, Adjutant General's Office, Records of the War Department.

[34] Johnston, *Life of Johnston,* p. 145.

Texas Planter and Oracle

〰〰〰〰〰〰〰〰〰〰〰〰〰〰〰〰〰

J OHNSTON RETURNED to a hero's welcome by wife and friends in Galveston. Expressing their "high sense
of Johnston's distinguished service," a group of the city's most prominent men sought to honor him with a testimonial dinner.[1] Unable
to attend because of personal business, he thanked his admirers with
these words: "Honor . . . has always been, in my opinion, the most
powerful incentive to action and should be esteemed . . . the highest
reward that can be accorded for public service. For my own part I
neither seek nor desire any other." He spoke as one who had received
no reward save honor.[2]

Johnston faced the painful decision whether to return to the
colors or to remain with his family. Before leaving to join Taylor's
force, he had promised Eliza that he would not re-enlist without her
consent. She now begged him not to leave her again, and other
circumstances also pressed upon him. China Grove lay tenantless
and idle; it ought at once to be returned to productivity. Moreover,

[1] Sam M. Williams [and others] to Johnston, November 1, 1846, Johnston
Papers, Barret Collection.
[2] Johnston to Williams [and others], November 24, 1846, *ibid.*

Johnston doubtless smarted over his failure to receive a command after the Battle of Monterrey. He made up his mind to stay with his family; if unable to find a tenant for his plantation, he would cultivate the place himself. In refusing to re-enlist, said Johnston, he was obliged "to resist the most powerful impulse of Nature and education." [3] Eliza was overjoyed. "Now . . . he will give to his family the attention they so greatly require," she wrote tartly, "so much more than his country." [4] At the end of November, 1846, Johnston and his family left Galveston for China Grove.

What they dignified with the name China Grove Plantation was in fact a crude frontier homestead. Situated on Oyster Creek about forty miles from Galveston, China Grove was a place of rich alluvial soil, but the bulk of it was in unbroken prairie, or in heavy forest that yet teemed with wildcat, occasional panther and bear, turkey, and deer. Wild flowers innumerable brightened forest and prairie. In the edge of the dense woods, under the shade of live oak and pecan, stood a double log cabin, covered with clapboard, and with a porch across the front. Its furnishings of roughhewn wooden tables, chairs, and beds would better have suited a camp than a residence, Johnston's son later wrote.[5] Here, subjected alike to the beauties and to the rigors of nature, Johnston and his family lived for three years.

Johnston worked with a will, toiling with his own hands to repair house, barn, and fences, and to grow crops of corn, cotton, sugar cane, fruits, and vegetables.[6] Assisting him were a slave family of husband and wife and two teen-age boys. Later he hired an Irish ditcher named John, who turned out to be as much tippler as worker. Johnston shot game in the forest to provide his table with meat. His family never wanted for food; their fare comprised venison, "with the fat two inches deep upon the saddle, fine fat Prairie hens and young wild Turkies," squash, artichokes, pie plant, cabbage, potatoes, yams, tomatoes, figs, cantaloups and melons. To all this was added the produce of poultry and dairy. There was abundance without stint.[7]

[3] Johnston, *Life of Johnston,* p. 157.
[4] Eliza Johnston to George Hancock, November 20, 1846, Johnston Papers, Barret Collection.
[5] Johnston, *Life of Johnston,* p. 146.
[6] Johnston to William Preston Johnston, May 16, 1849, Johnston Papers, Barret Collection.
[7] Eliza Johnston to Julia Davidson, August 20, 1849, *ibid.*

Johnston held high hopes for China Grove. Struck by its fertility, he believed that one day the place would produce great quantities of both cotton and sugar. During his first year on the plantation, he grew a small crop of cane, chiefly to test the soil. The experiment convinced him that the freshly broken ground was too rich for sugar cane, but that once "tamed" by cultivation, the land would grow cane superior to the finest of Louisiana.[8] His first harvest of corn yielded nine hundred bushels; besides this, he grew enough cotton to pay living expenses for the year, plus some expenditure for repairs and improvement. "Everything has prospered with us better than we had any right to anticipate," he wrote at the close of the first season.[9]

The Johnstons were at first supremely happy in their rustic home. They savored the beauties of woods and field; they knew the satisfaction that comes of physical labor and of observing the growth of plant and animal. They adorned their premises with the Cherokee rose and other flowers. Their pleasure was enriched with books: Eliza read *Godey's Lady's Book,* along with literature more serious; [10] Johnston reviewed mathematics and read Herodotus. Once he taxed his eyes beyond endurance with reading.[11]

Talented Eliza filled some of her scarce leisure with painting birds and flowers and brightened their evenings with music, as devotion to Texas grew in her. "I think myself as much of a fixture in Texas as one of its live oaks," she wrote from China Grove, "and have determined to be greatly astonished if I ever leave it even on a visit." [12] After almost five years of marriage to Eliza, Johnston said that no unkind word had ever passed between the two of them.[13] "Lizzie manages her part [of duties in the home] most admirably, and bears her privations with cheerfulness and courage which . . . cannot be surpassed." [14]

Their young son, Albert Sidney, was strong and full of childish mischief. "Like all healthy children," Johnston said with thinly concealed paternal pride, "[Sidney] is considered a prodigy, physi-

[8] Johnston to Hancock, February 28, 1847, March 22, 1848, *ibid.*

[9] *Ibid.,* March 22, 1848.

[10] Johnston to Mr. Godey, February 25, 1849, Johnston Papers, Barret Collection.

[11] Johnston to Henrietta Johnston, May 6, 1848, *ibid.*

[12] Eliza Johnston to Hancock, February 2, 1848, *ibid.*

[13] Johnston to Hancock, March 22, 1848, *ibid.*

[14] *Ibid.,* February 28, 1847.

cally and mentally. His mother will give you the facts sustaining this opinion, and can do it better than I can." [15] A second son was born a year after they went to China Grove. Albert Sidney's fair complexion resembled his father's, but this baby had Eliza's dark hair and eyes. "[He is] a much finer boy than Sid," Johnston wrote to his daughter in Kentucky, "although your Aunt . . . thought [Sid] non pareil." [16] They named the infant Hancock McClung after Eliza's uncle, George Hancock, and an esteemed brother-in-law of Johnston's.

The children were a source of profound joy and, at times, of trivial vexation. As Johnston wrote Hancock:

Sid . . . is a joyous merry little fellow. [He] can beat our "Army in Flanders" swearing; an accomplishment we know not where he picked up, but which he will soon forget, if his mother does not impress it upon his mind by rebuke or the more potent peach tree switch—This latter she threatens violently, but I think Sid will laugh her out of it.[17]

In January of 1850 a daughter was born. She was named Mary Hancock.[18]

The Johnstons lived lives of isolation at China Grove. Most of the time they were too busy for amusements, or for calling on friends or relatives. Between Christmas of 1846 and October of the following year Johnston left his plantation only twice, Eliza but once. In declining an invitation to visit relatives in Kentucky, Johnston explained, "The price of corn is eternal vigilance here." [19] Faulty mail service intensified the seclusion of China Grove. Mail was distributed by Postmaster General Cave Johnson through private contractors, who proved to be indifferent, if not incompetent; during the autumn of 1847 the "Cave Johnson Disease" left eastern Texas without mail for weeks.[20]

Yet the Johnstons did not live altogether to themselves. They paid occasional visits to friends—visits that became more frequent following the birth of McClung—and they sometimes entertained in their cabin home. Their nearest neighbors and most cherished companions were Colonel W. D. C. Hall and his family, who lived on a sugar

---

[15] Johnston to William Preston Johnston, July 7, 1847, Johnston Papers, Barret Collection.

[16] Johnston to Henrietta Johnston, January 4, 1848, *ibid.*

[17] Johnston to Hancock, March 22, 1848, *ibid.*

[18] Johnston, *The Johnstons of Salisbury*, p. 159.

[19] Johnston to Hancock, October 21, 1847, Johnston Papers, Barret Collection.

[20] Starr & Amory to Johnston, November 18, 1847, *ibid.*

plantation a few miles from China Grove. Inviting the Halls to visit China Grove, Eliza once penned this jingle:

> If Mrs. Hall will come to see
> My own "gude man" my boys and me
> She'll find the trees with ripe figs laden
> Enough for matron, man and maiden.
>
> .   .   .   .
>
> Tell Colonel Hall and Molly small
> Tell Mrs. A and Betty tall
> How glad we'll be themselves to see
> On figs to feast right merrily.[21]

From time to time the James Loves from Galveston were guests at China Grove. Perhaps infrequency added zest to such simple entertainments as the Johnstons enjoyed in their frontier home.

Johnston continued to observe the course of the Mexican War, which dragged on until February of 1848. But his old enthusiasm for the conflict was gone; he felt only contempt for President Polk, whom he considered an incompetent strategist and a political mountebank. When his brother-in-law, William Preston of Kentucky, prepared to enter the Army, Johnston spoke against it. "I do hope that [Preston] will not go to Mexico, if his family oppose it," he wrote.[22] "Their happiness is of more consequence to him than all else. . . . There [is] no special appeal to his patriotism." [23]

Eventually the Polk Administration adopted the general strategy that Johnston privately favored; in March of 1847 an army of ten thousand under General Winfield Scott took Vera Cruz and moved inland against Mexico City. Johnston still criticized the manner in which the war was being conducted. He scored the Administration for dividing its forces; he believed that Scott ought to have at least 50,000 men for the accomplishment of so hazardous a mission.[24] "War like any other business cannot progress prosperously in the hands of pidlers," he railed.[25] Even after Scott took Mexico City, Johnston remained critical of President Polk's strategy of dispersion.

---

[21] In Eliza Johnston's hand on back of letter from James Love to Johnston, May 23, 1848, *ibid.*

[22] Johnston to Hancock, November 1, 1847, *ibid.*

[23] *Ibid.*, October 21, 1847.

[24] Johnston to William Preston, August 3, 1847, Johnston Papers, Barret Collection.

[25] Johnston to Hancock, November 1, 1847, *ibid.*

An army the size of Scott's, isolated in the heart of the United States as Scott was isolated in Mexico, would never be able to extricate itself, he said. But he compromised the logic behind his criticism by saying, "But we cannot reason with regard to Mexicans as with regard to any other people." [26]

His admiration for General Taylor remained strong. When fear arose among Johnston's acquaintances that Taylor was in danger of being trapped and defeated before Buena Vista, Johnston accurately predicted that Taylor would emerge victorious.[27] Influenced by his own friendship for Taylor, and perhaps by the rising tide of Taylor's popularity throughout the country, Johnston so exaggerated the General's talents as to compare him to Hannibal, Caesar, and Napoleon.[28]

One of the brightest periods of the Johnstons' life at China Grove occurred during the winter and early spring of 1847, when sixteen-year-old William Preston Johnston spent three months with them on the plantation. Separation from his two elder children, who still lived with their grandmother in Kentucky, was a source of constant pain to Johnston; his hopes of having them live with him were always doomed to disappointment. William Preston was of a serious and studious nature. He lacked his father's powerful physique and seemed rather to have inherited his mother's tendency to frailty. Johnston supplied his son a tonic of physical exertion and outdoor life, ditching, planting hedge, and mending fence. Father and son rode often together, or tramped woods or prairie, and shot game. They talked of books and of life, as each profited from the presence of the other.[29] To Johnston's regret, he could not keep his son with him. Scarcely able to support an additional person at China Grove and altogether unable to provide facilities for education, he sent William Preston back to Kentucky in the spring. "I have no doubt you derived much advantage from a more enlarged view of men and things," he soon afterward wrote his son. "We miss you much more than either you or we could have imagined." [30]

Circumstance now kindled within Johnston a reflective mood out

---

[26] *Ibid.*, October 21, 1847.

[27] Johnston, *Life of Johnston*, p. 152.

[28] Johnston to Preston, August 3, 1847, Johnston Papers, Barret Collection.

[29] Johnston, *Life of Johnston*, pp. 148–149.

[30] Johnston to William Preston Johnston, July 7, 1847, Johnston Papers, Barret Collection.

of which came an interesting and often admirable philosophy of life. Maturity that came with age, opportunity to pause and look back upon his own career, the urge to provide counsel for a son and daughter in the trials of adolescence, and residence amid the beauty and solitude of his plantation—all united to bring about this pensive turn of mind. Letters to his children in Kentucky have the ring of a latter-day Polonius.

His attitude toward education told much about the man himself. Fearing that his son might become a bookworm, he once said, "I am not in favor of too much education. . . . A moderate knowledge of books and much knowledge of men makes the most successful man— Men who quit the arena for the closet are not able to contend with the trained and practised wrestlers." [31] Yet Johnston supported the education of his children with all available resources. Using the proceeds on property left them by their mother, he had their grandmother send them to private schools near Louisville. Later he sent William Preston to Yale College. "Education in the present age is a positive right," he wrote. Every parent was obligated to provide education for his children, he felt, though it cost toil and privation. "This is neither a humiliation nor a hardship; it is a labor of love." [32]

But when a kinsman suggested that Henrietta be sent to a fashionable school for girls in the east, and William Preston to Europe for study, Johnston vetoed both recommendations. His objections to European schooling were patriotic and practical. "As I place the American people above all others so I place their institutions," he said. Only in an American school, he thought, could William Preston absorb the spirit of America; only in this country could he form those ties of friendship essential to political advancement.

I know of no great man of any country who was educated away from his people [Johnston said]. An important part of education is the study of the temper and tendencies of ones own race. . . . One educated at home is recognized and received as a man of the people. . . . There is no disruption of those powerful bonds of sympathy without the power to arouse which the greatest mind would be powerless for any purpose.[33]

[31] *Ibid.*, November 17, 1847, in a postscript on a letter of that date from Eliza Johnston to William Preston Johnston, *ibid.*
[32] Johnston to William Preston Johnston, September 11, 1848, *ibid.*
[33] Johnston to Preston, July 21, 1847, *ibid.*

To his son he wrote, "I regard all Americans educated abroad as Mongrels whose hybrid minds will produce nothing." [34] Finally, Johnston feared that an overseas education would insinuate foreign ideas and manners into his son, that he might unconsciously imbibe feelings of social caste. "If my son could stand in the midst of any assembly in Europe & think or believe that there was present any nobler or bolder spirit than his own, I would scorn him as a craven," said he; "yet did he not they would deem him a fool." [35]

In equally strong language, he disapproved sending his daughter to an eastern school. "I do not wish her to cross the mountains," he wrote to his brother-in-law. "Your mind will at once cite our excellent wives as examples of the superiority of eastern schools; they are only exceptions. Thousands are made worthless by them." [36] He particularly objected to the school being considered for Henrietta. "I do not like Madame Segoignes [school], it is a catch penny . . . & besides is not American enough for my taste." [37]

In the end, Henrietta did not go to school at all the following year. Want of money may have been the chief reason why she remained at home,[38] but Johnston said that he preferred her not to enter school, that she needed relaxation more than formal education. She could well employ her time studying music and reading, he said; and associating with relatives and mingling in polite society would teach her good manners. He counseled:

Good manners are the offspring of benevolence, good sense & a high-toned mind, qualities not likely to be derived from your namby pamby posturers of New York or Philadelphia. There is so much nonsense & corruption in what is called good society there, that I would rather my daughter's manners should be formed upon a less ambitious model.[39]

Provincial as were some of these judgments, they at least distinguished sound training from sham. Johnston later encouraged his son to travel and study abroad. "He will be able to study his profession [law] as well," he said, "besides the advantage of a broader

[34] Johnston to William Preston Johnston, October 17, 1847, *ibid.*
[35] Johnston to Preston, July 21, 1847, *ibid.*
[36] *Ibid.*
[37] Johnston to Henrietta Johnston, January 4, 1848, Johnston Papers, Barret Collection.
[38] *Ibid.*, November 18, 1848.
[39] Johnston to William Preston Johnston, September 11, 1848, Johnston Papers, Barret Collection.

horizon in which to view the world. . . . His opinions & morals are now firmly American & I would not now fear a perversion by foreign travel." [40]

Johnston believed breadth of learning essential to refinement and to practical skills. Upon hearing that his son aspired to enter law, the father urged him to study all subjects thoroughly. Reading and meditation of good books enriches the mind, Johnston said; knowledge of mathematics develops the power of reasoning. "[Mathematics] is the helm of the mind, steering it over the shortest route from the point of departure to the destination—from cause to effect." Knowledge of chemistry and anatomy are often required to understand criminal cases, he pointed out to his son; knowledge of surveying is necessary to the settlement of many kinds of claims. Legal decisions frequently are not founded upon abstract justice, he wrote with a touch of pragmatic philosophy, but instead are derived from the wants of society and are dependent upon a multiplicity of causes. [41]

A man of temperate habits and self-discipline, Johnston urged his children to be the same. He feared that his son studied too much for good health. Daily reading and meditation must be balanced with physical exercise and relaxation, he advised. "However much I might desire the fame of learning," he said, "I would not give my eyesight to be the author of 'Paradise Lost.' The demands of nature must be satisfied; she unfailingly punishes every violation of her laws whether of excess or stint." [42] Success in life was the reward of moderation, Johnston believed.

Study moderately, exercise moderately, eat moderately, in fine let this be your rule and you will find in the end you know more. . . . Infinite magnitudes may be the accretion of infinitely small increments. Great learning may be the result of the daily acquirement of small items of knowledge. [43]

He repeatedly advised his son to take bodily exercise every day. Throughout life Johnston himself rode daily, for pleasure as well as health. To William Preston he recommended both riding and walking. Above all, he recommended fencing. Sword exercise contributed

[40] Johnston to Hancock, March 29, 1849, *ibid.*
[41] Johnston to William Preston Johnston, May 19, 1848, *ibid.*
[42] *Ibid.*, February 23, 1849.
[43] *Ibid.*, December 11, 1848.

to bodily strength and co-ordination, he said, and was a useful accomplishment. Perhaps recalling his own duelling experience, he suggested also that his son develop skill with the pistol. "Acquire [skill] in private & never . . . speak of it," he wisely advised. [44]

Johnston offered to his children precepts designed to mould character. Cautioning Henrietta against display of person or manner, he advised proportion in all aspects of life. Proportion is as necessary to the mind as to the body, he reasoned; just as one cannot admire a human nose a foot long, however shapely it may be, so one cannot admire exaggerated traits of personality. "Let us not admire those of your sex who 'o'er step the modesty of nature,'" he urged. "We ought rather to give our suffrage to those whose conduct is regulated by the approved notions of propriety among the wise & good." [45] When he learned that a school oration by his son had been applauded, he wrote, "I rejoice . . . [but] Beware the giddiness of success; now is the time when with you the mantle of humility may be gracefully and proudly worn." [46]

He extolled frugality. Live within your means no matter how limited they may be, he told his children. Doubtless with his own financial difficulties in mind, he warned that extravagance would lead to loss of independence, which in turn would arouse among friends and relatives such gossip and "doleful commisserations" as to render impossible any extrication through character or credit. In what must have been a moment of despondency he said:

Cherish friendship; it is a pleasant delusion. I will not do humanity the injustice to say that there are not very many capable of the most generous actions; I have known men who would risk life & fortune for a friend. But how many trials fail before such an one is found. Who shall sift the wheat from the chaff? [47]

Johnston's unhappiest moments over his son's welfare occurred about two years after William Preston's visit to China Grove. In the spring of 1849 the young man joined the staff of a small newspaper called the *Bon Ton*, newly established in Louisville. It was highly critical of leading citizens of the city and of Louisville society in general. When Johnston heard of his son's connection, he wrote

[44] *Ibid.*, May 19, 1848.
[45] Johnston to Henrietta Johnston, January 12, 1849, Johnston Papers, Barret Collection.
[46] Johnston to William Preston Johnston, May 27, 1848, *ibid.*
[47] *Ibid.*, February 29, 1848.

warning of pitfalls to be expected of the venture. He called the newspaper offensive; its insults had thus far been pocketed, he said, but the victims would surely seek retribution. Johnston's ingrained deference for womanhood was piqued by certain articles of the publication; to hold the female portion of the community up to ridicule was unmanly, he said.

Expounding another strain of his philosophy of life, he declared:

There is no power mental or physical equal to the task of . . . making society square their notions with our own. Horace with his keen, playful wit, Juvenal with his bitter sarcasm, Peter the Great with power over life . . . almost could achieve nothing. Time is the true & only honest reformer. He works those changes which are necessary & so gently as to prevent their being disagreeable.

He advised his son to sever ties with the newspaper. If the boatmen of early Kentucky ran into a pocket, he said, they backed out and took the true channel. "Now my son, if you think you are in a pocket, back out & take the right 'chute.' " [48] To his gratification, William Preston soon quit the *Bon Ton*.

Johnston burned with the American nationalism of his time. "However vain it may seem in us Americans," he once said, "we ought to 'lift our hands & thank God that we are not as other men.' " To the American political system he attributed American superiority in all things. "The well being of our population flows from a fostering government," he said, "which does not meddle *much* with private pursuits & taxes with great moderation." [49] An unrestrained admirer of Zachary Taylor, Johnston rejoiced when in 1848 the General was elected President of the United States. He believed that Taylor would curb the excesses of both major political parties, that he would moderate the high tariff of the Whigs and temper the expansionism of the Democrats. "Attempt to conceal it as they may," Johnston said, "a great & new party has arisen which like the 'rod of Aron has swallowed up all other rods.' " [50]

Though not given to flippancy or repartee, Johnston could relieve the gravity of conversation with a telling witticism. "[William] Griffin [Eliza's brother] is to be married in Jany to a young blonde of 22, fair as a lilly & having 70 or $80,000 in her own right," he once

[48] *Ibid.*, May 16, June 4, 1849.
[49] *Ibid.*, May 16, 1849.
[50] Johnston to Hancock, December 2, 1848, Johnston Papers, Barret Collection.

said, "which ought not to break off the match." [51] Closing a letter of fatherly admonition, he wrote, "Your own good sense, my dear son, has already suggested to you better counsel than I can give you; but it is the privilege of age to make youth suffer in that way, and you perceive I use my privilege." [52]

Johnston never became a communicant of any church; yet he had profound reverence for a supreme being. He seems to have been a deist, in the tradition of such great early Americans as Washington, Jefferson, and Franklin. In closing letters to relatives and friends, he frequently invoked God's blessing upon them. Eliza was a devout Episcopalian, and when later the Johnstons lived where she could attend religious services, Albert Sidney dutifully accompanied her. Expressing disappointment over being unable to have his elder children with him at China Grove, Johnston said, "We have learned to repine at nothing, believing that there is a power that orders all things for the best, that even those things that are seemingly to our finite mental visions a chastisement are ultimately for some good beyond our ken." [53] To his son, he once commented, "I trust in God; in that consists the sum of my religion." [54] But he had no concern with sectarian dialectics.

Despite an apparently auspicious beginning, Johnston lacked the capital and labor to profit from China Grove Plantation. Through his own exertion, along with that of his laborers, he was able to till only a part of the cleared land. Had he been free of debt, he presumably could slowly have improved the plantation, turned more of the prairie under the plow, and ultimately could have made China Grove pay handsomely. But he was not to be so fortunate. Of his original indebtedness on the place, $6,000 in principal remained unpaid, besides nearly five years of interest at 10 per cent. He could do little more than subsist his family and slaves on the plantation and rapidly fell farther behind in meeting his financial obligations as China Grove became a millstone about his neck. [55]

After two years there he was in poverty. When in the fall of 1848, Henrietta expressed a desire to join the family on the plantation,

[51] *Ibid.*

[52] Johnston to William Preston Johnston, May 19, 1848, Johnston Papers, Barret Collection.

[53] Johnston to Henrietta Johnston, May 6, 1848, *ibid.*

[54] Johnston, *Life of Johnston,* p. 243.

[55] Johnston to Hancock, October 21, 1847, Johnston Papers, Barret Collection.

Johnston had to reply that his cabin could not accommodate another person. Later he wrote that the most earnest wish of his heart was to have Henrietta with him, but that he could not then provide for her. "I am not the owner of a single horse," he confessed, "nor have I had one copper in my house since March." [56] Perhaps soon he would be better situated, he said. "Then how gladly will I call to me this lost star." [57]

Friends and relatives offered what assistance they could to extricate him from his difficulty or to relieve his immediate wants. Creditors, many of whom were his companions of early Texas days, long refused to press him for their money.[58] Some friends sent him money; [59] others authorized him to draw on their bank accounts.[60] James Love sought to arrange for him to manage Love's sugar plantation, hoping that Johnston eventually might become co-owner of the place.[61]

But sympathy and favors were of little avail. Poverty and anxiety slowly blighted Johnston's spirit. He grew careworn, sad, and thin. "You would be astonished at the great change in him," Eliza wrote to William Preston. "I try to persuade him that he takes his trials better than I know he does." Later Eliza feared that Johnston's "high spirit" was in danger of breaking. Her own outward serenity hid inner turmoil. Hopelessness brought bitterness in its wake, and she became so upset as to accuse her Kentucky relatives of indifference to the plight of herself and her family.

This is the last effort I will make to gain assistance in our troubles. If we have not been worthy of a strong firm friend who would make some little effort to stretch forth a helping hand to save us . . . let us go, but when once down I tell you it is not I who will fail in my efforts to scramble out and induce an effort to that effect on my husbands part.[62]

In the fall of 1849 Johnston's creditors brought suit against him. Although the suit was not settled until two years later, Johnston was still unable to pay the notes and saw China Grove sold at auction for

[56] Johnston to Henrietta Johnston, November 18, 1848, *ibid.*
[57] Johnston to William Preston Johnston, November 15, 1849, *ibid.*
[58] Johnston, "History of China Grove Plantation," *ibid.*
[59] Williams to Johnston, May 5, 1847, *ibid.*
[60] Johnston to Hancock, January 4, 1848, *ibid.*
[61] Love to Johnston, January 8, 1849, *ibid.*
[62] Eliza Johnston to William Preston Johnston, February 9, October 20, 1849, *ibid.*

$2,ooo. He was left owing $8,ooo.[63] Throughout the ordeal his behavior was exemplary. "In relation to Genl Johnston's matters," said the agent for the creditors, "I am happy to say that he has done nothing, nor omitted any thing, which would in any way detract from his high character and standing as a gentleman." [64] But the experience was an unforgettable humiliation.

Meantime, in spite of inability to meet his mortgage payments, Johnston's fortunes immeasurably brightened. He and his family were no longer living at China Grove when the place was sold at auction; his career was beginning a new phase. Ever since the election in 1848 of Zachary Taylor to the Presidency, Johnston and Eliza had hoped that Taylor would appoint Johnston to a command in the Army. Confident on the eve of the election that Taylor would win office, and doubtless confident of good things for her husband, Eliza expressed herself thus: "Then too [General Taylor] is *our cousing*. We must not forget that now he is President." [65]

To the Johnstons' disappointment, almost a year passed without any offer from the White House. When in the fall of 1849 Taylor named someone else to a vacant Army position that Johnston had thought might become his, Eliza could not conceal her feelings. Even should another vacancy occur, she wrote, "the old gentleman may still find good subjects for the exercise of his charity before he reaches Pa. . . . We have been so often disappointed . . . that we have become somewhat hardened to it." [66]

Johnston's attitude toward seeking appointment made getting a job difficult for him.[67] Though friends and relatives repeatedly offered to go to President Taylor on his behalf, he refused to approve of their intervention. He felt that the President ought not to be importuned by spoilsmen.[68]

The voluntary tender of an office by the President, without the solicitation of friends ought to be esteemed a high compliment [he wrote to a kinsman

[63] Johnston, "History of China Grove Plantation"; R. J. Townes to F. H. Merriman, February 4, 1852, both in *ibid.*

[64] Townes to Levi Jones, October 31, 1851, *ibid.*

[65] Eliza was distantly related to Taylor through the Preston family. Eliza Johnston to William Preston Johnston, November 17, 1848, *ibid.*

[66] *Ibid.*, October 20, 1849.

[67] Memucan Hunt to Johnston, May ?, 1848; October 20, 1849; Love to Johnston, March 19, 1849; A. T. Burnley to Love, June 9, 1849, all in Johnston Papers, Barret Collection.

[68] Johnston to Hancock, December 2, 1848, *ibid.*

who had the ear of the President]. When the party desiring an office is known to the President, it ought to be offered at the suggestion of his own judgement or not at all.[69]

To say this in the midst of poverty required more character than discretion.

Whether Johnston ever weakened and authorized his friends to approach President Taylor is not clear, but eventually they did do so, and with Johnston's knowledge. After an interview with the President, one of Johnston's Texas supporters, A. T. Burnley, wrote that Taylor was prepared to offer Johnston either a federal marshalship in Texas or the job of collector at the port of Galveston. When told that Johnston was not interested in either but desired a military command, Taylor then said he would make Johnston paymaster in the Army as soon as such a post should become vacant. "Think seriously . . . & decide like a man of sense & a gentleman," advised Burnley, in urging Johnston to accept an Army position other than a command. "When you doubt *consult your wife.*" [70]

In October of 1849 Johnston received Taylor's appointment as Army paymaster for a portion of the Department of Texas and was given the rank of major. Poverty and despondency over life at China Grove reinforced Eliza's pleas that he accept the position; in December, apparently after some hesitation, he did so. Ill of malaria, he was unable to report for duty for months. In the spring of 1850 he took his family to Kentucky, where he enjoyed a few weeks of reunion with his elder children and relatives. Then, temporarily leaving his entire family there, he reported to his new assignment in July. Whatever may have been his misgivings over the nature of the job, he must also have gone to it with gratification, for he returned to two of his strongest loves—Texas and the Army.[71]

[69] *Ibid.,* March 29, 1849.
[70] Burnley to Johnston, May 21, 1849, Albert Sidney Johnston Papers, Manuscripts Division, Kentucky Historical Society.
[71] Johnston, *Life of Johnston,* p. 170.

Frontier Paymaster

～～～～～～～～～～～～～～～～～～～～～～～～

UNITED STATES TROOPS guarding the Texas frontier held a line of posts almost identical to that Johnston had planned years before as Secretary of War of the Republic of Texas. Now he was to be paymaster for the posts from the upper Colorado to the upper Trinity—Austin, Fort Croghan, Fort Gates, Fort Graham, and Fort Worth. In July of 1850 he reported to San Antonio for duty. He was at liberty to live wherever he pleased, and the presence of friends in Galveston made him prefer it, but it was too far from the garrisons to be convenient for paying them.[1] He chose Austin and began to plan a house for his family and himself.[2] "This I intend when finished & paid for as a present for my wife," he said.[3] He had always admired the natural beauty of Austin's setting. A thousand nostalgic associations of earlier days spent in the outpost-capital must have filled his heart as he wrote Eliza where they were to live.

In September he traveled back to New Orleans, where he was to

---

[1] Johnston to George Hancock, August 19, 1850, Johnston Papers, Barret Collection.

[2] Johnston to William Preston Johnston, July 28, 1850, *ibid.*

[3] Johnston to Hancock, August 19, 1850, *ibid.*

secure the money—over $40,000—to pay the troops. In returning to Galveston by ship, he fell ill of what he thought to be the dread yellow fever; but his diagnosis was probably inaccurate, for after two weeks convalescing in Galveston, he recovered, and completed his first pay tour by mid-November.[4]

Writing Eliza to meet him in New Orleans with their three children, he returned for additional Army funds. Shock and grief awaited him. A few weeks earlier their baby girl, Mary, had died, probably of pneumonia; letters informing him had failed to reach him in Austin. With prodigious effort, Johnston kept his serenity.

Great as our distress is I can still thank God that my wife & my other children are left to me. It is not right to judge of his dispensations, nor do I, but bow with humble submission to decrees, the wisdom of which I cannot comprehend nor the justice of which I must not question.[5]

Sorrow filled the Johnston house in Austin for many months. Two-year-old Clungy (McClung) saw the missing baby sister in a small bright star in the heaven. Eliza lived in the "depth of agony." [6]

Johnston fell quickly into the routine of his exacting job. The troops were paid every two months with coin brought all the way from New Orleans. Three times a year he made the 1,100-mile round trip to New Orleans, journeying by stagecoach between Austin and Houston, by steamboat between Houston and Galveston, and by ocean steamer between Galveston and New Orleans. A single clerk accompanied him. Six times a year he traveled another 620 miles in going from Austin to the posts and back.[7] On these tours he was escorted by a group of ten or twelve dragoons under a noncommissioned officer. He made the journey to the posts in a mule-drawn wagon, or ambulance, carrying the money in a locked chest. Supplied from a provision and forage wagon, the little coin caravan would make its way across the Texas frontier, cooking, eating, sleeping, and living under the open sky.[8]

[4] Johnston to D. Randall, October 2, 1850, Letter Book, Albert Sidney Johnston Paymaster Records.

[5] Johnston to Hancock, December 14, 1850, Johnston Papers, Barret Collection.

[6] Eliza Johnston in postscript on letter from Johnston to William Preston Johnston, January 19, 1851, *ibid.*

[7] Johnston, *Life of Johnston*, pp. 170–171; Johnston to William Preston Johnston, July 28, 1850; Johnston to Hancock, August 19, 1850; Eliza Johnston to Willam Preston Johnston, May 11, 1851, Johnston Papers, Barret Collection.

[8] Johnston to T. P. Andrews, n.d., and Johnston to Randall, April 2, 1851, Letter Book, Albert Sidney Johnston Paymaster Records. After he had been

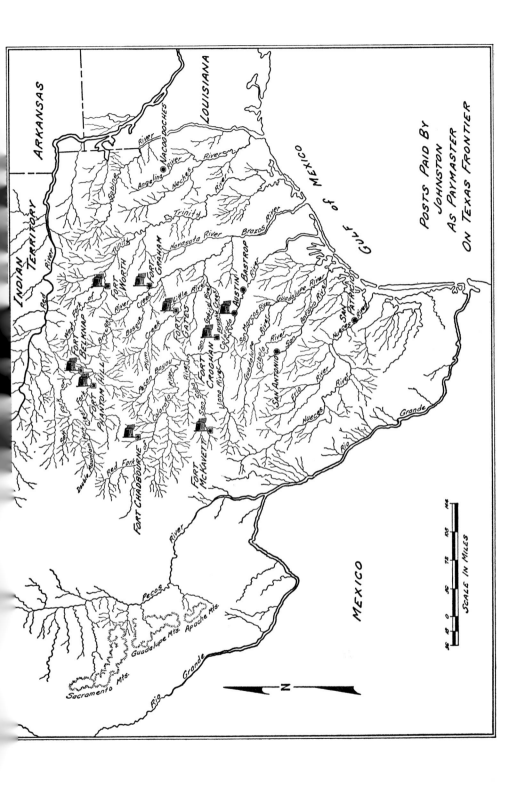

POSTS PAID BY
JOHNSTON
AS PAYMASTER
ON TEXAS FRONTIER

SCALE IN MILES

Johnston's pay journey took him over an expanse of wild and striking country. Much of the route traversed broad prairies or high plains, but it offered also a landscape broken by ranges of hills, stretches of oak and cedar, and numerous streams. A lover of nature, Johnston studied the manifold plant and animal life of the region.[9] He was up at dawn of each day, he wrote his daughter. "All that is beautiful and charming, and much that is magnificent or sublime, in scenery, daily feasts the eye." [10]

Yet he quickly wearied of the sights. "A first trip is delightful. But even this [magnificent scenery] becomes tiresome and uninteresting when seen too often." [11] And well it might. Each of the six yearly pay trips required more than a month.[12] Plodding thirty miles a day across the prairie, enduring the summer sun at more than 100 degrees or the howling norther at 10 degrees, sleeping on a buffalo skin at night, and daily eating cold bread and meat—these were experiences to blight the enthusiasm. Moreover, there were dangers. The great sums of money tempted bandits along the stage line to Austin, and the journey to the posts was beset with marauding Indian bands. Hazard, toil, monotony, and exposure provided an occupation of travail.[13]

Rich home life between pay trips eased the burden. Another daughter, Margaret Strother, was born a year after they arrived in Austin, and Maggie's laughter and presence went far toward assuaging the grief over Mary's death. "I feel that [Maggie's] coming is a comfort sent me by a good God," said Eliza.[14] Eliza exercised her talent and occupied her leisure in painting pictures of the plants

---

paymaster for a while, Johnston arranged to procure cash from lenders in Galveston, and later in Austin, by signing drafts on the paymaster general. This enabled him to pay the troops without journeying all the way to New Orleans. See Johnston to Andrews, July 31, 1852, Albert Sidney Johnston Paymaster Records.

[9] Johnston, *Life of Johnston*, pp. 173–174.

[10] Johnston to Henrietta Johnston, August 10, 1854, Johnston Papers, Barret Collection.

[11] *Ibid.*

[12] Johnston to B. F. Larned, April 8, 1852, Letter Book, Albert Sidney Johnston Paymaster Records.

[13] Eliza Johnston to George Hancock, July 9, 1851, Johnston Papers, Barret Collection.

[14] Eliza Johnston to William Preston Johnston, February 20, 1852; Eliza Johnston to William Preston Johnston on back of letter from Johnston to William Preston Johnston, September 10, 1852; Eliza Johnston to William Preston Johnston, September 10, 1852, all in Johnston Papers, Barret Collection.

and flowers of Texas. "Who knows that I may not make as much by [painting]," she said, "(if I conclude to honour the world by its publication) as Mrs. Beecher Stowe did by Uncle Tom's Cabin?" [15]

A great Newfoundland dog acquired by Johnston became the constant companion and guardian of the children.[16] Johnston was a father of patience and kindness; he loved his family dearly. Christmas was brightened, he said, "by the happy little faces round me." [17] When sickness came to the children, he would, if necessary, nurse them throughout the night.[18] He begrudged the time that had to be spent away from his family, and in the summer of 1852 he took them all with him on an outing for the first two hundred miles of his trip to the forts. Only the fear of Indians prevented him from taking them the entire way.[19]

Johnston was especially fond of his namesake, the mischievous Sid, who was said to be the strongest boy of his age in Austin.[20] Since Austin had no public school, Sid was tutored privately. In the summer of 1854 Johnston took Sid, then thirteen, with him over the entire pay journey. The boy swam and fished in almost every stream and reveled in the expanse and beauty of unsullied nature. Johnston's fatherly heart was full of pride as he observed his son's strength on the trail or the symmetry of his form in the water.[21]

To Johnston's supreme disappointment, he was never financially able to build the house he had planned for Eliza.[22] The presence of the state government in Austin made living there expensive, especially during sessions of the Legislature. Quoting the high prices of commodities, Eliza asked, "Do you not think New York would be cheaper for a poor soldier?" [23] When possible, the Johnstons purchased supplies in New Orleans. "Go to Holmes' on Canal Street as you come through New Orleans," Eliza once wrote to William Pres-

---

[15] Eliza Johnston to "My Dear Boy Willie," July 8, 1854, *ibid*.

[16] Eliza Johnston to Henrietta Johnston in postscript on letter from Johnston to Henrietta Johnston, September 10, 1852, *ibid*.

[17] Johnston to William Preston Johnston, December 23, 1854, *ibid*.

[18] *Ibid*., June 20, 1853.

[19] *Ibid*., August 7, 1852.

[20] Johnston to Henrietta Johnston, January 3, 1853, Johnston Papers, Barret Collection.

[21] *Ibid*., August 10, 1854.

[22] *Ibid*., January 3, 1853.

[23] Eliza Johnston to William Preston Johnston, November 15, 1851, Johnston Papers, Barret Collection.

ton before he paid them a visit, "and say to him that Genl Johnston of Austin who has been in the habit of dealing with him told you to get there a piece of Linen from 28 to 30 yds in piece at 50 cts pr yd." [24] Of his annual salary of $2,500 Johnston was able to save nothing.

In accepting the paymastership, he had fondly hoped that at last he could bring his entire family under his own roof. "If I can get you all together at my home," he once wrote to his elder children in Kentucky, "I shall feel that I have almost cheated destiny. I have sometimes thought that like the Bedouin I was fated to have no home, but to be a wanderer." His hope was vain; the elder children never lived permanently with their parent. [25]

Johnston's relationship with his elder children had entered a new phase as they approached maturity. At times Henrietta, given to extravagance, tried her father's patience. "Henny has no appreciation of the value of money," he once complained. [26] Just as he took over the paymastership, she underwent a spell of youthful jealousy toward Eliza. Henrietta yearned for her father's society and caresses, she said; as for Eliza, said Henrietta, "It is a dangerous and delicate matter for anyone to interfere with the feelings that exist between father and child." [27] Gradually she outgrew her jealousy and later spent long and pleasant visits in Austin with her father and Eliza. [28]

As Henny began to entertain suitors, Johnston's protective instinct bristled. Instructing his son to investigate one young man who was paying court to her, the strictly conventional father wrote: "He *has not* written to me. I wish him fairly dealt with. He ought to be accepted or discarded. It is a great injustice to a young lady to be bound by an engagement the fullfillment of which is indefinitely postponed." [29] When love letters for Henny arrived in Austin after her departure, Johnston forwarded them to his son with instructions to see that they were disposed of according to circumstance.

[24] *Ibid.*, February 13, 1853.

[25] Johnston to William Preston Johnston, October 19, 1852, Johnston Papers, Barret Collection.

[26] *Ibid.*, May 4, 1852.

[27] Henrietta Johnston to William Preston Johnston, December 1, 1850, Johnston Papers, Barret Collection.

[28] Henrietta's changing attitude is reflected in letters from Eliza Johnston to Henrietta Johnston, February 15, 1853, and William Preston Johnston to Henrietta Johnston, March 31, April 18, 1852, *ibid.*

[29] Johnston to William Preston Johnston, May 4, 1852, *ibid.*

I do not approve of this correspondence. If Henrietta intends to marry him, let him be so informed. . . . If she does not intend to marry him (and my opinion is that she cares but little for him) it would be dishonorable to delude him . . . and in that case his letters ought to be returned & he ought to be promptly informed. . . . I know nothing against the young gentleman and would in no case oppose the wishes of my daughter . . . unless there was some moral objection.

Poverty was no mark against a suitor to Johnston, who said that he would prefer a poor son-in-law who was temperate, intelligent, and industrious to a wealthy one who knew only how to waste an estate in riotous living.[30] About another qualification he had a stronger opinion, and his temper flared when he heard that Henny was seeing a young man of abolitionist views. Johnston spoke his mind.

Tell Henny if I did not know that there were other objections . . . being an abolitionist [should] make him despised by her as a viler traitor than Cataline; he had the redeeming trait of courage, these latter day Saints have no instincts above an assassin or incendiary.[31]

Johnston's ties with his eldest child, William Preston, grew stronger in spite of time and distance. He wanted his son to come to Austin to live.[32] Anticipating a long-deferred comradeship, he purchased a horse for William Preston and a pony for Sid. He planned to give William Preston his own case of pistols. But William Preston decided instead to enter Yale to prepare for a law career.

Notwithstanding his disappointment that his son would not be with him, Johnston warmly approved his decision to enter Yale. "Far . . . from finding fault with your course," he said, "I will be prepared to applaud you provided you do not injure your health." [33] With money earned on a job, plus a sum from the sale of property in Louisville, young Johnston entered Yale in the fall of 1850. When he received the Townsend Prize for English composition, his father added a typical bit of Johnstonian wisdom to his compliments: "It is said that college honors are a disadvantage, that the vanity of early success often shades the brightest faculties of mind. . . . The opinion is absurd. The mind capable of eminent success is in no danger of being overwhelmed by a minor success." [34]

[30] *Ibid.*, August 7, 1852.
[31] *Ibid.*, June 15, 1854.
[32] *Ibid.*, July 28, 1850.
[33] *Ibid.*, January 19, 1851.
[34] *Ibid.*, August 7, 1852.

William Preston Johnston was graduated high in his class in 1852, and when in the spring of that year he reached the age of twenty-one, Johnston welcomed him to manhood.

As an act of comity . . . [I] recognize you as a man. . . . With all the solemnity the occasion requires, [I] invest you with the "toga virilis." You have therefore the right in your sovereign capacity to make treaties of alliance, coin money, regulate & control your own happiness.[35]

After graduating from Yale, William Preston studied law at the University of Louisville for a year and then entered the practice of law in Louisville. His clientele was limited, but his father lectured him that every successful lawyer at first faced such discouragement. "Wait patiently & *prepare*," he wrote. "Your time will come. . . . Wait, but work, do not reject business because it is not important. 'Be faithful over a few (small) things & you shall be soon steward over many.' " [36]

When his son was to be married, Johnston approved both his decision and his choice, Rosa Duncan of New Orleans, and, speaking as one with experience in the vicissitudes of family finance, he gave realistic advice:

As this is the only opportunity I will have to speak of the expenses of your household without impertinence, I have to advise you that you regulate your outlay by the amount of your income. . . . The spirit of rivalry in display is the source of nearly all the miseries of life.[37]

William Preston's filial devotion shone brightest in his behavior toward his father's financial difficulties. During Johnston's residence at China Grove, the son had often expressed dismay over his parent's poverty, and when he reached manhood, he began to consider purchasing China Grove from Johnston's creditors in order to free his father of the debt that still lay upon him.[38] Whether Johnston himself suggested this course is not clear; certainly he encouraged it once the idea arose. Texas land must climb in value, he told his son with sincerity.[39] "I do not wish you to undertake anything . . . that

[35] *Ibid.*, May 4, 1852.

[36] *Ibid.*, December 23, 1854.

[37] *Ibid.*, August 7, 1852.

[38] Eliza Johnston to William Preston Johnston, February 20, 1852, Johnston Papers, Barret Collection.

[39] Johnston to William Preston Johnston, September 7, 1852, *ibid.*

would embarrass you, or in the least affect your prosperity," he said. "It would give me a degree of unhappiness to which my present embarrassment would bear no comparison." [40] But, he concluded, China Grove would one day pay handsome dividends. [41]

In the spring of 1852 William Preston Johnston bought China Grove Plantation. He agreed to give $12,234 for the property, the final installment to be paid on January 1, 1854. [42] In purchasing China Grove, he refused to heed his father's expressed wish that he not impair his own prosperity; [43] he apparently sold his Louisville holdings in order to acquire the Texas land. With great difficulty he paid off the last note a few months after it was due. "Perplexed in my affairs, I have been endeavoring to extricate my feet from the snares," he told a cousin at the time. "A man ought to be out of debt about this time. . . . My throat has not felt a cravat for a month, nor my soul the balm of calm." [44] Albert Sidney Johnston was at last free of obligation; and although for some time the burden of an idle plantation rested on the shoulders of his son, in the end Johnston's optimistic predictions came true: eight years later William Preston sold China Grove for $20,000. [45]

Johnston retained keen interest in the affairs of his friends, of Texas, and of the outside world. As he traveled from New Orleans to Texas and from post to post, he gave freely of his time and energy in doing favors for acquaintances. Accompanying his father on pay journeys in the springs of 1854 and 1855, William Preston was struck by the demands made upon Johnston's patience and benevolence. [46] The most trivial claim for adjustment of compensati n received close care, and Johnston willingly took orders from the troops for the purchase of horses, guns, boots, watches, and trinkets. [47] For friends

[40] *Ibid.*, October 11, 1852.

[41] *Ibid.*, December 4, 1852.

[42] William Preston Johnston, "Indenture," April 8, 1853, Johnston Papers, Barret Collection.

[43] William Preston Johnston to Johnston, August 17, 1854, *ibid.*

[44] William Preston Johnston to "Dear Stod," September 5, 1854, *ibid.*

[45] William Preston Johnston's indenture to Johnston's creditors was recorded May 21, 1853, in Book F, pp. 530–531, of the Records of the Clerk of Court, Brazoria County, Angleton, Texas; the subsequent act of sale of China Grove was recorded July 6, 1860, in Book J, pp. 493–494, *ibid.*

[46] William Preston Johnston Diary, March 13–April 6, 1855, Johnston Papers, Barret Collection. See also Arthur Marvin Shaw, *William Preston Johnston: A Transitional Figure of the Confederacy*, p. 57.

[47] Johnston, *Life of Johnston*, p. 176.

and acquaintances in other states, he paid taxes,[48] wrote descriptions of Texas topography and resources, and located land claims.[49] When his old comrade, United States Senator Thomas Jefferson Rusk, wished a description of the frontier country for the purpose of stimulating settlement, he called upon Johnston, whose word would command confidence among all who heard it, said Rusk.[50] Johnston served above and beyond the call of a paymaster's duty.

Praise of Texas came easily from Johnston's pen; his faith in the destiny of Texas never waned. Anticipating the prompt construction of a transcontinental railroad through the state, he said, "Then will commence an era of greatness for Texas that few would be bold enough to predict." He was himself bold enough to predict an immense empire of cotton, wheat, and cattle. "With these facts I leave you to elaborate the great future of Texas." [51]

When in 1850 a controversy arose between the federal government and Texas concerning the boundary of Texas and the projected New Mexico Territory, Johnston spoke as a Texan. He hoped that the United States government would avoid any collision with Texas authorities, he said, and would recognize the claims of Texas, "so often acknowledged by the Government." Then, he felt, the federal government could negotiate with Texas for whatever land was needed for the new territory, for nothing less would satisfy the people of Texas, he declared.[52]

Johnston now broke with his lifelong political persuasion. Repelled by the rise of abolitionism and Know-Nothingism in the Whig Party, he shifted his support to the Democrats.[53] Know-Nothingism was dangerou. to republican principles, he wisely said; proper safeguards on the suffrage could be achieved without resort to a secret organization that threatened religious toleration and the very genius of American institutions. "I hope your Uncle Wm [William Preston, who was now a Whig congressman from Kentucky] will not become entangled in any way in this Whig heresy," he told his son. "His

[48] Tax receipts for L. L. Fowler, October 24, 1853, in Johnston Papers, Barret Collection.

[49] A. T. Burnley to Johnston, March 3, 1854, Albert Sidney Johnston Papers, Manuscripts Division, Kentucky Historical Society. Also A. P. Skinner to Johnston, September 18, 1854, Albert Sidney Johnston Paymaster Records.

[50] Thomas J. Rusk to Johnston, December 8, 1853, Johnston Papers, Barret Collection.

[51] Johnston to William Preston Johnston, June 15, 1854, *ibid.*

[52] Johnston to Henrietta Johnston, August 9, 1850, *ibid.*

[53] Johnston to Hancock, December 4, 1852, and August 24, 1855, *ibid.*

position promises every thing for him that we could wish—Thane now, King hereafter." [54]

Johnston followed with critical eye the course of the Crimean War. "The great master of the art of war (Napoleon) would have made preparation commensurate with the object to be accomplished," he said. As Johnston plotted the Emperor's strategy, Napoleon would first have seized the neck of the peninsula; then the fortress of Sevastopol would have been besieged and taken without the threat of a Russian army of relief. Johnston's sympathy lay with the Russians. "We are all in favor of that good 'old Tzar.' The French & English are hostile to us (to liberty) to our progress & therefore we side with Russia." [55]

Johnston never enjoyed the job of paymaster; [56] he accepted it only out of necessity, and in the hope that it would open the way to an Army command. This hope seemed dead when five years passed with no change in the nature of his assignment. "Poor Pa!" wrote Eliza in the summer of 1854. "What a perfect drudge he is! [He] begins to show the effects of hard usage; he looks worn and thin. . . . He will not last long with this sort of life." [57] Johnston himself expressed his displeasure to the paymaster general: "This [journey] six times repeated during the year makes up an amount of travel, sleeping on the ground, privation, exposure to heat & cold not imagined by the framers of the law, nor encountered by a private soldier in time of war or peace." [58] Eliza also felt the strain of living alone with the children more than half of the time. Frequently she was left with great sums of Army money, $40,000 to $50,000, in her care. "I am *very brave,*" she said, "and have pistols, guns, etc., yet I try to make it understood that all is gone with Pa." [59] Presently Johnston's district was enlarged by the inclusion of Forts Belknap and Phantom Hill on the upper forks of the Brazos River, and Forts Chadbourne and McKavett near the upper Colorado and one of its

[54] Johnston to William Preston Johnston, October 19, 1854, *ibid.*
[55] *Ibid.,* December 23, 1854.
[56] Johnston to A. J. Coffee, October 18, 1853, Albert Sidney Johnston Paymaster Records.
[57] Eliza Johnston to William Preston Johnston, July 8, 1854, Johnston Papers, Barret Collection.
[58] Johnston to Larned, April 8, 1852, Letter Book, Albert Sidney Johnston Paymaster Record.
[59] Eliza Johnston to William Preston Johnston, July 8, 1854, Johnston Papers, Barret Collection.

tributaries, the San Saba.[60] This added another 250 miles to his tour. "Which will greatly increase his labour," said Eliza. "Gracious knows twas enough before." [61]

Misadventure added to the weight of the paymaster's burden. In spite of what he deemed to be meticulous care in guarding the money in his hands, hundreds of dollars mysteriously disappeared from time to time.[62] Over a period of two years about $3,900 was lost in this manner. Johnston made up the deficit out of his own pocket —a major cause of his continued financial extremity during the entire course of the paymastership.[63]

In the spring of 1855 William Preston accompanied his father on a pay tour and solved the mystery: a trusted Negro slave, John, had been stealing the money. Having acquired a duplicate key to the money chest, John had time and again simply helped himself to its contents. William Preston detected John's guilt by marking some of the coins, then discovering them in a search of the slave's possessions. Johnston refused to have the culprit whipped, said William Preston; instead he sold John for $1,000 to help repay the loss. "Whipping will not restore what is lost," said Johnston, "and it will not benefit the negro, whom a lifetime of kind treatment has failed to make honest." [64] Eliza had suspected John, but Johnston had refused to indulge a suspicion of one so close. His trust cost him dear.

All things conspired to chill Johnston's spirit in the paymastership. Loss of the Army funds determined him to give up the job if he could find any other means of support. Rumor spread in Texas that Sam Houston was about to quit the post of United States senator, and Johnston's friends spoke of him for the job. "They do not wish a word said of it," cautioned Eliza, "fearing old Sam will not resign if he knew such a thing is contemplated." Johnston would accept the

---

[60] Johnston to Larned, December 7, 1854, Letter Book, Albert Sidney Johnston Paymaster Records.

[61] Eliza Johnston to William Preston Johnston, September 6, 1854, Johnston Papers, Barret Collection.

[62] Johnston to William Preston Johnston, January 8, 1855, *ibid.*

[63] Eliza Johnston to William Preston Johnston, January 12, 1855, *ibid.*

[64] Johnston, *Life of Johnston*, pp. 178–179. In turning over his accounts to his successor, Johnston was $2,360.53 short of funds. He balanced the account with his own money. See Albert Sidney Johnston, "Account Current," April 15, 1855, Albert Sidney Johnston Paymaster Records. See also receipt by Lloyd I. Beall, April 21, 1855, Letters Received, Adjutant General's Office, Records of the War Department.

nomination, she said, if he could not get a regiment instead.[65] He still yearned for a command, and, having heard that the Army was about to be expanded, he yet had hopes of getting one. "I believe your Uncle Will [Congressman William Preston] & [Senator] Rusk will not forget me in that event," he said.[66] Presently the Army was expanded, and Johnston was not forgotten.

[65] Eliza Johnston to William Preston Johnston, January 12, 1855, Johnston Papers, Barret Collection.

[66] Johnston to William Preston Johnston, January 8, 1855, *ibid.*

The Second Cavalry Comes to Texas

~~~~~~

FATE SMILED upon Johnston just when his spirit was at the ebb. On March 9, 1855, he was appointed commander of the newly formed Second United States Cavalry Regiment, with the rank of colonel. After five years of drudgery in the paymastership, his fondest wish had suddenly come true.[1]

His good fortune came from various sources. It came from an expansion of the Army that required additional line officers; it came from Johnston's reputation as a competent and courageous soldier; and it came from the influence of friends and kinsmen in high places within the United States government.

Victory in the Mexican War had added an immense new territory to the United States, much of it inhabited by the Plains Indians, most formidable of North American tribes.[2] To cope with this foe, the Franklin Pierce Administration created two new mounted regiments, the First and Second Cavalry. Officers were drawn from regi-

---

[1] Jefferson Davis to Johnston, March 9, 1855, Johnston Papers, Barret Collection.

[2] Theophilus F. Rodenbough (ed.), *From Everglade to Cañon with the Second Dragoons,* p. 170.

ments already in existence, from staff assignments, and directly from civilian life through qualifying examinations.[3] In the spring of 1855 the Second Cavalry Regiment was in need of a commander; Albert Sidney Johnston was in search of a regiment.[4]

Johnston's record as a soldier supported his application for command. Experience in the Black Hawk War, in the Texas Army, in the Cherokee War, and the brief but spectacular display of leadership at Monterrey—all drew praise from friends who urged his appointment to head the new cavalry regiment. After debating sharply whether to recommend Johnston or Ben McCulloch, famed spy commander during the Mexican War, the Texas Legislature decided in favor of Johnston. Governor E. M. Pease of Texas did the same.[5] Years later McCulloch manfully said that Johnston was the right choice for the command.

Meantime, Johnston's wife, his relatives, and his personal friends waged an astute campaign in his support.[6] United States Congressman William Preston, Johnston's brother-in-law, wrote to Eliza:

Our diplomacy in behalf of Johnston, without consulting with him, has been crowned with success. I made Mag [Margaret Preston] write her prettiest possible letter to [the Secretary of War] . . . and enclose your letter. . . . [Senator] Rusk told me to write such a letter as I desired [endorsing Johnston] and he would sign it. I did so & made it as strong as poison & he signed it saying however he wished I had made it even stronger. . . . All the rest except yours and Mag's letters, were mere cotton and prunella. Johnston's merits should have given him a regiment years ago, but his pride & delicacy have always prevented him from pressing his claims. Mag is as happy as a queen. She did rare electioneering for Genl. Scott.[7]

Margaret Preston's influence for Johnston equalled that of two or three senators, wrote another observer.[8]

The Johnston lobby was formidable, but all of this probably was unnecessary, for the most influential figure in the entire transaction, the Secretary of War, the man who sponsored the creation of the new cavalry regiments, was Johnston's friend and admirer since youth—Jefferson Davis. Davis has long been accused of packing the

[3] George F. Price, *Across the Continent with the Fifth Cavalry*, pp. 16–22.
[4] Eliza Johnston to William Preston Johnston, February 19, 1854, Johnston Papers, Barret Collection.
[5] James H. Dearst [and others] to T. J. Rusk, January 8, 1854, *ibid.*
[6] James Love to Johnston, March 4, 1855, *ibid.*
[7] William Preston to Eliza Johnston, March 4, 1855, *ibid.*
[8] John S. Griffin to William Preston Johnston, February 24, 1855, *ibid.*

fresh cavalry formations with pet officers from the South; this he did in preparation for the coming Civil War, it has been said. The appointment of Johnston hurt some feelings, for it was done in preference to many who had served more time; but facts disprove the charge of Southern favoritism. Many officers of the two regiments were Northerners, including the initial commander of the First Cavalry, Colonel Edwin V. Sumner.[9] The new mounted units were Davis's pride; unquestionably he staffed them with what he thought was the cream of the officer corps.[10]

Johnston received the appointment with gratification. Friends heaped congratulations upon him: citizens of Austin and its surroundings held a testimonial dinner in his honor; [11] his old companion James Love expressed deep pleasure over the appointment, especially, he said, since Johnston had indicated that such a command was the object of his ambition.[12] Lieutenant Colonel Joseph E. Johnston, an army comrade of previous years, wrote:

It gives me great pleasure to be able to congratulate you upon your promotion—I have every reason to believe that the army generally feels as I do on the subject—& is sincerely glad that you have returned to the line in a high position. I have just received a note from [William J.] Hardee, who wishes to be assigned to your regiment. No one has that wish more strongly than I.[13]

At the end of spring, Johnston left Austin for Louisville, where he was to take command.[14]

He had reason to be proud of his command. With officers individually selected by Jefferson Davis, it perhaps had more military talent than any other regiment in American history. Colonel Johnston was at its head, Lieutenant Colonel Robert E. Lee was second-in-command, Majors William J. Hardee and George H. Thomas were next in rank; among the captains were Earl Van Dorn, Edmund Kirby Smith, Innis N. Palmer, George Stoneman; among the lieuten-

---

[9] John K. Herr and Edward S. Wallace, *The Story of the U.S. Cavalry, 1775–1942*, pp. 74–75.

[10] Price, *Across the Continent with the Fifth Cavalry*, p. 22.

[11] W. L. Hill [and others] to Johnston, April 16, 1855, Johnston Papers, Barret Collection.

[12] Love to Johnston, March 4, 1855, *ibid.*

[13] Joseph E. Johnston to Johnston, March 10, 1855, *ibid.*

[14] Samuel Cooper to Johnston, May 19, 1855, Letters Sent, Adjutant General's Office, Records of the War Department.

ants were John Bell Hood, Nathan G. Evans, Richard W. Johnson, Kenner Garrard, and Charles W. Field. All of these men were to achieve renown during the coming Civil War. Johnston, Lee, Hardee, Van Dorn, Hood, Smith, Evans, and Field would become Confederate generals; Thomas, Stoneman, Palmer, Johnson, and Garrard would rise to similar station in the Union Army.[15] In the words of a contemporary, the Second Cavalry was a "crack regiment."[16]

Johnston arrived in Louisville on May 28 to find the regimental headquarters already partially formed, with Lee temporarily in command. Already Lee had dispatched various regimental officers to recruit troops in designated cities throughout the nation. Johnston immediately took command and sent Lee to Jefferson Barracks, Missouri, where the companies were to be organized and instruction was to begin. Johnston spent more than a month in Louisville attending to regimental business and enjoying the company of his Kentucky friends and kinfolk.[17]

In July, Johnston and Major Hardee were ordered to Washington, D.C., to sit on a Cavalry Equipment Board to adopt the uniform and equipment to be used by the two new regiments.[18] The cavalry dress included gray trousers, short blue tunics with yellow trim, and black slouch hats with brims pinned up on the right side and ostrich plumes slanted back from the crown. Heavy gutta-percha cloaks gave protection against the rain, woolen greatcoats against the cold. Troopers were armed with carbines, navy revolvers, and sabers. Except for the cumbrous and slightly ridiculous hats, which soon were discarded in favor of visor caps, this was serviceable gear; it would distinguish the cavalry of the United States during the Civil War and for a number of years thereafter on the western plains.[19]

In early September Johnston moved his regimental headquarters from Louisville to Jefferson Barracks to complete organization and training while awaiting orders for field service. Recruiting was finished and fresh horses purchased during the late summer, and in-

[15] Price, *Across the Continent with the Fifth Cavalry,* pp. 26–27.

[16] Preston to Eliza Johnston, March 4, 1855, Johnston Papers, Barret Collection.

[17] Price, *Across the Continent with the Fifth Cavalry,* pp. 28–29.

[18] Cooper to Johnston, July 20, 1855, Letters Sent, Adjutant General's Office, Records of the War Department; Price, *Across the Continent with the Fifth Cavalry,* pp. 29–30.

[19] Herr and Wallace, *The Story of the U.S. Cavalry, 1775–1942,* pp. 76–78.

struction went forward rapidly. To Johnston's irritation, both he
and Lee were now ordered to Fort Leavenworth, Kansas, to sit on a
court-martial.[20] Hardee, left as acting regimental commander, perfected the formation of squadrons and inspected and reviewed the
troops. In spite of his vigor, regimental morale sagged and desertion
increased as equipment arrived tardily and cholera appeared in the
ranks. "I am much annoyed at my absence from the regiment at a
time when the presence of every officer is peculiarly needed," Johnston said. "It is really bringing form out of chaos to organize a
regiment of new recruits and prepare them for a long march."[21]
Hardee agreed. "I need not say that your . . . presence is indispensable," he wrote to his absent commander.[22]

While at Fort Leavenworth Johnston received orders assigning his
regiment to field service. Whether he was already aware of its destination is not known; whenever he learned it, he must have been
overjoyed. The Second Cavalry was ordered to proceed overland to
Fort Belknap on the Texas frontier.[23] Johnston seemed drawn by
fate to the soil of Texas.

The primary mission of the Second Cavalry was to guard the
frontier against the Comanche Indians. Peace between the Texans
and this fierce tribe appeared impossible. In 1852 the state had set
aside two reservations for the Indians, and a few of them had been
induced to settle on the smaller of the sites, a tract of 18,000 acres on
the Clear Fork of the Brazos River. This attempt at a peaceful
arrangement was futile. The reservation was popular with the Comanches during the winter months, when food elsewhere was scarce;
but Texans claimed that roving bands of braves used the reservation
as a base for raiding the frontier settlements, racing back to it for
sanctuary after forays. Widely spaced army garrisons occupying a
line from Fort Belknap on the Clear Fork to Fort Clark near the Rio
Grande could not hold all the savages out.[24] "Keeping a bulldog to
chase musquitoes would be no greater nonsense than the stationing
of six-pounders, bayonets, and dragoons for the pursuit of these red

[20] Price, *Across the Continent with the Fifth Cavalry,* pp. 30–31, 186.
[21] Johnston to William Preston Johnston, September 29, 1855, Johnston Papers,
Barret Collection.
[22] William J. Hardee to Johnston, September 26, 1855, *ibid.*
[23] Cooper to Johnston, October 1, 1855, Letters Sent, Adjutant General's Office,
Records of the War Department.
[24] W. Eugene Hollon, *Beyond the Cross Timbers: The Travels of Randolph B.
Marcy, 1812–1887,* pp. 184–185.

wolves," said the traveler Frederick Law Olmsted.[25] The new cavalry regiments were formed in the hope of solving this vexing problem.

Johnston and the people of Texas were equally impatient for the regiment to march. During the fall of 1855 Comanche outrages had filled the frontier settlements with terror;[26] the savages were bold enough to raid farms near San Antonio and along the Blanco River within twenty miles of Austin. Johnston had long complained of the government's negligence in protecting the settlers from harassment and depredation.[27] He was now welcomed as the defender of the frontier. "I know of no tidings that has been more grateful to myself and given as much general satisfaction, as the Knowledge that you will be again among us," wrote an acquaintance.[28] Texans remembered the Albert Sidney Johnston of the Cherokee War.

On October 27 the Second Cavalry filed out of Jefferson Barracks on the march to Texas.[29] Johnston looked with pride upon his formation; to enhance its appearance he had assigned horses by color to the various companies: grays to Company A, sorrels to B and E, and thus throughout the regiment. To his disappointment, he was unable to move out with his troops. His family was to accompany the march, but Eliza was ill of malaria, suffering a chill every other day, and the regiment moved out on her "chill day." Lee was still absent at Fort Leavenworth and did not make the march; Johnston gave Hardee the command and remained behind one day. He and his wife and children overtook the column on the evening of the second day.

The regiment was 710 men strong, and accompanying the troops were the wives, children, slaves, and hired servants of four officers, including Johnston. Trailing the column were twenty-nine supply wagons, an ambulance, and the privately owned teams and wagons of some of the officers; the formation looked something like an emigrant train bound for California.

[25] Frederick Law Olmsted, *A Journey through Texas,* II, 298.

[26] *Galveston Weekly News,* September 18, 1855.

[27] Johnston to William Preston Johnston, July 28, 1850; George Hancock to Johnston, September 27, 1855, Johnston Papers, Barret Collection.

[28] S. U. Swenson to Johnston, September 14, 1855, *ibid.*

[29] The best source on this famous march is the Eliza Johnston Diary, Johnston Papers, Barret Collection. See also Charles P. Roland and Richard C. Robbins (eds.), "The Diary of Eliza (Mrs. Albert Sidney) Johnston: The Second Cavalry Comes to Texas," *Southwestern Historical Quarterly,* LX (April, 1957), 463–500; and Price, *Across the Continent with the Fifth Cavalry,* pp. 31–35.

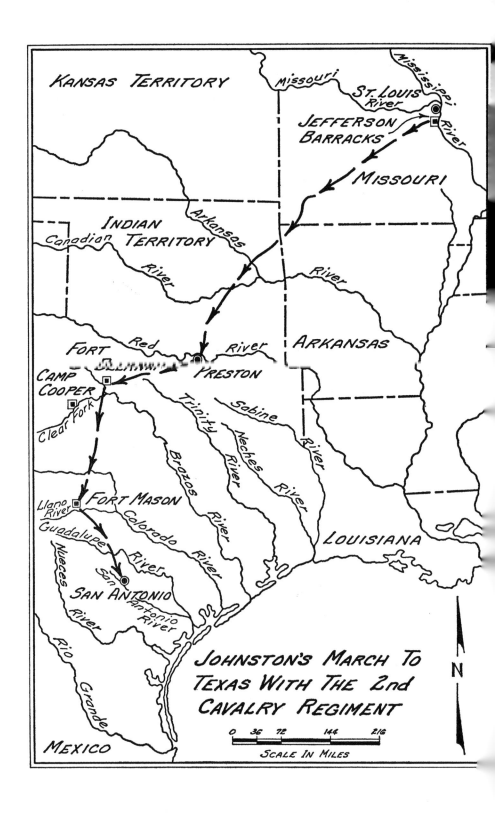

KANSAS TERRITORY

Missouri River

ST. LOUIS

JEFFERSON BARRACKS

Mississippi River

MISSOURI

Arkansas River

INDIAN TERRITORY

Canadian River

ARKANSAS

FORT

Red River

PRESTON

CAMP COOPER

Clear Fork

Trinity River

Sabine River

Neches River

Brazos River

Colorado River

FORT MASON

Llano River

Guadalupe River

LOUISIANA

Nueces River

San Antonio River

SAN ANTONIO

Rio Grande

JOHNSTON'S MARCH TO TEXAS WITH THE 2nd CAVALRY REGIMENT

N

MEXICO

SCALE IN MILES

0   36   72   144   216

During the march, Eliza kept a diary which is the best source of information on the movement. She described terrain, scenery, weather, marching conditions, inhabitants along the route, disease and injuries, births and deaths, philanderings, and gossip. Most interesting of all, she expressed her views of marching companions, many of whom would in a few years be immortalized in the saga of the Civil War.

Eliza wrote with feminine insight and complete candor; she disclosed the strengths and frailties of these officers when they were mere men, before they became national heroes. Upon hearing that Lieutenant Charles W. Field, who later would be a valiant Confederate general, had seduced the wife of a Missouri citizen, Eliza exclaimed, "Oh, you immoral men what should be your fate for all the sorrow you cause in this world." Of camp gossip, she said, "I get all my news from Mrs Capt Oaks who I veryly believe would cause trouble in Heaven, 'memo' I must beware of her moimeme. I listen to all, but say nothing." [30] When Lieutenant Colonel Lee refused to testify in court as strongly against an offender as Eliza thought he ought, she wrote with barbed pen, "I suppose the man [Lee] feared to become unpopular." [31]

From Jefferson Barracks the march led diagonally through Missouri, across the northwestern corner of Arkansas, and through Indian Territory.

The column moved from 10 to 20 miles a day, except when heavy weather or swollen streams temporarily halted it. On December 15 it crossed the Red River into Texas at Preston. From there it marched south to Fort Belknap above the fork of the Brazos River. Here, in obedience to a dispatch from the War Department, Johnston split his regiment; four companies under Hardee were ordered to proceed up the Clear Fork of the Brazos to a point near its head and there establish a post that would command the nearby Comanche reservation. Hardee departed with his troops and soon began the construction of Camp Cooper on the Clear Fork. Johnston, with the remainder of the regiment, then marched south for another 100 miles to abandoned Fort Mason near the Llano River, where his headquarters were pitched. After more than two and one-half months, the 750-mile trek was completed on January 14, 1856.[32]

[30] Eliza Johnston Diary, March 30–31, 1856, Johnston Papers, Barret Collection.
[31] *Ibid.*, March 31, 1856.
[32] *Ibid.*, January 14, 1856.

Mild weather cheered the early portion of the march. Especially pleasant were the scenes at night with hundreds of campfires blazing before as many tents, and soldiers seated on blankets, swapping stories, or tending kettles of boiling food. Later in the march, however, winter visited blizzards upon the troops, sending the thermometer below zero and blowing gales so fierce that fires were impossible. Horses froze to death at night on the picket lines; 113 oxen in the provision train died of cold. Even the stalwart Johnston, inured to hard living during the paymastership, felt the severity of these storms. Later he shivered at the memory of "the awfully Sublime roaring of the Texas norther." [33] Eliza and the children suffered severely, especially five-year-old Maggie [Margaret], who sat in her mother's lap and wept from cold.

Constant riding and life in the open soon hardened the men. Yet fatigue and exposure took their toll; a few troopers died on the march and were buried on the plain. "It was a sad thing," said Eliza after one burial, "for his comrades to march by his grave, and leave him in that great solitude." [34]

Johnston used every opportunity to shape his regiment into a fighting team. Though not a martinet, he was a stern disciplinarian when the occasion required sternness. Generally a man of patience and kindness, a father who never resorted to the rod with his own children, and a master who would not permit a thieving slave to be lashed, Johnston nevertheless used the harsh methods of the day to make soldiers out of recruits. Culprits were sometimes whipped and their heads shaven; then they were marched before the other troops to the tune of "Poor Old Soldier." Troopers who stole poultry from residents along the line of march were made to pay for the loot and to walk behind the mounted column all the next day. Training began as soon as the regiment closed into Fort Mason. "The officers get regular lessons & recite to the Col.," said Eliza; "a second West Point for them."

Under ordinary circumstances, Johnston treated subordinate officers and enlisted men with utmost courtesy and consideration; he did all within his power to provide amply for their needs. "Colonel Johnston . . . was one of the most unselfish men I ever knew, and one of the most just and considerate to those under his command," later

[33] Johnston to William Preston Johnston, January 17, 1855 [1856 ?], Johnston Papers, Barret Collection.
[34] Eliza Johnston Diary, January 9, 1856, *ibid.*

recalled a Union veteran, who had served under Johnston in the Second Cavalry before the Civil War. "The officers of the regiment not only respected but loved him." [35] "All the officers join their families after arriving in camp sooner than the Col.," Eliza complained, "as he is compelled to take care of the whole Reg whereas the Capts only take care of their Co's." Finding only four habitable rooms at Fort Mason, Johnston shared them with the families of the other married officers, though as regimental commander he could have demanded a house of his own.

He arranged for beef contractors to supply food for the regiment; sutlers supplied incidental necessities.[36] He prevailed upon the military authorities to permit his sutlers to sell whiskey to the troops. No degree of vigilance would prevent their obtaining alcohol from citizens along the route, Johnston said, and liquor provided by the sutlers would be of better quality than that bought at random across the countryside. Moreover, he argued with a sure knowledge of camp life, "The opportunity [to get whiskey from the sutlers] would dull the keen sense of desire" that otherwise would arise among the soldiers.[37]

Johnston was relaxed and convivial with subordinates when not on duty. On Christmas Day in a frigid camp near Fort Belknap he drank eggnog with his officers, and issued to each soldier a dram of whiskey. Through a blend of discipline, kindness, and competent provision, he earned the respect of his troops; in spite of toil and hardship, the regiment made its long march in high spirit.

Operations against the Indians began as soon as the weather permitted, and hostilities never ceased. Johnston sent scouting parties in all directions from Fort Mason; scarcely a week passed without a skirmish somewhere between small cavalry detachments and Indian raiding groups.

Shortly after reaching the frontier, Johnston fell ill of a violent intestinal disturbance that caused Eliza to fear for his life. After nine days he began slowly to recover.

On March 31 he unexpectedly received orders elevating him to temporary command of the Department of Texas in addition to his regimental command. "So rolls the wheel of fate," commented Eliza.

[35] Johnson, *A Soldier's Reminiscences in Peace and War*, p. 107.

[36] Johnston to Cooper, October 27, 1855, Letters Received, Adjutant General's Office, Records of the War Department.

[37] *Ibid.*, November 14, 1855.

"Last year at this time husband was travelling here as Paymaster, now . . . he is in command of the department." [38] On April 5, with his family and a cavalry escort, Johnston rode out of Fort Mason for departmental headquarters in San Antonio. Spring was in the air and on the countryside; Eliza's heart sang as they passed through the rugged and picturesque land toward their destination. Johnston must have been filled with gratification as he contemplated the sudden rise in his fortunes. In San Antonio he suffered a recurrence of his recent malady, so that for two weeks he was unable to take on his new duties, but soon he was on the job.[39]

As departmental commander, Johnston was now in position to deal with the Texas Indians according to his own views. He had long been critical of the Army's policy toward them. "With [the departmental commander's] orders, for mere defence he can accomplish nothing," Johnston once wrote when he was paymaster in Texas. "With such orders 5000 men could not prevent those predatory irruptions. To give peace to the frontier . . . the troops ought to act offensively, to carry the war to the homes of the enemy." [40] Indian Agent Robert S. Neighbors supported Johnston's ideas for dealing with the Comanches.[41] All Indians outside the reservations were hostile, said the agent; they would never settle on the reservations until they had been "chastized properly." [42] Johnston set about to administer the chastisement.

True to his purpose, he opened remorseless warfare upon his ancient foes. From every post along the frontier he kept scouting parties constantly in motion; time after time he dispatched combat groups deep into the Comanche country in an effort to cripple their forces beyond recovery. Pursue the savages "to the utmost limit of your means," Johnston instructed his subordinates; treat them "with rigorous hostility" whenever they are discovered.[43] The troopers searched and fought with steadfastness; expeditions frequently

---

[38] Eliza Johnston Diary, March 31, 1856, Johnston Papers, Barret Collection.

[39] *Ibid.*, April 30, 1856.

[40] Johnston to William Preston Johnston, July 28, 1850, Johnston Papers, Barret Collection.

[41] Robert S. Neighbors to Johnston, April 22, 1855, *ibid.*

[42] *Ibid.*, March 11, 1856.

[43] For Johnston's orders and instructions concerning operations against the Indians, see Special Order, Headquarters, Department of Texas, May 27, 1856; and Order No. 62, Headquarters, Department of Texas, September 13, 1856, both in Records of the War Department.

covered hundreds of miles through the formidable hill country along the headwaters of the Concho, Nueces, Brazos and Colorado rivers. Small but desperate encounters occurred repeatedly between the soldiers and the Comanches or their allies. The most extensive and most futile of these operations took place in the summer of 1856 when, upon Johnston's orders, Colonel Lee collected a force of four companies from Fort Mason and Camp Cooper.[44] Uniting his troops at Fort Chadbourne on June 18, Lee then led them in search of the Comanches along the upper Brazos and Colorado. A month of hard riding and harder living yielded no more than two Indians killed and one squaw captured.[45] The Comanches were wary antagonists.[46]

But by midsummer Johnston's exertions seemed to have been entirely successful in protecting the frontier. Congratulating him upon his accomplishment, a friend said that the people of Texas now knew that everything possible would be done to guard them against Indian raids.[47] Johnston breathed a sigh of relief. "So far, since my administration of the affairs of this Department our frontiers have been freed from Indian incursions," he wrote. "Our troops have driven them far into the interior, & I hope they will not soon venture in again." [48] The Comanches, however, had withdrawn only briefly to gain strength for renewed attacks.

Johnston's appointment to command the Second Cavalry, and temporarily the Department of Texas, ushered in the happiest life that he and his family had known. In San Antonio they lived in the quarters that had been occupied by the previous departmental commander, Brigadier General Persifor Smith. Surrounding the comfortable stone house on the bank of the bright San Antonio River was an acre of ground planted in pecan, mulberry, and peach trees, and in flowering shrubbery. The grove abounded in birds of pleasing song and plumage. Eliza could enjoy her music and painting as well as the company of a score of other army wives, and Johnston found

[44] D. C. Buell to R. E. Lee, May 27, 1856, Letters Received, Department of Texas, Records of the War Department.

[45] Lee to Buell, July 24, 1856, *ibid*.

[46] For reports on Johnston's operations, see Monthly Return, Department of Texas, January, 1857; and Johnston to Lorenzo Thomas, February 10, 1857, Letters Received, Department of Texas, Records of the War Department.

[47] Hamilton P. Bee to Johnston, July 11, 1856, Johnston Papers, Barret Collection.

[48] Johnston to William Preston Johnston, August 21, 1856, *ibid*.

more time than ever before for his family.[49] He was an indulgent father. His eldest son said that Johnston was no believer in the rod, which he thought made cowards and liars. His appeal, instead, was always to reason and moral suasion. Noble as this philosophy may have been in the abstract, or successful as it may have been in the end, Eliza was not convinced by it. Herself a believer in the rod, she was critical of her husband's softer methods.

My poor Sid is a sadly willful & imperious child [she wrote]. How to manage him seems a complete problem. . . . He has fine qualities but how to develop them, there is the difficulty   his willfulness seems to frustrate all my plans for his benefit   his perseverance is wonderful   I fear my dear husband was wrong in the first instance inducing me to waive my rules too frequently in his favor so that he imagines by importunity his father will interfere and beg for priviledges for him.[50]

Sid and Clungy were in a private school. Both were diligent students, though Johnston held their teachers' efforts in contempt. "There are few teachers any where fit for their calling," he railed. "The poor little devils that are sent to them, have but little help from them." [51] Yet Clungy studied so hard that Johnston feared for the child's health.[52]

Sid swam often in the beautiful river behind the dwelling, and Johnston set about teaching the two younger children to swim. "Having a strap of leather fastened to Clungy," said Johnston, "[I] sometimes float him about, like a fish bait trying to teach him to swim & have promised to Maggie a like instruction." [53]

In the spring of 1857 a third son was born. They named him Griffin Hancock in honor of Eliza's family and that of her uncle George Hancock, in whose home she had lived before her marriage. The Johnstons saw nothing objectionable in giving three of their children the name of Hancock. "This [name] is by way of compromise," Johnston explained, "which it is believed will allay all jealousies & quiet claims long standing. . . . So you see this young

[49] Eliza Johnston to William Preston Johnston, April 20, 1856; and Johnston to Henrietta Johnston, June 8, 1856, *ibid.*

[50] Eliza Johnston Diary, May 7, 1856, *ibid.*

[51] Johnston to William Preston Johnston, May 7, 1856, *ibid.*

[52] *Ibid.*, November 23, 1856.

[53] Johnston to Henrietta Johnston, June 8, 1856, Johnston Papers, Barret Collection.

American . . . has already been the subject of a profound diplomacy." [54]

They lived comfortably but frugally, for they were still in debt to William Preston Johnston and other kinsmen for loans made during the paymaster days. Johnston now from time to time made $1,000 payments to his eldest son. The family enjoyed good health, said Johnston, because of that simplicity of living that was necessary to a rigid economy. "After providing for our wants tho' not many, there is nothing left for hospitality," he said. "This gives me no uneasiness. I prefer rather that my creditors—now very few—should regard me as an honest man, than that the world should esteem me a generous fellow." [55]

Johnston responded as a Southerner and a slaveowner to the growth of abolitionism and the rising tide of sectional hostility. He left no explicit record of his philosophy on the morality or justice of slavery. Perhaps, like many other Southerners of his day, he subordinated such questions to the practical problems involved in eradicating the institution. Slaves were to be treated kindly, he believed, but they were to be treated as slaves. Though Eliza, always handy with the rod, would sometimes whip a slave, Johnston would not do so even under severe provocation.[56] But when his daughter's personal servant came to Texas from Kentucky, he frowned upon the maid's want of discipline. "A little work & cotton dresses go hard with her," he said. "She has the easy nonchalance of fraternity and equality, from free negro association which must be got rid of for this latitude." [57]

The bitterness of the slavery issue in the presidential campaign of 1856 filled him with gloom and wrath.

The best friends of the Union begin to feel apprehensions for its permanency [he exclaimed]. A disruption is too horrid for contemplation. War & its accompaniments would be a necessary consequence—a peaceful separation is impossible. . . . Our compact of union seems to be drifting towards a lee shore. . . . May divine interposition prevent the shock.[58]

[54] *Ibid.*, March 27, 1857.

[55] Johnston to William Preston Johnston, September 12, 1856; January 31, March 12, 1857, Johnston Papers, Barret Collection.

[56] Eliza Johnston to William Preston Johnston, July 8, 1854, *ibid.*

[57] Johnston to Henrietta Johnston, September 23, 1853, *ibid.*

[58] Johnston to William Preston Johnston, August 21, 1856, *ibid.*

Yet Johnston would rather accept disunion and war than submit to abolitionist demands. He explained:

We want the right & independence to the states & security to individuals guaranteed by [the] constitution. We claim immunity from intervention & interference. . . . Let [the abolitionists] cease to agitate a question which reaches our hearths (which should be sacred) disturbs our peace & produces a feeling of insecurity which is intolerable. . . . If these evils are to continue, rather than bear the degradation of suffering them, we say away with such an union only fair to behold, but foul in its embrace.

God gave the nation every source of happiness, said Johnston, but the extremists of the North would not rest "unless their Southron brothers will consent to lie upon a Procrustean bed they have constructed for them & suffer themselves to be stretched or cramped to fit it as their insane love of torture may suggest." Loss of the South and her cotton would wreck the Northern economy, he believed. Hence, "Why not let reason again resume its sway?" [59]

He was pleased by Democrat James Buchanan's victory in the election and wrote wistfully:

If our northern brethren will give up their fanatical, idolotrous negro worshiping we can go on harmoniously, happily & prosperously and also gloriously as a nation. We hope this, tho' we fear it is asking too much of poor human nature. It is more in accordance with human experience to believe that they will cherish their unhappy delusion, dandle & hug it to their bosoms—What a destiny, great almost without limit we would be if they would employ all the energy all the talent, all the genius, & all the resolution to build up beautify, adorn & strengthen our government which from the beginning they have used to cripple & destroy it. *Massachusetts* in particular.[60]

Thus he rendered judgment upon the land of his forebears.

Meantime, he could look with satisfaction upon a Texas frontier temporarily pacified through his relentless warfare upon the Comanches, but he was wise enough to know that there would be no permanent peace until the Texans should cease their westward expansion, or the Comanches should be wiped out. Despite the vigor of his forays into the interior, the Indians still lived; he sensed they would return. To his superiors, Johnston wrote that his regiment

[59] *Ibid.,* September 12, 1856.
[60] *Ibid.,* November 23, 1856.

was below regulation strength when it left Jefferson Barracks for Texas; now, he said, the organization was dangerously short of both men and horses to carry on the unremitting operations required against the Comanches.

Even as he expressed satisfaction over past achievements, he confessed his inability to bar the savages from the settlements. "There is nothing in the nature of the country offering any obstacle to their movements," he said. "The country . . . is as open as the oceans— They can come when they like, taking the risk of chastisement. If they choose therefore it need only be a question of legs." [61]

In the fall and winter of 1856 the Comanches chose to return. From the Brazos River on the north to the Rio Grande on the south, the border suddenly was again aflame with their raids. [62]

Since my return . . . I have literally been beset by my friends and constituents upon the subject of the depredations of the Indians [wrote a Texas Indian agent from Laredo on the Rio Grande]. From all quarters the same news comes. . . . They insist that I shall write to you, and appeal in the strongest terms . . . for assistance and protection.

Citizens of that area had begun to rebuild their ranches after deserting them, said the agent; now again they were refugees from the Indians, and could not even venture to seek their scattered cattle. [63] Similar calls came from settlements all along the frontier.

Johnston did all within his power to protect the people. Desperately he shuttled detachments from one stricken or threatened point to another, and again skirmishes between his troops and the savages raged across the countryside. [64] That anyone else could have done more is doubtful. But Johnston confessed his inability to quell the Comanches without a force many times the strength of the one at hand. "Four or five more regiments of mounted troops would hardly be enough to establish & keep up the degree of security, on the various frontiers, which should be maintained," he said. [65] Long after Johnston was gone from Texas, and even after his death, the Comanche barrier to white settlement would stand. Only in the mid-1870's would the remnants of this once indomitable tribe bow to

[61] *Ibid.*, August 21, 1856.

[62] William E. Jones to Johnston, November 25, 1856, Johnston Papers, Barret Collection.

[63] Hamilton P. Bee to Johnston, January 15, March 12, 1857, *ibid.*

[64] John B. Floyd, *Report of the Secretary of War*, p. 3.

[65] Johnston to Bee, February 14, 1857, Johnston Papers, Barret Collection.

overwhelming numbers and settle upon a United States Indian reservation.[66]

In the spring of 1857 Johnston was relieved of the position of acting commander of the Department of Texas; Brigadier General David E. Twiggs became permanent commander. Johnston did not relish going back to one of the frontier posts to command his scattered regiment. "This is rather a falling off," he complained privately. Nevertheless, in May he dutifully returned with his family to Fort Mason.[67]

After two months at Fort Mason, uneventful except for routine training and scouting, he suddenly received orders to report to the Secretary of War in Washington for a new assignment. Leaving Lee in command of the Second Cavalry, he departed from Texas at once; placing his family with relatives in Kentucky, he reported to the nation's capital as ordered. Whether he knew, or sensed, the nature of his coming duties is not revealed.[68]

Though Johnston failed to conquer the Comanches, Texas citizens and his troops believed he had done everything possible to protect the frontier with the force at his disposal. From fellow officers who one day would rank high in the nation's tradition of valor, Robert E. Lee and George H. Thomas, Johnston received letters of esteem.[69] Another subordinate of the Second Cavalry perhaps expressed the feelings of the regiment when he wrote to Johnston:

It seems to be generally believed that you will never join us again, but [will] succeed to the first vacancy in the general officers. While all would rejoice at your advancement we would deeply regret your loss, for the Cavalry arm can not replace you. . . . Your Regt. looks to you as its father and your reputation is the reputation of the 2 Cavalry. . . . All would be rejoiced at [an] order sending us to you.[70]

Johnston left his mark upon the officers who served under him in Texas.

[66] Richardson, *The Comanche Barrier to South Plains Settlement*, pp. 229, 338–397.

[67] Johnston to Henrietta Johnston, March 27, 1857, Johnston Papers, Barret Collection.

[68] D. E. Twiggs to Daniel D. Tompkins, July 29, 1857, Letters Received, Department of Texas, Records of the War Department.

[69] Lee to Johnston, August 1, October 25, 1857; George H. Thomas to Johnston, May 23, 1859, Johnston Papers, Barret Collection.

[70] R. W. Johnson to Johnston, November 3, 1857; August 24, 1858, *ibid.*

Federal Authority and Mormon Resistance

~~~~~~

A N EXTRAORDINARY MISSION awaited Johnston. Upon reporting to Secretary of War John Floyd, he received orders to take command of an expedition already on the march for Utah, in the far west, where the Mormon population was deemed to be in rebellion against federal authority.[1] That Johnston should be chosen for such a task was a measure of his rising prestige in the Army. "I consider it highly complimentary to you to be selected for this service over others more convenient & accessible," wrote Robert E. Lee, who knew of the assignment before it was announced to the public.[2] It was commonly known in the Army that Johnston was already in line for promotion to brigadier general, said another fellow officer, who then added, "Genl. [Winfield] Scott always speaks of you most flatteringly." [3] Johnston's star was in the ascendant.

He was to undertake a difficult and delicate task. The Mormons were aroused. Harried out of Ohio, Missouri, and finally Illinois, where their founder and leader, Joseph Smith, was lynched, in 1847 they shook the dust of the United States from their shoes and sought

---

[1] Samuel Cooper to Johnston, August 29, 1857, Johnston Papers, Barret Collection.

[2] Robert E. Lee to Johnston, August 1, 1857, *ibid.*

[3] Irvin McDowell to Johnston, August 22, 1857, *ibid.*

refuge in the wilderness of the west. After a prodigious trek across the Great Plains, led by Smith's successor, Brigham Young, they founded their Zion in the valley of the Great Salt Lake. There, protected by the towering Wasatch and Uinta mountain ranges, the Mormons worked with marvelous faith and industry; within ten years they had wrought a miracle of settlement.

They formed themselves into an independent theocracy later named the State of Deseret, after the word meaning "bee" in the Book of Mormon, their sacred scripture. The church-state was organized through an elaborate hierarchy of priestly orders topped by a Quorum (or Council) of Twelve Apostles and a First Presidency of three men. At the head of all the priesthood, including the First Presidency, was the President, or "Prophet, Seer, and Revelator"— Brigham Young.

Authoritarian organization gave purpose, cohesion, and discipline to the community. Rivers were dammed and turned from their courses in the lofty canyons and their waters brought through ingeniously designed canals to the thirsty soil of the valley; crops were grown where sagebrush had prevailed since time immemorial; homes, schools and temples were erected. Trade flourished in the sale of provisions to Oregon and California emigrants. Touched by Mormon energy, the desert was dotted with oases.[4]

Meanwhile, history overtook the Mormons. Their mountain fastness was part of the territory taken from Mexico by the United States at the end of the Mexican War. Two years later, as one of the measures in the famed Compromise of 1850, the United States Congress created the Territory of Utah. The Territory of Utah embraced the land of the Mormons.

At first this acquisition caused little concern among either the citizens of the states or of Utah. To most Americans, Utah was a remote place of slight interest; and Mormon fears were quickly relieved by President Millard Fillmore's appointment of Brigham Young as Territorial Governor. Soon, however, early harmony began to fade. The Mormon Church insisted upon nominating candidates for territorial office; Church members were obliged to support them

---

[4] This description of Mormon life and of the settlement of Utah is drawn from Leonard J. Arrington, *Great Basin Kingdom: An Economic History of the Latter-Day Saints, 1830–1900*, pp. 3–160; Thomas F. O'Dea, *The Mormons*, pp. 69–118; Nels Anderson, *Desert Saints: The Mormon Frontier in Utah*, pp. 28–135.

as a sacred duty.[5] Federal territorial judges, who were appointed by the President of the United States, were usually gentile (the Mormon name for non-Mormons), and these judges were at cross-purposes with the Mormon juries, who were told by Church authorities what decisions to reach. In a word, Utah remained a theocracy even after becoming a United States territory. Trouble was perhaps inevitable.[6]

Mormon anger flared over the nature and behavior of the federal judges, Indian agents, and other officials sent into the Territory. These representatives were frequently pompous men who made no effort to hide their contempt for the Mormons; some of them even were of disreputable character. The final blow to Mormon pride and patience was the activity of Territorial Judge W. W. Drummond, a man who had deserted his family to go to Utah, and whose consort there was said to be a prostitute. From the bench, Drummond attacked the territorial court system, which kept most jurisdiction under Church control; from his chambers, Drummond wrote letters to the United States Attorney General, charging the Mormons with despotism and sedition. Life was not secure for non-Mormons in Utah, Drummond said. A non-Mormon ought to be appointed governor of Utah Territory and supported by a federal army, he advised. At the same time, federal Indian agents accused the Mormons of inciting the Plains Indians against American settlements in the west.

Ultimately, the Mormons made life in Utah so miserable for Drummond and other gentile officials that a number of them, including Drummond, returned to the states, leaving their offices vacant. There, along with many other non-Mormons who had spent time in Utah, these exiles from territorial office became an instrument of propaganda for the disciplining of the Saints.[7]

Nor were the Mormons free of offense. Many of the accusations made by the exiles were true. Considered in the light of constitutional republicanism, the Church did practice a form of despotism over its adherents; unquestionably, non-Mormons were excluded

---

[5] Thomas B. H. Stenhouse, *The Rocky Mountain Saints*, pp. 279–291, 345–347.

[6] M. Hamlin Cannon, "The Mormon War: A Study in Territorial Rebellion" (Master's thesis), pp. 1–30; Anderson, *Desert Saints*, pp. 140–161.

[7] Norman F. Furniss, *The Mormon Conflict, 1850–1859*, pp. 45–61. Furniss gives the most recent and most authoritative account of the expedition against the Mormons. The present narrative draws heavily upon his work.

from voice in the public affairs of the Territory. If Church authorities did not sanction intimidation and, sometimes violence, against troublesome gentiles and apostate Mormons, the hierarchy at least permitted such actions to go unpunished.

Then there was polygamy. Introduced among the Mormons by Joseph Smith, this practice was carried on by Brigham Young, who proudly maintained his numerous wives and children in the commodious Lion House in the heart of Salt Lake City. Polygamy was not explicitly or officially given by Zion's refugee-critics as a cause of censure, since plural marriage was not then prohibited by federal law. Nevertheless, polygamy overshadowed all other Mormon customs in arousing hostility among the exiles and among the American people generally. Notwithstanding his doctrine of "popular sovereignty" for the territories, Democratic Senator Stephen A. Douglas of Illinois called Mormonism a "loathesome ulcer" that must be cut out of the body politic. The Republican Party platform of 1856 contained a pledge of opposition to America's "twin relics of barbarism"—slavery and polygamy.[8] Thus, like the people of Johnston's South, the Mormons practised a "peculiar institution" that plagued the conscience of a nation deeming itself otherwise without sin.

By 1857 the Democratic Administration of President James Buchanan was convinced that the Mormons were in rebellion. In May, Buchanan and his Cabinet decided to appoint a non-Mormon governor for Utah, along with a fresh group of territorial judges. To assure these officials of Mormon obedience, they were to be accompanied to Utah by a force of United States troops. After much delay, Buchanan appointed Alfred Cumming of Georgia as Territorial Governor; Delana R. Eckels, Charles E. Sinclair, and John Cradlebaugh were named federal judges of Utah. Initially assigned to command the armed forces was Brigadier General William S. Harney, one of the most famous Indian fighters of the Army.

Obstacles beset the course of the Administration. When asked for an appraisal of the military possibilities, General Winfield Scott was dubious. The Mormons could muster 4,000 defensive troops, he reckoned; to accumulate a sufficient United States offensive force would require many weeks, or even months. Because of the lateness of the season, the great distance to be covered across an uninhabited region, and the likelihood of severe cold in the mountains, the

[8] James Ford Rhodes, *History of the United States,* II, 184.

expedition ought not be started until spring of 1858.[9] General Harney also balked at the assignment. "General Harney is opposed to going, strongly so," wrote an officer of Harney's command. "He has written . . . that it is impossible to move with an army this season with any possible advantage, and it is the general impression . . . that we will not go." [10] In the end, Harney did not go; he was retained in Kansas where trouble brewed between proslavery and antislavery settlers. Nevertheless, the Administration ordered the Utah expedition forward; Albert Sidney Johnston was named to take Harney's place at its head.[11]

Johnston thus inherited confusion and blunder. He received the command in Washington on August 29; advance units of his force— eight companies of the Tenth Infantry under Colonel E. P. Alexander, with an attached battery of artillery under Captain John W. Phelps, and the Fifth Infantry under Colonel Carlos Waite, with an attached battery of artillery under Lieutenant Jesse Reno—were already more than a month out of Fort Leavenworth. They were almost to Fort Laramie in present Wyoming, fifteen hundred miles west of the army commander. The rear element of the expedition— six companies of the Second Dragoons under Lieutenant Colonel Philip St. George Cooke—was still at Fort Leavenworth. Between the head of the column and the tail were two companies of the Tenth Infantry marching from Minnesota to join the regiment, and a body of two hundred infantrymen and dragoons that for some reason had been separated from their commands. Hundreds of contractors' wagons laden with army supplies crept along the trail between Fort Leavenworth and Fort Laramie. The expedition stretched all the way across the Great Plains.[12]

Johnston left at once to join his far-flung column. Whether he again saw his family in Kentucky before departing for Utah is not known; possibly he stopped in Louisville on his way to Fort Leavenworth. In any event, he decided not to take his family with him on the march. A word on this subject from his friend Lee doubtless

[9] Furniss, *The Mormon Conflict*, pp. 95–97.

[10] Otis G. Hammond (ed.) , *The Utah Expedition, 1857–1858: Letters of Captain Jesse A. Gove*, p. 7.

[11] Cannon, "The Mormon War: A Study in Territorial Rebellion" (Master's thesis) , p. 30.

[12] Furniss, *The Mormon Conflict*, pp. 99–100. Copies of the most important military orders and correspondence of the expedition are in Leroy R. and Ann W. Hafen (eds.) , *The Utah Expedition, 1857–1858*, pp. 27–88, 139–177.

amused Johnston and confirmed him in his decision. "Tell Mrs. Johnston wives are a perfect drug out there," wrote Lee. "Besides Brigham's 50 female Saints will look upon her as a poor imposed on Sinner & she will not be appreciated in that Community." [13] Johnston took a house in Louisville for his wife and children during his absence on the Utah campaign.

The Mormons were on an outing in Big Cottonwood Canyon, celebrating the anniversary of their move to Salt Lake Valley, when they learned that a federal army was on its way to Utah. Undaunted by this prospect, Brigham Young and his associates immediately began to prepare Utah for defense. The United States Army was not to be permitted to enter the Territory. Young mobilized Mormon resources for war; he ordered out the Utah militia, which was identical with a Mormon force known as the Nauvoo Legion, and instructed Commanding General Daniel Wells to fortify the passes leading into the Valley.[14] Wells was to avoid a general engagement; if possible, he was to avoid shedding a single drop of blood. He was to impede and harass the advancing army by burning the grass along its line of march, by stampeding its livestock and by destroying its wagon trains. He was to ambush and cut off its outposts and detachments. "To waste away our enemies and lose none [of our own men] will be our mode of warfare," said the Mormon leader.[15] Young also recommended a measure that anticipated some of the efforts of psychological warfare in World Wars I and II: Wells was to take advantage of possible dissatisfaction in the enemy ranks by shouting invitations to the soldiers to desert and come into the Mormon

[13] Lee to Johnston, August 1, 1857, Johnston Papers, Barret Collection.

[14] Mormon preparations for defense are fully discussed in Furniss, *The Mormon Conflict*, pp. 119–147; Cannon, "The Mormon War: A Study in Territorial Rebellion" (Master's thesis), pp. 30–50; Lorna Bagley Allen, "A Study of the Alleged Mormon Rebellion" (Master's thesis), pp. 1–148; Don Richard Mathis, "Camp Floyd in Retrospect" (Master's thesis), pp. 1–25; Ralph Hansen, "The Nauvoo Legion in Utah" (Master's thesis), pp. 1–120; Hamilton Gardner, "The Utah Territorial Militia," Utah Historical Society Library, pp. 322–392; Nancy N. Tracy, "Narrative," Bancroft Library, University of California; Brigham Young to Daniel H. Wells, n.d., in "Journal History," Church Historian's Office, Salt Lake City; Miscellaneous Orders and Letters, Provo Military District Record; and Record of Orders, Returns and Courts-Martial of 2nd Brigade, 1st Division, Nauvoo Legion. Mormon preparations for defense are also shown in excerpts from Brigham Young's speeches, from Mormon diaries, and from newspaper accounts in Hafen and Hafen (eds.), *The Utah Expedition*, pp. 183–246.

[15] Young and Wells to William B. Pace, September 16, 1857, Provo Military District Record.

lines.[16] Both the United States Army and the Mormons indulged in an American naiveté—that the plain folk of the enemy do not have their hearts in the fight. The United States soldiers marched west under the mistaken belief that the oppressed masses of Utah would welcome liberation; Mormon leaders thought that the United States troops would seek the first opportunity to avoid service.

General Wells occupied Echo Canyon, which lay on the most direct route into the Valley, and began to fortify its narrows. The Mormon people were ready to fight; that, if necessary, they would have done so with courage and determination is beyond question.[17]

Johnston was not shaken by the difficulties that faced him. He would triumph, an old friend assured him, in spite of the blunder of the Administration in starting the expedition too late in the year. "I do not fear that disaster will overtake you, because I have abiding faith in the purity and loftiness of the motive that controls you," he was encouraged.[18] Johnston arrived at Fort Leavenworth during the second week of September. He found the rear guard of the expedition under Lieutenant Colonel Cooke ready to march. Governor Cumming and his wife, along with the new judges and other territorial officials, were to accompany Cooke.[19] On the day the rear guard moved out, Johnston, accompanied by an escort of forty horsemen, left to gain the remote head of the column. "[I shall be] prepared to make the journey in about 35 days," Johnston said, "and will arrive at Salt Lake Valley, say 20th October." [20] He embarked upon his mission with optimism; disillusionment awaited him in the mountain barriers of the kingdom of the Saints.

Aware that he was racing against the seasons, Johnston hastened with his escort across the Great Plains. On September 29 he crossed

[16] Young to Wells, n.d., "Journal History," Church Historian's Office, Salt Lake City.

[17] For expression of prevailing attitudes among the Mormon people, see J. D. T. McAllister Diary, August 13, October 18, 1857; Winslow Farr Diary, July 22–24, 1857; Jesse W. Crosby Diary, September 25, 1857; Charles L. Walker Diary, January 15, 1858; Lorenzo Brown Diary, July 24, September 28, December 1, 1857; Wandle Mace Journal, July 24–August 17, 1857.

[18] N. J. Eaton to Johnston, September 8, 1857, Johnston-Eaton Letter Book, Johnston Papers, Barret Collection.

[19] Johnston to Eaton, September 16, 1857, *ibid.*

[20] Johnston to McDowell, September 16, 1857, Letters Sent, Department of Utah, Records of the War Department. Copies of Johnston's official correspondence from the Utah expedition are in notebooks in the Johnston Papers, Barret Collection.

the South Fork of the Platte. His optimism was beginning to fade. He wrote that upon reaching his advance units he would at once carry out his mission, "unless prevented by the destruction of the grass on the route by cold, or the filling up of the passes by snow." [21] Eight days later, he arrived at Fort Laramie, still believing he might beat the winter in crossing the mountains. But he sent instructions for Colonel Cooke to use his own judgment about advancing beyond Fort Laramie once the rear guard reached that post.[22] Then he pressed on across the high, barren plateau of southern Wyoming.

After Johnston had left Fort Laramie, rumors reached him of Mormon attacks upon the vanguard of his expedition. These rumors reached the wagon trains also, frightening the conductors and drivers and stopping or slowing their progress. Johnston stirred them into action as he overtook them on the trail, bringing order out of chaos even before he was in position to assume personal command of the campaign. Wrote Major Fitz John Porter, Johnston's adjutant general:

Experienced on the Plains and of established reputation for energy, courage, and resources, [Johnston's] presence restored confidence at all points, and encouraged the weak-hearted and panic-stricken multitude. The long chain of wagons, kinked, tangled, and hard to move, uncoiled and went forward smoothly.[23]

On October 13 Johnston reached the Sweetwater River near South Pass. That day he received dire tidings from Colonel Alexander, an indecisive and timid officer, known to his subordinates as the "Old Woman." In September Alexander had met Captain Stewart Van Vliet of the Army returning from Salt Lake City. Van Vliet was a special envoy sent by order of the Administration to apprise the Mormons of President Buchanan's intentions, and to convey the Mormons' response to General Harney and the President. Alarmed by Van Vliet's report of Mormon determination to resist, Alexander had stopped on Ham's Fork and entered into a fruitless correspondence with Brigham Young.

On September 15 Young issued a proclamation of defiance, placing Utah under martial law and forbidding all armed forces to enter the Territory. Two weeks later the Mormon Lion wrote to Alexander:

[21] Johnston to McDowell, September 29, October 5, 1857, Letters Sent, Department of Utah, Records of the War Department.

[22] Johnston to Philip St. George Cooke, October 5, 1857, *ibid.*

[23] Johnston, *Life of Johnston,* p. 211.

Brigadier General Albert Sidney Johnston, U.S.A.

Mrs. Albert Sidney Johnston, in a photograph
made years after Johnston's death.

A pen-and-ink sketch by Eliza Johnston of the Johnston home in Austin in
1851–1852, showing the old Capitol in the background and a double log cabin
once occupied by the Department of State.

Cactus in bloom

Turk's Cap

Bluebonnet   *Firewheel*

Paintings of Texas flowers by Eliza Johnston

Courtesy Library of Congress

United States Military Academy in the 1820's

Battle of the Bad Axe

View of Monterrey in the Mexican War

Review of Texas Troops in the Mexican War

The March to Fort Bridger

Fort Bridger in the Winter of 1857–1858

The Battle of Shiloh

I now . . . direct that you retire forthwith from the Territory by the same route you entered. Should you deem this impracticable, and prefer to remain until Spring . . . you can do so in peace, and unmolested, on condition that you deposit your arms and ammunition with . . . [the] Quarter Master General of the Territory and leave . . . as soon as the condition of the roads will permit.[24]

While this palaver was going on, Alexander had left a gap of thirty miles between his regiment and the Fifth Infantry, with his supply trains between the two. On October 4, Mormon horsemen under Major Lot Smith slipped past the Tenth Infantry and burned three of the trains, seventy-two wagons in all. Alexander at last knew that he was at war, and frantically uniting the two regiments and their supporting artillery, he began to march northwest toward the valley of the Bear River on October 7, hoping thus to enter Salt Lake Valley in a roundabout way that would bypass Mormon fortifications in the canyon directly ahead. This was the information brought to Johnston on the Sweetwater.[25]

Johnston was greatly perturbed. Leaden skies portended the immediate onslaught of winter; the thermometer was falling. On September 16 he ordered Alexander to return to his former position on Ham's Fork. Johnston intended to concentrate his entire command there preparatory to establishing winter quarters in a suitable location. Warned by flurries of snow, Alexander was already on his way back to his old camp when Johnston's message reached him. On the morning of the eighteenth, Johnston's camp on the Sweetwater was blanketed with snow and the thermometer read 16 degrees. He wrote to his superiors:

I greatly regret that the impossibility of concentrating the troops destined for this service, and their supplies, will prevent a forward movement before spring. It is now manifest that before the force can be united that the autumn will be too far advanced to move with a probability of success, tho' not opposed by the Mormons.

He went on to recommend an expedition into Utah from the Pacific coast, to be coordinated with his advance in the spring.[26] He had lost his race against the seasons.

---

[24] Stenhouse, *The Rocky Mountain Saints,* pp. 358–359, 366.

[25] Furniss, *The Mormon Conflict,* p. 109. A vivid description of the stampeding of army mules by the Mormons is in John L. Ginn, "Mormon and Indian Wars," Collection of Western Americana, Yale University Library.

[26] Johnston to McDowell, October 13, 16, 18, 1857, Letters Sent, Department of Utah, Records of the War Department.

Johnston waited at South Pass for all units he had overtaken since leaving Fort Laramie to catch up with him and for Alexander to retrace his steps. He forbade all further communication with the Mormons and commandeered and attached to his army two merchant wagon trains bound for Salt Lake City. Once the rear elements caught up with him, Johnston planned to hasten them over the remaining ninety miles to make junction with Alexander; then he would seek the best available haven against the winter. Retarded by snow, the rear columns and supply trains were nine days in reaching him. On October 26 he began the march from the Sweetwater; eight days later he joined Alexander on Ham's Fork. Save for the dragoons under Cooke, the entire army was at last concentrated.[27]

Johnston's objective was now Fort Bridger thirty-five miles to the west. Built by Mountain Man Jim Bridger, this well-known station on the Oregon Trail now belonged to the Mormons; Bridger said they had forced him to sell it to them. Fort Bridger was located on Black's Fork 125 miles northeast of Salt Lake City. It offered sufficient water for Johnston's troops and livestock, and as it lay between the Rocky Mountains on the east and the Wasatch on the west, it was somewhat sheltered from the fiercest blasts of the mountain winter.

Johnston found Alexander's men dangerously low in supplies and morale. His presence immediately lifted their spirits, but they were in such need of winter clothing and tents, and their livestock in such need of forage, that Johnston took two precious days to distribute these and to organize his column for the march to Fort Bridger. Considering his information and expectations, this delay was perhaps justified; to push on pell-mell without preparation or organization was to invite disaster from the Mormons or the weather, or both. As events turned out, however, the delay proved almost fatal. On November 6, as the column started for Fort Bridger, a mountain blizzard struck.[28]

A struggle for survival began. Amid blinding snow and intense cold the troops fought their way forward a few miles each day. Temperature in the middle of the day was 2 degrees above zero; at

[27] *Ibid.*, November 5, 30, 1857; Johnston to Eaton, February 5, October 11, 1858, Johnston-Eaton Letter Book, Johnston Papers, Barret Collection.

[28] Johnston to McDowell, November 30, 1857, Letters Sent, Department of Utah, Records of the War Department; Johnston to Eaton, February 5, 1858, Johnston-Eaton Letter Book, Johnston Papers, Barret Collection.

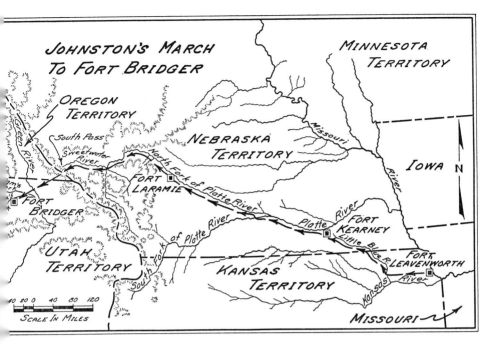

JOHNSTON'S MARCH TO FORT BRIDGER

night it fell to 16 degrees below. Grease froze on the axles of moving wagons and caissons, and horses, mules, and oxen died by hundreds. It became necessary to shuttle the remaining draft animals back and forth, pulling some of the wagons a few miles forward one day, then returning to bring up the rest the next. On November 9 a soldier wrote:

Made about 7 miles [today]. Animals lying along the road every rod, almost, and daily and hourly dying as they are driven along the road. . . . No fire except what we can make from the sage bushes. It was awful. Never were men more exposed or had a harder tour of duty.[29]

Meanwhile, Colonel Cooke was making an even more severe march from Fort Laramie. Caught by the storm at South Pass, he led his suffering troops, along with the civil officials of the Territory, toward Fort Bridger through temperatures that dropped to 44 degrees below zero at night.[30]

Both Johnston and Cooke displayed superb leadership under stress. The only human casualty of the bitter march was a soldier of

[29] Hammond (ed.), *The Utah Expedition,* pp. 92–93.
[30] Cooke to "Sir," November 21, 1857, Letters Received, Adjutant General's Office, Records of the War Department.

Cooke's regiment who died of tetanus. In tribute to Johnston, a subordinate wrote:

The will which moved this force . . . [was] brighter and stronger as the constitution became weaker, and if he had said on—on we would have gone, feeling that what he would direct would be right. The assurances . . . of confidence in my commander have been more than realized, and he now has, I believe, the unbounded confidence of the army.[31]

Notwithstanding his fifty-four years and his partial lameness from Felix Huston's old bullet wound, Johnston led his troops on foot through the blizzard. His willingness to share hardship endeared him to all. A captain of the Tenth Infantry spoke for the entire Utah army when he said, "Col. Johnston . . . is a man." [32]

Johnston, with the advance units of the expedition, reached Fort Bridger on November 17, to find only a burnt ruin left by the withdrawing Mormons. Cooke's dragoons and retinue of civilians arrived two days later. The Utah army was at last concentrated. Johnston did not exaggerate when he wrote, "The army under my command took the last possible step forward at Bridger, with the animals then alive and in condition they were in." [33]

They made camp—which Johnston named Camp Scott in honor of his commanding general—on Black's Fork above the remains of Fort Bridger. The civilian territorial officials made a camp of tents and huts adjacent to Camp Scott, and named this cluster of dwellings Eckelsville, in honor of the territorial chief justice.

Their situation remained perilous, for the force was lodged in a barren and frigid land almost a thousand miles from reinforcement or source of supply. More than four thousand head of beef cattle had been lost by freezing or by Mormon raids; immense quantities of clothing, medicine, and rations had been burned with the wagon trains. Artillery batteries had fewer than half their horses left, and the dragoons were almost without mounts. Johnston was desperately short of everything needed to support his troops. Courage and ingenuity of high order were required to mend the wounds of the

[31] ——to "Dear Major," November 29, 1857, Johnston Papers, Barret Collection.

[32] Hammond (ed.), *The Utah Expedition*, pp. 92–93. See also Robert E. Stowers and John M. Ellis (eds.), "Charles A. Scott's Diary of the Utah Expedition, 1857–1861," *Utah Historical Quarterly*, XVIII (April, 1960), 167.

[33] Johnston to McDowell, April 17, 1858, Letters Sent, Department of Utah, Records of the War Department; "Extracts from the Diary of Major Fitz John Porter," November 17, 1857, Fitz John Porter Papers.

forlorn army, to sustain its morale, and to shape it into a true striking force.[34]

Johnston tackled these problems resolutely. By repairing Fort Bridger, arming it with cannon, and occupying it with infantry, and by ordering scouting parties to search the surrounding countryside for enemy activity, he made his command secure against attack.[35] Against the advice of his guide, Jim Bridger, he sent Captain Randolph Marcy with a small body of troops to proceed south through the Uinta Mountains to acquire horses and draft animals from the commander of Fort Union in New Mexico Territory.[36]After a heroic struggle against the elements, Marcy made it to his destination and returned in the spring with the needed animals.[37] To preserve the livestock that survived the march to Fort Bridger, Johnston distributed the herds in neighboring creek valleys to feed upon what scanty vegetation remained. Colonel Cooke and his dragoons were ordered to guard them. From nearby mountain men, Johnston purchased hundreds of beeves. He also sent a civilian agent, B. F. Ficklin of one of the wagon companies, to purchase horses and beeves from the Flathead Indians of the upper Missouri, but Ficklin's mission was not successful.[38]

Johnston had to contend with apathy and bureaucratic entanglement in keeping open his direct line of supply across the plains. Upon learning that Forts Laramie and Kearney had been unaccountably removed from his authority by War Department order, he protested vigorously, and when the commander of Fort Laramie indicated that he could not fill Johnston's requisition for rations to be brought to Camp Scott in the spring, Johnston assumed authority to order him to do so. Writing that he had issued his orders before he learned of the transfer of Fort Laramie to another department—the Department of the West—Johnston said:

---

[34] Special Order, November 24, 1857, Letters Sent, Department of Utah, Records of the War Department; John H. Dickenson to Porter, November 24, 1857, Letters Received, Adjutant General's Office, Records of the War Department.

[35] *New York Daily Tribune,* January 18, 1858; Johnston to Eaton, February 5, 1858, Johnston-Eaton Letter Book, Johnston Papers, Barret Collection.

[36] Johnston to John Garland, November 25, 1857, Letters Sent, Department of Utah, Records of the War Department.

[37] "Extracts from the Diary of Major Fitz John Porter," April 11, 1858, Porter Papers.

[38] Johnston to McDowell, April 17, 1858, Headquarters Book, Army of Utah, 1857, Johnston Papers, Barret Collection.

But [this knowledge] would have had no influence in issuing [my] orders, inasmuch as they were dictated by necessity and regard for the safety of this command and the honor of our country, and their fulfilment is of such importance as to admit of no delay for reference to higher authority. . . . [I] will continue to give you orders—but only such as are necessary for the good of the service, and [I] expect them to be obeyed as implicitly as when you were in this Department, or if issued by the commander of the Department of the West.[39]

He also wrote urgently to the War Department, which replied by sending fresh supply trains and herds of beef to Fort Laramie to be forwarded to Johnston's troops; but these would not reach Camp Scott until early June of 1858.[40]

Improvisation and rationing stretched meager supplies through the winter. To spare the few weakened horses that remained alive, Johnston had soldiers draw wagons to procure wood for the camp.[41] When clothing wore out, soldiers made stockings out of coat sleeves, and patched their pantaloons from discarded garments, and Johnston put groups of men to mending shoes and fashioning moccasins out of skins, Indian style.[42] He reduced the flour ration by one half, and even slaughtered draft oxen for meat, but when the army ran out of salt, he spurned an offer of resupply from Brigham Young.[43] The troops ate their victuals unsalted; or, at exorbitant price, purchased salt smuggled into camp from Mormon sources. "Beef is so tough that the dogs cannot and will not eat it unless you cook it," said one campaigner; "and then even they are compelled to do so or starve." Nevertheless, for months the army subsisted largely on such fare, supplemented with "desiccated vegetables" and some fresh fruits and garden produce sold in camp by friendly Indians.[44]

[39] Johnston to Major Isaac Lynde, March 10, 1858, Letters Sent, Department of Utah, Records of the War Department.

[40] Johnston to McDowell, December 13, 1857; February 5, 1858; Johnston to Assistant Adjutant General of the Army, January 4, 1858; Porter to William Hoffman, November 13, 1857, all in *ibid.*

[41] *New York Daily Tribune*, March 23, 1858.

[42] Furniss, *The Mormon Conflict*, p. 150.

[43] Young to Johnston, November 26, 1857, Letters Received, Adjutant General's Office, Records of the War Department; "Extracts from the Diary of Major Fitz John Porter," December 2, 7, 1857, Porter Papers; Hammond (ed.), *The Utah Expedition*, p. 103. Before Johnston's arrival, Colonel E. P. Alexander had accepted Young's courtesies—for example, copies of the Mormon newspaper, *Deseret News*. See Henry Maynadier to Young, October 10, 1857, Letters Received, Adjutant General's Office, Records of the War Department.

[44] Hammond (ed.), *The Utah Expedition*, pp. 142, 155.

Some of the officers fared much better, at least occasionally, than did the troops. On Christmas Day one of the officers' wives served eggnog made with eggs from hens she had brought along in coops.[45] From private stores brought with the expedition, Captain Jesse Gove, of the Tenth Infantry, entertained sumptuously from time to time; his board included oyster soup, boiled tongue, tripe, rice croquettes, and cakes. The service was silver; and liquers topped off the meal. Gove invited his regimental commander, Colonel Charles F. Smith, and second-in-command, Colonel E. R. S. Canby, along with Canby's wife and daughter and others, but Johnston was not among his guests.[46]

Knowing that morale is as important as rations to an army, Johnston called forth every trick at his disposal to brighten the spirits of his men. He encouraged the establishment of a camp theater, which was soon in production. Band concerts and photography provided entertainment; one of the regiments set up a library of books brought along on the march.[47] Johnston held formal guard mountings and reviews to keep an edge on his command. There is something at once absurd and heroic in the vision of this band of ragged, hungry, and bored soldiers, isolated in their remote snow-bound fastness, going through the exaggerated precision movements of the parade ground. One is reminded of the legendary Englishman dining in formal attire in the midst of the jungle. Yet these trappings of glory appealed to at least some of the troops in the Utah expedition. "You ought to see the parade passing in review," wrote a junior officer, with as much enthusiasm as if he had been on the Plain at West Point.[48]

To keep his soldiers fit and alert, Johnston put them in training every day that the weather permitted. He had officers hold schools in tactics for the instruction of their subordinates. He caused the various units of the command to practice tactical exercises of the regiment and the brigade. He was wise enough to know that a busy and well-trained soldier is likely to be a soldier of high morale and good behavior.[49]

[45] Journal, December 25, 1857, J. W. Phelps Papers.

[46] Hammond (ed.), *The Utah Expedition,* pp. 124, 136.

[47] *New York Daily Tribune,* March 23, 1858.

[48] Hammond (ed.), *The Utah Expedition,* pp. 162–163.

[49] General Order, May 24, 1858, Order Book, Army of Utah (copy), Johnston Papers, Barret Collection; Hammond (ed.), *The Utah Expedition,* p. 132.

Johnston's efforts to preserve decorum and morale through training, assigned labor, and organized diversion were, on the whole,
successful; yet no system could entirely overcome the effects of such
isolation and boredom as the Utah army underwent, or the inherent
perversity of some of the troopers. Gambling flourished in camp and
about the outskirts. Whiskey was a constant source of difficulty;
some of the men literally drank themselves to death.[50] To assure
order in the camp, Johnston assigned an officer as provost marshal,
with a provost guard of husky sergeants.[51] The mere existence of this
organization tended to keep the camp orderly.

Nevertheless, serious disorders sometimes occurred. In January of
1858, for example, when the private soldiers were permitted to hold
a ball in the camp theater, a group of the men got drunk at the ball
and fell to fighting; a sergeant was waylaid and severely beaten on
his way back to his quarters; several other soldiers were injured in a
general melee. Furious at this gross breach of temperance and discipline, Johnston tried the culprits by court-martial, which sentenced
them to be confined at hard labor until the expiration of their
enlistment. Then they were to be branded over the left hip with the
letter *M,* their heads were to be shaven, and they were to be
drummed out of service.[52] After such an example there were no more
riots, although drunken and boisterous parties were held from time
to time in Judge Eckels's quarters in Eckelsville, which was not under Johnston's control. "The Judge has some womenfolk at his establishment," an officer commented on one of these occasions, "who are
probably at the bottom of the affair." [53]

Johnston exacted stern discipline, but he was neither martinet nor
tyrant. He freely used the court-martial to keep troops in line, but
he frequently lightened the sentences of the courts. Sometimes he
restored deserters to duty without trial. Except in cases of extreme
provocation, he struck out those parts of sentences that called for
whipping, branding, the wearing of irons, or shaving of the head.
Johnston always weighed extenuating circumstances in meting out
punishment and expected less of men who were new than of vet-

---

[50] Journal, December 31, 1857; April 2, June 12, 1858, Phelps Papers.
[51] Porter to "Dear Major," January 21, 1858 (copy), Johnston Papers, Barret
Collection.
[52] Hammond (ed.), *The Utah Expedition,* pp. 114, 123.
[53] "Extracts from the Diary of Major Fitz John Porter," April 2, 1858, Porter
Papers.

erans. He distinguished between willful disobedience and thought-lessness. "Believing that leniency towards the prisoner will be properly appreciated by him," he wrote in reviewing one case, "and that his future behavior will be such as to give no ground of complaint . . . [sentence] is remitted." [54]

Under Johnston's watchful eye, the Utah force became campaign-worthy. The entire command, men and officers, was 2,000 strong. In addition to the regulars, Johnston had enlarged his army by creating a volunteer battalion of over 300 men enlisted from among a group of civilian road builders that he had overtaken near South Pass, and from among the idle teamsters of the destroyed wagon trains. Besides adding strength to the command, this wise move gave employment and subsistence to men who would have been on army rations any-way, and it contributed to order in camp by bringing them under military discipline.[55] The troops were remarkably healthy through-out the winter; [56] fewer than 4 per cent were reported sick at any one time.[57] In the spring Johnston could truthfully write, "The army is healthy, efficient, well disciplined & ready & willing to perform any duty." [58]

Johnston's alertness and efficiency impressed his command. "Col. Johnston . . . sees everything, knows everything and everybody, nothing escapes his notice," wrote a junior officer to his wife.[59] The universal hope of the expedition was that Johnston soon would be promoted to brigadier general, wrote a newspaper correspondent from Camp Scott. Johnston's qualifications were acknowledged by all, said this observer; "The Administration have for once put the right man in the right place." [60] Johnston was esteemed and loved by officers and men alike, one of the campaigners later recalled. "Had there been a battle with the Mormons, [Johnston] would have gotten all the fight out of his men that was in them." [61] His bright young

[54] Special Orders, December 7, 1857; January 15, February 19, March 6, 1858, Order Book, Army of Utah (copy) , Johnston Papers, Barret Collection.

[55] *New York Daily Tribune,* March 1, 1858.

[56] Hammond (ed.) , *The Utah Expedition,* p. 126.

[57] Monthly Returns, February, 1858, Letters Received, Department of Utah, Records of the War Department.

[58] Johnston to William Preston Johnston, April 17, 1858, Johnston Papers, Barret Collection.

[59] Hammond (ed.) , *The Utah Expedition,* p. 149.

[60] *New York Daily Tribune,* July 7, 1858.

[61] Charles Becker, "History of the Expedition against the Mormons in 1857," Church Historian's Office, Salt Lake City.

adjutant general, Major Porter, spoke for the Utah army when he said:

Col. Johnston has done everything to add to the efficiency of the command—and put it in a condition to sustain the dignity and honor of the country—More he cannot do. . . . Don't let any one come here over Col. Johnston—It would be much against the wishes and hopes of everyone here—who would gladly see him a Brigadier General.[62]

The decision to spend the winter at Camp Scott had been endorsed by all, or virtually all, of the command. One or two subordinate officers may have suggested an audacious plan for taking the Mormon valley from the rear without delay. A newspaper correspondent later wrote from Utah that during the previous winter one officer had wished to attempt a march into the Mormon redoubt by way of a southern route along the Provo River and Provo Canyon; the effort was to be made with a small combat force of one battalion of infantry supported by a section of light artillery and a squadron of dragoons.[63] Years afterward, Colonel Cooke scoffed at Johnston for failing to press on to Salt Lake City during the winter.[64] But there is no contemporary record that anyone proposed such a movement at the time.

Since this strategy was not attempted, its feasibility cannot be known. Possibly it would have been successful. From time to time the winter abated long enough for such a march to have been accomplished; it might have taken the Mormons by surprise. But Johnston's decision seems to have been the sound one. Time was his ally: spring would bring him supplies and reinforcements, but to the Mormons it would bring no added strength. Moreover, Johnston could not predict the winter's vagaries; a mountain blizzard could have, without warning, brought disaster to an expedition on the move. A heavy snowfall occurred at Camp Scott as late as June 10. Of Johnston's leadership an admirer said, "The reputation which [he] has gathered during this expedition, is derived from the display of traits of character more solid than brilliant."[65] Johnston's course

---

[62] Porter to "Dear Major," January 21, March 14, 1858 (copies), Johnston Papers, Barret Collection.

[63] *New York Daily Tribune*, November 26, 1858.

[64] Rodenbough (ed.), *From Everglade to Cañon with the Second Dragoons*, p. 192.

[65] *New York Daily Tribune*, July 7, 1858.

in wintering at Camp Scott was neither daring nor brilliant; yet it seems to have been wise.[66]

One incident that occurred at Camp Scott presented Johnston's character at its best. From one of the contractors selling supplies to the army he received a Christmas gift. Upon opening the package and discovering that it contained a valuable silver service, Johnston wrote to the contractor, saying that it could not be accepted. He said that he had at first thought the gift

some trifle in value offered in a spirit of kindness, which I might properly receive. . . . I beg that you will believe that in declining to receive this token of your regard (but which will also be considered as an evidence of your approbation of my conduct as commander) that I am actuated by no other feeling than a sense of military propriety—Your own reflections, without any elaboration of argument on my part, will inform you how injurious to the discipline & well being of the service would be the [acceptance of the gift].[67]

The troops were not to be disappointed in their desire for Johnston's promotion. His superiors in Washington also looked with high favor upon his conduct of the campaign. General in Chief Winfield Scott in January commended Johnston for having "manfully conquered" all difficulties. His recommendation of a diversion, or cooperating expedition, from the Pacific coast would be launched in the spring, said Scott, with the General in Chief himself in command.[68] Scott urged that Johnston be promoted without delay.[69] If Johnston should at once be made brevet brigadier general, said Scott to President Buchanan in February, Johnston would be a

[66] Gardner, "The Utah Territorial Militia," p. 418, Utah Historical Society Library. Even the Mormons later said that Johnston was wise not to have risked the blizzards in a winter march to the valley; they applauded his ability to keep his troops fit through the mountain winter. "It takes a cool brain and good judgment to maintain a contented army and healthy camp through a stormy winter in the Wasatch Mountains," said the Salt Lake City *Deseret News*, October 13, 1858.

[67] ———to Howard Livingston, January 2, 1858, Johnston Papers, Barret Collection. The last page of this letter is missing; it is written in Johnston's hand. Whether the letter was actually sent, or the gift returned, cannot be determined from the documentary evidence. Johnston later told his son that the gift was returned. According to the unanimous testimony of friends and acquaintances, such an action would have suited his character.

[68] George W. Lay to Johnston, January 23, 1858, Johnston Papers, Barret Collection.

[69] McDowell to Johnston, January 19, 1858, *ibid.*

major general before the campaign ended.[70] Johnston was not so fortunate as to gain two promotions while on the Utah expedition; but on April 10, 1858, he became a brevet brigadier general.[71]

His customary poise and self-control did not prevent an occasional yielding to vanity. Upon learning that his conduct in the campaign was criticized by some congressmen and newspaper editors, Johnston permitted articles supporting him to leak out to the press, and he looked in the other direction when a junior officer voluntarily wrote letters praising him and sent them to the *New York Herald* for publication.[72] One subordinate irreverently said that Johnston's voice grew deeper after he received his promotion to brigadier general.[73]

Johnston's attitude toward the Mormons before taking command of the Utah expedition is not known. Quite probably he shared the popular aversion for them. Whatever his earlier views may have been, he came to look upon them as rebels against the nation. Captain Van Vliet's report of Mormon defiance, Brigham Young's presumptuous letter ordering the army to retire from the Territory, the burning of the army trains—these kindled in Johnston a determination to treat the Mormons as enemies.

They have with premeditation placed themselves in rebellion against the Union and entertain the insane design of establishing a form of government thoroughly despotic and utterly repugnant to our institutions [he wrote to the assistant adjutant general of the Army]. The people of the United States must act now, or submit to an usurpation of their Territory and the engrafting upon our institutions [of] a social organization and political principles totally incompatible with our own.[74]

The ordeal of winter at Camp Scott also had hardened Johnston's heart against the Mormons. Considering the "treasonable temper" of their leaders, he said, he felt that no concessions ought to be made to them. They should be obliged to submit unconditionally to federal authority; an agreement with them on any other terms would be

[70] Eaton to Johnston, February 21, 1858, *ibid.*

[71] Cooper to Johnston, April 10, 1858, *ibid.* Plans for an expedition from the Pacific coast were soon dropped. See Lay to Johnston, February 4, 1858, Letters Received, Adjutant General's Office, Records of the War Department.

[72] Hammond (ed.), *The Utah Expedition,* pp. 156–157, 182.

[73] Journal, May 19, 1858, Phelps Papers.

[74] Johnston to McDowell, November 5, 1857, Letters Sent, Department of Utah, Records of the War Department.

useless. "Their threat to oppose the march of the troops in the spring will not have the slightest influence in delaying it," Johnston said; "and if they desire to join issue I believe it is for the interest of the Government that they should have the opportunity." [75] To a friend he said, "The people of the Union must now . . . act with the vigor and force . . . which the honor and dignity of the Government require should be exerted against those who raise a parricidal hand against their country." [76] And to his son he wrote, "I have not learned yet to call crimes by soft names & I never intend to aid & abet in compounding a felony—I will call a traitor a traitor & have him punished for his treason if I can." [77] This resolve was an ironic paradox in Johnston's career: he now was willing to risk his life to support federal authority; later he would give his life in opposing it.

He and his troops were inflamed against alleged atrocities of the Mormons. Members of the expedition were determined to exact justice for the Mountain Meadows Massacre, which had occurred in southern Utah while Johnston was on his way to take command of the army. This massacre was a hideous affair in which more than one hundred emigrants to California—men, women, and children—were ambushed and slain by Indians, who were supported by a few Mormons. That the Church hierarchy was involved in this crime has never been demonstrated; a careful historian has said that the Church leaders were only "accessories after the fact." [78] But the men of the Utah expedition were easily convinced that Brigham Young and his associates were parties to it.[79] Countless tales of Mormon inhumanity were told at Camp Scott by gentile and apostate-Mormon refugees. They described a band of Mormon terrorists called the Destroying Angels whose supposed duty was to exterminate heretics and backsliders; a Mormon husband was said to have cut the throat of his doubting wife when advised to do so by Young.[80] A book filled with alleged Mormon abominations—John Hyde's *Mormonism: Its Leaders and Designs*—circulated in

[75] *Ibid.*, January 20, 1858.
[76] Johnston to Eaton, February 5, 1858, Johnston-Eaton Letter Book, Johnston Papers, Barret Collection.
[77] Johnston to William Preston Johnston, April 17, 1858, Johnston Papers, Barret Collection.
[78] Furniss, *The Mormon Conflict*, p. 88.
[79] J. W. Phelps to "Dear Charles," May 23, 1858, Phelps Papers.
[80] *New York Daily Tribune*, June 26, July 1, 1858.

the camp, and the campaign threatened to become a crusade of righteous vengeance against a people thought to be beyond compassion.[81]

Chief Justice Eckels shared the army's views toward the Mormons. Stooping to the sophistry that Utah Territory was still under Mexican law, since it had not been explicitly repealed, Eckels contemplated trying the Mormons for polygamy under the Mexican legal code.[82] Shortly after going into winter quarters, Eckels opened court in his hut and impaneled a grand jury from among the few civilians in Eckelsville; in what would appear to have been a travesty upon the judicial process, the jury promptly indicted Brigham Young and other Church leaders for treason. Full retribution seemed to await the rebellious Saints.[83]

While Johnston and his troops grew ever more bitter toward the Mormons, the Buchanan Administration grew ever more anxious to bring the expensive and embarrassing conflict to a close without hostilities. Two men principally served the Administration in achieving this aim. The first of these was Colonel Thomas L. Kane of Pennsylvania. Kane had long been a friend of the Mormons. With "unofficial" approval from President Buchanan, Kane traveled via Panama and California to Salt Lake City, where he prevailed upon Brigham Young to permit him to go through the Mormon lines and negotiate with the civil and military authorities at Camp Scott. After an exhausting ride, he arrived at camp on the night of March 12, 1858.[84]

Kane's mission was distasteful to Johnston, who burned to punish the Mormons for their sins, and Kane's manners quickly alienated him personally from Johnston. In reporting to Johnston, Kane rode his horse into the entrance of Johnston's quarters so close that in coming out, the General found himself wedged between horse and tent.[85] Kane seems also to have been full of his own importance;

---

[81] Hamond (ed.), *The Utah Expedition*, p. 165.

[82] Journal, April 2, 1858, Phelps Papers.

[83] Furniss, *The Mormon Conflict*, pp. 166–167. For orders for the arrest of Mormons apprehended by the Army, see *House Executive Document 71, 35th Congress, 1st Session*, Vol. X, pp. 55–56, 68.

[84] Alfred L. Zobell, "Thomas L. Kane: Ambassador to the Mormons" (Master's thesis). Kane's correspondence pertaining to his mission to Utah is in Hafen and Hafen (eds.), *The Utah Expedition*, pp. 265–293.

[85] Journal, March 13, 1858, Phelps Papers.

Major Porter considered him an ass.[86] From the first, Johnston held himself aloof from Kane, whom he considered a tool of the Mormons, if not a spy; most of the contact between the two men was by letter, though they occupied tents only a few hundred yards apart.

Kane made the mistake of repeating Brigham Young's offer of salt, plus other provisions, to the "destitute" army.[87] Johnston replied in scorn, saying that his supplies were adequate until they could be replenished from the proper sources. "Whatever might be the need of the Army under my command for food," Johnston told Kane, "we would neither ask nor receive from President Young and his confederates, any supplies while they continue to be enemies of the Government." [88]

Kane found in Governor Cumming the other person who would play a vital role in preventing hostilities between the United States and the Mountain Saints. Finding Johnston unshakeable in his determination to punish the Mormons, Kane appealed to the Territorial Governor to accompany him back to Salt Lake City; there, he said, Cumming could observe for himself whether his subjects were law-abiding citizens or red-handed rebels and murderers. Cumming gave ear to this appeal.[89]

Tension mounted at Camp Scott. Kane's presence was known and resented by the entire army. On March 14 Adjutant General Fitz John Porter promised, "I think [Kane] an imposter and will find him out today." [90] When Kane had first entered camp, Johnston assigned a sergeant of the provost marshal's command to protect the envoy from molestation. The sergeant got the idea, possibly from Major Porter, that he was to keep Kane under surveillance. Sensing that he was virtually under arrest, and angered by overhearing an orderly say, "Keep an eye on this d——d Mormon," Kane sent Johnston a letter hinting at an invitation to a duel.[91] Johnston

[86] "Extracts from the Diary of Major Fitz John Porter," March 13, 1858, Porter Papers.

[87] Young to Kane, March 9, 1858 (copy); Kane to Johnston, n.d. (copy), in "Extracts from the Diary of Major Fitz John Porter," *ibid.*

[88] Johnston to Kane, March 15, 1858, Letters Sent, Department of Utah, Records of the War Department.

[89] Zobell, "Thomas L. Kane: Ambassador to the Mormons" (Master's thesis).

[90] Porter to "My Dear Major," March 14, 1858 (copy), Johnston Papers, Barret Collection.

[91] Kane to Johnston, March 16, 1858 (copy), *ibid.*

soothed ruffled feelings by explaining that the sergeant had received garbled orders and that Kane was under no restraint while in the camp.[92]

Tempers had scarcely cooled from this incident when another occurred. Returning to camp after dark from a consultation with his Mormon escort, Kane foolishly fired some shots to notify the army pickets of his presence. Thinking they were being attacked, the outpost company beat the long roll and sprang to arms. A patrol moved out and soon discovered Kane. Before he could identify himself, or before he was permitted to do so, a soldier fired point-blank at him; miraculously the shot went wild. "We all think [the soldier] did it, that is, tried to shoot Kane on purpose," said the outpost commander with approval.[93] "Pity they did not rid him of life," commented Porter. "It would have saved one fool from troubling us." [94] Kane returned to his quarters, an angry and shaken man.[95]

In spite of the antipathy of Johnston and his soldiers, Kane partially accomplished his mission in coming to Camp Scott; after a week of exhortation, he persuaded Governor Cumming to go with him to Salt Lake City. On April 5 they set forth on their week's journey. Johnston frowned upon Cumming's going into Salt Lake City ahead of the army; he feared that the Governor was not strong enough to withstand the wiles of the Mormons. The officers said openly that Cumming had "compromised the honor of his country by seeking peace on such terms" as they chose to suppose he had.[96] Mrs. Cumming pouted that Johnston had quit calling upon her because he disapproved of her husband's mission to the Mormon capital.[97]

Cumming was heartily received as he entered the Mormon country, and was saluted with parades, bonfires, and "The Star-Spangled Banner." Soon he was in conference with Brigham Young and other

---

[92] Johnston to Kane, March 17, 1858 (copy), *ibid.*

[93] Hammond (ed.), *The Utah Expedition*, p. 135.

[94] "Extracts from the Diary of Major Fitz John Porter," March 20, 1858, Porter Papers.

[95] For Johnston's explanation of the affair, see Johnston to Alfred Cumming, March 17, 1858, Letters Sent, Department of Utah, Records of the War Department. Copies of the official correspondence between Johnston and Cumming are in the Cumming Papers.

[96] Mrs. Cumming to Cumming, April 21, 1858, Cumming Papers.

[97] *Ibid.*

leaders of the Church.[98] The hierarchy acknowledged Cumming as Governor, at least in name; despite the Mormons' hot words over the approach of the Army, Cumming still sought for a peaceful settlement. Ten days after leaving Camp Scott, he was able to inform Johnston that his authority as Governor was now recognized throughout Utah Territory. Then Cumming repeated to Johnston accusations by the Mormons that Indian Agent Garland Hurt had incited the Indians to attack the Mormons; [99] the implication was that Johnston had supported this alleged activity.

Cumming's reference to Johnston's relations with the Indians touched a sore spot. The Mormons had persistently accused Johnston of trying to turn the tribes against them. Johnston vehemently denied this charge; he believed instead that Mormon leaders urged the Indians to steal army livestock and otherwise hinder his advance. Both accusations were partly true; both sides courted the favor of the Indians. Mormon General in Chief Wells told his subordinates, "Instruct the Indians that our enemies are also their enemies & how they [the United States troops] are continually fighting against them somewhere." [100] Johnston contemplated using the Uinta Indians as auxiliaries against the Mormon armed forces, should his advance be resisted in the spring.[101]

Perhaps the mere presence of a threatening army encouraged some Indians to commit violence against the Mormons; during the winter a Mormon missionary post on the Salmon River was raided by Bannock and Snake Indians. But, according to the testimony of all of Johnston's associates, he did not incite the Indians to prey upon the Mormons. Rather, he was said to have advised a number of Indian chiefs who came into camp to remain neutral in the contest between the United States and the Saints.[102] Indian Agent Jacob Forney, though a supporter of Governor Cumming, nevertheless denounced these Mormon charges as "false and slanderous." [103] Johnston encouraged no Indian atrocities against the Mormons.

[98] For descriptions of Cumming's welcome by the Mormons, see David Candland Diary, April 6, 1858; Charles L. Walker Diary, April 25, 1858; Lorenzo Brown Diary, April 7, 1858.

[99] Cumming to Johnston, April 15, May 21, 1858, Cumming Papers.

[100] Wells to Pace, August 13, 1857, Provo Military District Record.

[101] "Extracts from the Diary of Major Fitz John Porter," January 14, 1858, Porter Papers.

[102] B. F. Ficklin to Porter, April 21, 1858 (copy) ; Garland Hurt to Cumming, April 21, 1858 (copy) , both in Johnston Papers, Barret Collection.

[103] J. Forney to Cumming, April 21, 1858 (copy) , *ibid.*

Johnston's heart was not softened by Cumming's message that the Mormons had accepted United States authority. A Mormon army was still in the field, reasoned Johnston; the Mormon press still railed against the United States government and its army and representatives; Mormon leaders still accused the army of inflaming the Indians to rapine and massacre; and the Mormons themselves still importuned the Indians to steal army livestock and burn army trains. Johnston was convinced that the Mormons were insincere in their professions of loyalty and peace. He advised:

> To compromise with these people on any other terms, than an unconditional surrender would in my opinion be unsafe, unwise and impolitic. The Government can make no compromise with treason with safety. . . . These people are bound together by rebellion and polygamy and are governed according to their wish, despotically, except the few who are helpless.[104]

The army shared its commander's antipathy for Cumming's attempts to preserve the peace and was sure the sins of the Mormons must be purged in fire.[105]

Seeing Johnston's determination, and knowing that he surely would march as soon as horses and supplies arrived at Camp Scott, Cumming rightly feared bloodshed. He hastened back to Camp Scott in the hope that he could stay the army's advance. Johnston gave him a cool reception. The two remained aloof from each other in the camp; they communicated only by mail.

Meantime, the Buchanan Administration made other moves toward settling the Mormon imbroglio without combat. In early April Buchanan appointed two commissioners, Lazarus W. Powell and Ben McCulloch, to open talks with Mormon leaders; the commissioners were to offer pardon for "seditions and treasons heretofore committed," provided the Mormons would pledge acceptance of federal authority and obedience to federal officials. The commissioners arrived at Johnston's headquarters at the end of May. Impressed more by Johnston's reasoning than by Cumming's, and doubtless hostile to the Mormons beforehand, the commissioners wrote Secretary of War Floyd that the presence of the army was the chief inducement to Mormon peace and submission.[106]

[104] Johnston to McDowell, April 22, 1858, Letters Sent, Department of Utah, Records of the War Department.
[105] Furniss, *The Mormon Conflict*, pp. 184–186.
[106] *Ibid.*, p. 194.

Three days later the commissioners left for Salt Lake City; Governor Cumming and his wife followed shortly. A series of meetings occurred between the commissioners and the leaders of the Church. Young and his colleagues realized that, having failed to dislodge or starve Johnston's command during the winter, further open resistance would be disastrous. Finally, disguising "their capitulation behind a flood of face-saving rhetoric," the hierarchy accepted Buchanan's terms.[107] On June 12 the commissioners invited Johnston to bring his army into the valley of the Saints.[108]

Even before he heard from the commissioners, Johnston was on the move. In the early days of June he had received word that the long-awaited horses and provisions were almost to Camp Scott;[109] on the fifth he issued orders alerting his command for the advance. Within the next week the expected reinforcements and supplies arrived. Escorted by Colonel W. W. Loring and two hundred troopers, Captain Marcy came into camp from New Mexico with 160 horses and almost 1,000 mules; Lieutenant Colonel William Hoffman brought in a train of 52 wagons of supplies from Fort Laramie; units of the First Cavalry and of the Third, Sixth, and Seventh Infantry joined the Utah army, bringing with them 52 other wagons of provisions. Johnston's force was now amply equipped and almost three thousand strong. On the eleventh a junior officer accurately observed, "The ball is about to open."[110] Two days later the army broke camp and marched for the Mormon valley.

Word of Johnston's move incensed Governor Cumming and the Mormon leaders and caused concern to Commissioners Powell and McCulloch.[111] Johnston had told the Governor and the commissioners before they left Camp Scott that he would not march before hearing from the commissioners. Having interpreted this statement

[107] *Ibid.*, pp. 194–197. The Mormon people were convinced that the United States commissioners had engaged in "face-saving rhetoric." See Hosea Stout Diary, June 16, 1858; Oliver B. Huntington Diary, n.d.; *Deseret News*, June 23, 1859.

[108] "Journal History," June 12, 1858, Church Historian's Office, Salt Lake City.

[109] Johnston to McDowell, June 4, 1858, Letters Sent, Department of Utah, Records of the War Department; "Journal History," June 11, 1858, Church Historian's Office, Salt Lake City.

[110] Hammond (ed.), *The Utah Expedition*, p. 172.

[111] Cumming to Johnston, June 15, 17, 1858, Cumming Papers. Even before Johnston marched, Church leaders were aware of his preparations to move.

as a pledge by Johnston to remain idle until he was invited to advance, Cumming upbraided the General for his action. Johnston replied that he had made the statement believing that the army would be unable to march before the commissioners could reveal to him the outcome of their talks with the Mormons. He had never intended it to bind him to inactivity if it should conflict with sound military judgment, he said, nor did he believe that Cumming and the commissioners had so construed it at the time.[112]

At the time of his agreement with Cumming and the commissioners, Johnston unquestionably believed that he would hear from them before the arrival of fresh mounts and supplies. But when he found himself prepared to move, with still no word from Salt Lake City, he began the march; he was probably convinced that this procedure was in the original understanding. The unexpected move had no effect on the military situation. The Mormons had already decided not to resist, and the United States commissioners had already written Johnston to come into the Valley. But his move, before he had received this message, further embittered relations between Johnston and Cumming, and between Johnston and the Mormons.[113]

The army was in camp on the Bear River two days' march west of Fort Bridger when Johnston received the commissioners' message to come into the Valley. Wishing to allay Mormon fears as much as possible, Buchanan's emissaries asked for a statement reassuring the people that they would not be harmed. Johnston complied with this request.

I . . . feel it incumbent on me, and have great satisfaction in doing so [he proclaimed], to assure those citizens of the Territory who, I learn, apprehend from the army ill-treatment, that no person whatever will be in anywise interfered with or molested in his person or rights, or in the peaceful pursuit of his avocation; and, should protection be needed, that they will find the army (always faithful to the obligations of duty) as ready now to assist and protect them as it was to oppose them while it was believed they were resisting the laws of their Government.[114]

---

[112] Johnston to Cumming, June 19, 1858, **Cumming Papers.**
[113] Young to "Dear Colonel," August 6, 1858, Brigham Young Papers.
[114] Proclamation, June 14, 1858, in *House Executive Document 2, 35th Congress, 2nd Session,* Vol. II, Pt. II, pp. 167–168.

To the commissioners, he wrote that the army would not interfere with the Mormons "if no obstruction is presented to the discharge of [its] duties." But he indicated that he now expected the people of Utah to show "a more just appreciation of their relations to the general government." [115]

Johnston pressed on to his destination. On June 21 his column filed through now unguarded Echo Canyon. The canyon lived up to its name; music of the regimental bands reverberated among the rocks in a fashion beyond anything the soldiers had ever heard. The troops gazed in awe upon "stalwart walls" rising hundreds of feet on either side of the narrow defile, and cut at right angles by innumerable fissures that reached to the floor of the valley. Nature had given the place formidable strength; beyond question, a determined Mormon defense could have exacted heavy toll of any assailant. Having gained the pass without a fight, the campaigners looked with contempt upon abandoned Mormon trenches and hasty fortifications. The marchers were crestfallen, wrote one of them, for having lost during the previous autumn an opportunity to take the position.[116]

Into Salt Lake Valley the army advanced without incident. Halting on June 25, Johnston issued orders for the observance of strict discipline: soldiers were to keep rank meticulously; private property was not to be trespassed upon. At ten o'clock on the morning of the twenty-sixth, riding at the head of his column, Johnston entered the city of the Saints.

Leading his army through the forbidden city must have gratified him, but he found the place virtually deserted. In deciding not to oppose the advance of the army, Church leaders resolved also upon a remarkable accompanying course of action; they determined to lead the entire population of northern Utah into the southern end of the valley until they were convinced of the army's good behavior. Tales had circulated in Salt Lake City of lust and intemperance among the soldiers; they were said to have boasted that all Mormon men would be put to the sword, and that Mormon women would be saved "for [the soldiers'] own vile purpose." If necessary, threatened the Church

---

[115] Johnston to Commissioners, June 14, 1858, Headquarters Book, Department of Utah (copy), Johnston Papers, Barret Collection. Correspondence of the United States commissioners is in Hafen and Hafen (eds.), *The Utah Expedition*, pp. 329–359.

[116] J. Cecil Alter (ed.), *The Utah War: Journal of Albert Tracy*, pp. 22–24.

leaders, the Mormons would make a new exodus and build a new Zion in the Mexican state of Sonora, beyond persecution by American gentiles. "I would rather see this city in ashes," said Brigham Young to his brethren, "than have one good Elder killed." [117]

Protesting, but obedient to their leaders, the people had packed their belongings on carts and abandoned their homes. Throughout the spring they had streamed south to the town of Provo forty miles below Salt Lake City. Young went with them. He arrived in Provo on April 30 with his wives, children, and household goods borne in a caravan of twenty-two wagons. "From the appearance of the family, he had cleared the Lion house," said an observer.[118] Young asked the bishop at Provo to provide him with four houses for the use of his family, but the masses of the people were not so fortunate. Thousands of them lived for months in shanties, tents, and even holes in the ground on a plain adjoining Provo, anxiously awaiting word of the army's conduct and of their leaders' decision for the future. A handful of chosen men remained in Salt Lake City with orders to apply the torch if the army should turn to looting.[119]

Through the dead city Johnston led his army with bands playing and flags flying.[120] Rigid order was preserved; Mormon property was untouched, save for some accidental and unavoidable trampling of fields by army herds.[121] When the column reached Young's residence, the Lion House, the band struck up a ribald camp song named "One-Eyed Riley." [122] On this incongruous note Johnston rode through Salt Lake City and pitched camp beyond the Jordan River on the west. It was a queer triumphal march.

[117] "Journal History," December 7, 1857; March 21, 1858, Church Historian's Office, Salt Lake City.

[118] *Ibid.*, April 30, 1858.

[119] For Mormon accounts of the exodus, see William M. Egan Journal, n.d.; George Morris, "Autobiography," pp. 83, 84; John Clark Dowdle Diary, n.d.; Esaias Edwards Diary, August 8, 1858; Hannah Hood Hill Romney, "Autobiography"; Azariah Smith Journal; Allen Joseph Stout Journal; Silas Haris, "A Sketch of Silas Haris' Life"; John Langston, "History of John Langston"; Orvill S. Cox Diary; Edwin Harley Diary, March 28, 1858; Henry W. Bigler Journal, April 24, 1858; Nancy N. Tracy, "Narrative"; Jane Richards, "Reminiscences"; Franklin D. Richards, "Narrative"; Mary Horne, "Migration and Settlement of the Latter-Day Saints"; Mrs. Hubert H. Bancroft, "Utah Notes."

[120] Johnston to Assistant Adjutant General, June 27, 1858, Letters Sent, Department of Utah, Records of the War Department.

[121] Young to "Dear Colonel," August 6, 1858, Young Papers.

[122] Alter (ed.), *The Utah War: Journal of Albert Tracy*, p. 27.

Military Occupation and
Latter-Day Theocracy

~~~~~~

J OHNSTON RODE OUT of Salt Lake City to begin one of history's most unusual military occupations. Since the Mormons offered no overt resistance either to the new territorial officials or to the Army, his primary duty was to stand by on call. Leaving the troops encamped across the Jordan River from Salt Lake City, he, with a small group of officers, reconnoitered the surrounding countryside in search of a permanent camp site.[1] He sought a place with sufficient water for his thousands of men and animals, and with enough grass for his numerous mounts and herds. To prevent the occurrence of incidents and provocations between troops and citizens, he wisely desired to establish base as far as possible from the centers of Mormon population.[2] Captain Van Vliet had been instructed by the War Department the previous

---

[1] Mathis, "Camp Floyd in Retrospect" (Master's thesis) , pp. 28–36.
[2] Johnston to Alfred Cumming, June 19, 1858; Johnston to Irvin McDowell, July 8, 1858, Letters Sent, Department of Utah, Records of the War Department.

summer to look for such a location; [3] and Commissioners Powell and McCulloch had assured Mormon leaders that the Army would not trespass upon their cities.[4] Yet Johnston must be in position to move troops quickly to any point in the valley, should their presence be required.

For a permanent camp, he selected a site in Cedar Valley about thirty-five miles southwest of Salt Lake City. Wishing to avoid irritating brushes between the Army and the population, most of whom were still encamped at Provo, Johnston delayed marching south until the Mormons had been given opportunity to return to their homes. When by July 6 they had not done so, Johnston began his move to Cedar Valley. His hope of preventing contact with the Mormons was now dashed; the Army met refugees by thousands trudging north to Salt Lake City and the upper valley.[5] Fortunately no clashes occurred. The Mormons regarded the soldiers with sullen dislike; the soldiers looked upon the Mormons with mingled contempt and pity. Johnston ordered that the Mormons be treated with civility and that they be given the windward side of the road to protect them from the dust.[6]

After camping for a few days in the mouth of West Canyon, where water was scarce and dust intolerable, Johnston in early July marched his army to the village of Fairfield near the western edge of Cedar Valley. Across a small stream from this community, he established his permanent station, which he named Camp Floyd in honor of the Secretary of War.[7]

Some of Johnston's subordinate officers sharply criticized his choice of a camp site.[8] Colonel Cooke, who already had entered into an altercation with Johnston regarding the duties of the dragoons, later said that Johnston had apparently looked for "the most complete desert" in which to locate his army.[9] This was carping.

---

[3] A. Pleasanton to Stewart Van Vliet, July 28, 1857, *ibid.*

[4] Lazarus W. Powell and Ben McCulloch, "Notes on Conference," June 12, 1858 (copy), Johnston Papers, Barret Collection.

[5] *New York Daily Tribune*, August 13, 1858; *New York Times*, August 13, 1858.

[6] J. W. Phelps to "Dear Levine," July 7, 1858, Phelps Papers; *Senate Executive Document No. 11, 35th Congress, 1st Session*, Vol. III, pp. 27–28.

[7] Mathis, "Camp Floyd in Retrospect" (Master's thesis), pp. 28–36.

[8] Alter (ed.), *The Utah War: Journal of Albert Tracy*, pp. 70–71.

[9] Rodenbough (ed.), *From Everglade to Cañon with the Second Dragoons*, p. 192.

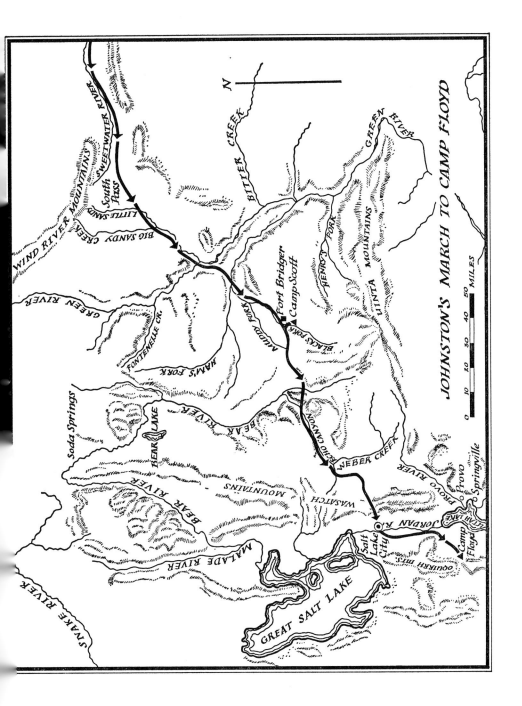

JOHNSTON'S MARCH TO CAMP FLOYD

Aside from areas irrigated by Mormon-built canals, and occupied by the civilian population, the Salt Lake basin had no wholly desirable sites for so sizeable a body of troops. Lying at the base of the cedar-girt Oquirrh Mountains, bordered by a running stream, and surrounded by grassland, the site of Camp Floyd provided the essentials of water, wood, and forage. Almost equidistant from Salt Lake City and Provo, but forming a triangle with them, and flanking the route to Fillmore City in southern Utah, Camp Floyd was so situated that in an emergency Johnston could interdict Mormon communications or dispatch troops easily to any major community in the Territory. The place had shortcomings; Johnston himself was never happy with it. But it seems to have been as good as any other in the basin would have been.[10]

Determined that his command should not spend another winter in tents, Johnston at once set about getting huts constructed for living quarters at Camp Floyd. Much of the building was done by the soldiers themselves, but most of the materials were acquired from their erstwhile enemies, the Mormons. Reassured by Johnston's firm discipline, and lured by the promise of handsome profits, Church leaders cooperated in building the camp. Since Congress had not then authorized the establishment of such quarters, Johnston assumed the responsibility of using Army funds for this purpose. He did so with reluctance. Yet he would not shrink from it, he said. "As I do not one thing which my conscience does not approve as beneficial to my country, I shall always be without fear & as I hope without reproach." [11]

Soon hundreds of Mormon workmen were busy making adobes (crude clay bricks), and Brigham Young's sawmills were supplying the camp with lumber from the mountains.[12] Many months were required to finish the construction, but eventually Camp Floyd was a neat military cantonment of almost four hundred adobe huts, each housing a group of six or eight soldiers. Besides the huts, there were

[10] Johnston to McDowell, July 8, 22, 1858, Letters Sent, Department of Utah, Records of the War Department.

[11] Johnston to William Preston Johnston, September 23, 1858, Johnston Papers, Barret Collection. For additional information on the building of Camp Floyd, see Johnston to McDowell, July 8, 28, 1858, Letters Sent, Department of Utah, Records of the War Department; and *Valley Tan* (Salt Lake City), November 5, 1858.

[12] *New York Daily Tribune*, August 27, 1859.

extensive warehouses, headquarters buildings, mess halls, smithies, and stables.[13] While construction was in progress, and afterward, the soldiers freely purchased fruit and vegetables from the Mormons, and hired them as blacksmiths and craftsmen. Instead of destroying the Mormons, the Army vastly enhanced their prosperity with its trade.[14] "The army is still quietly concentrated in Camp Floyd," observed Brigham Young in November, "obviously more to the benefit and gratification of the people of Utah than to itself or the public at large."[15] One of Johnston's officers deplored what he looked upon as Mormon profiteering. "Mormonism is a monstrous cross between Religion and Mamon," he wrote; "between New England Puritanism and New England tact, cunning and shrewdness in money getting."[16] The irony of this situation doubtless was not lost on Johnston, but his main concern was not with such quirks of providence. He needed comfortable quarters for his men; he got them the best way he could.

On November 9 Camp Floyd was formally dedicated with a grand review and flag raising. At twelve o'clock noon, before the entire army assembled in formation, a 40-foot United States flag was run up a 100-foot flagstaff which had been prepared from a mountain pine, the regimental bands struck up "Hail Columbia," a thirty-two-gun salute of artillery was fired, and the entire command, "led by their gallant General," greeted the flag with three hearty cheers.[17]

Johnston's command slowly increased in numbers; by fall of 1858 he had about 2,900 men at Camp Floyd, and another 400 at Fort Bridger building roads and guarding communications with the east.[18] He did everything in his power to keep the army fit and in high morale. Drill, tactical exercises, reviews, and parades all went on regularly. With Johnston's encouragement, the soldiers organized a camp theater (starring Mormon actresses brought from Salt Lake City), a chapter of the Masonic Lodge, a circus, and a singing club.[19] From time to time the General joined his officers and their wives in

[13] Mathis, "Camp Floyd in Retrospect" (Master's thesis), pp. 39–40.

[14] Arrington, *Great Basin Kingdom*, pp. 196–199.

[15] Brigham Young to W. H. Hooper, November 17, 1859, Young Papers.

[16] Phelps to "Dear Levine," April 13, 1859, Phelps Papers.

[17] *New York Times*, December 15, 1858. For other accounts of the flag raising, see Phelps to "My Dear Lily," November 9, 1858, Phelps Papers; *Valley Tan*, November 12, 1858; and *Deseret News*, November 10, 1858.

[18] Furniss, *The Mormon Conflict*, pp. 205–206.

[19] Mathis, "Camp Floyd in Retrospect" (Master's thesis), pp. 46–54.

attending concerts and plays in the camp theater.[20] On special occasions each man was issued a gill of whiskey from the commissary stores; invariably some of them became intoxicated.[21]

Johnston's numerous measures to uphold the spirits of his men had good effect, but no human power could completely relieve the awful loneliness and boredom of such a station. The campaigners were thousands of miles away from home, they lacked a positive mission to claim their enthusiasm and energies, and they were surrounded by a hostile civilian population. Moreover, though Camp Floyd offered shelter and sustenance, it was a forlorn place.[22] In winter it froze in temperatures that fell below zero. In summer it parched under the glaring sun and lay enveloped in clouds of dust that rose a mile toward the sky. With bitter humor, the soldiers named these dust storms "Johnsoons" in honor of their commander for selecting such a camp site.[23] Such conditions taxed Johnston himself almost beyond control. "This is the most sterile & worthless country I have ever seen or imagined," he damned it.[24]

Small wonder that many of the soldiers sought escape in diversions outside of camp. A few minutes only were required to find lustier amusements than those of Camp Floyd's Military Dramatic Association or the Germania Singing Club. Just across the creek from camp, the village of Fairfield (renamed Frogtown, or Dobietown) quickly grew into a raucous community of 3,000 people. Its residents were largely gentile camp followers of one sort or another, plus a sprinkling of Mormons who had a taste for such company. Frogtown offered a wide variety of entertainments—gambling of many forms, saloons serving a potent whiskey, called Valley Tan, made of a combination of wheat alcohol and tobacco, and women of easy virtue.[25]

---

[20] Johnston to Henrietta Johnston, February 15, 1860, Johnston Papers, Barret Collection. Other descriptions of the Camp Floyd theater are in F. Frank to Johnston, September 3, 1859, *ibid.*; and the *Valley Tan*, December 10, 1858; July 13, December 7, 1859.

[21] Journal, Phelps Papers, December 25, 1858.

[22] Johnston to Henrietta Johnston, August 15, 1859, Johnston Papers, Barret Collection.

[23] Alter (ed.), *The Utah War: Journal of Albert Tracy*, p. 68.

[24] Johnston to William Preston Johnston, August 5, 1859, Johnston Papers, Barret Collection.

[25] For descriptions of Frogtown, see the *Valley Tan*, March 1, December 7, 1859; Journal, Phelps Papers, June 8, 15, 17, 1859; Mathis, "Camp Floyd in Retrospect" (Master's thesis), pp. 58–60; Anderson, *Desert Saints*, pp. 193, 209–210.

Johnston required passes for leaving camp, he patrolled the adjacent community with provost sergeants,[26] and a group of the more sober men of the command formed a chapter of the Sons of Temperance to combat the evils of drink.[27] But the fleshpots of Frogtown mocked all efforts to impose sobriety and continence upon men who lived in misery; soldiers crossed the creek at every opportunity.

Johnston left no record of his personal attitude toward affairs in Frogtown; his own conduct would indicate an abhorrence of such intemperance and vice. Since the town was a civilian community beyond camp limits he had no jurisdiction over it. Apparently he made no effort to bar soldiers altogether from visiting there, though by requiring passes he did restrict the number of troops in Frogtown at any one time. He could not very well keep the entire command in camp all the time, and Mormon antipathy made life anywhere else in Utah uncomfortable, if not dangerous, for the soldiers. But Frogtown was a primary source of difficulty for Johnston. Shootings, knifings, and beatings were commonplace there. The registry of trials by courts-martial in the Department of Utah during Johnston's command records hundreds of cases. Charges ranged in seriousness from murder to such trivialities as impertinence to an officer. Many of the cases arose out of Frogtown brawls, which claimed the lives of a number of soldiers who are buried in the Camp Floyd cemetery.[28]

Yet, considering the nature of service in Utah, Johnston kept his troops remarkably well disciplined and cheerful. He considered his men to be of high intelligence and acceptable decorum.[29] When he left Utah, he could sincerely commend them for "a lasting respect for discipline" under trying circumstances.[30]

True to the promise that he had made in his proclamation before entering Salt Lake Valley, Johnston exercised firm control over his command in the protection of citizens and their property. When the enlistment terms of the volunteer battalion expired, Johnston ordered most of the men back to Fort Leavenworth for discharge, lest they cause strife in Utah. No one was mustered out in Utah who

---

[26] General Order, January 24, 1860 (copy), Order Book, Department of Utah, Johnston Papers, Barret Collection.

[27] Mathis, "Camp Floyd in Retrospect" (Master's thesis), p. 60.

[28] Registry of Trials by Garrison and Regimental Courts-Martial, Department of Utah, Adjutant General's Office, Records of the War Department.

[29] Johnston, *Life of Johnston*, pp. 242–243.

[30] General Order, February 29, 1860 (copy), Order Book, Department of Utah, Johnston Papers, Barret Collection.

could not give proof of immediate and steady employment, or show that he intended to go at once to California.[31]

Even the Mormons admitted their respect for Johnston and agreed that the army, in general, conducted itself with propriety.[32] A Church newspaper, the *Millennial Star,* editorialized in rare tribute from the Mormon camp:

> Against the Army we have no ill feeling nor prejudice. The Army of Utah is as well and gallantly commanded and officered and efficiently disciplined as it is superiorly equipped and generously sustained. . . . They appear to respect the feelings of the citizens and content themselves with their garrison limits. The compliments to their discipline and good behavior are all well deserved.[33]

Johnston's rigid protection of Mormon life and property belied his feelings toward Mormon ways—a loathing which increased with time and proximity. The presence of territorial officials and federal troops had in no manner abated Mormon offenses against republican institutions, he observed. Theocracy still prevailed; the people still obeyed the orders of the hierarchy; juries still rendered verdicts according to Church instructions. "Where is the remedy?" Johnston insisted, "There is none." Only federal legislation could right these wrongs, he declared. "Are the Mormons right in their endeavor to establish a local theocratic Government within our Union. If so sustain them—If not pass a law for its abrogation & cause it to be carried into effect." [34]

Johnston admitted that, in the absence of federal laws against Mormon institutions, the Army had no right to interfere with local practices. But he yearned to see Church leaders brought to justice for past crimes he believed them guilty of committing. In the spring of 1859 an opportunity arose for him to assist in settling some of these accounts.

---

[31] Johnston to McDowell, July 8, 1858 (copy), Headquarters Book, Department of Utah, 1858, Johnston Papers, Barret Collection.

[32] Mormon expressions of respect for Johnston are in John Taylor to George Q. Cannon, January 12, 1859 (copy), "Journal History," Church Historian's Office, Salt Lake City; Young to Thomas L. Kane, November 22, 1858; Young to Hooper, November 1, 1859, both in Young Papers; *Deseret News,* October 13, 1858.

[33] Quoted in Allen, "A Study of the Alleged Mormon Rebellion" (Master's thesis), p. 192.

[34] Johnston to William Preston Johnston, September 1, 1858, Johnston Papers, Barret Collection.

Scorning Governor Cumming's policy of conciliation, the territorial judges had set about to investigate charges against the Mormons and to bring them to trial where the evidence suggested guilt. Impaneling a grand jury in Salt Lake City, Associate Justice Sinclair began to consider allegations ranging all the way from destruction of a lawyer's library in a privy fire to treason by Church leaders. Meanwhile, Associate Justice Cradlebaugh prepared to open court in Provo and to begin a probe of the circumstances surrounding the fatal shooting the preceding spring of a Mormon apostate and his son and a companion—the Parrish-Potter murders. Two days before proceedings were to start, Cradlebaugh asked Johnston for a detachment of soldiers to guard prisoners who were to be arrested. Such a provision was necessary, said the judge, because there was no jail in which prisoners could be housed in Provo.[35] Johnston at once ordered Captain Henry Heth, with his company, to Provo to carry out Cradlebaugh's assigned purpose.

The Mormons accused Johnston and Cradlebaugh of conspiring to destroy them.[36] Johnston unquestionably applauded Cradlebaugh's efforts to render judgment upon the Mormons and may have welcomed making a demonstration of force in support of these efforts. He could not rightly refuse Cradlebaugh's requisition, for Johnston's orders from General Scott were to provide troops upon the call of the governor, the judges, or the federal marshals.[37] Notwithstanding his personal views, Johnston entered into no conspiracy to destroy the Mormons. He demonstrated his restraint with respect to them shortly when a group of Mormons at Springville, near Provo, petitioned him for protection against Church tyranny. Though formally acquiescing in the civil law, said the petitioners, Church leaders actually continued to enforce despotic ecclesiastical law upon the people. Johnston believed this to be true.

All is smooth on the surface [he wrote his superiors], but I fear there is an undertow that sweeps away every principle of liberty and the basis of our own code of morals.

[35] John Cradlebaugh to Fitz John Porter, March 6, 1859 (copy), *ibid.*

[36] Mormon sentiments are given in Daniel Wells, "Narrative," Bancroft Library; George W. Bean, *Autobiography of George Washington Bean*, p. 136; and Young to Kane, November 22, 1859, Young Papers.

[37] Johnston was to follow the orders previously issued to General Harney. See George W. Lay to W. S. Harney, June 29, 1857 (copy), Johnston Papers, Barret Collection; also *House Executive Document, 35th Congress, 1st Session*, Vol. X, p. 79.

Reluctantly, Johnston withheld troops from Springville, saying:

However intolerable [the tyranny] may be, and however much it may excite
our sympathy, the military arm cannot . . . without a much more dangerous
violation of law than that of which they complain, be interposed.

Johnston curbed his own desire to employ force directly against the
Church; instead, he meticulously observed the limits of his military
authority.[38]

Heth moved to Provo in early March and established his command
next to the building in which Cradlebaugh had opened court. Johnston had instructed Heth to preserve strict decorum among his
troops and to perform no service except to guard the prisoners. At
first the citizens were not excessively alarmed. Two days after his
arrival, Heth reported the town quiet and assured Johnston that
every precaution would be taken not to give offense to the inhabitants. Nevertheless, tension mounted as Cradlebaugh proceeded with
his investigation. On March 11, complaining of "military occupation" and the intimidation of citizens, Mayor B. K. Bullock and the
town council petitioned Cradlebaugh to remove the troops. He
refused to do so.[39]

A week later, acting under Cradlebaugh's instructions, United
States Marshal Peter Dotson arrested Mayor Bullock himself, along
with two others, for implication in the murders the year before. The
town was inflamed. "Missouri, Carthage, and Nauvoo are still fresh
in [Mormon] minds," wrote a Mormon, "and with a mob court held
without authority of law backed up by the army of the United States
. . . [they] feel like preparing for the worst." [40]

Parties of armed Mormons began to pour into Provo. Heth informed Johnston that he could hold his position against attack, but
the junior officer obviously was growing nervous.[41] The next day
Johnston ordered Major Gabriel R. Paul, with eight companies of
the Seventh Infantry, a battery of artillery, and a squadron of cavalry, to march to the vicinity of Provo in order to relieve Heth's
command if it should be assailed. Major Paul was to enter the town
only if Heth should call for aid. Moreover, cautioned Johnston,

[38] Johnston to Lorenzo Thomas, March 10, 1859, Letters Sent, Department of
Utah, Records of the War Department.
[39] Furniss, *The Mormon Conflict, 1850–1859*, p. 215.
[40] Elias Smith Journal, March 23, 1859.
[41] Henry Heth to "Sir," March 18, 1859, Johnston Papers, Barret Collection.

"You will be careful not to permit your command to interfere with the rights of the citizens, and, on no pretense whatever will you make an attack upon any body of citizens except in sheer self defence."[42] Major Paul marched at once; despite the restrictions of his orders, hostilities between troops and Mormons threatened.

Johnston did not bother to inform Governor Cumming of the use of troops at Provo. He considered it unnecessary to do so; certainly his orders did not oblige him to do so. Yet it was unfortunate and injudicious that he failed to confer with the chief executive before taking a step that was sure to throw the civilian population of the territory into panic and rage. Relations between Johnston and Cumming remained cool during the entire period of occupation; Johnston looked upon Cumming as a toady to the Mormons. Probably because he anticipated opposition by Cumming to the employment of troops at Provo, he refused to notify the Governor of the plan.

When Cumming learned of conditions in Provo, he hastened there. Convinced by his own investigation that the troops ought to be withdrawn, he requested Johnston to order them back to Camp Floyd.[43] Replying that Judge Cradlebaugh needed soldiers to guard the prisoners, and that Johnston's own orders required him to send troops upon the call of a federal judge, Johnston refused to recall the troops. He loftily wrote Cumming:

I am under no obligation whatever to conform to your suggestions with regard to the military disposition of the troops in this department, except only when it may be expedient to employ them in their civil capacity as a posse; in which case, should the emergency arise, your requisition for any portion of the troops under my command will be complied with.[44]

Cumming responded by publishing a proclamation saying that the presence of the troops tended to terrify citizens, subvert justice, and intimidate witnesses, and ending with a formal protest against the use of troops without his approval.[45]

[42] Porter to G. R. Paul, March 19, 22, 1859, Letters Sent, Department of Utah, Records of the War Department.

[43] Cumming to Johnston, March 20, 1859 (copy), Cumming Papers.

[44] Johnston to Cumming, March 22, 1859, Letters Sent, Department of Utah, Records of the War Department.

[45] Cumming, Proclamation, March 27, 1859 (copy), Johnston Papers, Barret Collection. For other accounts of this imbroglio, see *Senate Executive Document 2, 36th Congress, 1st Session*, Vol. II, pp. 149, 151–152; Walker Diary, March 22, 1859; Brown Diary, April 9, 1859; *Valley Tan*, March 15, 24, April 5, 12, 1859.

Impasse at Provo kindled to new heights Johnston's antipathy for Mormon ways, and his contempt for any compromise with them.

Judging from the tone of administration papers [he complained to his son], our government is about to or rather has yielded to the people of this territory the right to establish a priestly autocracy & their vile polygamous institution. . . . The Mormons have not changed; the theocracy is the same, sustained by the same bloody code as before. . . . There is no more recognition & enforcement of the civil law than there was before.

The United States government had appointed three able and honest men (the federal judges) to administer justice, said Johnston, but under the circumstances they had been unable to do so. "Cradlebaugh from Ohio seems to be a noble fellow; [he] is now making every effort to bring criminals to justice, but he will fail." Crimes of the most monstrous nature, including the Mountain Meadows Massacre, had been committed with Church sanction, believed Johnston; justice could not be rendered without military protection of the courts.[46]

Johnston disavowed any feeling of vindictiveness against the Mormon people. Their mores presented legal and social problems of the deepest gravity, he observed; to solve them demanded the best ability of the nation, "aided by the wisdom of experience to determine it." Yet the problem could not be ignored. An ecclesiastical despotism was in the midst of the republic, he felt; to tolerate it would be to create a government within a government.

This cannot be—How then can the change be made without violence, without perhaps cruelty. Yet we must make their government and social organisation conform to ours and it is also our solemn duty to do this tenderly & without vindictiveness; yet it is a duty to be performed and cannot be avoided.[47]

Federal military and civil authorities in Utah were now in open discord. Rumors were abroad that Johnston planned to seize Salt Lake City and to order an artillery bombardment on Provo. Emboldened by Cumming's proclamation, the Mormons redoubled their preparations to resist. Heth's sentries were stoned one night, but not again after he sternly threatened to open fire if the deed was re-

[46] Johnston to William Preston Johnston, March 31, 1859, Johnston Papers, Barret Collection.
[47] *Ibid.*, April 14, 1859.

peated.[48] Amid the agitation, Judge Cradlebaugh finally saw the futility of attempting to indict his prisoners. Mormon witnesses either fled or refused to talk; Mormon grand jurors refused to act. On April 2, Cradlebaugh adjourned court in defeat and disgust. The troops left for Camp Floyd, taking their prisoners with them.[49]

Mormon jeers and catcalls followed the column as it marched out of Provo. Cheers greeted it at Fairfield and Camp Floyd, where the soldiers waited in great excitement. "It is by no means improbable, that, without the strict discipline in which they were held, they would have seized, and lynched the Mormon prisoners on the spot," reported a member of the Provo detachment.[50]

Even as tempers flared over the employment of troops at Provo, another incident occurred to embitter the army and the Mormons against each other. On March 23 a fight took place between a soldier and a citizen of Utah. The affray grew out of an order by Johnston that the Mormon be evicted from an Army grazing reserve in Rush Valley.

Upon establishing Camp Floyd, Johnston had set aside a number of areas in the national domain, including Rush Valley, for the use of government herds. In taking this action, he seems to have observed as carefully as possible the needs of the inhabitants; when in the fall of 1858 he received complaints that government herds were encroaching upon grazing grounds of the citizens of Nephi City, he ordered the government herds removed.[51] When Governor Cumming asked permission for a prominent Mormon, Daniel Spencer, to leave his cattle in Rush Valley until the following spring, Johnston honored the request.[52] Upon learning in March, 1859, however, that Spencer's place was being used to sell whiskey to the soldiers, Johnston ordered Spencer ousted at once. When a detachment of troops sought to carry out the General's orders, Spencer's nephew, Howard Spencer, resisted and threatened Sergeant Ralph Pike with a pitch-

---

[48] Heth to Porter, March 27, 1859 (copy), Johnston Papers, Barret Collection.

[49] Furniss, *The Mormon Conflict*, pp. 216–217. Other descriptions of the Provo crisis are in the *Valley Tan*, April 5, 12, 1859; Brown Diary, April 9, 1859; Edwards Diary, October 9, 1859.

[50] Alter (ed.), *The Utah War: Journal of Albert Tracy*, pp. 65–67. See also Journal, Phelps Papers, April 5, 1859.

[51] Porter to Henry Little, November 28, 1858 (copy), Adjutant General's Book, Department of Utah, Johnston Papers, Barret Collection.

[52] Daniel Spencer to Johnston, March 31, 1859 (copy), Porter Papers.

fork; Pike then struck Spencer a near-fatal blow on the head with his rifle.[53] At least this is the way Johnston believed the affair took place. To the Mormons it was an instance of wanton brutality upon an innocent citizen.

When he had recovered from the blow, young Spencer brought charges in the United States District Court against Sergeant Pike for assault with intent to commit murder. Johnston sent Pike under Marshal Dotson, and accompanied by a small military escort, to Salt Lake City to stand trial. There, on August 11, while walking down the street under custody of Marshal Dotson, Pike was shot from behind by an assailant who quickly escaped into the surrounding crowd of Mormons. Pike said the man who fired the shot was Spencer; a few hours later Pike died.[54]

The murder of Sergeant Pike kindled an almost irrepressible rage among the soldiers at Camp Floyd. With the greatest difficulty Johnston held them in check. By assigning special guards, he prevented all violence except for a single raid in which some Mormon property was destroyed by a group of Pike's comrades in the nearby village of Cedar Fort.[55] Pike's body was returned to Camp Floyd and buried with military honors. Johnston, with the entire command, attended the funeral. Pike's bitter epitaph read:

Ralph Pike . . . fell the victim of Mormon assassination in Great Salt Lake City in open day, having gone there in obedience to the mandate of the civil authorities.[56]

A junior officer reflected the feeling of the whole army when he wrote, "The feeling left upon the minds of all has struck deep." [57]

Johnston's imbroglio with Governor Cumming over the Provo affair obliged the Buchanan Administration to issue explicit instructions regarding the authority to use troops in Utah. Both Johnston

[53] Johnston to Cumming, March 26, 1859, Letters Sent, Department of Utah, Records of the War Department.

[54] Porter to Johnston, August 15, 1859 (copy), Adjutant General's Book, Department of Utah, Johnston Papers, Barret Collection.

[55] These soldiers were tried, convicted, and punished. See General Order No. 2, January 24, 1860, Order Book, Department of Utah, Johnston Papers, Barret Collection.

[56] "Journal History," August 17, 1859, Church Historian's Office, Salt Lake City.

[57] Alter (ed.), *The Utah War: Journal of Albert Tracy*, pp. 73–74. For Mormon accounts of the shooting of Sergeant Pike, see Brown Journal, August 15, 1859; Stout Diary, August 11, 1859.

and Cumming had asked for clarification. Urging support of the judges, Johnston lectured his superiors on the misdeeds of the Mormons. He reminded them of

the horrible crimes which have been perpetrated in this territory, crimes of a magnitude and of an apparently studied refinement in atrocity, hardly to be conceived of, and which have gone unwhipped of justice—These if the judges are sustained they will endeavor to bring to light. . . . The Mormon polity and their social organization . . . are anomalies which our government . . . will correct. . . . If I err in presenting these views, not strictly within the scope of my duty, it is because I fear to err more by neglecting to present them, because in my opinion the question of Mormonism is one which involves the integrity of our country, and the morality of a great nation.[58]

Johnston believed the Mormons guilty of a multitude of atrocities; he was convinced that a test of strength was required to settle whether federal authority or local autonomy was supreme in Utah; he was prepared to back up the judges with whatever force the situation demanded.

To Johnston's dismay, the Buchanan Administration supported Cumming, not the judges. Conciliation was the chief quality of President Buchanan's nature; as he would shun a resort to arms in the secession crisis two years later, so now he shunned coercion of the Mormons. Plagued by the aftermath of the Panic of 1857, by the heavy expense of the Utah expedition, and by fierce opposition in Congress, he decided not to run the risk of provoking hostilities.

On May 6 Secretary of War Floyd, much against his own wishes, issued to Johnston new instructions in keeping with a decision taken by the President and his Cabinet a few days before. Since peace was now restored to Utah, said Floyd, the judiciary no longer required military assistance. Services of the troops were unnecessary, except to aid the governor in executing the laws. Only upon written application of the governor for the use of troops as a *posse comitatus* was Johnston to employ his command to keep domestic peace. "The fidelity with which you have obeyed the instructions of this Department heretofore given you," said Floyd in conclusion, "is the fullest guarantee that you will with the same zeal and efficiency conform to these."[59]

Floyd was right in assuming that Johnston would obey orders.

[58] Johnston to Thomas, March 31, 1859, Letters Sent, Department of Utah, Records of the War Department.

[59] John B. Floyd to Johnston, May 6, 1859, Johnston Papers, Barret Collection.

Thereafter he refused all calls for troops, except requisitions by Governor Cumming. But Johnston never wavered in his conviction of Mormon guilt, or in his belief that ultimately the United States government would be obliged to adopt stern measures to bring the Saints under federal authority. The changed instructions were wise, he wrote his son, in view of the premises assumed by the Secretary of War. He warned, however:

But these are not the law abiding people the administration believes them to be, and [Floyd] will find that henceforward the law here is a nullity. ... I have conscientiously discharged my duty in sustaining the judiciary, and the people will applaud me for it, for the time is not far away when they will know the utter incompatibility of the concurrent existence of Mormon institutions and those our own people are pledged by every obligation of duty & honor to establish & cherish in every part of our broad territory.[60]

Johnston's altered instructions from the War Department stayed his rod of punishment against the Mormons. He would remain in command of the Utah army for almost another year—a year of loathing for Mormon customs and of disdain for Governor Cumming. Training, drill, and reviews went on with regularity on the dust-shrouded plain of Cedar Valley; brawls and carousals in Frogtown continued to give numerous troops a measure of relief from the maddening ennui of life in Camp Floyd. "Why were we sent here?" was the question on every tongue. "A fettered, suspected, watched, distrusted Army—an Army which must do nothing—must not even be asked to do anything. ... Why, then, not withdraw it?"[61]

Johnston himself never visited Salt Lake City; he seems never to have gone far from the limits of Camp Floyd. According to Mormon folklore, he often sat before the door of his quarters, smoking his pipe in silence and contemplation. He repeatedly asked in vain to be relieved of the Utah command and returned to his regiment in Texas. Yet the Utah army kept smart and fit; Mormon prisoners at Camp Floyd said the troops there were the best-disciplined soldiers they had ever seen. That this could be true, under the circumstances, was high tribute to Johnston's character and leadership.[62]

[60] Johnston to William Preston Johnston, June 10, 1859, *ibid.*
[61] *New York Daily Tribune*, August 27, 1859.
[62] "Journal History," April 19, 1859, Church Historian's Office, Salt Lake City.

Duties other than guarding Mormons claimed some of Johnston's attention in Utah. He and his army rendered notable service in western pathfinding and in protecting emigrant wagon trains from the Indians. Through Johnston's orders, detachments of the Utah force explored and opened new and easier routes into the Salt Lake basin from the east, and beyond the basin to the Pacific coast.[63] Captain Marcy's expedition from Fort Bridger to New Mexico and back, B. F. Ficklin's journey to the Snake River valley, construction of a supply road from Fort Bridger to Camp Floyd by way of the Provo River valley, and the explorations by Captain James H. Simpson of a shorter route to California by way of Hasting's Pass in the Humboldt Mountains and then Carson Valley—these were major achievements in trail blazing.[64] Of Captain Simpson's work alone, a careful student of the Utah expedition has said, "It would have been enough if the Army for Utah had accomplished nothing more than this one reconnaissance." [65] Western roads laid out under Johnston's directives have served generations of Americans from the day of the ox wagon and stage coach through that of the diesel locomotive and family automobile.

With a strong force in Utah, the United States Army was for the first time in position to give to the California and Oregon emigrant trains adequate protection against the Indians. Johnston cheerfully undertook this task, for he had long felt it a service owed the settlers by the government. He repeatedly dispatched dragoons to escort caravans through Indian territory; seeking to anticipate attacks upon the trains, he temporarily stationed garrisons on the Humboldt River and at other points considered dangerous along the route.[66]

---

[63] *Senate Executive Document No. 1, 35th Congress, 2nd Session,* Vol. I, pp. 203–206; *House Executive Document, No. 2, 35th Congress, 2nd Session,* Vol. II, pp. 1301–1302.

[64] James H. Simpson, *Report of Explorations across the Great Basin of the Territory of Utah,* pp. 44–148 and map following p. 495.

[65] Mathis, "Camp Floyd in Retrospect" (Master's thesis), p. 99. Other descriptions of Johnston's role in pathfinding are Johnston, *Life of Johnston,* p. 241; and the *Valley Tan,* July 6, 1859.

[66] For Johnston's orders and reports concerning his precautions against the Indians, see Johnston to McDowell, October 12, 1858; and Johnston to Thomas, November 2, 1859, both in Letters Sent, Department of Utah, Records of the War Department; Porter to Lt. Col. Morrison, October 5, 1858; Porter to "Officers in command on Sevier River," November 11, 1858; and Porter to Isaac Lynde, June 5, 1859 (copies), Adjutant General's Book, Department of Utah, Johnston Papers, Barret Collection.

When in August of 1859 Governor Cumming requisitioned soldiers to punish marauding Indians along the northern trail to California, Johnston curtly and with petty legalism replied that his new instructions forbade him to answer the Governor's call except for the use of troops as a *posse comitatus*. Nevertheless, on his own authority, Johnston at once ordered out a punitive expedition against the guilty Indians.[67] He did so, he explained to Cumming, not in compliance with the Governor's requisition, but because of the information that Cumming had supplied regarding Indian misdeeds, ". . . as [I] would do should the like information come from any source entitled to credit." [68] Johnston did all within his power to make safe the paths of westward migration.

Still other services occupied Johnston's time in Utah. To his hands came inquiries, sometimes from foreign lands, concerning persons said to have been abducted by the Mormons, and requests for assistance in returning these persons to their homes. He passed all such matters on to the proper civil officials in the Territory.[69] One exceptionally sad duty befell him. In the summer of 1859 he received from Indian Agent Forney the eighteen young children who had survived the Mountain Meadows Massacre of two years before. Johnston arranged for matrons to care for the orphans and provided ambulances to carry them back to the east, with an escort of dragoons for their protection.[70]

Life in Utah stimulated Johnston's abiding interest in the mysteries of nature. At Fort Bridger he had supported the investigations of an ornithologist who accompanied one of the wagon trains in search of information on the birds of the area.[71] From Camp Floyd, Johnston now sent collections of rare fossils to the Academy of Natural Sciences in Philadelphia.[72]

[67] Special Order No. 65, August 5, 1859 (copy), Order Book, Department of Utah, Johnston Papers, Barret Collection.

[68] Johnston to Cumming, August 5, 1859, Letters Sent, Department of Utah, Records of the War Department.

[69] Johnston to J. I. McCormic, July 27, August 11, 1858 (copy), Headquarters Book, Department of Utah; Special Order, June 25, 1859 (copy), Order Book, Department of Utah, both in Johnston Papers, Barret Collection; and Johnston to Samuel Cooper, September 16, 1858, Letters Sent, Department of Utah, Records of the War Department.

[70] *New York Daily Tribune*, July 28, 1859.

[71] Johnston, *Life of Johnston*, p. 220.

[72] W. G. Binney to Johnston, November 4, 1858, Johnston Papers, Barret Collection.

Out of admiration for Johnston's conduct in Utah, many of his friends began to talk of nominating him on the Democratic ticket for President of the United States. From St. Louis, Johnston's West Point classmate and lifelong admirer, N. J. Eaton, condemned the Buchanan Administration for indecision and political opportunism. Said Eaton:

I take the ground . . . that God in His kind providence has been so ordering the events of your life as to bring you prominently & favorably before the people of this nation, to the end that you may be our Chief Magistrate . . . that we as a people may once more see the benefit of pure and unselfish administration.[73]

From Washington a fellow Texan wrote Johnston not to be surprised if he were nominated for the Presidency at the Charleston convention, that in the capital Johnston's name was freely mentioned for this honor.[74]

One of Johnston's subordinate officers calculated Johnston's chances for election to be favorable.

As a Kentuckian of good family he would be popular in the Southwest [reasoned this officer]. As a moderate man and not a fire eater he would suit the Northwest. At the same time as he is a slave holder and a representative of Filibusters thru his Texas antecedents, he would take both with fire eaters and Filibusters; and altogether he has more available qualities than any other candidate.[75]

Johnston's head was not turned by this praise; to all such overtures he said no. "If success were certain," he told his son, "I still have honesty & patriotism enough to say that there are others more capable & more fit for the station, who ought to have precedence." [76] To Eaton he wrote that he had neither ambition nor taste for political life. Eaton was mistaken in believing that the ills of the nation could be cured by electing Johnston to the Presidency, said Johnston; these ills were like a severe disease that only nature could remedy. "Time will, I trust, restore to us a sound and healthy basis of moral

[73] N. J. Eaton to Johnston, October 17, 1858; January 16, 1859, Johnston Papers, Barret Collection.

[74] J. S. Holman to Johnston, March 18, 1859, *ibid.*

[75] Journal, Phelps Papers, July 1, 1859.

[76] Johnston to William Preston Johnston, November 3, 1858, Johnston Papers, Barret Collection.

action, such as we set out with as a people in the days of Washington and the elder Adams." [77] Johnston stuck to soldiering.

He felt keenly the long separation from his family that the Utah campaign obliged him to endure. His letters to them were filled with fatherly admonition and expressions of endearment. He cautioned his son against starting his own childern's schooling too early. "They & all other children have to & do learn more before they are 8 years old, when they ought to go to school, than ever afterwards," said their grandfather. He encouraged his son to work hard in his profession in order to secure the independence of his family.

My example ought not with you to be a precedent. My vices & errors should rather serve as a beacon to warn [you] from dangerous shoals—If I had pursued a different course myself I would not now be under the necessity of asking protection for a helpless family from whoever will give it.

He kept his family informed on affairs in Utah, even sending them copies of official correspondence, and freely expressing his own views regarding the Mormons and the Buchanan Administration. When Eliza fondly but unwisely published some of this correspondence, her husband threatened to censor his letters.[78]

Upon hearing that his brother-in-law, William Preston, had been appointed Minister to Spain, Johnston advised against his accepting the position. Spain was in decline, said Johnston, and a ministry there would bring no real honor. Preston hoped to acquire Cuba from Spain through diplomacy. This would never come to pass, said Johnston. "Cuba will be ours when the people will it & the right man is at their head." The United States had no right to Cuba, he reasoned, except on the ground of national security. "This is the question to be well considered & reflected upon at every man's fireside and if the whole with one mind & one heart respond affirmatively, then she will be ours and rightfully, as soon as they can apply their Leviathan power." Johnston still believed in the "manifest destiny" of the American nation.[79]

When critics of the Buchanan Administration turned their censure upon Johnston also, saying that he was appointed through political favor to command the Utah army, he replied indignantly that he had not sought the command. He was in need of surgery at

---

[77] Johnston to Eaton, December 15, 1858, *ibid.*

[78] Johnston to William Preston Johnston, September 1, 1858; January 7, April 14, 1859, *ibid.*

[79] Johnston to William Preston Johnston, September 1, 1858, *ibid.*

the time of his appointment, he said, and his family required his presence for support and protection. The assignment was repugnant to him because it called for the enforcement of laws upon a portion of his fellow citizens.

Nor had he solicited promotion to brevet brigadier general, Johnston affirmed; yet he felt that his services in the battle of Monterrey and elsewhere entitled him to the honor.

I am by some pointed out as . . . a person but a short time in service, [he said]. My experience in the service runs back more than thirty years; I claim that my life and my means (not small) have been devoted to the service of my country. It is true that I was out of the army for some years, but I was not idle; I was laboring on another field [Texas] the benefits, not less than an empire in extent enured to the Government. To this result I contributed my humble aid. It was not my good fortune to be present at the battle at which was won the independence of Texas by a band of heroic men; but I served long and faithfully to assist to maintain that independence, and in so doing I think the interest of the United States was well subserved.[80]

Separation from Texas had in no way diminished Johnston's love for his adopted state; if anything, it made his heart grow fonder of her. In the summer of 1859 his son wrote, upon the advice of Texas attorneys, advising Johnston to enter suit in federal court for the recovery of the Blossom League in Harrison County from the squatters living on it.[81] Federal judges would be more favorably disposed toward Johnston's claim than would state judges. But in order to secure this advantage, Johnston must renounce his Texas citizenship. Johnston's reply was immediate and unequivocal.

My citizenship in Texas was obtained at the cost of the bloom of health & the prime of life spent in the service of the state [and of] property which if I had now would constitute a princely estate—I will not give it up now, tho' I should lose in consequence every foot of land I have in the state, this I would regard as a mere mess of pottage in comparison with my citizenship.

Johnston considered himself a Texan for time and for eternity.[82]

The General enjoyed robust health in Utah—at 194 pounds he

---

[80] Johnston to Eaton, October 11, 1858 (copy), Johnston-Eaton Letter Book, *ibid.*

[81] Clough and Lane to William Preston Johnston, June 28, 1859, Johnston Papers, Barret Collection.

[82] Johnston to William Preston Johnston, August 27, 1859, *ibid.*

weighed more than ever before [83]—but physical well-being brought little peace of soul; duty in Utah wore grievously upon his patience throughout the waning months of 1859. Boredom and loneliness among the soldiers set tempers on edge; a small minority of Johnston's subordinates grew bitterly critical of him. They complained of favoritism toward certain officers and of discrimination against others.[84] One of them even accused Johnston of immoderate drinking—a charge not substantiated by any other evidence.[85]

Johnston gave voice to his own frustration, saying:

I have . . . no hopes of escapeing from this infernal region—It is to me worse than any imagined horrors of a Siberian exile. . . . The scenery [of the Utah mountains] which is sublime and magnificent preserved its novelty to me for a long time but that now is gone & it has resolved itself into a huge prison wall, a barrier to cut me off from all those I love. . . . For a long time I have tried to believe that I was an exception and backed up by a pseudo Philosophy I have fancied myself sometimes content. . . . But in the midst of this monotony my Philosophy has been thrown overboard and I find myself no more content . . . than the rest of mankind.

Christmas merriment of balls, dinners, theatricals, and sleigh rides at Camp Floyd palled upon him. "How much pleasure & happiness could I have had, had my destiny permitted my being in the midst of my family," he wrote.[86]

Relief came sooner than expected; in February Johnston received orders relieving him of the Utah command and granting him an extended leave of absence before reporting for fresh assignment.[87] On March 1 he reviewed the Utah army for the last time. Addressing the troops from the saddle, and praising them for their patriotism and devotion to duty under great stress, he relinquished the command to Lieutenant Colonel Charles F. Smith, then wheeled his horse, bared his head, and rode out of Camp Floyd while the regimental bands appropriately played "Come out of the Wilderness." [88]

---

[83] Johnston, *Life of Johnston,* p. 243.

[84] Journal, Phelps Papers, September 19, 1859. Phelps had become bitterly hostile to Johnston over the slavery issue also.

[85] Alter (ed.), *The Utah War: Journal of Albert Tracy,* pp. 75, 81–82.

[86] Johnston to Henrietta Johnston, August 15, 1859; January 4, 1860, Johnston Papers, Barret Collection.

[87] Cooper to Johnston, January 11, 1860, Letters Sent, Adjutant General's Office, Records of the War Department; General Order, February 29, 1860, Order Book, Department of Utah, Records of the War Department.

[88] Alter (ed.), *The Utah War: Journal of Albert Tracy,* pp. 81–82.

Johnston left Utah as he had entered it, implacably hostile to Mormon institutions. His analysis of relations between federal and Church officials was accurate; for many years, federal authority in Utah remained a shadow. But in the end, Buchanan's policy of conciliation proved the wiser course. Ultimately, federal legislation and judicial pressure without bloodshed destroyed polygamy and brought local administration into line with national practice. In 1896 Utah became a state.

Like much of Johnston's previous career, his experience as commander of the Utah expedition was one of enthusiasm turned to frustration. He gave up the command feeling that his true mission in Utah was unfulfilled. Yet he had grown immensely in the eyes of the American Army and people. "It is generally remarked," wrote a newspaper correspondent upon Johnston's departure from Utah, "that no other military commander of the American army ever left a military department carrying with him so universally the high regards and good wishes of those under his command, as well as their approval of his official conduct." [89] Johnston's heart was filled with relief and gladness as he rode toward California to take ship for the long journey that would carry him to his waiting wife and children.

[89] Unidentified newspaper clipping, in Scrapbook, Johnston Papers, Barret Collection.

Pacific Service and Desert Anabasis

~~~~~~

AFTER A SEPARATION of almost three years, Johnston joined his wife and children in Louisville in the spring of 1860. Granted an extended leave of absence from duty, he remained there for the next seven months. Little is known of how he occupied himself while on leave, but he must have found this one of the most gratifying periods of his entire career. Not only was he again with his own beloved immediate family; he was also reunited with his eldest son, William Preston, and his son's wife and children, and with his own daughter Henrietta. Besides these, he was surrounded in Louisville by numerous kin and associates of bygone years. Among them all, Johnston was a hero returned from a difficult and distant mission admirably pursued.

Johnston's reputation in the United States Army was now at its zenith; superior and subordinate alike looked upon him as perhaps the foremost officer of the service. Both publicly and in private, General in Chief Winfield Scott commended Johnston's ability, and expressed his intention to place Johnston in command of a military department as soon as a vacancy should occur.[1] From New York

[1] Fitz John Porter to Johnston, August 7, 1860, Johnston Papers, Barret Collection.

wrote Major Fitz John Porter, now assistant adjutant general of the Army:

I think your services will be regarded as so essential to the country that your anticipated rest will be denied you—The ambition which stirs your soul will not permit your declining what may be offered, while we think you should sacrifice much that the great aim may be attained of being General Scott's successor, which all wish you.[2]

Sending Johnston a dress sword as a testimonial of friendship, Porter expressed his "esteem, admiration and love for one whose rare virtues can only be fully known and appreciated by those, who, like myself, have fortunately been as intimately associated." [3] "Take care old fellow," wrote a Texas friend, "or you will be President after awhile, a station no honest man in these desperate days ought to hold." [4] Abiding in the love of family, in the admiration of friends, and in the commendation of colleagues, Johnston found his cup of happiness overflowing.

Johnston and Major Porter continued to exchange letters of friendship and information; Porter was in the confidence of General Scott, and thus was in excellent position to support Johnston's professional advancement. Porter relayed news from the army in Utah, including gossip about indiscretions between certain officers and their housckeepers. With a measure of vindictive satisfaction, Porter quoted to Johnston a statement by Governor Cumming saying that Utah was in near anarchy. "I hope thorns are not only in the crown he [Cumming] wears," said Porter, "but in a certain part of his unmentionables." [5]

When Johnston ran afoul of Army bookkeeping, Porter came to his rescue. After Johnston had left Utah he received notice from the United States Treasury Department that he owed money for horses and equipment turned over to B. F. Ficklin, a civilian, for Ficklin's mission to the Indians during the winter at Fort Bridger.[6] Irritated at what he considered penny pinching, Johnston complained to Porter. The faithful former subordinate wrote Johnston not to be vexed by the affair; he would go down to Washington, said Porter,

[2] *Ibid.*, May 4, June 10, 1860.
[3] *Ibid.*, December 9, 1860.
[4] James Love to Johnston, June 11, 1860, Johnston Papers, **Barret Collection.**
[5] Porter to Johnston, May 4, 1860, *ibid.*
[6] P. J. Morris to Johnston, November 14, 1860, *ibid.*

and prevail upon Secretary Floyd to take care of it. "I have engineered worse matters than that through the Treasury," Porter assured his onetime chief. "If you have nothing worse than this ever to trouble your pillow, you will have the rest I and many friends wish you." [7] Presumably, Porter "engineered" this charge to Johnston's satisfaction.

Uppermost in Johnston's mind was the question of his next assignment. Rumor said that he was now to become quartermaster general of the Army and that General Scott had filed a recommendation for Johnston to succeed him as general in chief.[8] Johnston's ever-faithful supporter, N. J. Eaton, urged Johnston to turn down the quartermaster post and to remain a commander in the line. Eaton acknowledged that Eliza would be happier living in Washington than in some remote spot, or perhaps even separated from her husband once more. But if Johnston should become quartermaster general, said Eaton, his chances of becoming head of the Army would be dimmed, "to say nothing of a position still higher." [9] In the end, Johnston did not have to decide whether to accept the position; Secretary of War Floyd appointed Colonel Joseph E. Johnston to it.

The likeliest assignment for Johnston was to the command of the Department of Texas. Before he left Utah, friends in Texas were expressing their hope for his return there.[10] Every Texan in Washington was now urging this, wrote James Love from the nation's capital, for they believed that Johnston was the only officer who understood how to fight the frontier Indians.[11] This unsolicited support bore fruit; in November, the adjutant general of the Army wrote that Secretary Floyd had directed that Johnston be appointed to the Texas command and that he was to report to Washington for instructions as soon as he could with convenience do so.[12]

Ordinarily Johnston would have welcomed returning to his adopted state. He had always considered service there a privilege; one of the happiest periods of his life had been spent in San Antonio as temporary commander of the Department of Texas before leaving for Utah. Oddly, now he was reluctant to take the Texas command.

[7] Porter to Johnston, November 28, 1860, *ibid.*
[8] Love to Johnston, June 11, 1860, *ibid.*
[9] N. J. Eaton to Johnston, June 14, 1860, *ibid.*
[10] S. U. Swenson to Johnston, October 7, 1859, *ibid.*
[11] Love to Johnston, June 8, 1860, *ibid.*
[12] Samuel Cooper to Johnston, November 1, 1860, *ibid.*

Johnston's son later quoted him as saying that he sensed the coming secession of the state and that he was determined to avoid having to choose loyalties between a federal government that he revered and a state that he loved. That Johnston could so accurately foretell events which lay months in the future seems hardly credible. Yet, for some reason, even before he returned from Utah, he had indicated an aversion to duty in Texas. "My own recollection of your views are that you would not care much about Texas at the present time," wrote Major Porter in the summer of 1860.[13] For whatever reason, and it may have been the fear of secession, Johnston left for Washington in November, determined not to accept the Texas command. He would resign his commission first, he told his son.[14]

Fortunately, he was not forced to this unhappy alternative. Shortly before leaving for Washington, he learned of the death of the commander of the Department of California. "How would you like to succeed [as commander of] California?" asked Porter. "Every effort here [at General Scott's headquarters] will be made to unite the two departments [California and Oregon]—Please reply by Telegraph —and keep the fact a secret that your wishes were consulted." [15] Johnston replied in the affirmative; General Scott at once requested the Secretary of War to name him to the California command.[16] When Johnston arrived in Washington and expressed his preference, Floyd appointed him to command the Department of the Pacific (embracing the two former Departments), with headquarters in San Francisco.[17]

Johnston prepared to leave for California as soon as possible. Since he would take his family with him, he arranged his personal affairs accordingly. To his son William Preston he granted power of attorney to sell any Texas land to which he had lawful claim.[18] Because California was a free state, Johnston and Eliza felt obliged to dispose of their two Negro slaves. A young woman slave named Mary was sold to William Preston Johnston for $1,200.[19] When John-

[13] Porter to Johnston, August 7, 1860, *ibid.*
[14] Johnston, *Life of Johnston,* pp. 247–248.
[15] Porter to Johnston, October 30, 1860, Johnston Papers, Barret Collection.
[16] H. L. Scott to Johnston, November 2, 1860 (copy), *ibid.*
[17] Johnston, *Life of Johnston,* pp. 247–248.
[18] Albert Sidney and Eliza Johnston to William Preston Johnston, December 13, 1860, Johnston Papers, Barret Collection.
[19] Albert Sidney and Eliza Johnston, Certificate of Sale, December 13, 1860, *ibid.*

ston's young man slave named Ran (Randolph Hughes) expressed a wish to accompany the family to California, Johnston emancipated him, but bound him by contract to five years of additional service at wages of $12 a month, plus upkeep.[20] Major Porter booked passage for Johnston and his family out of New York on the steamer *North Star;*[21] on December 21, 1860, they sailed via the Isthmus of Panama for California and new experiences.

The three-week voyage was rough; seasick most of the time, Eliza reached port "much reduced & feeble." But the harrowing journey was soon forgotten in the entire family's enthusiasm for their new environment. Johnston praised the San Francisco schools and the salubrious climate. "The [winter] weather here is like the October weather in Kentucky," he wrote his son. "This is a climate that would suit you, the air is bracing at all seasons."[22] Eliza found many things she liked about life in California. She desired her children to cast their lot there, she said; California was a thriving country, free of internal strife. "There are the fewest number of free negroes. One hardly ever sees one here in the streets, that is a good feature in the population for where the darky is in any numbers it should be as slaves."[23] Southern attitudes accompanied the Johnstons to the Pacific.

On the day after his arrival in San Francisco, Johnston took command of the Department of the Pacific.[24] He remained in this position for only three months—a period during which no military operations of significance occurred there. Serving a remote section of the country at a time when secession and impending civil war filled the national mind, Johnston found himself in a neglected command. His quartermaster was destitute of funds, he wrote the adjutant general shortly after reaching California, the other branches of the department nearly so.[25] "The Government has allowed every department of the staff here to fall into a state of pauperism," he confided to Major Porter, "making the military arm as impotent

---

[20] Randolph Hughes, Contract, December 10, 1850, *ibid.*
[21] Porter to Johnston, November 28, 1860, *ibid.*
[22] Johnston to William Preston Johnston, January 17, 1860 [1861], *ibid.*
[23] ———[Eliza Johnston] to "Dear Uncle," March 3, 1861, *ibid.*
[24] Order No. 1, Department of the Pacific, January 15, 1861 (copy), *ibid.*
[25] Johnston to Cooper, January 17, 1861, Letters Sent, Department of the Pacific, Records of the War Department.

for action here as the greatest enemy of the republic could desire to have it. . . . Is our Government absolutely stupefied?" Vainly he urged that money in the San Francisco mint be authorized for the use of his command.[26]

One situation only required military action during Johnston's command of the Pacific Department. In the spring of 1861, settlers in Mendocino, Humboldt, and Trinity counties of California (an area in northern California lying between the Coast Range Mountains and the Pacific) complained of Indian outrages. Though Johnston anticipated no extensive Indian uprising, he at once took steps to protect the whites.[27] From military posts near the troubled region he ordered small parties of troops to scout constantly between the mountains and the sea, to guard the settlements, and to punish any Indians actually guilty of wrongdoing.[28] Carefully he cautioned the ranking officer of the expedition that there must be "no indiscriminate slaughter of the guilty with the innocent." [29] Soon he learned that the earlier accounts of Indian outrages had been exaggerated; the remainder of his period of command was free of Indian problems.

Johnston commanded the Department of the Pacific with his characteristic intelligence and fairness. When he learned that a certain commissary agent had signed a contract whereby officers could purchase food at lower cost than could enlisted men, Johnston rebuked the agent and cancelled the contract.[30] He offered wise counsel to his superiors regarding a disciplinary affair that he inherited from his predecessor. Two years earlier, in an expedition against the Mohave Indians, soldiers of one of the California regiments (the Sixth Infantry) had discovered and seized a cache of provisions that had been stored by a road construction company. Ordered by the Secretary of War to make the troops pay for the provisions with money from their company funds, Johnston interceded in behalf of the soldiers. They had been in need of rations at the time, he argued, and the provisions would probably never have been used by the

[26] Johnston to Porter, February 25, 1861, Johnston-Porter Letter Book, Johnston Papers, Barret Collection.

[27] Johnston to John G. Downey, March 12, 1861, Letters Sent, Department of the Pacific, Records of the War Department.

[28] Johnston to Lorenzo Thomas, March 23, 25, 1861, *ibid.*

[29] W. W. Mackall to C. L. Lovell, April 13, 1861, *ibid.*

[30] Mackall to F. F. Flint, April 16, 1861, *ibid.*

owners anyway. He urged that the soldiers be relieved of accountability, and that the War Department assume the debt.[31]

Events beyond Johnston's control now cast an ominous shadow across his life. For years he had feared a disruption of the Union because of the bitter controversy over slavery. His worst fears now began to be fulfilled. South Carolina seceded from the Union while Johnston was on his way to California; six other states of the lower South, including his own state of Texas, quickly followed the example of South Carolina. With foreboding and heartache Johnston watched these events. Though he believed in the right of a state to secede as a final redress of grievance, and had on an earlier occasion said that the South might be driven to exercise the right, he felt no joy over the South's action.

All of his life Johnston had been an ardent nationalist; he had served in two wars to uphold his concept of national honor; he had been an implacable advocate of imposing national authority upon the Mormons.

No one could have been more distressed [over secession] than he [Eliza later wrote]. He said again & again that he could not see that secession was a remedy for the evils of which the south complained. In either case (should ie she succeed or be defeated) he feared that it would lead to a military & despotic Government.[32]

Desperately, but vainly, Johnston yet hoped that the Union might be peaceably preserved. Describing a great Union meeting held in San Francisco in late February, he said, "I would that there were no other sentiments within the broad expanse of our country." [33]

Because of Johnston's high military authority, and because he was a Southerner and former slaveowner, his name became involved in various rumors of conspiracy and disloyalty in California.[34] An estimated 7 per cent of the population of California had migrated from the South; at least two Confederate secret societies—the Knights of the Golden Circle and the Knights of the Columbian Star—were active in California during the Civil War.[35] These groups hoped to

[31] Johnston to Thomas, March 27, 1861, *ibid.*

[32] Eliza Johnston to William Preston Johnston, August 13, 1871, Johnston Papers, Barret Collection.

[33] Johnston to Porter, February 25, 1861, Johnston-Porter Letter Book, *ibid.*

[34] Johnston, *Life of Johnston*, pp. 270–271.

[35] Benjamin F. Gilbert, "The Confederate Minority in California," *California Historical Society Quarterly*, XX (June, 1941), 154–156.

form an independent Pacific republic which would give assistance to the Southern Confederacy. Johnston was reputed to be in league with these societies; it was said that at the right moment he was to turn over to them the principle fortresses defending San Francisco (Alcatraz Island and Fort Point), along with the arms in the Bernicia arsenal.[36]

Knowing of Johnston's ties with the South, the Confederate societies in California doubtless hoped to gain his collusion. According to a later account by one of their leaders, a committee of them called upon Johnston to determine whether he could be approached on the matter. Before they could make known the purpose of their visit, Johnston is said to have declared:

There is something I want to mention. I have heard foolish talk about an attempt to seize the strongholds of the government under my charge. Knowing this, I have prepared for emergencies, and will defend the property of the United States with every resource at my command, and with the last drop of blood in my body. Tell that to all our Southern friends.[37]

Whether this conversation actually took place cannot with certainty be known. If it did take place, Johnston would seem to have been unaware that he was addressing members of a Southern conspiracy. Shortly before he quit the Pacific command, Johnston wrote his son that he had not talked with anyone who even so much as desired to establish a Pacific republic.[38]

So prevalent became the rumors concerning Southern conspiracies in California that Governor John G. Downey called upon Johnston to express his fears. Johnston assured the Governor that the fortifications and arms of the Pacific Department were secure.

I have spent the greater part of my life in the service of my country [he told Governor Downey], and while I hold her commission [I] shall serve her

[36] Benjamin F. Gilbert, "The Mythical Johnston Conspiracy," *ibid.*, XXVIII (June, 1949), 166–167. Tales of Johnston's complicity in such plots have continued to be peddled almost to the present day. See *San Francisco Daily Herald*, n.d. (clipping), in Scrapbook, Johnston Papers, Barret Collection; Charles M. Dustin, "The Knights of the Golden Circle," *Pacific Monthly*, XXVI (November, 1911), 495–504; Elijah R. Kennedy, *The Contest for California in 1861*, pp. 194–208; "A Copy of the Original Military Records Written by Colonel Orlando Hurley Moore," *Oakland Tribune*, April 7, 1935; Editorial, *Pony Express Courier*, XIV (March, 1948), 2.

[37] Gilbert, "The Mythical Johnston Conspiracy," *California Historical Society Quarterly*, XXVIII (June, 1949), 167.

[38] Johnston, *Life of Johnston*, p. 271.

honorably and faithfully. I shall protect her public property, and not a cartridge or a percussion cap belonging to her shall pass to any enemy while I am here as her representative. There is no man in the Union more sorely afflicted than I am at the occurrences now taking place. I have been long identified with Texas, her interests and public men, and her action may control my future destiny. But in any event I shall give due notice and turn over intact my department to my successor.[39]

Sympathetic as Johnston was with the aggrieved South, he never wavered in his own sense of honor or of responsibility to the federal government as long as he held a commission under it. "Should I prove unfaithful to my trust here," he told a kinsman who inquired his intentions in case of an insurrection by Southerners in California, "how could I expect to be trusted elsewhere?" [40] He was as good as his word. Though he believed that the fear of conspiracy in California was exaggerated, he took steps to guard his command against surprise. He strengthened the security forces of all installations and ordered 10,000 additional muskets with suitable accoutrements and ammunition to be transferred from the Bernicia arsenal to the impregnable fortress of Alcatraz Island.[41] To the commander of Fort Alcatraz, Johnston issued orders that the position be defended against all attempts to seize it, "from whatever direction such efforts may be made." The numbers and appearances of boats and passengers in the harbor were to be closely observed, lest a disguised assault take the island fortress unaware.[42] Doubtless with heavy heart, Johnston stood ready to repel any Southern move against the peace of California.

Though Johnston's sense of honor impelled him to secure the federal installations against suspected plots, his own sympathy for the South grew stronger with every passing day. He resolved that he could not bear arms against the people of Texas; if she should finally cast her lot with the Confederacy, he would resign his commission in the United States Army.[43] On April 9 he received information that a Texas convention had carried into effect its own earlier

---

[39] *St. Louis Globe-Democrat,* n.d. (clipping) , Johnston Papers, Barret Collection.
[40] Eliza Johnston to William Preston Johnston, July 9, 1875, *ibid.*
[41] Mackall to Thomas Swords, February 17, 1861, Letters Sent, Department of the Pacific, Records of the War Department.
[42] Mackall to J. Stewart, February 20, 1861, *ibid.*
[43] Mackall to William Preston Johnston, January 7, 1876; Eliza Johnston to William Preston Johnston, July 9, 1875; December 16, 1884, Johnston Papers, Barret Collection.

decision, supported by a popular referendum, to withdraw from the Union and join the Confederacy.[44]

Johnston now acquiesced in secession. Until this time, he said, he had believed that the slave states could, through joint action, obtain from the North sufficient guarantees to make secession unnecessary; that in this way the Union could be preserved and all interests be protected.

But the persistent obstinacy of the Republican party, in refusing to concede anything whatever for the sake of the Union up to the hour of the adjournment of the Senate, seems to indicate that the action of the South was based upon a correct understanding of the true sentiments of the North and their unbending character. It [the South] seems instinctively to have seized the right conclusion. . . . I felt, as soon as I learned the course adopted by my State (Texas) that it was my duty to conform to her will.[45]

That day Johnston submitted his letter of resignation.[46]

Word of Johnston's intention to resign stirred consternation among his many Unionist friends and admirers. Their pleas that he remain in the United States service cut him to the heart. If Johnston at this time corresponded with his lifelong comrade, N. J. Eaton, no record remains of what was said. Eaton was a Unionist. When he learned of Johnston's decision he wrote in sorrow to Johnston's son:

Since these troubles commenced, there has hardly been a day, that I have not thought of your father & my heart has bled for him, & still bleeds for him. I know how much he loved the Union. I know how just he is. I know how kind hearted he is, & I know too that there is no malice or revenge in his nature, and knowing all this, I have felt that his situation was more trying & I have not been able to see how he could consent to shed the blood

---

[44] S[usan Preston Hepburn] to William Preston Johnston, April 27, 1861, *ibid.*

[45] Johnston, *Life of Johnston,* pp. 271–272.

[46] Johnston to Thomas, April 9, 1861, Letters Received, Adjutant General's Office, Records of the War Department; also United States War Department, *The War of the Rebellion: A Compilation of the Official Records of the Union and Confederate Armies,* Ser. I, Vol. L, Pt. I, p. 433 (cited hereinafter as *Official Records*). The day before Johnston submitted his letter of resignation, Major Porter wrote from Texas that secession there was supported by only about one third of the people, that coercion and intimidation had caused many who opposed separation to vote for it. Porter to Johnston, April 8, 1861 (copy), Porter Papers.

of his countrymen. On the other hand, feeling, as I know he did, that the Republican party denied to the South its rights, his sense of justice would be strongly appealed to to induce him to throw his sword into the scale of the South. . . . Come what may, I shall struggle to still love my old friends.[47]

The most poignant exchange of views concerning Johnston's resignation took place between himself and Eliza Gilpin, his beloved sister-in-law, widow of Josiah Stoddard Johnston, the elder brother to whom Johnston once said he owed more than to any other man. From Philadelphia, Eliza Gilpin wrote urging him not to resign.

Remember your dear Brothers love for the union [she pleaded], his exalted patriotism—& his many virtues—you are his representative now—& will remain by our beloved Flag. . . . My love for my country is such that I care not who rules for four years, we must all unite now, in guarding its honour, & preserving our beloved Flag. . . . Do not resign. . . . God bless you my dear Brother & direct you in the right way.[48]

Johnston replied that his letter of resignation was already in the hands of the President.

No one could feel more sensibly the calamitous condition of our country than myself. Whatever part I may take hereafter it will be always a subject of gratulation with me that no act of mine ever contributed to bring it about—I suppose the difficulties will now only be adjusted by the sword—in my humble judgement that was not the remedy. I hope my dear sister you are in good health and that you may long live to enjoy the good things providence has placed in your hands—Such is the prayer of yr affectionate Brother.[49]

A few days later Eliza Gilpin wrote to Johnston's son, "I truly grieve for the necessity of your father's resignation. Still, I cannot blame him. He has always been the soul of honor; and so he will be, in my estimation, while I live." [50]

Meantime, something occurred that filled Johnston with personal bitterness against the Lincoln Administration. Before Johnston wrote his letter of resignation, rumors from many sources

[47] Eaton to William Preston Johnston, June 5, 1861, Johnston Papers, Barret Collection.
[48] Eliza Gilpin to Johnston, April 15, 1861, *ibid.*
[49] Johnston to Eliza Gilpin, June 1, 1861, *ibid.*
[50] Johnston, *Life of Johnston*, p. 274.

had reached the ear of President Lincoln that he was not to be trusted, that he was plotting to surrender the California forts and arms to Southern conspirators. Fresh in Lincoln's mind was the surrender by General Twiggs of the federal posts in Texas. Unable to determine at once the truth about Johnston, and unwilling to run the risk of losing California, Lincoln on March 23 ordered Johnston relieved of command by Brigadier General E. V. Sumner.[51] As a precaution, Sumner was to sail unannounced to California to take over the Pacific Department. On April 25, two weeks after Johnston had mailed his letter of resignation but before the War Department had had time to reply to it, General Sumner arrived in San Francisco and presented his orders to Johnston. Until Sumner showed up at his headquarters, Johnston was unaware of the transaction.[52]

Johnston did not at first realize that he was under suspicion. Shortly, however, he read articles in the newspapers that revealed to him the true state of affairs. Outraged to learn that he had not been trusted, he expressed satisfaction over having already resigned; the government's action made it impossible for anyone with a spark of honor to serve longer, he said.[53] His acquaintances in California agreed with him. "Johnston . . . is a gentleman, and incapable of treason," said a Unionist newspaper. "There is no question that he will be heard of again." [54]

Even before General Sumner had reached San Francisco, and before Johnston's resignation reached Washington, the Lincoln Administration decided that it had erred in suspecting Johnston of treachery in his command. According to a later account by Montgomery Blair, word was received of Johnston's steadfastness in securing the forts against Southern conspirators.[55] Johnston's supporters in the Army now strove diligently to retain his services. Major Porter wrote from Washington:

[51] *Official Records,* Ser. I, Vol. L, Pt. I, p. 456.

[52] Johnston to Eliza Gilpin, June 1, 1861, Johnston Papers, Barret Collection. Various accounts are given as to how the rumors of Johnston's alleged plotting reached President Lincoln. See Gilbert, "The Mythical Johnston Conspiracy," *California Historical Society Quarterly,* XXVIII (June, 1949), 166; *Sacramento City and Its Resources: A Souvenir of the Bee,* p. 156; Erasmus D. Keyes, *Fifty Years' Observations of Men and Events, Civil and Military,* p. 420.

[53] Johnston to Eliza Gilpin, June 1, 1861, Johnston Papers, Barret Collection.

[54] *San Francisco Evening Bulletin,* April 25, 1861.

[55] Montgomery Blair to William Preston Johnston, December 4, 1875, Johnston Papers, Barret Collection.

I take the greatest pleasure in assuring you for the Secretary of War, that he has the utmost confidence in you, and will give you the most important command and trust on your arrival here—Sidney is appointed to the military Academy. I hope soon to see you and with a heart glowing with pride and pleasure for my commander and friend.[56]

A report soon arrived in Washington from General Sumner that he had received the Pacific command from Johnston in good order.[57] Major Porter now wrote to his fellow assistant adjutant general, Irvin McDowell, saying:

You must see that General Johnston's resignation is not accepted till he comes and is heard from in person. He will not resign to take service— He cannot be bribed by any power on Earth—He is the only man to save us next to General Scott and if we lose him—God knows what a calamity it will be—to our country.[58]

All was to no avail; Johnston's fateful decision had already been made. On May 6 the War Department formally approved his resignation.[59]

Johnston's resignation from the Army left him without the means to sustain himself and his family. "It brings us face to face with poverty," he said. "There is no dishonor in this; but, to serve without the proper animus would be." [60] Johnston's San Francisco landlord later wrote that Johnston prevailed upon him to cancel his lease, and, with "tears in his eyes," begged for even so much as a clerk's position in the man's business.[61] That Johnston was reduced to such humiliation is unlikely, however, for he had many generous friends in California, and his wife's brother, John Griffin, was a prosperous physician and property owner in Los Angeles. From friends in San

[56] Porter to Johnston, April 18, 1861, *ibid.* Sidney had previously been passed over in the appointments to the United States Military Academy. See Porter to Johnston, April 8, 1861 (copy), Porter Papers.

[57] E. V. Sumner to E. D. Townsend, April 28, 1861, Letters Received, Adjutant General's Office, Records of the War Department.

[58] Porter to "My Dear Major" [Irvin McDowell], May 6, 1861 (copy), Johnston Papers, Barret Collection.

[59] Adjutant General's Office to Johnston, May 6, 1861 (copy), *ibid.*

[60] Johnston, *Life of Johnston,* pp. 271–272.

[61] Years later, Johnston's San Francisco landlord published a severely hostile account of Johnston's last days in that city, implying that Johnston was in league with Southern conspirators and accusing Johnston of leaving the rented house filthy and badly damaged. Casper T. Hopkins, "The California Recollections of Casper T. Hopkins," *California Historical Society Quarterly,* XXVI (September, 1947), 253–266.

Francisco, Johnston received a fine silver service;[62] from various quarters he received offers of hospitality and succor.[63]

When Johnston left the service he seems to have been resolved to join neither Union nor Confederacy in the impending conflict. To one relative he wrote that he desired never again to hold office;[64] to another he said that he would accept any form of civilian employment that would support his family.[65] He yet hoped that hostilities could be prevented between North and South, that "there were Patriots enough on both sides to avoid the issue of war."[66] A comrade of the Mexican War quoted him as saying at this time "that he never could give up the old flag he had followed all his life. Nor could he take sides against his own people and that he should soon leave the Army, go to Los Angeles and buy a Rancho in the neighborhood of Dr. Griffin."[67] A week after he was relieved of command, Johnston and his family left San Francisco to go to the home of the Griffins in Los Angeles.

In believing that he could remain passive in faraway California while the two sections of the nation grappled in mortal combat, Johnston failed to reckon with his lifelong enthusiasm for independence movements, with his fierce devotion to Texas and the South, and with his latent but powerful fighting instinct. News came of the bombardment of Fort Sumter and the call to arms in North and South. He grew more restless with every passing day, cruelly torn between the desire to stay out of the conflict and the urge to be in the thick of it.

It seemed impossible in the excitement of the times for him to "beat his sword into a ploughshare" [recalled Eliza]. The two sections of the country North & South being opposed to each other and the intense bitterness of the struggle already commenced caused his sympathy for his own people, who needed every arm that could handle a gun, to influence his decision.[68]

[62] Eliza Johnston to William Preston Johnston, September 23, 1875, Johnston Papers, Barret Collection.
[63] Richard H. Coolidge to Johnston, April 29, 1861; and ——— to Johnston, June 16, 1861, *ibid.*
[64] Johnston to Eliza Gilpin, June 1, 1861, *ibid.*
[65] Johnston, *Life of Johnston,* p. 272.
[66] Eliza Johnston to William Preston Johnston, July 9, 1875, Johnston Papers, Barret Collection.
[67] Joseph Hooker to William Preston Johnston, June 3, 1875, *ibid.*
[68] Eliza Johnston to Colonel Stevenson, December 16, 1884; Eliza Johnston to William Preston Johnston, December 8, 1872; July 9, 1875, *ibid.*

After a month of soul searching, Johnston knew that he must cast his lot with Texas and the Confederacy.

"It seems like fate," he said, "that Texas has made me a Rebel twice." [69]

Johnston prepared to leave at once for the Confederacy. At first he planned to sail to New York, and from there make his way south to Virginia. His family was to accompany him on the journey. But shortly he learned that he could not travel through the North, that his arrest had been ordered by the Secretary of War.[70] Knowing of a group of California Southerners that had been organized by Captain Alonzo Ridley to march overland back to the Confederacy, Johnston asked to join this company. Delighted to learn Johnston's decision, Ridley offered the company as an escort. With becoming modesty, Johnston said he would march simply as a member of the organization.[71]

His decision to go overland with Ridley's company was taken with reluctance. Eliza was expecting another baby within a few weeks; neither she nor the younger children could endure such a march. He must leave his loved ones behind, to join him later by ship and rail. The sorrow of family parting is not recorded. On June 16, 1861, Johnston bade his wife and children goodbye and rode out of Los Angeles toward an unknown destiny.[72]

Drawn by inescapable ties of kin and sentiment, he and his comrades made their way laboriously toward Texas and the Confederacy. Across eight hundred miles of desert and plain—traversing the southern portions of California and the present states of Arizona and New Mexico—they marched. The route led from Los Angeles to Yuma on the Colorado River, then up the Gila River and across the

[69] Eliza Johnston to William Preston Johnston, July 9, 1875, *ibid.*

[70] Eliza Johnston to Colonel Stevenson, December 16, 1884, *ibid.* The order for Johnston's arrest was issued June 3, 1861. See *Official Records,* Ser. I, Vol. L, Pt. I, p. 496.

[71] Alonzo Ridley to William Preston Johnston, November 11, 1875, Johnston Papers, Barret Collection. Ridley was an officer in a California militia company. He armed his group headed for the Confederacy with rifles requisitioned from state armories. Johnston had nothing to do with forming Ridley's company. Whether Johnston knew or approved the taking of this public property cannot be determined. See J. M. Scammell, "Military Units in Southern California, 1853–1862," *California Historical Society Quarterly,* XXIX (September, 1950), 229–240.

[72] Eliza Johnston to Colonel Stevenson, December 16, 1884, Johnston Papers, Barret Collection.

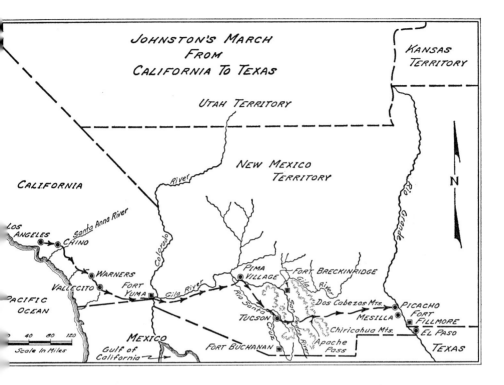

JOHNSTON'S MARCH
FROM
CALIFORNIA TO TEXAS

plain to Tucson, then through Apache Pass between the Chiricahua and Dos Cabezas Mountains to Mesilla on the upper Rio Grande.

Accompanied by his Negro servant Ran, Johnston rode horseback most of the time; a light covered wagon, or ambulance, drawn by mules, carried his provisions. The march was made in the scorching heat and sand of midsummer; temperatures often went to 120 degrees in the shade, and shade was almost nowhere to be found. Survival depended upon the most stringent rationing of water, for water was life itself. Johnston called the stretch from Warner's Ranch in southern California to Tucson a "horrid inhospitable desert"; it was four hundred miles of soda dust that threatened to smother men and animals. "It would have been quite impossible for you to have made this journey," he wrote Eliza. "Maggy & Griff would have perished in the heat & dust & long night marches." [73]

Notwithstanding his fifty-nine years, Johnston bore with patience and steadfastness the hardships of the march, calling upon stamina, trailcraft, and self-control acquired in long seasons of riding and

[73] Johnston to Eliza Johnston, July 21, 1861, *ibid.*

camping on the Texas frontier.[74] His presence was a source of inspiration to his younger comrades. When, during the nights of late June, a great comet lit the sky, Johnston interpreted it as a favorable portent in the heavens. Near Yuma one night Captain Ridley ordered a member of the company to ride back along the road to carry water to a straggler whose horse had broken down. Exhausted and frayed of nerve, the man refused to obey. As tempers and voices rose, Johnston quietly volunteered to go. Stung in their pride, a dozen men then stepped forward, and the disciplinary crisis was over.

Johnston refused to take advantage of age or rank to escape the labor of the camp. At wells along the route he took his turn in drawing water for the spent and thirst-crazed animals. "I could not but remark the patience and endurance of our general," said a member of the company in describing a particularly severe portion of the march. "[He] at all times bore himself with cheerfulness and dignity, and set an example of fortitude and self-denial." [75] When on one occasion the marchers were obliged to clean an abandoned well of refuse and dead rats before using the water, Johnston drank the first cup and jauntily announced to his hesitant companions, "This water tastes like the White Sulphur Springs in Virginia." [76] The entire company drew strength from this strong man in their midst.

More than once his character and judgment prevented the company from committing acts of depredation or otherwise straying from its mission of joining the Confederacy without delay. Finding Fort Yuma held by a mere handful of United States troops, some of the marchers wished to seize and plunder it. Johnston objected, saying that inasmuch as they did not yet have official status, the action would be the equivalent of piracy on the high seas. Southern sympathizers at Tucson proposed to join forces with Ridley's company in an attack upon four nearby companies of United States troops. Again Johnston dissuaded his comrades from injudicious action.

Only once on the march did the company resort to force, or a show of force. At Apache Pass they met a group of Texas Unionists on their way to California. A dispute arose over the use of water from

[74] This description of the return from California is drawn from Johnston's letters to Eliza (cited in footnotes below) ; from Ridley to William Preston Johnston, November 11, 1875, and George W. Gift to William Preston Johnston, November 17, 1875, all in Johnston Papers, Barret Collection; and from Johnston, *Life of Johnston*, pp. 275–291.

[75] Johnston, *Life of Johnston*, p. 289.

[76] *Ibid.*

the trail-side spring. "We were too thirsty, tired, and bad-tempered to argue long," recalled one of the Confederate marchers. "We had the force, and our necessities were great. We took the water." [77]

Much of the route led through Apache country. This fierce tribe was now tempted to renewed belligerency by the withdrawal of troops from the western posts; twice the column came upon pathetic evidence of stage coach massacres, but vigilance and march discipline preserved the Southerners from being molested.

The greatest threat to the Southern marchers, and especially to Johnston, was that of capture by United States troops, who were on the lookout for them. This danger became acute as they neared the end of their march. At Fort Fillmore, on the Rio Grande above El Paso, a Federal regiment was stationed; the Southerners employed great caution to avoid being trapped by this force. On July 27, as the company approached the village of Picacho on the Rio Grande it prepared a ruse to be employed should it be discovered by the Federals: the bulk of the company was to engage the United States soldiers while Johnston and two picked companions escaped on fresh mounts by riding across the Mexican border forty miles away.

Fortunately, they were not compelled to resort to this stratagem. Ridley and a companion rode into Picacho, where they discovered a Mexican who, believing that they were scouts of the United States force, warned them, "The brush is full of Texans, creeping about like cats in every direction." Ridley returned to his group; that night the company entered the village. Upon being hailed in Spanish, Ridley replied that they were United States troops. "By all means go north at once," advised the Mexican spokesman, "for the Texans only yesterday captured all the troops, and have all the guns, horses, and stores." [78] Johnston at first doubted this account; but shortly a Texan scout was brought in to confirm that Texas state troops led by Colonel John R. Baylor had indeed taken prisoner the entire United States regiment. Johnston's long march to Texas was over.

The California group now joined the Texas troops at nearby Mesilla. There Colonel Baylor prevailed upon Johnston to take temporary command of the entire body of Southerners in an effort

[77] *Ibid.*, p. 285.
[78] Ridley to William Preston Johnston, November 11, 1875, Johnston Papers, Barret Collection.

to intercept and capture a United States detachment known to be marching from New Mexico to Fort Fillmore. Johnston chafed at this delay, but Ridley said he confided privately "that it was like being asked to dance by a lady—he could not refuse." [79] Warned, however, that Fort Fillmore was held by Texans, the quarry escaped Johnston's trap by destroying artillery and trains and marching north to a post still in Federal hands.

On the march from California Johnston recorded a clear view into his nature. At rare intervals along the way he was able to post letters back to Eliza; they bared the heart of a man called by fate and an irrepressible sense of duty from the home of his rich love.

Can I better testify my love for you & my children than by this journey? Love & hope cheer me on to discharge a great duty which may in the end benefit you.[80]—Accept for yourself dear wife the homage of a devoted heart & give my love to Sid & Hancock [McClung], Maggy & Griff.[81]— You know how much I love you & that I will not change, could not, if I would, I will always love my dear wife—Kiss my dear children. Pa misses Griff every night.[82]

Devotion turned his thoughts often to his family. After a hard ride with poorly adjusted gear he sent his children a word of advice, drawn, as was all his counsel, from an intermingling of practical experience, history, and abstract reasoning.

Tell Sid & Hancock and master Griff that the stirrup leather should be long enough to let the foot rest in them without bearing any weight. They should only support the weight of the leg; in this position the rider should be able to rise a little in the saddle, by straightening his legs when necessary—when the leathers are too short they will fatigue & cramp the legs—The riders of India are usually represented on horseback with very short stirrup leathers, this position I should think good for battle, allowing them to rise in their saddles to deliver a sabre blow & tolerable for a short time, but uncomfortable for a journey.[83]

---

[79] *Ibid.* For a detailed account of this episode, see Martin H. Hall, "Albert Sidney Johnston's First Confederate Command," *The McNeese Review*, XIII (1962), 3–12.

[80] Johnston to Eliza Johnston, June 26, 1861, Johnston Papers, Barret Collection.

[81] *Ibid.*, July 21, 1861.

[82] *Ibid.*, July 1, 1861.

[83] *Ibid.*

A parental valedictory contained much of his philosophy of life; it lifted the curtain of the future for a glimpse at what his own conduct would be in the climactic scene of his career.

I have nothing to say to my boys that has not been already said. I have perfect confidence that they will be all that ought to be desired, or expected, besides our solicitude leads us to give too much thereby wearying [them] and making [them] listless, like too much drilling. I have been looking (in my cadetship) at the instructor, saw that he was talking but heard not a word—I am glad that Sid refrains from teasing Maggy & being over solicitous for her, she will love him and heed his advice just in proportion as he is kind & considerate for her—One man by an exhibition of physical power can control but few, it is by moral power alone that numbers of minds are controlled and directed by one mind, by not preserving his equanimity, he throws away his moral power—A man who cannot control himself cannot control others—He will know when to feel & show a proper resentment, and it is only on grave occasions that this is necessary—Napoleon knew the value of a scene, but his judgment rather than his passion dictated it.[84]

In spite of the darkness of the moment, he looked with hope to the future: "The sun shines none the less brightly tho' dark clouds interpose [and] will I feel sure shine brightly for us again." [85] He urged his wife to share this view.

We should not borrow trouble by apprehension of danger in the future, but nerve ourselves to meet them bravely should they come—I am happy that . . . I can discharge my duty in whatever position fortune may assign me, with equanimity & cheerfulness with the hope that there is much good in store for us.[86]

Buoyancy of spirit helped Johnston to overcome the ache of loneliness; it sustained him through the desert anabasis; it strengthened him to meet whatever trials might lie ahead.

"May God preserve you dear wife & sustain you in your trials," he wrote to Eliza from Mesilla. "After this trip the mail will cease to go. Give my love to our dear children." [87]

---

84 *Ibid.*
85 Johnston to John Griffin, June 26, 1861, Johnston Papers, Barret Collection.
86 Johnston to Eliza Johnston, June 26, 1861, *ibid.*
87 *Ibid.*, August 7, 1861.

Confederate Command

~~~~~~

JOHNSTON TARRIED at Mesilla for more
than a week in his effort to capture
the oncoming Federal troops; all
the while his eagerness grew to be on the way to Richmond. "Great
events are transpiring," he wrote to Eliza, "and we feel called on to
hurry on." [1] On August 8 he left Mesilla for El Paso. From there he
traveled by stage coach to San Antonio, and then on to Houston.
Unable to proceed by sea because of the Federal blockade on the
Gulf, he continued to New Orleans by land, arriving in early September. Word of Johnston's march out of the west had preceded him
by pony express and telegraph; his appearance in Texas was greeted
with elation by Texans and other Southerners. The authorities of
Houston sought to honor him with a public reception and a ban-
quet, but, in haste to get to the scene of action, Johnston turned

[1] Johnston to Eliza Johnston, August 7, 1861, Johnston Papers, Barret Collection.

down the invitation.[2] Southern newspapers extolled his prowess and predicted great things of him in the stern days to come.[3]

Johnston at once left New Orleans by rail for Richmond, where he arrived some time between the first and the tenth of September. President Jefferson Davis was ill in the Confederate White House when Johnston rang and was admitted to the hall. Davis later said that he raised himself from the sickbed at the sound of the tread below. "That is Sidney Johnston's step," he is supposed to have exclaimed. "Bring him up." A moment later Johnston strode into the room.[4]

A scene of deep but restrained emotion must have followed; Johnston's appearance renewed with striking drama a friendship of near a lifetime. Perhaps the two indulged in brief reminiscence—a recalling of faraway days together on the campus of Transylvania University, of life together as cadets at West Point, where, according to Davis, Johnston treated him like a younger brother, of service together on the Illinois frontier in the Black Hawk War, of braving together the shot and shell of Monterrey, or the repulse of the Mexican lancers, or the tense moment at the barricade on the way to General Ampudia's headquarters. These were men who had shared enough of life to justify a moment of nostalgia even as they stood on the threshold of their supreme adventure.

Soon they must have come to the exigencies of the day. Victories at Manassas in Virginia and Wilson's Creek in Missouri had given the Confederacy a season in which to mobilize her full resources for defense, but she faced on all fronts hostile armies of great and rapidly increasing strength. The South had urgent need for good soldiers and good generals.

There is no evidence that Johnston was promised anything if he would join the Confederacy. Davis said that Johnston came without herald or pretension of claim to any position, that "he simply offered himself to the cause." [5] Yet a man of Johnston's training, experience,

[2] *Daily True Delta* (New Orleans), September 8, 1861.

[3] Unidentified newspaper clipping, n.d., in Johnston Papers, Barret Collection; and *Daily Delta* (New Orleans), August 29, 1861.

[4] Jefferson Davis, "Address," 1878, in Dunbar Rowland (ed.), *Jefferson Davis, Constitutionalist: His Letters, Papers and Speeches*, VIII, 232. Much of the material in this chapter and the one following has been previously published. See Charles P. Roland, "Albert Sidney Johnston and the Loss of Forts Henry and Donelson," *Journal of Southern History*, XXIII (February, 1957), 45–69.

[5] *Ibid.*

and reputation, and with his ties to the Confederate President, was certain not to be overlooked in assigning rank. In Davis's mind, the South could not have received a more valuable gift than the service of Albert Sidney Johnston.[6]

He came and by his accession I felt strengthened, knowing that a great support had thereby been added to the Confederate cause. . . . I hoped and expected that I had others who would prove generals; but I knew I had one, and that was Sidney Johnston.[7]

The only question was where to place Johnston to gain the most from his skill, and Davis quickly reached a decision. Confederate forces in Virginia were led with assurance by Generals Joseph E. Johnston and P. G. T. Beauregard, victors of Manassas. Confederate forces west of the Appalachians had no officers of comparable stature; the Mississippi Valley was vulnerable. Already a citizens' committee from Memphis had petitioned for Johnston to be appointed commander in the west.[8] The ranking Confederate general in the west, Lieutenant General Leonidas Polk, had written Davis, "I know of no man who has the capacity to fill the position, who could be had, but General [Albert Sidney] Johnston." [9] A Kentuckian by birth and a Texan by adoption, Johnston seemed the ideal choice for this assignment. Thus it was agreed. On September 10 an order was issued naming Johnston to command Confederate Department Number Two—an immense area stretching from the Appalachian Mountains on the east through Indian Territory on the west. It included the states of Kentucky and Missouri, which had not seceded but were thought to be about to do so, Tennessee and Arkansas, and the northern portions of Alabama, Mississippi, and Louisiana.[10]

Johnston was appointed a full general with rank second only to Adjutant General Samuel Cooper, who was considered too old for command. The President's exalted estimate of Johnston's capacity was shared by virtually all with any knowledge of military affairs—

[6] Davis to John F. Elliott, July 29, 1884; Davis to J. William Jones, November 22, 1883; Davis, "Address on the Occasion of Laying the Corner Stone of the Monument Tomb of the Army of Tennessee," April 6, 1883, all in Rowland (ed.), *Jefferson Davis, Constitutionalist*, VIII, 232; IX, 292, 270, 206.

[7] Johnston, *Life of Johnston*, p. 291. See also Hudson Strode, *Jefferson Davis: Confederate President*, pp. 153–155.

[8] F. Titus and others to Davis, September 9, 1861, Johnston Papers, Barret Collection.

[9] Parks, *General Leonidas Polk, C.S.A.*, p. 180.

[10] *Official Records*, Ser. I, Vol. III, pp. 687–688; Vol. IV, p. 405.

friend and foe alike.[11] Years after the Civil War, General U. S. Grant would say of Johnston: "His contemporaries at West Point, and officers generally who came to know him personally later and who remained on our side, expected him to prove the most formidable man to meet that the Confederacy would produce." [12] General Scott was known to have offered him high command in the Union Army; Generals Taylor [13] and Worth [14] of Mexican War fame both were said to have called him the finest soldier that they knew. Johnston had an awesome reputation to uphold; his people expected miracles of him in the field.

He left at once to take command of his Department, arriving by rail in Nashville on September 14. The citizens greeted him with enthusiasm and called for a public appearance. Johnston spoke briefly, addressing his hearers as "Fellow Soldiers" of the reserve corps. His implication was not lost on the perceptive members of the audience: the Confederacy was engaged in a people's war and could be sustained only by them. "This was a well-timed remark," observed a Nashville editor, "and showed that, as a military man, he knew what was coming. The South will need all of her force. Every able-bodied man may as well make up his mind to it, and that soon." [15]

In Nashville, Johnston met his son William Preston, who was on his way to join his Kentucky regiment in northern Virginia. For a few brief hours the two talked of family and of public affairs; Johnston described his California career and the march across the plains. Associates urged Johnston to appoint his son to his staff; he refused to do so, for he wished to avoid the appearance of favoritism. This meeting between father and son was undoubtedly happy, and the parting sad; parental and filial bonds between the two were exceptionally strong, perhaps in measure to compensate for their having lived apart during most of the son's life. They were not to meet again.[16]

---

[11] *Daily True Delta*, September 8, 1861.

[12] Grant, *Personal Memoirs of U. S. Grant*, p. 187.

[13] Richard Taylor, *Destruction and Reconstruction: Personal Experiences of the Late War*, p. 283.

[14] Editorial, *Harper's Weekly*, II (January 30, 1858) , 72–74.

[15] Stanley F. Horn, *The Army of Tennessee*, p. 56.

[16] Johnston, *Life of Johnston*, pp. 306–307. William Preston Johnston subsequently had a varied and interesting career. He soon became aide-de-camp to Jefferson Davis, held this position for the remainder of the war, and was captured with Davis at the end of the conflict. Later he wrote a biography of his

Johnston at once turned his mind to the military task that confronted him. A grave decision was required immediately: whether to advance his line into Kentucky in an effort to secure her for the Confederacy or to consider the state untenable and dispose his forces for the most advantageous defense of Tennessee. The people of Kentucky were sharply split in their loyalties to the Union and the Confederacy; for months the state administration had attempted to remain neutral. This precarious neutrality had already been violated by both contestants. On September 1, Federal troops under General Robert Anderson had moved into Louisville, where Anderson established his headquarters, and pro-Union militia units throughout the state were placed under Federal army commanders; three days later Confederate Lieutenant General Leonidas Polk marched from western Tennessee and seized Columbus, Kentucky, on the Mississippi River at the northern end of the Mobile and Ohio Railroad. Even before reaching Nashville, Johnston had ordered Brigadier General Felix Zollicoffer to move his command of about 4,000 from Knoxville to Cumberland Ford in eastern Kentucky to guard the Cumberland Gap through the mountains from Virginia. The Kentucky Legislature now demanded that the Southern troops be withdrawn.

After consulting with Governor Isham G. Harris of Tennessee concerning "facts, political and military," Johnston decided to ignore the demand of the Kentucky Legislature, and instead to advance his forces as far into Kentucky as possible. The only defensible line in front of Nashville was that of the Barren River in central Kentucky, said Johnston. To give up this line to the Federals, and to withdraw from Columbus and Cumberland Ford would expose the important city of Nashville and the entire state of Tennessee to immediate invasion. To the requirements of military strategy were added the requirements of political and economic necessity, felt Johnston, and the Confederacy ought to do all within its power to gain the adherence of Kentucky. He predicted:

---

father, General Johnston, which was published in 1878. He taught under Robert E. Lee at Washington College, Lexington, Virginia, and was at his bedside when Lee died. From 1880 until 1883 William Preston Johnston was president of Louisiana State University. In 1884 he became the first president of the Tulane University of Louisiana, a newly organized private university which had grown out of the old state University of Louisiana. Johnston served with distinction as president of this school until his death in 1899. Shaw, *William Preston Johnston,* pp. 72, 80, 94–106, 157–191, 192–221.

The Government of the United States fully appreciating the vast resources to be obtained by the subjugation of Kentucky will make its greatest efforts here for this purpose. If we could wrest this rich fringe from his grasp the war could be carried across the border and the contest speedily decided upon our own terms.[17]

Johnston now ordered Brigadier General Simon B. Buckner, with the 4,000 Confederate troops stationed in Nashville, to occupy Bowling Green without delay. Buckner left Nashville with his troops on September 17; traveling by the Louisville and Nashville Railroad, they took Bowling Green before noon of the eighteenth. Buckner made a preliminary statement of reassurance to the people of Kentucky, and issued stringent orders to his troops against molesting citizens or property. On September 22 Johnston published a formal proclamation of his purposes and intentions in entering the state. The Confederate Army was in Kentucky because of the prior Federal occupation of a part of the state, he said, and he pledged to withdraw if the Federals would do the same. Southern troops felt no hostility toward citizens of Kentucky, said Johnston; rather, the presence of these troops would enable the people to follow the path of their choice in the war. They might either continue their neutrality, or they might join ranks with the Confederacy. Or they might make common cause with the North. "But if it be true . . . that a majority of those people desire to adhere to the United States and become parties to the war," he declared, "then none can doubt the right of the other belligerent to meet that war whenever and wherever it may be waged." [18]

Union commanders in Kentucky believed that Johnston was striking for Louisville and the line of the Ohio River. If he had possessed the strength for such a blow, he doubtless would have attempted it. Johnston was an advocate of offensive warfare; earlier in his career he had urged it against the Mexicans, against the Indians, and against the Mormons. He now hoped that ultimately he would be able to carry the war into the North; he was said to have remarked that, with sufficient numbers, he would march to the Great Lakes. But Johnston was painfully aware that for the present he lacked the strength for offensive warfare; even as he ordered Buckner to Bowl-

[17] Johnston to Samuel Cooper, October 17, 1861, "Headquarters Book of Albert Sidney Johnston."

[18] *Official Records*, Ser. I, Vol. IV, pp. 420–421.

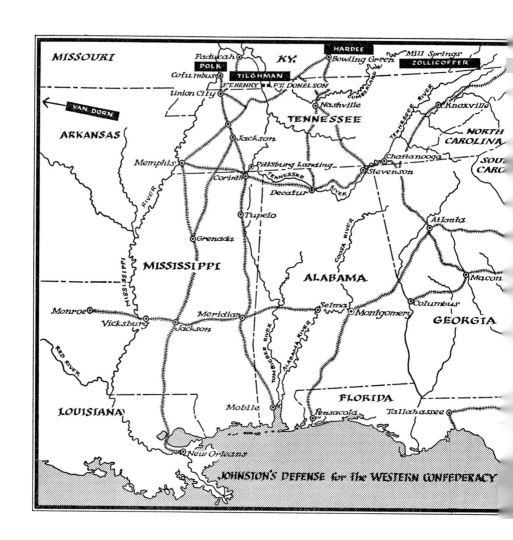

MISSOURI

KY.

HARDEE

Paducah
POLK
Columbus
Union City

Bowling Green

Mill Springs
ZOLLICOFFER

TILGHMAN
FT. HENRY FT. DONELSON

CUMBERLAND RIVER

Nashville

Knoxville

VAN DORN

TENNESSEE

ARKANSAS

Jackson

TENNESSEE RIVER

NORTH
CAROLINA

Memphis

Corinth

Pittsburg Landing

Chattanooga

Stevenson

SOU
CARO

TENNESSEE RIVER

Decatur

Tupelo

MISSISSIPPI RIVER

Grenada

COOSA RIVER

Atlanta

MISSISSIPPI

ALABAMA

Macon

Monroe

Vicksburg

Meridian

Jackson

Selma

Montgomery

Columbus

GEORGIA

RED RIVER

TOMBIGBEE RIVER

ALABAMA RIVER

LOUISIANA

Mobile

FLORIDA

Pensacola

Tallahassee

New Orleans

JOHNSTON'S DEFENSE for the WESTERN CONFEDERACY

ing Green he wrote urgently to Davis that he had not more than half enough troops required to hold this advanced line.[19] Johnston had pressed forward to the utmost limit of his capabilities; he planned now to dig in and hold long enough for Confederate authorities to send reinforcements and for Southern leaders in Kentucky to rally her citizens to the Confederate cause.[20]

Seizure of Bowling Green created a Confederate line of defense for the Mississippi Valley.

Bowling Green was fortified [Johnston explained] for the reasons that in my judgment . . . it was the most defensible point that could be selected to cover Nashville and our Southern line of defence extending from Cumberland Gap to the Mississippi River. It is naturally strong, a salient point on the railroads and turnpike roads passing through Kentucky, and the most difficult point to turn by an aggressive enemy that could have been selected.[21]

Johnston's forces were now deployed from the Appalachians to the western border of Arkansas—an expanse of more than 500 miles.

Johnston commanded somewhat fewer than 40,000 troops present for duty, and they were poorly armed and virtually untrained. They were disposed as follows: 4,000 under Zollicoffer at Cumberland Ford in eastern Kentucky, 4,000 under Buckner at Bowling Green, 11,000 under Polk at Columbus, with skeleton garrisons at Fort Henry on the Tennessee River and Fort Donelson on the Cumberland, 10,000 under Sterling Price in southwestern Missouri where he had remained after the Confederate victory at Wilson's Creek in August, 7,000 under Ben McCulloch in northwestern Arkansas, and a handful of troops under Johnston's old subordinate and comrade of the Second Cavalry, William J. Hardee, at Pocahontas on the Black River in northeastern Arkansas.[22]

Johnston faced a Union force of half again his own strength. In central and eastern Kentucky (the Union Central Department) were some 20,000 Northern troops led by Johnston's erstwhile friend, General Robert Anderson of Fort Sumter fame; from St. Louis,

---

[19] Johnston to Davis, September 16, 1861, *ibid.*, pp. 193–194.

[20] Johnston to Cooper, October 17, 1861, "Headquarters Book of Albert Sidney Johnston."

[21] "Questions Propounded to Genl. A. S. Johnston by the Special Committee of the House of Representatives, and Answers"; and Johnston to "Sir," March 17, 1862, both in War Department Collection of Confederate Records.

[22] *Ibid.*

General John C. Frémont, the celebrated Pathfinder and antislavery politician, commanded approximately 36,000 Federal soldiers distributed throughout Missouri and at Cairo, Illinois, and Paducah, Kentucky. Frémont's detachments at Cairo and Paducah were under the immediate command of Brigadier General U. S. Grant.[23]

Johnston's line was arranged to take advantage of the railroads that served his Department. If supplied with adequate locomotives and cars, he could easily transfer troops and supplies via the Memphis, Clarksville and Louisville Railroad and the Memphis and Charleston Railroad from Bowling Green to Columbus, or to points between that might be threatened. Bowling Green and Nashville were connected by the Louisville and Nashville Railroad, as well as by an improved turnpike. The Mobile and Ohio Railroad and the New Orleans, Jackson and Great Northern linked Johnston's forward positions with the Gulf Coast; the Memphis and Charleston Railroad and the Southern of Mississippi provided lateral transport at intervals of 150 miles behind the forward line. Johnston's rail communications were as good as the Confederacy could provide.

Yet his position, geographically, was dangerously exposed and weak. The broad frontier committed to his care was without a significant natural obstacle to the enemy; no narrow pass would enable him to stand favorably against superior numbers. Instead, the rivers, the most important features of the prevailing terrain, seemed almost to have been plotted by some Brobdingnagian strategist preparing to invade the South. The Mississippi, Tennessee, and Cumberland rivers all flowed into or out of Johnston's sector and all came together in Northern territory. The Mississippi split his defense zone and rendered difficult any coordination of forces east and west of the great stream. The Tennessee and Cumberland both penetrated his line in western Tennessee and, lying generally paral-

---

[23] Exact troop strength as of September, 1861, is not in all cases available. As late as November the Confederate forces in Kentucky were fewer than 32,000 troops present for duty. *Official Records,* Ser. I, Vol. IV, pp. 425, 554, 557. Under Price and McCulloch in Arkansas were about 17,000 men. *Ibid.,* Ser. I, Vol. III, p. 748. Confederate troops present for duty were about 65 per cent of the total, present and absent. Frémont's aggregate in September, present and absent, was 55,693. His total present for duty, reckoned at 65 per cent of this figure, would have been roughly 36,000. *Ibid.,* p. 493. The aggregate strength of the Union force in central and eastern Kentucky in November (then under General William T. Sherman) was 49,586—an estimated 32,000 present for duty. *Ibid.,* Ser. I, Vol. IV, p. 349.

lel, curved behind his Bowling Green position. The Cumberland led directly to Nashville, major center of population and industry of his Department. The Tennessee described a great arc that cut twice across the entire state of Tennessee, touched the northeastern corner of Mississippi, and went through the northern portion of Alabama. The bottom of this arc ran for 100 miles within easy marching distance of the major transverse railroad of the Confederacy—the Memphis and Charleston—and twice crossed the railroad in northern Alabama.

The Ohio River, forming the northern boundary of Kentucky, protected the states of the northwest from the threat of invasion, and made junction with the Mississippi, Tennessee, and Cumberland within a space of seventy-five miles, behind the Union line. From a central point—Cairo, Illinois—Federal troops could be moved rapidly by water against Columbus on the Mississippi or against Confederate positions on the Tennessee or Cumberland rivers; in an emergency the Ohio could be used to transfer reinforcements quickly from one wing of the Union army to support of the other. Overwhelming Northern superiority in gunboats and transports converted these rivers into a formidable military advantage against the South.

Dangerous weaknesses in Johnston's line were at the points where the Mississippi, Tennessee, and Cumberland rivers entered it. The General recognized this deficiency, and set about at once to remedy it. As soon as Buckner was firmly lodged in Bowling Green, Johnston went from Nashville to Columbus to see that the Mississippi was made safe against Federal penetration. There he felt the gladness of being reunited with his West Point roommate and lifelong friend, General Leonidas Polk. Long before, Polk had left the army to become an Episcopal minister; in time he had risen to become Episcopal Bishop of Louisiana, but upon the outbreak of war Polk laid aside his clerical attire to don the gray uniform of the Confederacy. After a brief period recalling past years and associations, the two turned to the business of fortifying Columbus. Johnston found that Polk was already at work emplacing batteries along the bluff to combat enemy gunboats and laying out field works to protect against attack by land.[24] Soon Columbus would become a powerful fortress, bristling with 140 heavy guns, and known to the Confederates as the

---

[24] Parks, *General Leonidas Polk, C.S.A.*, pp. 186–187.

"Gibraltar of the West." Below Columbus other fortifications were being prepared at Island No. 10, New Madrid, and Fort Pillow. The Mississippi seemed secure for the Confederacy.[25]

Johnston remained at Columbus for only a few days. His presence there had its characteristic striking effect upon the troops, lifting their spirits to new heights. Without playing the martinet or resorting to bluster, he brought firm discipline to a hitherto slack command. Ostensibly riding daily for his health, he continuously inspected men, camps, weapons, and instruction. To judgment, courtesy, and quiet efficiency, Johnston added a touch of timely daring for the benefit of the fresh recruits. When one day a Federal gunboat dropped down the river and exchanged a few rounds with the shore batteries, the General stood immobile as shells burst nearby. Warned by a subordinate of the danger to his person, Johnston replied, "We must all take our risks." The soldiers broke into cheers as they observed his conduct under fire.[26]

On another occasion, as he was about to ride out of camp, he was stopped by a sentry because he had no pass from headquarters. Johnston refused to "pull rank"; instead, he tipped his cap and said, "You are right my young soldier—I commend you for your obedience—I am glad to command such a soldiery." [27] Again, he might pass a wry pleasantry to draw his subordinates closer to him. When the names of General Frémont's numerous staff were published, including such as Kalmanuezze and Zagonyi, Johnston remarked with a smile, "There is too much tail to that kite." With these and other words and deeds Johnston created between himself and his subordinates those mystic bonds of respect and sentiment that transform an aggregation of men into a true army. "The entire army, as by some instinct, soon conceived the greatest admiration of and confidence in him," said an associate.[28]

At Columbus, Johnston created a staff to support him in command. The staff was organized into a Department of Orders, with Lieutenant Colonel W. W. Mackall as ranking assistant adjutant general (Mackall had occupied this same position under Johnston

[25] James L. Nichols, *Confederate Engineers*, p. 51.

[26] Thomas C. Reynolds to William Preston Johnston, November 13, 1875, Johnston Papers, Barret Collection.

[27] L. W. Finlay, "Account of the Shiloh Campaign," attached to letter from G. B. Peters, Jr., to William Preston Johnston, July 5, 1877, in *ibid*.

[28] Reynolds to William Preston Johnston, November 13, 1875, *ibid*.

in California), a Quartermaster Department under Major Albert J. Smith, a Commissary Department under Captain Thomas K. Jackson, and an Engineer Corps under Lieutenant Joseph Dixon. This staff lacked such modern staff departments as Operations and Intelligence, and there was no chief of staff to coordinate its work, but it was set up along logical lines. Colonel Mackall acted, in part, as chief of staff.

Johnston added another department, the Personal Staff, whose very existence throws light on his concept of strategy and operations.

In addition to an aide-de-camp, the Personal Staff included a number of volunteer aides. Among these were George W. Johnson and Thomas C. Reynolds, Confederate "governors in exile" of the states of Kentucky and Missouri; later, Governor Isham G. Harris of Tennessee was added to this group. There was also Samuel Tate, president of the Memphis and Charleston Railroad.[29] The presence of these political leaders indicates Johnston's awareness of the close relationship between military strategy and politics. Said Governor Reynolds:

This [appointment of political figures to the staff] was one of the many incidents which showed me that he was a complete general, for, while no true soldier will permit any merely political influences around him, yet an able commander should always take into consideration, and be minutely and accurately informed of, the condition, resources, etc., of the country in which he operates.[30]

The presence of Samuel Tate revealed Johnston's awareness of the new but vital role of the railroad in warfare. Johnston was wise beyond the narrow sense of the canons of military science.

He found fortifications already under construction to guard the Tennessee and Cumberland rivers. Fort Henry on the Tennessee and Fort Donelson on the Cumberland lay in Tennessee about ten miles south of the Kentucky line. The two forts were between the rivers at a point where the streams are about eleven miles apart. The ideal location would have been farther downriver where the streams flow within two miles of each other. But this spot was in Kentucky.

---

[29] Order No. 2, Headquarters, Western Department, September 26, 1861, Leonidas Polk Papers, Manuscript Division, Library of Congress.

[30] Reynolds to William Preston Johnston, November 13, 1875, Johnston Papers, Barret Collection.

Building of the forts had been begun by the state of Tennessee at a time when Kentucky declared herself neutral; hence, political exigencies rather than requirements of strategy or terrain governed the selection of the sites.

Almost until Johnston's arrival, Confederate authorities continued to respect the neutrality of Kentucky and went ahead, though perfunctorily, with strengthening Forts Henry and Donelson. When Johnston took command, he considered the advisability of beginning new fortifications at more favorable sites in Kentucky. On September 17 he sent Lieutenant Joseph Dixon, a gifted young topographical engineer, to survey the positions and recommend whether to move the forts or complete them where they were. Dixon reported that the positions were not the best possible, but that, under the circumstances, they ought to be completed. Johnston approved this decision; considering the need for haste, he had hardly any other choice. But he realized that the forts were vulnerable to a determined attack by land or water, and that, recessed as they were behind his advanced positions at Columbus and Bowling Green, they created a dangerous re-entrant in the Southern line.[31]

On October 13, Johnston left Columbus for Bowling Green, where Buckner reported Union forces threatening. There he had the pleasure of renewing another fond acquaintance, that of General Hardee, whose command he had ordered from Arkansas a few days earlier. About 12,000 troops were now concentrated at Bowling Green. This strength was achieved by drawing Hardee's force from Arkansas, by bringing Terry's Texas Rangers, at their request, from Louisiana, and by enrolling a number of Kentucky volunteer regiments into the Confederate Army. Johnston organized the Bowling Green army into two divisions, the First under Hardee and the Second under Buckner. Johnston himself at first took direct command of the entire Bowling Green force. Hardee's division was ordered forward to the Green River about eighteen miles above Bowling Green; Buckner's division was held ready to be sent wherever it was needed. Later Johnston gave the Bowling Green force the name of Central Army of Kentucky, and placed Hardee in command.[32]

Lacking the strength to attack, Johnston organized his entire command east of the Mississippi River so as to meet anticipated Federal

---

[31] Nichols, *Confederate Engineers*, pp. 42–43; Horn, *The Army of Tennessee*, pp. 74–79.

[32] *Official Records*, Ser. I, Vol. VII, p. 814.

advances. These would come, he believed, on one or more of three lines: along the Louisville and Nashville Railroad against Bowling Green, with Nashville as the objective; against the Cumberland Gap; or along the line of the Mississippi River, perhaps using the Tennessee River to support this movement.[33] Johnston split his front into three sectors of responsibility against these expected enemy operations. He held the Bowling Green army ready to block any advance along the Louisville and Nashville; Polk was responsible for the defense of the Mississippi, Tennessee, and Cumberland river lines; and Zollicoffer was responsible for the defense of Cumberland Gap and the roads leading from eastern Kentucky into Nashville.[34]

In advancing into Kentucky, Johnston adopted what in modern warfare has been called an "arrogant display of power." It was a bluff; he knew that he would not be able to hold this line indefinitely, to say nothing of taking the offensive, without strong reinforcement. But he shrewdly reasoned that a bold front might deceive the enemy into believing that the Southern army was stronger than it actually was. If this could be accomplished, Johnston would be able to gain precious time for the Confederacy to build up strength in the west. For almost six months this strategy was remarkably successful.

Johnston maneuvered the little army at Bowling Green with deceptive confidence, instructing Hardee to dispose his troops so as to make the enemy feel that a Confederate advance was about to begin.[35] Reconnaissance and raiding expeditions were told, "Create the impression that this force is only an advanced guard." Cavalry sorties were to be conducted in the same manner.[36]

Johnston's ruse had the desired effect. "The Yankees had a vague idea that we were their superiors in courage and skill," Hardee wrote.[37] At his headquarters in Louisville, General Anderson was convinced that the Confederates were poised to march upon that

[33] Johnston to Cooper, October 27, 1861, "Headquarters Book of Albert Sidney Johnston."

[34] *Ibid.* See also William J. Hardee to "My Dear Friend," October 11, December 4, 5, 1861, William J. Hardee Papers.

[35] W. W. Mackall to Hardee, October 21, 1861, "Headquarters Book of Albert Sidney Johnston."

[36] Johnston to Hardee, November 9, 1861, *Official Records,* Ser. I, Vol. IV, p. 531.

[37] Hardee to "My Dear Mrs. Stover," January 23, 1862, Hardee Papers.

city; instead of attacking the light Southern column at Bowling Green, Anderson ordered his subordinate, Brigadier General William T. Sherman, to occupy Muldraugh's Hill near Elizabethtown in order to defend Louisville. Anderson's resolve collapsed almost immediately before Johnston's pressure. On October 5 Anderson turned his responsibilities over to Sherman, saying that "he could not stand the mental torture of his command any longer, and that he must go away or it would kill him."

Sherman fared no better. As the weeks went by he more and more exaggerated Johnston's strength, which actually was decreasing in proportion to his own. Sherman was convinced that any forward movement by the Union forces was impossible; he lived in fear of a stroke by Johnston. If Johnston should combine his Bowling Green force with that of Zollicoffer, Sherman believed, the Confederates could take Louisville. Sherman continued after the war to say that Johnston at first could have "walked into Louisville"; but he confessed that at the time he was "unnecessarily unhappy" about the danger of an advance by Johnston.[38] Ultimately Sherman's nerves, too, gave way; on November 15 he was relieved of command by Brigadier General Don Carlos Buell.

Johnston's strategy of the bold front moved a Northern editor to write:

[Johnston] perpetually threatened our army with assault and annihilation, kept Louisville, and even Cincinnati, for a time in a state of perturbation, and delayed the progress of our arms until it seemed his end was on the eve of accomplishment.[39]

Ultimately Johnston's ruse came to naught. But it must be credited with achieving what it was meant to achieve: it purchased half a year of grace for the Confederacy in the west.

The enemy might be deceived about the true strength of Confederate forces in the west; but Johnston was fearfully cognizant of his weakness. Even as he published exaggerated figures on his armies, and gave them out to individuals who would pass them on to Federal officers, Johnston constantly warned the Richmond authorities of the imminent peril of a Federal advance against his line. "We have not over half the armed forces that are now likely to be required for our security against disaster," he wrote in his first letter from Nash-

[38] William T. Sherman, *Memoirs of General William T. Sherman,* I, 199.
[39] Johnston, *Life of Johnston,* p. 726.

ville to Davis. Every subsequent communication to his superiors repeated the urgent necessity for strengthening the Confederate forces in the west.[40]

He did not, however, sit idle to await reinforcement by the War Department. At the same time that he informed the Administration of his weakness, he set about vigorously to remedy it. At first he believed that he would have plenty of men; so eager had Southerners volunteered during the preceding spring and summer that tens of thousands were turned away by the enrolling officers for want of arms and equipment. "I feel assured that I can command the requisite number of men," Johnston wrote to Davis, "but we are deficient in arms." Already, he was searching his Department for weapons. On the day after his arrival in Nashville he had dispatched staff officers to Major General Braxton Bragg at Pensacola and to the governors of Alabama and Georgia, asking for small arms to equip infantry and cavalry. Four days later, he telegraphed Davis that he had information of the arrival at Savannah of a shipload of arms and that the western army needed 30,000 stand.[41]

All replies to these requests were disappointing. Governor A. B. Moore of Alabama feared that his own Gulf Coast was threatened; Governor Joseph E. Brown of Georgia, stormy petrel of state rights, answered that all of his arms had been sent to the defense of Virginia, Florida, and the Georgia coastline.[42] General Bragg wrote in a solicitous tone, saying that all of the efforts on the Gulf Coast were being wasted, that Mobile and New Orleans were being fortified at great expense while their true protection lay in the strength of Johnston's army. But Bragg had no arms, he said, that he could send to Johnston.[43] Davis wrote that the steamer at Savannah was a merchant vessel bringing some arms but that only a fraction of them could be spared the western department. "Rely not on rumors," Davis admonished Johnston.[44] Of the 30,000 arms that Johnston needed, he got but 1,000.[45]

---

[40] Johnston to Davis, September 16, 1861, "Headquarters Book of Albert Sidney Johnston."

[41] *Official Records,* Ser. I, Vol. IV, p. 416. Johnston's troops were also short of clothing, especially of overcoats. See Hardee to "My Dear Mrs. Stover," November 21, 1861, Hardee Papers.

[42] *Official Records,* Ser. I, Vol. IV, p. 412.

[43] *Ibid.,* pp. 419–420.

[44] *Ibid.,* p. 417.

[45] *Ibid.,* p. 430.

He was no more successful in securing enough troops than in obtaining enough arms. He was authorized by the Confederate government to call upon the state governments of Arkansas, Tennessee, and Mississippi for men. He was also to accept troops from Kentucky and Missouri, states of divided loyalties, which did not secede. Johnston was sorely disappointed in expecting the men of these two states to flock to the Confederate cause; few troops joined his army from either state.

The coolness of the Kentuckians was especially bitter because of his Kentucky birth and associations; more to the point, he was disappointed because his advance into Kentucky had been made largely in the hope that it would draw the resources of that state to the support of the Confederacy.[46]

We have received but little accession to our ranks since the Confederate forces crossed the line [he wrote to Secretary of War Judah P. Benjamin]; in fact, no such demonstrations of enthusiasm as to justify any movements not warranted by our ability to maintain our own communications. . . . [The people] appear to me passive, if not apathetic. . . . I shall, however, still hope that the love and spirit of liberty are not yet extinct in Kentucky.[47]

In invading Kentucky, Johnston had misjudged the temper of his native state.

He at once appealed for men to the governors of the Confederate states within his Department. Estimating his need at an additional 50,000, he called upon Tennessee for 30,000, and upon Mississippi and Arkansas for 10,000 each, saying he preferred men who were enlisted for the duration of the war, as they would be better trained and more dependable than short-term volunteers. Nevertheless, because of the urgency of the situation, he offered to accept twelve-month volunteers.[48] This possible solution was blocked; on October 25 Secretary of War Benjamin informed Johnston that the acceptance of unarmed men for periods of less than the duration of the war was a violation of Confederate policy. Johnston was ordered to disband those who recently had come into his army in response to his "unlucky offer." [49] To a man as desperate for troops

[46] *Ibid.,* p. 469.

[47] Eliza Calvert Hall, "Bowling Green and the Civil War," *The Filson Club History Quarterly,* XI (October, 1937) , 251.

[48] *Official Records,* Ser. I, Vol. IV, pp. 417–418, 421–423.

[49] *Ibid.,* pp. 473–474.

as Johnston was now becoming, this order made little sense, but he reluctantly obeyed it.

Even as he complied with the Secretary of War's interdiction, Johnston sought ways to get around it legally. He called upon the states for their militia companies, which already possessed weapons. He also worked out with energetic Governor Harris of Tennessee a method of arming short-term volunteers who came to the service unarmed. Johnston continued to accept volunteers who were temporarily without arms, while Governor Harris induced the Tennessee Legislature to impress privately owned weapons from the citizens of the state.[50] Impressed weapons suitable for use were immediately placed in the hands of the recruits, and unserviceable arms were altered and repaired. Meantime, the unarmed men were organized into military units and their training was begun.

The Government thus secured their services [Johnston explained to the Secretary of War]. Otherwise they could not have been procured; and the time between mustering in and arming was profitably employed in giving the men all practicable instruction in their duties as soldiers. This, it will be readily perceived, was quite as necessary to their efficiency in the field as placing arms in their hands.[51]

Johnston's methods anticipated the "wooden-guns" drilling of unarmed American soldiers in wars of the twentieth century.

Johnston's call upon the states brought only a trickle of men, woefully short of the 50,000 asked for. Again, and now more urgently, he appealed to the state governors for reinforcement. A message to Governor John J. Pettus, of Mississippi, read:

If troops are given to me, if the people can be made to feel how much suffering and calamity would be avoided by the presence now in my camp of 10,000 or 15,000 more brave men, so that I could attack the enemy, and not, from a disparity of force, be compelled to await it—it seems to me that the same generous ardor that induced them to embark in the great struggle for our independence would give me such succors that victory would be certain. . . . A decisive battle will probably be fought on this line; and a company on that day will be worth more than a regiment next year. If the enemy does not attack, the North embarrassed at home, menaced with war

---

[50] For accounts of Governor Harris's efforts, see Isham G. Harris to Davis, October 15, 1861; Harris to Johnston, December 31, 1861; Harris to Judah P. Benjamin, January 8, 1862, all in Harris Letter Book.

[51] Johnston to Benjamin, January 12, 1862, "Headquarters Book of Albert Sidney Johnston."

by England, will shrink foiled from the conflict, and the freedom of the South will be forever established.[52]

Similar messages went to the other chief executives in Johnston's area.

In spite of his efforts to raise troops, the Confederate army in the west gained strength slowly; it failed to keep pace with its foe. The initial flush of Southern patriotism had waned; the number of new enlistments fell below Johnston's expectation. "I am disappointed in the state of public sentiment in the South," Johnston said to one of his staff officers. "Our people seem to have suffered from a violent political fever, which has left them exhausted. They are not up to the revolutionary point." [53] In early January, 1862, he wrote forebodingly to Secretary Benjamin:

I have hoped to be able to raise an adequate force by the aid of the Governors of the several States of this department; but, notwithstanding zealous efforts on their part, thus far I have been able to draw to this place only a force which, when compared in number to the enemy, must be regarded as insufficient.[54]

As Johnston sought to strengthen his army through volunteers, he sought also to impress upon the Richmond government the strategic importance of the Mississippi Valley. Preoccupied with the defense of Richmond, Davis seems to have been insufficiently aware of the danger through the broad western approach. Johnston saw it with clarity. A powerful Federal army was about to march south from Kentucky, he warned Benjamin.

They [the Federals] have justly comprehended that the seat of vitality of the Confederacy, if to be reached at all is by this route. It is now palpable that all the resources of that government will, if necessary, be employed to assure success on this line.[55]

At the same time he attempted a greater concentration of available Confederate forces in the support of his line. Confederate troops were lamentably scattered, many of them stationed at points of comparatively slight importance or danger in the interior or along

[52] Johnston to J. J. Pettus, December 24, 1861, *ibid.*
[53] Edward W. Munford, "Albert Sidney Johnston," n.d., Johnston Papers, Barret Collection.
[54] *Official Records,* Ser. I, Vol. VII, p. 825.
[55] Johnston to Benjamin, January 8, 1862, "Headquarters Book of Albert Sidney Johnston."

the seacoast of the South. Beset by the doctrine of state rights, and importuned by state governors and other political leaders to protect every foot of Confederate territory, Davis was never able to achieve an effective concentration of forces.

Johnston realized that complete concentration was impossible, and his requests were modest. Yet he did call upon Davis to send reinforcements from other departments not similarly threatened by the enemy. "If the public service would permit," he wrote to the Secretary of War, "I beg leave to suggest that a few regiments might be detached from the several armies in the field and ordered here, to be replaced by new levies." [56] To the adjutant general, he analyzed:

The enemy will probably undertake no active operations in Missouri and may be content to hold our forces fast in their position on the Potomac for the remainder of the winter, but to suppose with the facilities of movement by water which the well filled rivers of the Ohio, Cumberland, and Tennessee give for active operations, that they will suspend them in Tennessee and Kentucky during the winter months is a delusion. All the resources of the Confederacy are now needed for the defence of Tennessee.[57]

In his urgency, Johnston went outside the normal chain of command to present his views to Davis; in mid-January, 1862, he dispatched Colonel John R. Liddell directly to the President. Speaking for Johnston, Liddell urged Davis to send troops to Kentucky from Virginia, Charleston, Savannah, Pensacola, and New Orleans. The plea was futile. Liddell found Davis careworn and irritable. "My God!" Davis exclaimed. "Why did General Johnston send you to me for arms and reinforcements, when he must know that I have neither. He has plenty of men in Tennessee, and they must have arms of some kind—shotguns, rifles, even pikes could be used." The next day Davis was more sympathetic, but he dismissed Liddell, saying, "Tell my friend, General Johnston, that I can do nothing for him; that he must rely on his own resources." Thus the Confederacy failed to concentrate its forces for the defense of the Mississippi Valley.[58]

Though pressed by the cares of his command, Johnston's mind turned often to his family. "You & the children occupy every thought not devoted to business," he wrote to Eliza. For months Johnston

---

[56] *Ibid.*

[57] Johnston to Cooper, January 22, 1862, *ibid.*

[58] St. John R. Liddell, "Liddell's Record of the Civil War," *Southern Bivouac,* I NS (December, 1885), 417–419.

heard nothing from his loved ones, so difficult was it to get mail to and from California. His last recorded word from them was a letter from his son Sid, written September 6. He endured a bitter silence. In spite of the impending birth of a child, when Johnston left Eliza in June she had expected to join him soon by sailing to New York and coming south through the military lines. At year's end Johnston believed that she and the younger children were in Louisville with her relatives. At last he learned that this was not so, that Eliza had been unable, for some reason, to make the journey, and that she was still in Los Angeles. His relief upon learning that his wife and children were all right assuaged the disappointment of knowing that they could not join him within any determinable period of time. "I was rejoiced to know that you & the dear little ones were all safe & well," he said. "I pray God that you have so continued since then." [59]

In early January, 1862, Johnston wrote his last known letter to Eliza. It was characteristic of the man. He expressed his love for her and for the children; then he talked of the times. The people of California ought to be thankful that they were spared the hardships brought by war to North and South, he said. Eliza must be courageous and remain hopeful for the future.

The boys must go on in their studies and be encouraged to read history & other proper works of literature and as far as possible be prepared for the station they will be called on to fill when they are old enough to enter the arena of life. . . . Kiss each boy & each girl. I shall love the youngest better if you give her your own name—May God bless you & them & preserve you free from all harm.[60]

Johnston penned words of encouragement to his wife, but his own spirit must have been heavy as he wrote. He now realized he had small prospect of increasing his force to equal his mission; and powerful enemy columns were ready to march against his slender line.

[59] Johnston to Eliza Johnston, December 29, 1861, Johnston Papers, Barret Collection.

[60] *Ibid.*, January 6, 1862. The Johnstons' last child was born August 30, 1861—a daughter. His wish concerning her name had been more than fulfilled even before he wrote this letter. She was named Eliza Alberta Johnston. See Johnston, *The Johnstons of Salisbury,* p. 160, and Hancock M. Johnston to E. G. Littlejohn, July 29, 1902, in Texas Historical Society Papers, Manuscripts Division, Rosenberg Library. Eliza Johnston continued to live in Los Angeles for the remainder of her life. She died there in 1896. See Alberta Johnston Denis, "Mrs. Albert Sidney Johnston," *Texas Magazine,* I (May, 1897), 427–430.

Defeat at the Rivers

BY MID-NOVEMBER Johnston's strategy of bold maneuver to conceal weakness was beginning to lose effect. The Union generals in the west—Henry W. Halleck, who had replaced Frémont in Missouri, Grant in Cairo, and Buell in Kentucky—were now certain that Johnston lacked the strength to attack with any hope of success, that he must wait for them to strike the first blow. This knowledge alone was an incalculable advantage to the Federal commanders, enabling them to choose the time and place for their stroke. Johnston had lost the tactical initiative in the west.

The first Northern thrust against Johnston's line came on November 7. It was launched by Grant, a then obscure brigadier general whose rugged fighting qualities would in time carry him to the supreme command of the Union armies, and ultimately to victory in the war. Grant decided upon a blow against one of General Polk's outposts located in the village of Belmont, Missouri, across the Mississippi River from the fortress Columbus. Landing his steamboat transports about three miles above Belmont early on the seventh, Grant then marched his column of 3,000 directly against the

Confederate position. He also sent small forces from Cairo and Paducah to search for Confederates under Jeff Thompson in Missouri and to demonstrate against Columbus.[1]

Polk, learning of Grant's movement, meantime sent 2,500 reinforcements across from Columbus to Belmont under the command of Brigadier General Gideon Pillow. Fighting began at 10:30 in the morning and continued briskly for four hours. Slowly the Confederates gave ground and seemed at last on the point of disaster when Polk himself arrived with additional troops. Now the tables were turned. Exhausted from fighting and disorganized from looting the captured Southern camp, Grant's outnumbered column was flanked and driven back in near rout. Late in the afternoon Grant, with extreme difficulty, embarked his worn command on their transports and steamed upstream to Cairo. Both sides uttered cries of victory; but the lines of the two armies in the west remained unchanged.[2]

For more than two months after Belmont the western front lay quiet except for minor skirmishes here and there. Then, in mid-January, Johnston suffered his first defeat in the field. It occurred at the eastern extremity of his line. Displaying more spirit than wisdom, General Zollicoffer had, in early December, moved his army to Beech Grove, Kentucky, on the north side of the Cumberland River.[3] Johnston foresaw the hazard of such a move; on December 4 he wrote his impetuous subordinate to select a point from which he could observe the river "without crossing it." Zollicoffer replied on the tenth saying that he inferred from Johnston's letter that he should not have crossed the stream but that since he lacked the boats to recross it, he could not now attempt to do so in the presence of the enemy.[4]

By this time another Confederate general was on the scene in eastern Kentucky. Major General George B. Crittenden, ordered by the Confederate War Department to take command of the area, had set up his headquarters in Knoxville on November 24. In his first instructions to Crittenden, Johnston called attention to Zollicoffer's

[1] Accounts of the Battle of Belmont are in Parks, *General Leonidas Polk, C.S.A.*, pp. 190–193; Kenneth P. Williams, *Lincoln Finds a General*, III, 75–100; Bruce Catton, *Grant Moves South*, pp. 75–84; Horn, *The Army of Tennessee*, pp. 63–66; *Official Records*, Ser. I, Vol. III, pp. 304–310, 317.

[2] For Polk's report, see Leonidas Polk to W. W. Mackall, November 10, 1861, Polk Papers, Manuscript Division, Library of Congress.

[3] *Official Records*, Ser. I, Vol. VII, p. 753.

[4] Johnston, *Life of Johnston*, p. 396.

position, with the enemy in front and the river behind; but he did not explicitly order Crittenden to retire.[5] In abstaining from doing so, Johnston was faithful to his theory of command. Once he turned over an area to a subordinate, and explained the mission and general instructions, he withheld detailed orders and instead relied upon the subordinate's judgment as to how the mission could best be accomplished at that point.[6] This "mission concept" of command was partially the result of Johnston's inexperience in commanding a large army on a vast and exposed front. Yet it had much to recommend it. Such a policy worked splendidly with lieutenants of great skill and daring—men like "Stonewall" Jackson or Nathan Bedford Forrest; with soldiers of less skill, it was disastrous.

Crittenden did not arrive in person at Zollicoffer's position until early January. When he got there, he immediately began to prepare boats for recrossing the Cumberland. But he was too late and too slow. On the eighteenth he wrote Johnston that he faced a superior enemy force, that to attempt to pass back over the river would be excessively hazardous, and that he planned to fight where he was.[7]

Meantime, the Federal commander in Kentucky moved to strike this isolated Confederate body before it could gain the security of the south bank of the Cumberland. On December 29 Buell ordered Brigadier General George Thomas at Lebanon, Kentucky, and Brigadier General Albin Schoepf near Somerset to join forces in an attack upon Zollicoffer. By January 17 Thomas was at Logan's Cross Roads ten miles from the Confederate camp, awaiting the arrival of Schoepf.

Crittenden decided to take the offensive, to fall upon Thomas while the two Union forces were divided by the rising waters of Fishing Creek. The Confederates—above 6,000 strong—marched at midnight of January 18 against an opponent of about equal strength. Everything went wrong for the Southern attack. Moving in a downpour of rain, Zollicoffer's brigade struck Thomas by surprise at daylight, but after an initial success the Confederates fell into complete disorganization and were halted by stubborn resistance. The nearsighted Zollicoffer, clad in a white raincoat, was shot dead by a Federal whom he had mistaken for a Confederate officer. In the

---

[5] *Ibid.*

[6] Mackall to Felix Zollicoffer, October 3, 1861, "Headquarters Book of Albert Sidney Johnston."

[7] *Official Records,* Ser. I, Vol. VII, p. 103.

confused fighting that followed, the Southern troops were defeated and driven back into their entrenchments. With great difficulty, Crittenden got his disorganized army back across the Cumberland, abandoning artillery and supplies to the enemy.[8]

The Battle of Mill Springs (or Fishing Creek, or Logan's Cross Roads, as it was variously called) was a serious reverse to Confederate arms and an ominous harbinger of things to come. Cumberland Gap and the railway from Tennessee to Virginia were thereby exposed to a possible Northern thrust, the eastern flank of Johnston's position at Bowling Green was turned, and the roads from eastern Kentucky into Nashville were open to the enemy. Though a public outcry arose against Crittenden,[9] Johnston spared his subordinate all recriminations; ultimately Crittenden was exonerated of fault by a board of inquiry. Instead of railing against Crittenden, Johnston strove to reinforce the shattered army guarding his eastern flank, meantime increasing the fervor of his pleas to Richmond for additional men and arms. It was at this moment of defeat that he wrote General Cooper that all the resources of the Confederacy were needed for the defense of Tennessee.[10]

The Richmond authorities were unable or unwilling to send Johnston the reinforcements that he sorely needed. The only troops dispatched in response to his calls were two brigades from western Virginia, which arrived in Bowling Green on January 5.

Instead of troops, Davis sent Johnston another general—General P. G. T. Beauregard. A Louisiana Creole, Beauregard was the *beau sabreur, beau frappeur* of the Confederacy; he was the hero of Fort Sumter and of First Manassas. But Beauregard and Davis were at odds with each other. In ordering Beauregard to the west as Johnston's subordinate, Davis may have been sending him into exile. On February 4 Beauregard reported to Johnston at his Bowling Green headquarters. Johnston received the celebrated Louisiana general warmly and took him fully into his confidence.[11]

[8] For reports of the engagement, see *ibid.*, pp. 79–82, 102–110.

[9] E. C. Walthall to William Preston Johnston, March 11, 1877, Johnston Papers, Barret Collection.

[10] Johnston to Samuel Cooper, January 22, 1862, "Headquarters Book of Albert Sidney Johnston."

[11] Alfred Roman, *The Military Operations of General Beauregard in the War between the States, 1861 to 1865,* I, 213–215.

Beauregard brought with him a plan of operations he had conceived in Virginia from studying the situation in the west. As a zealous advocate of the Napoleonic principle of the concentration of force, Beauregard now proposed to mass the majority of Confederate strength at Forts Henry and Donelson, leaving only light garrisons at Columbus and Bowling Green. He hoped through this maneuver to be able to crush Grant's relatively small command should it advance upon the forts, then to turn upon Buell in central Kentucky; he would thus defeat the enemy "in detail." But Beauregard came to the west under the impression that Johnston's army was far stronger than he found it to be. When on the evening of his arrival Beauregard learned the disparity in the strength of the opposing forces, he was dismayed, and declared that his presence in Kentucky was useless. With difficulty Johnston dissuaded him from returning to Virginia.[12]

Beauregard had cause for alarm over the weakness of Johnston's army; by now the comparative strength of the western forces was about as follows: In or near Bowling Green under Hardee were 24,574 troops present for duty; at Columbus under Polk were 22,061 men; and at the Tennessee forts were approximately 5,000 under Brigadier General Lloyd Tilghman, who three months before had been ordered by the War Department to this command. Thus Johnston had fewer than 52,000 men available east of the Mississippi River. In Arkansas, and therefore within Johnston's Department, were an additional 20,000 Confederate troops, but they were too far away to be of use in the defense of Kentucky; moreover, to transfer them east of the Mississippi would have completely stripped the trans-Mississippi states of defenders against the Federal column in southwestern Missouri.

Federal numerical strength in the west had outpaced Confederate strength during the five months that Johnston had been in command. Buell lay south of Louisville, and in position to march upon Bowling Green and Nashville, with more than 73,000 men present for duty. At Cairo and Paducah were Grant and his force of 20,000 who were within Halleck's command. Stationed at various points in

---

[12] T. Harry Williams, *P. G. T. Beauregard, Napoleon in Gray,* pp. 114–115. See also Beauregard to Charles Villere, January 30, 1863, P. G. T. Beauregard Papers.

Missouri was the remainder of Halleck's army, perhaps an additional 60,000 men.[13] Beauregard estimated that 30,000 of these Missouri troops were in position, by ferrying the Mississippi River, to strike the Confederate stronghold of Columbus. Johnston's line in Kentucky and Tennessee faced numerical odds of well over two to one.[14]

Even as Johnston and Beauregard examined the Bowling Green fortifications, Union forces under Grant were moving upon Fort Henry on the Tennessee River. The Union command had found the weakest point in Johnston's line.

In spite of much effort on Johnston's part, Fort Henry was ill-prepared for assault. Throughout early fall Johnston had repeatedly urged General Polk to look to the defense of Fort Henry and to occupy and fortify the high ground overlooking the fort from the opposite (Kentucky) side of the Tennessee River, where a stronghold to be named Fort Heiman was planned. When in mid-November Brigadier General Tilghman was placed in command of Forts Henry and Donelson, Johnston ordered him to complete these works with the utmost speed. Tilghman was to call upon surrounding citizens for slave labor, for which he was to issue certificates of indebtedness. Meantime, Johnston sought in Memphis, Richmond, and elsewhere for artillery to arm the forts.[15]

All plans went awry. Few slaves could be hired. "I regret to say that the response to my appeal for laborers has not, thus far, been as flattering as I had hoped and expected," advised Governor Isham G. Harris of Tennessee. An adequate number of guns was not available;

---

[13] Troop numbers, Northern and Southern, are controversial. For Confederate strength, see *Official Records*, Ser. I, Vol. VII, pp. 852–855. For Buell's figure, see *ibid.*, p. 616. As early as October 10, 1861, Frémont reported the total strength of the Federal Western Department, which included troops in Missouri and at Cairo and Paducah (and a handful in New Mexico), as 93,131 men, present and absent. See *ibid.*, Ser. I, Vol. III, p. 530. Reckoning Frémont's active strength at 65 per cent of the total, he is estimated to have had above 60,000 present for duty. By the end of March, 1862, Halleck had 107,781 troops present for duty, excluding Buell's army. See *ibid.*, Ser. I, Vol. VIII, pp. 649, 652. Perhaps Halleck's strength as of early February fell somewhere between his March figure and Frémont's October figure—about 84,000 present for duty.

[14] Roman, *Military Operations of General Beauregard*, I, 213–214. Ignoring the Confederate troops in Arkansas and the Federal troops in southwestern Missouri, Beauregard estimated that Johnston had a total of 45,000 men of all arms and conditions and that he was opposed by 130,000 Northern soldiers. This estimate exaggerated the disparity somewhat, but not much.

[15] Nichols, *Confederate Engineers*, pp. 42–45. For Johnston's orders and reports, see *Official Records*, Ser. I, Vol. IV, pp. 476, 506, 544–545, 416–424.

Tilghman was dilatory in carrying forward the designs of fortification drawn by Johnston's engineers. Finally, burdened with a thousand cares elsewhere, Johnston failed to give to the construction of the Tennessee forts the personal attention that coming events would prove required; Governor Harris complained mildly that Johnston had not answered his inquiries as to how many laborers were needed, and for how long a time.[16]

On January 17 Johnston learned that little was being done to complete the armament of Fort Henry or the works at Fort Heiman. He wired Tilghman: "Occupy and intrench the heights opposite Fort Henry. Do not lose a moment. Work all night." A few days later Johnston withdrew his chief engineer, Colonel Jeremy Gilmer, from the planning of obstructions on the Cumberland River and sent him to inspect the Tennessee River forts. Gilmer found Fort Henry ready for action but Fort Heiman yet unfinished and without guns. The Tennessee River was weakly held as Grant's force drew near.[17]

Grant's plan was to transport his army of 17,000 on steamboats to a point above Fort Henry. There he would lead one column in an assault on Fort Henry; at the same time, Colonel Charles F. Smith was to command another column in the seizure of Fort Heiman on the opposite bank. These attacks were to be supported by the fire of Flag Officer Andrew H. Foote's flotilla of seven gunboats.[18]

Tilghman's 5,000 troops were at first about equally divided between the Tennessee River forts (Henry and Heiman) and Fort Donelson. On the afternoon of February 4 he began to telegraph Johnston of Grant's landing and apparent intention to attack the forts. At midnight of the fifth, Tilghman urged Johnston to send reinforcements at once, saying that with them he could overwhelm the enemy. When by the morning of the sixth he had received no additional troops, Tilghman and his subordinates decided that Fort Henry could not be held. He had already abandoned Fort Heiman. Now ordering most of the Fort Henry garrison to retire to Fort Donelson eleven miles away, Tilghman remained with his gunners to hold off the Federal assault as long as possible.

---

[16] Isham G. Harris to Johnston, December 31, 1861, Harris Letter Book.

[17] Johnston, *Life of Johnston*, pp. 407–428.

[18] Accounts of the attack on Fort Henry are in Williams, *Lincoln Finds a General*, III, 199–206; Catton, *Grant Moves South*, pp. 138–144; Horn, *The Army of Tennessee*, pp. 80–83; Jesse Taylor, "The Defense of Fort Henry," in *Battles and Leaders of the Civil War* (R. U. Johnson and C. C. Buel, eds.), I, 370.

At 11:00 A.M. of February 6, Foote's gunboats opened fire. Tilghman's artillerists replied, and a Confederate shot soon disabled the gunboat *Essex*. But Confederate resistance was short-lived; one by one the guns burst, were disabled by Foote's fire, or were abandoned by their crews; water from the rising Tennessee River threatened to inundate the position. At 2:00 P.M., after valiantly serving one of the guns with his own hands, Tilghman surrendered to Foote. The action ended before Grant could deliver his assault.[19]

The fall of Fort Henry breached Johnston's line. The loss was more than merely that of a fortress from which the defenders could retire to the next natural obstacle and establish a new position. The Tennessee River, an indestructible thoroughfare curving through western Tennessee, across the northeastern corner of Mississippi, and into northern Alabama, now lay open to the Federals, navigable to gunboats and transports as far as the Muscle Shoals at Florence, Alabama. The establishment in Tennessee of a defense in depth was rendered virtually impossible to the Confederates, since Federal forces could be landed, reinforced, and supplied behind any point where the Confederates might attempt a stand. Within two days after the capture of Fort Henry a Union flotilla reconnoitered the Tennessee as far as Florence, Alabama.[20]

Could Johnston have saved Fort Henry without yielding positions elsewhere that were equally vital? He left no record why he chose not to defend the fort more heavily than he did. Twenty years later Beauregard gave an account of the western campaign in which he said that during his inspection of the Bowling Green defenses in February of 1862 he urged upon Johnston the plan formed by him in Virginia, that he advised Johnston to mass his army for a blow against Grant, leaving a reduced garrison at Columbus on the Mississippi, and a small bridgehead north of the Barren River above Bowling Green. Beauregard said that Johnston turned down this strategy on the ground that if the Confederates should fail to defeat Grant at the forts, they would be crushed between the armies of Grant and Buell, and that even if victorious over Grant, the weakened and disorganized Southern force would then be incapable of keeping Buell's strong army out of the vital city of Nashville.[21]

---

[19] For Tilghman's messages to Johnston, see Johnston, *Life of Johnston*, pp. 428–433. See also *Official Records*, Ser. I, Vol. VII, pp. 131–152.

[20] *Official Records*, Ser. I, Vol. X, Pt. II, p. 8.

[21] Roman, *Military Operations of General Beauregard*, I, 216–218.

There is no contemporary evidence that Beauregard proposed such measures to Johnston; possibly his account was another of the innumerable expositions of post-bellum strategy that occupied the twilight years of many Federal and Confederate leaders.[22] If, however, such a plan was feasible, whether or not it was urged by Beauregard at the time, Johnston ought to have conceived and executed it. Johnston also was an advocate of the military principle of concentration. He had done all within his power to prevail upon the Richmond authorities to concentrate their resources for defense of the Mississippi Valley by sending troops there from relatively quiet theaters of the Confederacy.

Moreover, Johnston explicitly revealed his appreciation of the application of this principle on his immediate front. In October he had written to General Cooper:

[The enemy's] command of the Ohio and all the navigable waters of Kentucky, and better means of transportation give them great facilities of concentration. As my forces at neither this [Bowling Green] nor either of the other points threatened are more than sufficient to meet the force in front I cannot weaken either until the object of the enemy is fully pronounced.

Johnston understood that premature concentration without regard to enemy dispositions is futile; he clearly intended to concentrate his forces at what he considered the right place at the right time.[23]

Ought Johnston to have gathered most of his troops at the Tennessee and Cumberland river forts before Grant's advance began? Possibly so, since this would have created a centrally located striking force capable of being moved by rail to the support of Columbus, or by water to the defense of Nashville. Yet this would not have insured Confederate success. Johnston concentrated the majority of his troops at the points most seriously threatened by Federal strength. The Confederate position at Columbus was exposed to a

---

[22] In 1866 one of Beauregard's former staff officers, Colonel Thomas Jordan, wrote a book in which he suggested that by massing the Confederate army at the Tennessee forts Johnston might have defeated Grant. Jordan makes no mention of Beauregard's having proposed this to Johnston at Bowling Green, although, years later, Jordan strongly supported Beauregard's claim that he had urged Johnston to adopt this measure. Thomas Jordan and Roger Pryor, *The Campaigns of Lieut. General N. B. Forrest and of Forrest's Cavalry*, pp. 94–98.

[23] Johnston to Cooper, October 17, 1861, "Headquarters Book of Albert Sidney Johnston."

Federal army across the Mississippi and to Grant's army at Cairo. The Bowling Green position and the direct route to Nashville were threatened by Buell's force, which was larger than Johnston's entire army. To weaken either of these positions significantly was simply to open the door to the Mississippi River or to Nashville, for Johnston's adversary was capable of pinning him down with an army larger than his entire main body and of flanking him at the same time with another equally as strong.

Johnston anticipated the very strategy then being urged upon the Union command by President Abraham Lincoln. On January 13 Lincoln had written to Buell that the Union had the greater numbers but the Confederacy the greater facility of concentrating troops at points of decision, that therefore a proper strategy for the Union was to menace the Confederacy with superior forces at different points at the same time, that if the Confederate commander should weaken one point in order to strengthen another, then the Union ought to withhold attack from the strengthened point but attack the weakened one. Lincoln was only partially right: along the Kentucky line the Union command had the advantage of both numbers and facilities of transportation. Prior concentration at any point would have made Johnston's army vulnerable to Lincoln's strategy.[24]

Perhaps Johnston's likeliest possibility of destroying Grant's army would have been to rush the bulk of his Bowling Green force to Fort Henry as soon as Grant's landing on the Tennessee River was reported. Johnston received word of the landing on February 5. Had he ordered Tilghman to concentrate all of his troops at Fort Henry and make a determined stand there, Johnston might have been able to fall upon Grant with superior numbers brought from Bowling Green. Again, however, such reasoning is problematical. This strategy would have abandoned to Buell's army the road to Nashville so that Johnston could attempt to engage a relatively small segment of the Union forces at Fort Henry. Moreover, Grant was not obliged to remain immobile before Fort Henry to be attacked by Johnston's stronger force. Grant could, and probably would, have adopted Lincoln's formula; he could have withdrawn his troops in their transports as soon as Johnston's move became apparent. Grant had done precisely this at Belmont when faced by a reinforced Confeder-

[24] Lincoln to Don Carlos Buell, January 13, 1862, *Official Records,* Ser. I, Vol. VII, pp. 928–929.

ate army there. "Who controls the sea [or, in this case, the rivers] is at liberty to take as much or as little of war as he wills."

Encouraged by easy success at Fort Henry, Grant immediately turned his eyes to nearby Fort Donelson on the Cumberland River. If this stronghold could be taken, the way to Nashville would be open and Johnston's line would be irreparably broken. Shortly after the capture of Fort Henry, Grant wired Halleck, "I shall take and destroy Fort Donelson on the 8th, and return to Fort Henry." Johnston faced a grave command decision.

On February 7, after receiving word of the surrender of Fort Henry, Johnston met at the Covington House (Beauregard's Bowling Green quarters) with Beauregard and Hardee to discuss the plight of the western army and to fashion a strategy for the immediate future. As a result of this meeting Johnston adopted a plan of supreme portent for his own force and for the entire Confederacy. Assuming that the Kentucky-Tennessee line could no longer be held against the forces pressing upon it, he decided to withdraw his army to undetermined positions south of the Tennessee River. Columbus, Bowling Green, and Fort Donelson were to be abandoned; if necessary, even Nashville was to be given up, temporarily, to the enemy.

The two major wings of the army, the forces then at Columbus under Polk and those at Bowling Green under Hardee, were, for the time, to act as independent armies; ultimately they were to be reunited farther south. The eastern segment was to retire to Nashville and then to Stevenson, Alabama (on the Memphis and Charleston Railroad), and "thence according to circumstances." The western force was to pull back to Humboldt, Tennessee, and then to Grand Junction, in order to defend Memphis. Until they could be joined, Beauregard was to command the western wing. If Memphis could not be held, this section of the army was to retreat southward to Grenada, Mississippi, and if necessary to Jackson. The Mississippi River was to be defended by a series of fortifications supported by a small fleet of Confederate gunboats under Commander George N. Hollins, first by a desperate stand at Columbus, then in succession at Island Number 10, Fort Pillow, and finally at Memphis.[25]

The decision was a grave step. It meant surrendering, at least for the present, the states of Kentucky and Tennessee; it surely would blight the morale of these states, and of the entire South. It would

[25] *Official Records,* Ser. I, Vol. VII, pp. 861–862.

turn to Unionism those who yet wavered in their loyalty to the Confederacy. The "provisional" (Confederate) governor of Kentucky, who was a member of Johnston's staff, implored Johnston not to give up the Kentucky line. Such a move, said the Kentuckian, would place the enemy upon the vitals of the South; it would "spread dismay over the whole Confederacy." [26]

But Johnston's mind was made up. He felt that he must withdraw from an untenable position in order to save his army for a blow at the enemy under more favorable circumstances. Right or wrong, this decision required moral courage; the General knew that it would produce demoralization and furor among both soldiers and civilians. On February 11 the Bowling Green army began to evacuate that city; by nightfall of the fifteenth it approached Nashville.

Johnston and his subordinate generals in the Covington House conference had declared Fort Donelson untenable; mindful of the fall of Fort Henry, they believed Fort Donelson vulnerable to enemy gunboats alone. But it was then still intact and held by the 5,000 troops concentrated there according to General Tilghman's previous orders. Brigadier General Bushrod Johnson was now in command. What defense, if any, was to be made at this point? In deciding this question, Johnston made the most grievous error of military judgment of his career. Either the fort ought to have been defended with all the resources at his command, in the hope that reinforcements would be rushed to the Cumberland River from throughout the Confederacy, or it ought to have been stripped of all but a "sacrifice" garrison left to fight as long as possible in order to cover the withdrawal of the Bowling Green army. Johnston did neither. In spite of his previous declaration that Fort Donelson could not be held, and of his plan for a general withdrawal from the Kentucky-Tennessee line, he made the fatal decision to reinforce the doomed fort.

Even before Grant advanced into Tennessee, Johnston had moved some of his forces into position to defend the line of the Cumberland River. General Gideon Pillow with his brigade had been stationed at Clarkesville, Tennessee; Generals John B. Floyd (former United States Secretary of War) and Buckner had been sent to Russellville, Kentucky, with a total of 8,000 troops. [27] Increasingly troubled by the prospect of sacrificing Fort Donelson without a determined stand,

[26] George W. Johnson to Johnston, n.d. (copy), Johnston Papers, Barret Collection.

[27] Johnston, *Life of Johnston*, pp. 433, 438.

Johnston in effect now reversed his earlier strategy and resolved to send Pillow, Floyd, and Buckner to the defense of the fort. On February 7 he ordered Pillow to Fort Donelson. Johnston at first gave Floyd his discretion whether he would oppose the Federals at Fort Donelson or elsewhere on the Cumberland. But on February 12, urged by Pillow to come to the fort, Floyd decided to do so, and, at the same time, Johnston ordered him to do so. On the morning of February 13 Floyd arrived at Fort Donelson with his and Buckner's units; as ranking general, Floyd took command of the 17,000 troops gathered there.[28] Johnston later wrote Davis, "I determined to fight for Nashville at Donelson, and gave the best part of my army to do it." [29] There lay the rub; for this defense had to be all or nothing at all.

Meantime, Grant had been delayed in moving against Fort Donelson on March 8, as he had planned. Not until the morning of the twelfth was he able to march out of Fort Henry, but he moved swiftly, and by the next day had invested the Confederate position with about 15,000 men. As Grant moved by land, Foote's flotilla steamed up the Cumberland River to support the assault. The Battle of Fort Donelson was about to begin.

Fort Donelson was not a Fort Henry. Donelson occupied a 100-foot bluff on the west bank of the Cumberland; skilfully located by engineers Dixon and Gilmer, the fort's thirteen guns commanded the river to the north. To protect the position from attack by land Gilmer had laid out a semicircular line of rifle pits running for three miles along the ridges west of Fort Donelson. Enclosed within this line was the village of Dover, Tennessee. If resolutely manned by the troops now assembled there, Fort Donelson would require a siege to take it.[30]

At 3:00 P.M. of the fourteenth, Foote steamed his five serviceable gunboats confidently toward Fort Donelson and opened fire.[31] Deceived by his success at Fort Henry, he anticipated another easy

[28] Horn, *The Army of Tennessee*, pp. 83–85.

[29] Johnston to "My Dear General," March 18, 1862, Johnston Papers, Barret Collection; and Johnston to "Sir," March 17, 1862, War Department Collection of Confederate Records.

[30] Nichols, *Confederate Engineers*, pp. 48–50.

[31] An account of the Battle of Fort Donelson is in Horn, *The Army of Tennessee*, pp. 87–98. Official messages and reports are in *Official Records*, Ser. I, Vol. VII, pp. 261, 265, 267, 270, 278, 285, 301, 327–328, 383–387, 418.

victory. When the flotilla was within sure range, the guns of the fort suddenly replied with great effect. For more than an hour the gunboats and the fort duelled furiously. One by one the vessels were disabled and drifted down river out of range. At 4:10, bleeding and tearful, Foote gave up the contest. Fort Donelson must be taken by Grant's army.

The story of the short-lived defense of Fort Donelson against Grant can hardly be matched in the annals of warfare. It is one of courage and timidity, of decisiveness and vacillation, of brilliance and stupidity—a tactical comedy of errors turned into high tragedy for Johnston and for the South. Floyd and Buckner doubted that the fort could be held; the repulse of Foote's gunboats did not change their minds. During the night of the fourteenth, all three generals decided to fight their way out of the trap at Fort Donelson and rejoin Johnston at Nashville. This was what Johnston had instructed Floyd to do if he could not hold the fort.

Before daybreak of the fifteenth, Pillow's division struck the Federal line guarding the road to Nashville. Soon Buckner's troops joined the attack. The Confederates were fortunate enough to attack while Grant was absent in conference with Foote. By early afternoon they had broken the enemy ranks and laid open the route of escape. To Buckner's astonishment, and over his vehement protest, Pillow now proposed to return to the fort. Floyd agreed first with one, then with the other, and finally ordered the entire army back into its old position. That night, while the realistic Buckner brooded over this turn of events, Floyd and Pillow exultantly wired Johnston that they had won "victory complete and glorious." [32]

As the night of the fifteenth wore on—a miserable night with temperature well below freezing—the three Confederate generals bickered over the condition of their army. Aware that Grant was being reinforced, Floyd and Pillow now came over to Buckner's belief that their position could not be held. At last they decided to surrender the fort and its defenders without further resistance or effort to escape. Because of his former political connections, and because of charges of treason being made against him in the North, Floyd felt that he could not permit himself to fall into Union hands. He proposed to turn over the command to Pillow and to make his own getaway. Pillow was by nature a fighter; he said he would under

[32] Johnston, *Life of Johnston*, p. 495.

no circumstances surrender the fort. Finally this unpleasant task fell upon Buckner.

With bewildering rapidity the three generals enacted an *opera bouffe* transfer of command. Floyd said, "General Pillow, I turn over the command." Pillow at once passed it to Buckner. The unhappy Buckner sent for bugler, pen, ink, and paper in order to open negotiations for capitulation. Floyd, with his staff and Virginia troops, left for Nashville by steamboat; Pillow and his staff crossed the river in a small boat and got away; a then unknown cavalry colonel, Nathan Bedford Forrest, led his command out through the icy backwaters and escaped. At dawn Buckner surrendered unconditionally to Grant.[33]

The surrender of Fort Donelson completed the penetration of Johnston's line and exposed the heart of the western Confederacy to the enemy. One fourth of Johnston's entire army east of the Mississippi River was gone, captured in Fort Donelson. Nashville was now indefensible. The two wings of the army were almost two hundred miles apart with a strong Union force between them on the Cumberland and Tennessee rivers; powerful Northern columns were advancing upon both flanks. The Confederate army in the west faced disaster.[34]

Could Johnston have saved Fort Donelson and restored his Kentucky-Tennessee line after the fall of Fort Henry? General Beauregard later claimed that at the historic conference in the Covington House on February 7, he again pressed upon Johnston a plan for concentrating against Grant at Fort Donelson. Beauregard reasoned that the fort could have been held and Grant's army defeated even then if Johnston had rushed most of the Bowling Green army to Fort Donelson, leaving only a token force to delay Buell's advance in central Kentucky. According to Beauregard, this concentration at Fort Donelson could have been accomplished by February 10. If so, Grant's isolated army of 15,000 men could no doubt have been annihilated or captured by a Confederate force of approximately

[33] Horn, *The Army of Tennessee*, p. 95. See also Albert Sidney Johnston, "Partial Report of Operations around Bowling Green, 1861"; and Johnston to "Sir," March 17, 1862, both in War Department Collection of Confederate Records.

[34] Acting under Johnston's orders, Colonel Jeremy F. Gilmer had tried unsuccessfully to obstruct the Cumberland River between Fort Donelson and Nashville.

twice the Union strength. With Grant's army destroyed, said Beauregard, Buell would not have dared undertake an offensive against Johnston.[35]

Only the memories of Beauregard and his staff officers years after the event support his claim of having offered this alternative to withdrawal from Fort Donelson. There is much evidence that he did not do so. The day after the Covington House conference Johnston wrote to Secretary of War Benjamin, "Genls Beauregard and Hardee are equally with myself impressed with the necessity of withdrawing our force from this line at once." [36] A month later Johnston wrote to Jefferson Davis, "I . . . laid . . . before [Beauregard] my views for the future, in which he entirely concurred, and sent me a memorandum of our conference, a copy of which I send to you." [37]

Beauregard had indeed signed the memorandum referred to by Johnston, indorsing the plan of withdrawal. Moreover, on February 12, before Grant's army reached Fort Donelson, Beauregard had written Johnston saying unequivocally that the loss of Fort Henry made Confederate retreat unavoidable; Beauregard made no reference in this letter to any other suggested plan of operations.[38] Ten days after the fall of Fort Donelson, Hardee wrote that the evacuation of Bowling Green had been unanimously decided upon in the Covington House conference; Hardee mentioned no other recommendation by Beauregard.[39] Perhaps in the Covington House meeting the Creole general did mention the possibility of concentrating upon Grant at Fort Donelson; apparently he did not urge it with the conviction that his memory seemed to indicate.[40]

Yet, whether or not Beauregard advised this plan, if a prompt shift of the Bowling Green army to Fort Donelson held promise of victory over Grant, Johnston must answer for failing to take the step. Could Johnston have moved his Bowling Green army to Fort Donelson in time to meet Grant? Johnston could have transported

---

[35] Roman, *Military Operations of General Beauregard*, I, 218–219, 227–228.

[36] Johnston to Judah P. Benjamin, February 8, 1862, "Headquarters Book of Albert Sidney Johnston."

[37] Johnston to Jefferson Davis, March 18, 1862, Johnston Papers, Barret Collection.

[38] Roman, *Military Operations of General Beauregard*, I, 221–223.

[39] William J. Hardee to "My Dear Mrs. Stover," February 25, 1862, Hardee Papers.

[40] Williams, *P. G. T. Beauregard*, p. 118.

his men on trains to a point only a short march from the fort.[41] How many shuttles this movement would have required, or how long it would have taken, cannot be determined. Colonel Robert W. Woolley of Johnston's staff denied that Johnston had enough trains to shift his troops in the time estimated by Beauregard. "The railroad was almost bare of transportation," said Woolley. "The locomotives had not been repaired for six months, and many of them lay disabled in the depots." [42] Johnston himself said that he lacked the transportation to move the Bowling Green force to Fort Donelson in time to strike Grant.[43] Considering the inadequacies of Confederate transport, it seems unlikely that Johnston could have made the move in the time estimated by Beauregard.

But if Johnston had been able to complete the move to Fort Donelson by February 10, he would not have found Grant there. Grant, with his army, was still at Fort Henry, delayed by high water.[44] The Confederate army would have had another ten miles to walk before reaching the enemy—another half day's march. It could not have covered this distance and deployed for attack before nightfall of the eleventh.[45]

Even without the caprice of nature that held Grant in Fort Henry until February 12, Johnston could not reasonably have expected to find the Union army at Fort Donelson on the tenth. Only by keeping Grant ignorant of the Confederate build-up at Fort Donelson could Johnston have anticipated finding him there, unless Grant was so inept as to leave his forces exposed to a blow in the open by twice their numbers. Grant could easily have withdrawn into the Fort Henry defensive position.

Had Grant chosen to fight at Fort Henry, Johnston probably would have been unwise to attack him there. The position was by

[41] See *Official Records*, Ser. I, Vol. VII, pp. 164–165, for General Simon B. Buckner's correspondence showing that trains were arriving in Russellville, Kentucky, to transport his troops to Fort Donelson.

[42] Johnston, *Life of Johnston*, p. 485.

[43] Johnston, "Partial Report of Operations around Bowling Green, 1861," War Department Collection of Confederate Records.

[44] *Official Records*, Ser. I, Vol. VII, p. 596.

[45] William Preston Johnston, "Defense of Genl A. S. Johnston against the Strictures of Genl Beauregard," Johnston Papers, Barret Collection. See also Roland, "Albert Sidney Johnston and the Loss of Forts Henry and Donelson," *Journal of Southern History*, XXIII (February, 1957), 45–69, for an elaboration of the difficulties opposing the strategy that Beauregard said he recommended.

then completely surrounded by high water; for Johnston to deploy and attack through such a barrier would seem well-nigh impossible, and Grant was strong enough to withstand any assault that Johnston could have delivered against him at Fort Henry. Grant at first had 17,500 troops there;[46] during the night of February 11 he received six regiments of reinforcements.[47] By morning of February 12, Johnston's army of 30,000 would have faced a foe of 22,500, entrenched in Fort Henry, surrounded by water, with flanks and rear secure on the Tennessee River, and lines of communication maintained by gunboats and transports. Only if Johnston could have destroyed Grant at a blow would an attack upon him have saved the Confederate army; that Johnston could have done so is extremely doubtful.

Failure to annihilate Grant at a single stroke would have thrown Nashville open to Buell and exposed Johnston's army to destruction. Buell was on the move to reinforce Grant and seize the Tennessee capital.[48] Johnston reasoned that even if he should defeat Grant at the forts, his weakened army could not withstand Buell's powerful column. Only by retiring below the Tennessee River, thought Johnston, could he save his army for continued resistance.

General Grant wrote in his memoirs that Johnston ought to have brought his entire Bowling Green army to Fort Donelson, as the final result could not have been worse for him even if he and all of his troops had been captured there.[49] That Johnston was remiss in not taking personal command at Fort Donelson is true. Had he done so, he might have been able to inflict defeat upon Grant's leaderless army on the morning of February 15; certainly Johnston could have escaped with most of the men who were lost through Floyd's indecision. In electing to retire with the Bowling Green troops, Johnston exaggerated the immediate threat of Buell's advance on that line. But Grant erred in saying that the capture of Johnston and all of his troops would have been no greater disaster than the capture of Fort Donelson and a part of the troops. Grant ignored the vital role played later by Johnston and the Bowling Green troops in checking the Federal thrust into the lower Mississippi Valley. Grant, of course,

---

[46] Grant, *Personal Memoirs of U. S. Grant*, p. 152.

[47] *Official Records*, Ser. I, Vol. VII, p. 612.

[48] For the movements of Buell's army see *Official Records*, Ser. I, Vol. VII, pp. 461, 578, 585, 612, 932, 937, 940–941; and Henry M. Cist, *The Army of the Cumberland*, pp. 25–26.

[49] Grant, *Personal Memoirs of U. S. Grant*, p. 166.

wrote in retrospect; Johnston anticipated a different outcome when he decided to abandon his advanced line.

Johnston thus lost the states of Kentucky and Tennessee. That any action by him could have saved them is doubtful; Union advantages probably were too great to be overcome by strategy. "It was impossible for any General to have defended the line from Columbus to Bowling Green with the forces at the command of Genl Johnston," Hardee judiciously wrote immediately after the fall of Fort Donelson.[50] But if the forward Confederate line could not have been held, then the Confederate army ought all to have been saved. Instead, Johnston lost both the line and a substantial portion of his army. He failed to act with the audacity and decision required by the crisis that he faced.

[50] Hardee to "My Dear Mrs. Stover," February 25, 1862, Hardee Papers.

Retreat and Recovery

~~~~~~

O N THE NIGHT OF February 15, while the generals at Fort Donelson floundered in indecision, Johnston encamped his Bowling Green force at Edgefield on the Cumberland River opposite Nashville. At midnight he went to bed, heartened over Floyd's message of victory. Before daybreak he was awakened to learn that Fort Donelson and its defenders were to be surrendered at dawn. Stunned by this somber intelligence, and aware that he and his troops were in danger of being trapped north of the Cumberland, he declared, "I must save this army." During the remainder of the night he moved his men across the river and into the city of Nashville.[1]

The city greeted Johnston with cries of victory, for the morning newspapers carried the glad false tidings of Floyd's premature message of the night before. Soon, however, came the bitter news of defeat, and in its wake came rage and panic. Rioting broke out

[1] Munford, "Albert Sidney Johnston," Johnston Papers, Barret Collection. Most of the material in this chapter and the one following has been previously published. See Charles P. Roland, "Albert Sidney Johnston and the Shiloh Campaign," *Civil War History,* IV (December, 1958) , 355–382.

among the citizens; on the evening of the sixteenth an angry and drunken mob pressed into Johnston's headquarters, demanding to know his intentions. With extreme difficulty, staff officers dispersed the crowd.[2]

Having been deceived by exaggerated accounts of Confederate strength, the people of Tennessee and the South now blamed Johnston for the defeat, and turned upon him. The newspapers clamored for his dismissal. The Southern army was totally demoralized, one prominent citizen wired Davis; only the President's personal presence in Tennessee could save the state. Others besought Davis to take command of the western army, or to turn it over to Beauregard, Bragg, or Breckinridge. The false rumor spread that Johnston was drunk when Fort Donelson fell. The Tennessee Legislature sent a delegation to Davis demanding Johnston's removal "because he is no general." [3] But Davis's faith in Johnston remained unshaken. "If [Johnston] is not a general," Davis replied, "we had better give up the war, for we have no general." [4]

Perceiving that their city could not be defended and must soon be surrendered to the enemy, many of the people of Nashville fell to looting and destroying. Soldiers mingled with civilians in the pillage; shouts, curses, and shots rang in every direction. "It seemed as if the bonds of discipline would be cast off altogether," recorded an observer.[5] On February 17 Johnston withdrew from Nashville with most of his troops; he appointed Floyd, whom he received with courtesy from the disaster of Fort Donelson, as commander of the rear guard left in the city until the arrival of the Union advance forces. When on the following day Forrest arrived in Nashville from Fort Donelson, Floyd turned the job over to him. Forrest was a fortunate choice; the redoubtable cavalryman quickly returned Nashville to a semblance of calm. Acting under orders given by Johnston to Floyd, Forrest shipped out by rail vast stores of rations, clothing, ammunition, and other military supplies. On February 22, as Buell's army moved into Edgefield across the river, Forrest and his

---

[2] Horn, *The Army of Tennessee,* pp. 100–102.

[3] Johnston, *Life of Johnston,* pp. 496–500.

[4] Munford, "Albert Sidney Johnston," Johnston Papers, Barret Collection; and Strode, *Jefferson Davis: Confederate President,* p. 221.

[5] Munford, "Albert Sidney Johnston," Johnston Papers, Barret Collection. See also Jeremy F. Gilmer to "My Dear Loulie," March 15, 1862, Jeremy F. Gilmer Papers.

troops abandoned Nashville and rode to rejoin Johnston's army.[6]

Leaving Floyd and his detachments in Nashville, Johnston on February 17 and 18 led his main body thirty-five miles southeast to Murfreesboro. Demoralization hung upon the marching column. Soldiers wept to leave Nashville to her fate; others urged that the city be burned and only her ashes left to the enemy. Disdaining to "run away from the Yankees," many clamored to stay and fight. "Some of the troops were disheartened," Johnston later wrote to Davis.[7] Masterful understatement; all of the troops were disheartened. Even Hardee and Johnston's adjutant general, Colonel W. W. Mackall, had lost faith in their commander.[8] Whereas Johnston felt that to remain in Nashville would destroy what discipline was still in the army, Hardee believed that the "precipitate" retreat from the city aggravated the demoralization of the troops. "In my judgment," wrote Hardee, "nothing can save us except the presence of the President, who ought to come here, assume command, and call on the people to rally to his standard." [9] To restore the morale of this army seemed to Johnston the most pressing need of the hour.

While Johnston was losing Fort Donelson and abandoning Nashville, Beauregard had undertaken to dispose the western body of the army according to the plan adopted at the Covington House conference in Bowling Green on February 7. These troops were principally Polk's command and were still concentrated in the fortified city of Columbus, Kentucky. Having decided that with Fort Donelson untenable, Columbus could no longer be held, Beauregard wrote Johnston on February 12 urging that he be authorized to abandon Columbus at once in order to establish a prompt defense of western Tennessee.[10]

Two days later Johnston met Beauregard in Nashville for a last conference before Beauregard departed for his new responsibilities. Except for an account by Beauregard long after the war, no record remains of this meeting. Johnston reaffirmed his conviction that the

---

[6] John Allan Wyeth, *Life of General Nathan Bedford Forrest,* pp. 58–60.

[7] Johnston to "My Dear General," March 18, 1862, Johnston Papers, Barret Collection.

[8] Liddell, "Liddell's Record of the Civil War," *Southern Bivouac,* I NS (December, 1885) , 530.

[9] William J. Hardee to "My Dear Mrs. Stover," February 25, 1862, Hardee Papers.

[10] Roman, *Military Operations of General Beauregard,* I, 221–223.

Confederate army must withdraw to a line south of the Tennessee River, said Beauregard. Johnston also supported abandoning Columbus immediately but said that Beauregard must get War Department approval of the move before taking it. Johnston planned to retreat with the eastern wing of the army along the railroad from Nashville to Stevenson in northern Alabama. As the two parts of the army were widely separated, and an enemy force likely to be thrust between them, Johnston gave Beauregard independent command of the western section. That evening Beauregard left Nashville for Decatur, Alabama, and Corinth, Mississippi.[11]

A more complete knowledge of what was said at this meeting would throw light upon the subsequent course of the campaign. If Beauregard's memory was accurate, the discussion was scarcely more than a repetition of the Covington House conference. But it seems highly probable that the two generals would also have discussed an ultimate junction of the two wings of the army.

Beauregard proceeded from Nashville to Corinth and then to Jackson, Tennessee, where he established his headquarters. Obtaining the approval of the War Department, he at once withdrew Polk's force from Columbus and deployed that wing of the army along a new line extending from Island No. 10 in the Mississippi River through Union City, Humboldt, and Jackson, Tennessee, and terminating at Corinth in northern Mississippi. He then set about energetically to concentrate as many troops as possible to meet the anticipated thrust of the Northern army up the Tennessee River. He sent letters and messengers to the governors of the states of the western Confederacy, and to Generals Braxton Bragg at Mobile, Mansfield Lovell at New Orleans, and Earl Van Dorn in Arkansas. All were urged to send or bring troops to Beauregard's support.[12]

Meanwhile, Johnston remained at Murfreesboro with the eastern segment of the army. There he gathered together the troops from Bowling Green, the small force under General Crittenden from eastern Kentucky, and, on February 23, the rear guard of the army from Nashville.[13] These groups, comprising somewhat fewer than 20,000 men, were reorganized into a compact army of three divisions commanded by Hardee, Crittenden, and Pillow, with a reserve under

---

[11] *Ibid.,* p. 223.
[12] *Official Records,* Ser. I, Vol. VII, pp. 899–901.
[13] *Ibid.,* p. 889.

Breckinridge. The Texas Rangers and Forrest's cavalry were left unassigned. Johnston took command of the whole.[14]

Johnston has been censured for remaining with this eastern fraction of his army. He ought to have gone to Memphis, or Corinth, say his critics, where he could have supervised more expeditiously the coordination of the entire army. In other words, Johnston ought to have done just what Beauregard was doing. This is a telling criticism of Johnston's behavior, if it be assumed that Johnston could have accomplished a more effective concentration than Beauregard did, and that someone else, perhaps Hardee, could have conducted the retreat from Nashville as well as Johnston did. Both operations were vital to the future success of the Confederate army in the west.

Johnston had already attempted the very concentration that Beauregard was now achieving. But Johnston's efforts had been futile because Confederate authorities were unwilling at the time to strip other departments to strengthen Johnston's line. Had his earlier calls been heeded, the present crisis might not have been upon the South. Johnston's earlier failure to secure reinforcements seems to have discouraged him from renewing the effort.

But Johnston's reluctance was misguided; stirred at last by the calamity of losing Forts Henry and Donelson, Davis and Benjamin now approved a heroic massing of troops to check the Federal drive down the Mississippi Valley. Immediately after the fall of Fort Henry, General Bragg had written to Benjamin, asking the question raised three weeks before by Johnston, "Should we not give up the seaboard now and concentrate all our means on the vital point?" [15] General Lovell had detached four regiments from his command at New Orleans and sent them north under Brigadier General Daniel Ruggles. Johnston, on February 10, had ordered these troops to join Beauregard.[16] When Beauregard's emissary to General Bragg reached Mobile on February 28, he found that Bragg had already been authorized by the War Department to reinforce Johnston and was preparing to leave the next day. By early March, Bragg's 10,000 well-drilled men were in Corinth,[17] and new regiments raised by the

[14] Johnston, *Life of Johnston*, p. 508.
[15] *Official Records*, Ser. I, Vol. VI, pp. 826–827.
[16] Johnston to Mansfield Lovell, February 10, 1862 (copy), Johnston Papers, Barret Collection.
[17] *Official Records*, Ser. I, Vol. VI, p. 894.

governors of the southwestern states were also assembling there. Finally, Johnston himself led the eastern body of troops from Murfreesboro to join the forces collected by Beauregard at Corinth.

Johnston offered no explanation why he persisted in keeping with the column withdrawing from Nashville. Some feel that the disaster of losing his troops at Fort Donelson, and the sound and fury that broke from the people over this defeat, stunned and paralyzed him, that he was groping in a fog, unable to discern his true strategic course.

This may at first have been so. Certainly he was not insensible to the bolts of criticism aimed at him from all quarters. But such a reaction would not explain why he remained with the retreating body once he had resolved to attempt a junction with Beauregard at Corinth. His letters and messages from that moment on indicate perfect clarity of purpose and confidence in the outcome of the endeavor. "The General wears a very anxious face," wrote Colonel Gilmer, Johnston's chief engineer. "Still he expresses confidence that better fortune awaits us." [18] Johnston seems to have felt that his presence with the eastern wing was required to restore its morale and will to fight, perhaps even to assure that it reached its destination, for Hardee, Mackall, and Gilmer believed the movement to Corinth impossible. The spirit of these troops needed rekindling; the measure of discipline restored at Murfreesboro began to vanish again as the column once more moved south. Dissatisfaction broke out afresh; unaware of the grand strategy to concentrate and strike a counterblow against the enemy, both officers and men denounced Johnston's leadership unsparingly.[19] Aware of the demoralization of his subordinates, Johnston perhaps trusted no one else to bring the army to its rendezvous.

Whatever his motives, he worked tirelessly while on the march to restore the spirit of his men, and fashion them into an effective striking force. The Civil War was to witness no more remarkable transformation than he achieved in this effort. Imposing a stern

---

[18] Gilmer to "My Dear Loulie," March 6, 1862, Gilmer Papers.

[19] Basil W. Duke, *History of Morgan's Cavalry*, pp. 118–119. Hardee wrote that one of his friends was "excessively denunciatory" of Johnston, but Hardee left no doubt of his own loss of confidence in Johnston's leadership. Hardee now looked to Beauregard and Bragg to restore Confederate fortunes. See Hardee to "My Dear Mrs. Stover," March 22, 1862, Hardee Papers.

march discipline upon the column, Johnston moved it with efficiency and deliberation toward its objective.[20] The General's quiet dignity and unostentatious air of confidence gradually spread to his subordinates.[21] By the time they were halfway to their destination, Johnston was able to write Beauregard, "The force here is in good condition and fine spirits. They are anxious to meet the enemy." [22] The conduct of these soldiers in the contest that awaited them testified to the effectiveness of Johnston's leadership during the retreat and to the accuracy of his insight into the character of his men.

As Johnston moved south, he parried and measured his opponent with the tentacles of his army—the cavalry. Johnston's use of cavalry in reconnaissance and as a protective screen for his march was a lesson in the employment of this arm; perhaps he learned it in tracking the Comanches on the Texas frontier. The hard-riding troopers of John Hunt Morgan and J. S. Scott swept the countryside between Johnston's line of withdrawal and the city of Nashville, keeping Buell's army under constant surveillance and masking the Confederate march. Morgan was especially active; he rode to the very outskirts of Nashville, drove in the Northern pickets, and observed the operations of the enemy.[23] From the reports of his cavalry commanders, Johnston determined that Buell was not on the move, either to join the western force of the Union army or to intercept the Confederate retreat. When Buell at last left Nashville to join Grant on the Tennessee River, Johnston's cavalry kept him informed on the progress of the Federal column, and burned the bridges along Buell's line of march in order to retard his movement.[24] Johnston's skilful use of cavalry helped him to outdistance Buell and to unite

---

[20] Lawson to Mrs. M. E. Duncan, March 7, 1862, Johnston Papers, Barret Collection.

[21] Edwin Porter Thompson, *History of the First Kentucky Brigade*, p. 79.

[22] *Official Records*, Ser. I, Vol. X, Pt. II, p. 310. Johnston's successful march and subsequent strategic decisions restored Hardee's confidence in his leadership. On the eve of the Battle of Shiloh, Hardee wrote, "[Johnston] has made a successful movement in concentrating the two armies & if he gains a great battle will, I hope, fully reinstate himself in public confidence." Hardee later wrote that he went into the Battle of Shiloh with a "light heart." Hardee to "My Dear Mrs. Stover," April 3, 1862; and to "My Dear Friend," May 19, 1862, Hardee Papers.

[23] John Hunt Morgan to Johnston, March 10, 1862, Johnston Papers, Barret Collection.

[24] J. S. Scott to Johnston, March 19, 1862, "Headquarters Book of Albert Sidney Johnston."

the wings of the Confederate army before the Union forces could make junction.[25]

Johnston took other measures that confused the Union command and delayed the concentration of Union forces in western Tennessee. By withdrawing southeast to Murfreesboro instead of directly south to Franklin, and by sending part of his ordnance and quartermaster stores to Chattanooga, he led his opponents to believe that Chattanooga was his objective.[26] He had mail for his troops addressed to the Quartermaster Department in Chattanooga.[27] Beauregard wrote on March 6, urging Johnston to spread rumors that he was on his way to Chattanooga; [28] but that impression was already abroad. On February 25 Grant had reported that Johnston was falling back on Chattanooga; [29] on March 2 Buell said the same.[30] As late as March 7 a Confederate spy reported to General Bragg at Corinth that the Federal commanders thought Johnston on his way to Chattanooga.[31] The advantage was now won; Johnston was already ten days on the march to Corinth.

Corinth, Mississippi, was one of the most valuable strategic sites in the western Confederacy. It lay at the junction of two major Southern railroads, the Mobile and Ohio and the Memphis and Charleston; and it was scarcely twenty miles from the Tennessee River, which Johnston sensed was to be the Union line of penetration. The town's important situation was obvious to all. Two days before the fall of Fort Donelson, Brigadier General Leroy Pope Walker had written Johnston from Florence, Alabama:

It is not only the Tennessee River up to this point which is threatened, but also the Memphis and Charleston Road at Corinth, Miss. These roads constitute the vertebrae of the Confederacy. . . . A large proportion of the population of the counties of Hardin and Wayne [Tennessee] is in sympathy with the enemy, and either Savannah or Hamburg, in Tennessee, or Eastport, in Mississippi, will be made the base of his operations.[32]

[25] Don Carlos Buell, "Shiloh Reviewed," *Century Magazine,* XXXI (February, 1886) , 751.

[26] Johnston to Judah P. Benjamin, February 27, 1862, and Johnston to Mr. Perkins, February 25, 1862, "Headquarters Book of Albert Sidney Johnston."

[27] Gilmer to "My Dear Loulie," March 2, 1862, Gilmer Papers.

[28] P. G. T. Beauregard to Johnston, March 6, 1862, Johnston Papers, Barret Collection.

[29] *Official Records,* Ser. I, Vol. VII, p. 666.

[30] *Ibid.,* p. 679.

[31] Braxton Bragg to Johnston, n.d., Johnston Papers, Barret Collection.

[32] *Official Records,* Ser. I, Vol. VII, pp. 887–888.

After the war, Johnston's son and friends argued long and bitterly with Beauregard and his supporters over who selected Corinth as the base of Confederate operations.[33] Beauregard claimed that he first chose the site, then sent an emissary to Murfreesboro to persuade a bewildered and undecided Johnston to bring his troops there.[34] It is true that Johnston at first was not sure of his objective; indeed, he could not be. Major Gilmer wrote his wife from Murfreesboro that the army would withdraw to Decatur, Alabama (which lay on the route to Corinth), or to Chattanooga, or to some other point south.[35] Johnston apparently had a number of alternate goals in mind, depending upon the action of the enemy. He was wise to maintain flexibility, for the Federals were capable of interdicting his movement to Corinth. Precisely when Johnston determined to attempt reaching Corinth cannot be ascertained; his adjutant general said that Corinth was his objective even before he reached Murfreesboro, and therefore before he talked with Beauregard's staff officer.[36] Probably both Johnston and Beauregard independently selected Corinth as the point of junction, then came to an agreement on plans when Beauregard's emissary talked with Johnston in Murfreesboro.

As Johnston's army retreated through Tennessee, Confederate authorities pressed him for an explanation of the loss of Forts Henry and Donelson. The Confederate Congress made an investigation; President Davis requested details from Johnston. Without directly saying so, Johnston implied in his answer that he lost the forts because he wanted the strength to hold them, that he lost the troops because of the misjudgments of his subordinates.

But his reply to Davis revealed Johnston's self-control under adversity. He withheld censure of Floyd and Pillow, who had been relieved of command by Davis's order; and he refused to indulge in self-pity or in bitterness against the public for its outcry against him. Floyd might have been able to lead his command out of Fort Donelson, said Johnston, "but justice requires to look at events as they appeared at the time and not alone by the light of subsequent information." Loss of Fort Donelson and its defenders had been

---

[33] William Preston Johnston, "Plan of Shiloh Campaign," *Johnston Papers*, Barret Collection.

[34] Roman, *Military Operations of General Beauregard*, I, 505–506.

[35] Gilmer to "My Dear Wife," February 22, 1862, Gilmer Papers.

[36] Roman, *Military Operations of General Beauregard*, I, 505–506.

disastrous and almost without remedy, said Johnston; for this reason he had previously remained silent about the consequences.

I observed silence, as it seemed to me to be the best way to serve the cause and the country. The facts were not fully known, discontent prevailed, and criticism or condemnation were more likely to augment than to cure the evil. I refrained well knowing that heavy censures would fall upon me, but convinced that it was better to endure them for the present and defer to a more propitious time an investigation [of Floyd and Pillow]. . . . The test of merit in my profession with the people is success   it is a hard rule but I think it right.

If he should succeed in uniting the two wings of the army, he concluded, the popular discontent would abate.[37]

Johnston was less perturbed than was Beauregard over the need for haste in joining the two Confederate forces. On March 2, Beauregard wrote that the great battle of the war would soon be fought at or near Corinth; [38] in subsequent letters and telegrams he pressed Johnston to speed his movement by rail to the point of junction. Johnston knew that time was precious, but he had with him great quantities of artillery, ammunition, and provisions that could be moved only by rail. Wanting the facilities to transport troops and supplies together, he decided to march the troops and ship the supplies.[39] After the war Gilmer explained:

It was simply impossible [to ship the men by rail] without sacrificing the supplies and munitions on which the subsistence and armament of the command depended. The entire transportation capacity of the railroads was taxed to the utmost, and even then immense quantities of meat and other commissary supplies were left at [points along the line of march].[40]

Severe weather and widespread sickness among the troops added immeasurably to the difficulties of the march. "We live and move in mud and water," wrote a staff officer, "and the roads have come to such a pass that we cant move much longer." [41] The sick were transported by freight car and hospitalized in makeshift infirmaries

[37] Johnston to "My Dear General," March 18, 1862, Johnston Papers, Barret Collection.
[38] Beauregard to Johnston, March 2, 1862, Johnston Papers, Barret Collection.
[39] M. H. Wright to William Preston Johnston, February 2, 1878, *ibid.*
[40] Gilmer to William Preston Johnston, January 18, 1878, *ibid.*
[41] Gilmer to "My Dear Loulie," March 15, 1862, Gilmer Papers.

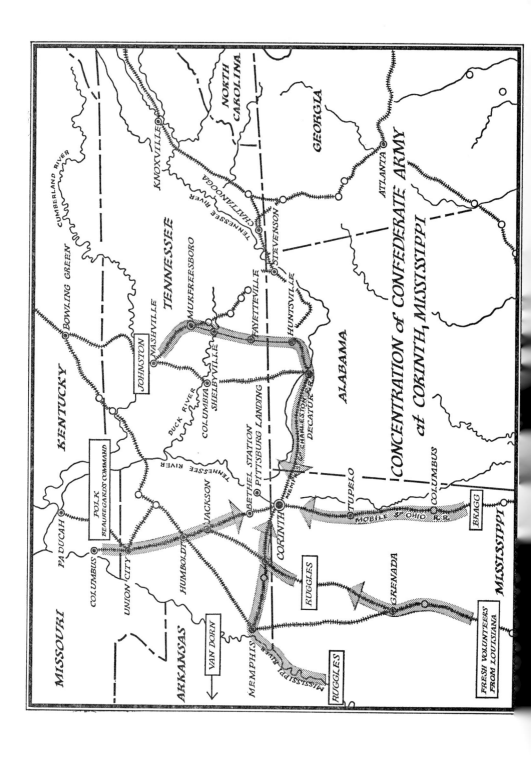

CONCENTRATION of CONFEDERATE ARMY at CORINTH, MISSISSIPPI

and private homes along the route.[42] Against the advice of every other officer of his command, Johnston took the calculated risk that his adversary would remain immobile long enough to enable him to move in this fashion.[43] From Murfreesboro he led his column to Shelbyville, thence to Fayetteville, and thence to Huntsville and Decatur, Alabama, on the Memphis and Charleston Railroad. From Decatur, he shuttled his men by rail to Corinth. His arrival there with both troops and supplies before the enemy was concentrated vindicated his judgment on the manner of the movement.

As the Southern troops concentrated at Corinth, Federal General Halleck, now in command of all Northern forces in the west, made his next move. He ordered an army of about 40,000 men up the Tennessee River to a point where the Confederate line of communications—the Memphis and Charleston Railroad—could be attacked. On March 13, Brigadier General Charles F. Smith landed this force at Savannah, Tennessee; three days later he established camp near Pittsburg Landing nine miles upriver from Savannah and twenty-five miles by road from Corinth. Grant arrived from Nashville the next day and took command of this army of five divisions. Making his headquarters at Savannah, Grant awaited the arrival of Buell's column from Nashville. Halleck had ordered Grant not to move against Corinth until he was reinforced by Buell.[44]

Johnston saw clearly the necessity of uniting Confederate forces for a counterattack against this fraction of the enemy that now lay isolated and exposed at Pittsburg Landing. Yet he made another strategic miscalculation in seizing the opportunity offered by Halleck's move when he failed to bring together all available troops for the stroke. In Arkansas were 20,000 men under General Earl Van Dorn who could have been added to the army at Corinth.

Van Dorn had been appointed in January by President Davis to take command of the Trans-Mississippi District, which included the states of Missouri (considered by Confederate authorities a part of the Confederacy), Arkansas, Indian Territory, and Louisiana as far south as the Red River. Van Dorn was also to draw upon Texas for troops. The precise nature of Van Dorn's assignment is not known;

---

[42] I. B. Ulmer, Jr., to "My Dear Mother," March 14, 1862, I. B. Ulmer, Jr., Papers. See also R. P. Boswell to E. Lee, March 29, 1862, R. P. Boswell Letters.

[43] William Preston to William Preston Johnston, April 18, 1862, Johnston Papers, Barret Collection.

[44] Catton, *Grant Moves South,* pp. 210–214.

no record of his instructions from Davis is available. Van Dorn's district was in Johnston's Department and under his general authority; yet Van Dorn seems to have received from Davis either orders, or approval of a plan, for mounting a bold offensive against the Federal army in Missouri. St. Louis was to be the object of this attack. On his way to the new post, but before receiving any instructions from Johnston, Van Dorn wrote exuberantly to his wife, "I am now 'in for it,' as the saying is—to make a reputation and serve my country conspicuously or to fail. I must not, shall not, do the latter. I must have St. Louis—then Huzza!" Van Dorn had reported to Johnston at Bowling Green late in January. What the two said is not recorded, but Van Dorn's subsequent messages and actions indicate that Johnston approved his plans.[45]

Van Dorn had assumed command of the Arkansas forces on January 29 and begun to apply himself vigorously to preparing his offensive; but he was there only two weeks when the entire situation in the west was altered by the loss of Forts Henry and Donelson and the withdrawal of Johnston's army below the Tennessee River. On February 21, while Johnston was at Murfreesboro, Beauregard wrote to Van Dorn from Jackson, Tennessee, suggesting that Van Dorn's troops be joined with Beauregard's in a great counteroffensive to take Kentucky and capture Cairo, and possibly St. Louis. The troops with Johnston were not to be included in this venture. "What say you to this brilliant programme," asked Beauregard, "which I know is fully practicable if we can get the forces?"[46]

Van Dorn thought little of the "brilliant programme"; he refused to budge. He proposed, instead, to defeat the Union army in Arkansas under General Samuel R. Curtis; by seizing or threatening St. Louis, he felt, he could create a diversion that would favor Johnston's strategy east of the Mississippi.[47] On February 24 Van Dorn informed Johnston that he was moving at once against Curtis.[48] If Johnston made any reply, it has been lost; either he approved the attack, or Van Dorn took silence to mean assent. On March 6 Van Dorn struck Curtis in the Battle of Pea Ridge (or Battle of Elkhorn Tavern). Van Dorn was defeated; the diversion had failed.

[45] *A Soldier's Honor: With Reminiscences of Major-General Earl Van Dorn,* pp. 62–63.

[46] *Official Records,* Ser. I, Vol. VII, pp. 900–901.

[47] *Ibid.,* Vol. VIII, pp. 750–752.

[48] *Ibid.,* p. 755.

Van Dorn's idea appears to have been sound. It was more practicable than Beauregard's grand strategy of recapturing Kentucky, plus Cairo and St. Louis, with the meager forces then available. Van Dorn had reason to believe that he could defeat Curtis. The forces were about equal. If Van Dorn had won at Pea Ridge, Halleck would have diverted to Missouri some of the troops that instead were moved up the Tennessee River to Grant; Halleck said that he had intended to do so.[49] But Johnston was remiss in failing to order Van Dorn east of the Mississippi immediately, once the Battle of Pea Ridge was lost. Again, on March 19, Beauregard appealed to Van Dorn to make this move, but the appeal was unheeded.[50] Johnston and Van Dorn apparently continued to hope for a successful diversion west of the Mississippi. Only after Johnston arrived in Corinth and discussed the situation with Beauregard and Bragg did he order Van Dorn to join him.[51] It was then too late; inadequate transportation delayed Van Dorn's coming until after the great test of arms in the west.

Johnston reached Corinth on March 23. Some of his troops had preceded him there; the remainder arrived within the next two or three days. His aim was accomplished: the two wings of his army were now united, while those of his adversary were still apart.

Johnston greeted Beauregard and Bragg with unrestrained gratitude for the roles they had played in concentrating a Confederate force at Corinth. To Bragg he exclaimed, "Your prompt and decisive move, Sir, has saved me, and saved the country. But for your arrival, the enemy would have been between us."[52]

To Beauregard, Johnston offered the command of the army. Johnston would continue as head of the Department, he said, but would retire his headquarters to Memphis or Holly Springs; Beauregard thus would be left in charge of operations in the field.[53] Why did Johnston make such a gesture? Some feel that he sought to shift from his shoulders the heavy responsibility of the coming campaign. But

---

[49] *Ibid.*, Vol. X, Pt. II, pp. 27, 354.

[50] *Ibid.*, Vol. VIII, pp. 789–791.

[51] Earl Van Dorn to his wife, April 6, 1862, quoted in *A Soldier's Honor*, p. 71.

[52] Bragg to Elise Bragg, March 25, 1862, Braxton Bragg Papers, Manuscript Division, Library of Congress.

[53] Roman, *Military Operations of General Beauregard*, I, 266; Munford, "Albert Sidney Johnston," Johnston Papers, Barret Collection; *Official Records*, Ser. I, Vol. VII, p. 912.

this explanation does not square with Johnston's behavior in that campaign; for then he would override Beauregard's judgment and alone take his most momentous decision. Johnston's son explained his father's proposal as a mere *beau geste*—a courteous posture by a gentleman to an esteemed colleague.[54] Such an offer was unusual but not unique. Only a few weeks before, in asking for Bragg's army to be ordered north, Beauregard had offered to serve under Bragg, who was his junior in command experience, prestige, and rank.[55]

Beauregard gave the most convincing reason for Johnston's conduct. Johnston tendered him the offer of command, said the Creole general, because he felt that the army and people no longer trusted his leadership and that the Confederate cause would be better served with Beauregard in command. Johnston knew that to give up the command would deprive him of all opportunity to retrieve his reputation as a general. His friends urged him not to do it.

You must not do this [wrote George W. Johnson, Confederate Governor of Kentucky]. I beg that you will not do it, both for your own fame and the good of our country. If I hear that you are resolved upon this course, I will despair of our cause. It will sink under the curse of Heaven, upon a people, who joined like wolves . . . to hunt down the noblest and purest man it has been my good-fortune to know.[56]

Nevertheless, Johnston made the offer. In making it, if Beauregard's explanation is sound, Johnston placed the welfare of his country above the opportunity for personal glory.

Beauregard chivalrously declined the offer of command. Johnston then assumed command of the entire force, and named Beauregard second-in-command.

Johnston at once determined to strike Grant's army at Pittsburg Landing before the arrival of Buell from Nashville; Beauregard and Bragg supported this proposal. Beauregard later implied that he initially made this important decision and persuaded Johnston to it after he reached Corinth.[57] Again Beauregard's memory seems to have been confused; Johnston required no such persuasion. Indeed, it is questionable that Beauregard at the time believed this the best

---

[54] Johnston, *Life of Johnston*, p. 550.
[55] *Official Records*, Ser. I, Vol. VII, p. 912.
[56] George W. Johnson to Johnston, March 26, 1862, Johnston Papers, Barret Collection.
[57] Roman, *Military Operations of General Beauregard*, I, 267.

strategy, for shortly before, he had informed Bragg that the Confederate forces ought to adopt a "defensive-offensive" that would lead the enemy away from the Tennessee River and expose him to attack at a distance from his base.[58]

Johnston's ingrained theory of strategy called for a direct counter-stroke against the Federals on his front. "You have some of the high and rare qualities of a good General," he once wrote to his daughter in chiding her for negligence in writing. "You know when to take the initiative. You anticipated my attack by making one." [59] As early as March 11, four days before Buell left Nashville, and before Grant's advance reached Savannah, Johnston had predicted a junction there of the forces of Buell and Grant. He scarcely could have had any other motive in uniting his own army than to fall upon the divided forces of the enemy.[60]

Both President Davis [61] and General Robert E. Lee wrote to Johnston expressing their confidence in his judgment, and recommending the very strategy that he had already resolved to use. "I need not urge you when your army is united, to deal a blow at the enemy in your front if possible, before his rear gets up from Nashville," said Lee. "You have him divided now, keep him so if you can." [62]

Having decided to attack, Johnston and his colleagues began vigorously to prepare the army for the blow. The task was a mighty one. At or near Corinth were between 40,000 and 50,000 troops, never before assembled as a body; many had only recently entered the ranks and were entirely without training. Most of the officers were as unseasoned as their men. Johnston did not have a true army; he had an unorganized multitude in the elementary stages of instruction, and short of all sorts of arms and equipment. Worse, these soldiers labored under the burden of recent defeat. Johnston faced the awful responsibility of organizing, training, arming, and inspiring this ill-assorted body of Southerners, then of leading them in an offensive against a victorious and confident foe. And he had less than two weeks in which to accomplish this miracle.

---

[58] Beauregard to Bragg, March 17, 1862 (copy), Johnston Papers, Barret Collection.

[59] Johnston to Henrietta Johnston, February 27, 1856, *ibid.*

[60] *Official Records*, Ser. I, Vol. X, Pt. II, p. 310.

[61] Jefferson Davis to Johnston, March 21, 1862, Johnston Papers, Barret Collection.

[62] Robert E. Lee to Johnston, March 26, 1862, *ibid.*

He met the situation with "cool, quiet self-control." [63] To his ranking subordinates, Beauregard and Bragg, he delegated many of the details of preparation. He authorized Beauregard to draw up a plan for the organization of the forces. Beauregard did so at once, and Johnston accepted his proposals. All Confederate troops in and about Corinth were combined into the Army of the Mississippi. The Army was divided into three corps commanded by Polk (First Corps: 9,136 men), Bragg (Second Corps: 13,589 men), and Hardee (Third Corps: 6,789 men). Three reserve brigades, amounting to 6,439 men, were placed under Crittenden, who shortly was replaced by Breckinridge. The reserve was encamped at Burnsville, Mississippi, fifteen miles from Corinth on the Memphis and Charleston Railroad. Most of the cavalry and artillery were left unassigned, and under the direct command of the army commander. [64] After the war Beauregard took full credit for this organization, which is praised for its compactness and simplicity of command. Beauregard said that Johnston accepted his plan without alteration. [65] This is doubtless true, but the general principles of the plan were discussed with Johnston before it was submitted in writing; furthermore, it strikingly resembled the organization that Johnston gave to the eastern wing of the army while he was yet in Murfreesboro.

Johnston named Bragg as chief of staff of the army, as well as commander of one of the corps. Bragg was an excellent choice; few men, if any, in the Confederacy had his talents as an organizer and disciplinarian. The army at Corinth tested these qualities to the utmost. He faced a bewildering variety of arms and equipment in the hands of the raw troops. "Rifles—rifled and smooth bore muskets, some of them originally percussion, others hastily altered from flint locks by Yankee contractors, many still with the old flint and steel, and shot guns of all sizes and patterns," said Bragg, "held place in the same regiments." [66]

To Bragg's precise mind, the entire body of men was an unruly mob; he looked with especial disfavor on the troops that had re-

[63] Braxton Bragg, "General Albert Sidney Johnston and the Battle of Shiloh," *ibid.*

[64] Johnston to "The President," March 30, 1862, "Headquarters Book of Albert Sidney Johnston"; and *Official Records*, Ser. I, Vol. X, Pt. I, p. 396.

[65] Roman, *Military Operations of General Beauregard*, I, 267–268.

[66] Bragg, "General Albert Sidney Johnston and the Battle of Shiloh," Johnston Papers, Barret Collection.

treated from Kentucky under Johnston and Polk, whom Bragg considered slack disciplinarians.[67] "It was a heterogeneous mass," Bragg said truthfully, "in which there was more enthusiasm than discipline, more capacity than knowledge, and more valor than instruction. . . . The task of organizing such a command in four weeks and supplying it . . . was simply appalling." [68] Nevertheless, under Bragg's stern and competent supervision this "heterogeneous mass" of soldiers was hastily equipped and brought to fighting edge.[69]

Johnston was busy with other preparations for the forthcoming offensive. He secured local inhabitants familiar with the roads and terrain to guide his columns into position for attack [70] but turned down the offer of a citizen to raise an independent guerrilla company to scour the countryside and destroy Union communications. Johnston refused to use any troops that were not subject to the articles of war or were outside the regular military organization.[71]

He attempted to solve one problem that continues to vex American military commanders today; he sought to release for combat as many as possible of the troops of the rear echelon. Johnston estimated that an additional brigade of riflemen could be formed of the cooks, teamsters, and other noncombatant soldiers of his army, provided their duties behind the lines could be taken over by someone else. Hoping to replace these troops with Negro slaves from the neighboring plantations, he sent his staff officers throughout the countryside in an effort to hire the Negroes. To his chagrin, the planters refused to let him have them.

Those people have given their sons freely enough [he said], but it is folly to talk to them about a negro or a mule. I regret this disappointment; a single

[67] Bragg to Elise Bragg, March 20, 1862, Bragg Papers, Manuscripts Division, Duke University Library; and Bragg to Elise Bragg, March 25, 1862, Bragg Papers (photostatic copies), Manuscript Division, Library of Congress.

[68] Bragg, "General Albert Sidney Johnston and the Battle of Shiloh," Johnston Papers, Barret Collection.

[69] The most authoritative student of Bragg's career feels that Johnston should have left Bragg in the position of chief of staff during the battle. See Grady McWhiney, "Braxton Bragg at Shiloh," *Tennessee Historical Quarterly* (March, 1962), pp. 19–30.

[70] Edward W. Munford to James E. Mathews, March 26, 1862, Johnston Papers, Barret Collection.

[71] Munford to E. J. Saunders, March 30, 1862, "Headquarters Book of Albert Sidney Johnston."

brigade may determine the fate of a battle. These people do not seem to be aware how valueless would be their negroes were we beaten.[72]

Johnston spoke with foresight; a single brigade might indeed have decided the fate of the contest that lay ahead.

On the night of April 2 Johnston ordered the attack; he could delay no longer, either for the additional training of his troops or for the arrival of Van Dorn from Arkansas. Johnston took his decision under these circumstances: During the night of the second, General Polk received a message from Brigadier General B. F. Cheatham, commander of a Confederate division posted at Bethel Station on the Mobile and Ohio Railroad above Corinth, saying that a portion of the Union army was advancing upon his position. Polk sent the message to Beauregard at about 10:00 P.M. Inferring that the enemy force was now divided, Beauregard sent the message to Johnston with the recommendation, "Now is the moment to advance, and strike the enemy at Pittsburg Landing." [73] The letter was delivered to Johnston by Colonel Thomas Jordan, formerly Beauregard's chief of staff, now serving as adjutant general of the Army of the Mississippi. Years later, Jordan wrote that upon receiving the message, Johnston was strongly averse to moving against the enemy at the time. He protested that his troops were in no condition for battle, and only after Jordan had parried Johnston's arguments did the reluctant commander give his consent for the offensive, said Jordan.[74]

But Jordan's accounts omit much of the story; indeed, his various narratives after the war contradict each other in certain particulars in describing this episode.[75] Johnston certainly expected to move against his adversary at any moment. The day before Cheatham sent his message, Johnston had issued the following instructions: "The troops of the First and Third Army Corps and of the several detached brigades of the forces will be placed in readiness for a field movement and to meet the enemy within twenty-four hours." [76] This order could hardly have come from a commander who had to be

---

[72] Munford, "Albert Sidney Johnston," Johnston Papers, Barret Collection.

[73] Roman, *Military Operations of General Beauregard,* I, 270–272.

[74] Jordan and Pryor, *Campaigns of Lieut. General N. B. Forrest,* p. 108.

[75] Compare Jordan's "Notes of a Confederate Staff Officer at Shiloh," in *Battles and Leaders* (R. U. Johnson and C. C. Buel, eds.) , I, 594–595, with his account in *Campaigns of Lieut. General N. B. Forrest,* p. 108.

[76] *Official Records,* Ser. I, Vol. X, Pt. II, p. 381.

coaxed into launching the attack. At about the time that Cheatham's message arrived, or possibly earlier, Johnston received from Colonel Nathan Bedford Forrest the information that Buell was marching quickly to join Grant on the Tennessee River.[77] In advising President Davis of his decision to move, Johnston did not mention the division of the enemy force. Instead he said:

General Buell is in motion, 30,000 strong, rapidly from Columbia by Clifton to Savannah. Mitchel behind him with 10,000. Confederate forces, 40,000, ordered forward to offer battle near Pittsburg. . . . Hope engagement before Buell can form junction.[78]

Other circumstances may have influenced Johnston in his decision to advance, but it is clear that he was moved primarily by the knowledge that Buell was about to join forces with Grant.

To Beauregard, Johnston delegated the preparation of the orders for the advance and attack. Verbal orders were at once given to the corps commanders: they were to begin marching before dawn toward Pittsburg Landing. Written orders concerning the particulars of deployment and attack would reach them on the march.[79]

Five of Grant's divisions (about 37,000 men) lay encamped beyond the high bluff overhanging Pittsburg Landing. Lew Wallace's division was at Crump's Landing four miles downriver.[80] The main camp ground took the shape of a rough parallelogram, bordered on the east by the Tennessee River, and on the north and south by Owl Creek and Lick Creek. The western end of the camp site was open. Two roads (the Ridge Road and the Monterey Road) led from Corinth to a point of convergence about five miles from Pittsburg Landing, entering the Union camp from the west. Lateral roads connected these in three places before they ran together.

Beauregard planned to move the three main Confederate corps over these roads during the day of April 3 so as to bring them together in the vicinity of a farmhouse called Mickey's located about seven miles from the landing. Here the three corps would bivouac during the night of April 3. Cheatham's division from Bethel Station was to join its parent corps (Polk's) on the march; the reserve

---

[77] Wyeth, *Life of General Nathan Bedford Forrest*, pp. 74–75.

[78] *Official Records*, Ser. I, Vol. X, Pt. II, p. 381.

[79] Bragg to William Preston Johnston, December 16, 1874, Johnston Papers, Barret Collection.

[80] Grant received an additional division in early April. See Catton, *Grant Moves South*, p. 218.

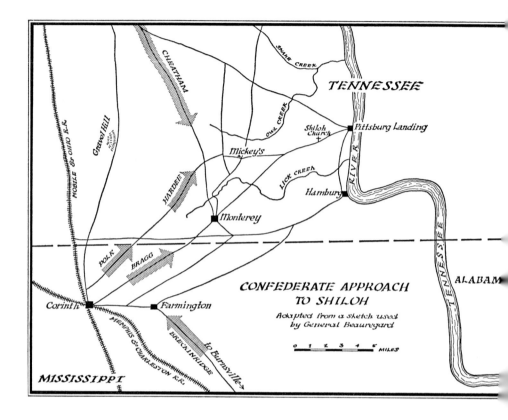

CONFEDERATE APPROACH
TO SHILOH

Adapted from a sketch used
by General Beauregard

0 1 2 3 4 5 MILES

brigades under Breckinridge were to move from Burnsville and make junction with the main body of the army at Mickey's. Before dawn of the fourth, Hardee was to deploy across the entire army front, a width of about three miles; he was to attack at dawn. His left flank was to guide on Owl Creek and his right on Lick Creek. Bragg was to follow Hardee at 1,000 yards, also deployed across the army front. Polk and Breckinridge were initially to follow Bragg in reserve. The main effort in the attack was to be made by the Confederate right; the object was to cut the Union army off from its base at Pittsburg Landing and drive it into the Owl Creek bottom to be scattered and destroyed.[81]

The movement fell short of the plan. Hardee's column was blocked in the streets of Corinth by Polk's troops and wagons, and did not clear the town until the afternoon of the third. Hardee bivouacked on the road and did not reach Mickey's until the morn-

[81] *Official Records*, Ser. I, Vol. X, Pt. I, pp. 392–397.

ing of April 4, twelve hours late. Bragg was even slower; by noon of the fourth his bulky corps was only at the village of Monterey, about halfway from Corinth to his destination. Breckinridge did not clear Burnsville until 3:00 A.M. of the fourth.[82] Johnston soon realized that the attack could not be made on the morning of the fourth, although he seems for a time to have continued in the hope that it could be made later that day. Finally, at 5:00 P.M. of the fourth, in a conference at Monterey with Beauregard and Bragg, Johnston reset the attack for the morning of April 5.[83]

During the night of the fourth, torrential rain fell upon the struggling columns.

It was dark as Eribus and raining tremendously [wrote a soldier]. We were drawn up on the edge [of the road]. As we stood there, troops tramped by in the mud and rain, and darkness. . . . To us who were simply standing in line in the rain it was bad enough, but those men who were going by were wading, stumbling and plunging through mud and water a foot deep.[84]

Hardee was unable to move on schedule the morning of the fifth. As his corps moved into position, the men committed all the errors to be expected of green and nervous soldiers on the eve of their first combat. Many discharged their weapons to test whether the powder would still fire; scampering rabbits were favorite targets. Upon flushing a deer out of the woods, the men gave a shout that could be heard for miles.[85] Not until midmorning was Hardee deployed for attack.

Even then Bragg's corps was not in position; one of his divisions was lost on the road. Johnston repeatedly urged Bragg to hasten his deployment; still Bragg could not get the missing unit up. At last, shortly after noon, Johnston's patience was exhausted. "This is perfectly puerile!" he cried. "This is not war! Let us have out horses." [86] He and a part of his staff rode back along the route looking for the lost division. He discovered it standing still, blocked on the road by

[82] Johnston, *Life of Johnston*, pp. 555–566; Roman, *Military Operations of General Beauregard*, I, 272–276.

[83] William Preston Diary, April 4, 1862, in War Department Collection of Confederate Records. See also Preston, "Memoranda of A. S. Johnston's Death," in Johnston Papers, Barret Collection.

[84] S. R. Latta to "My Dear Mary," April 10, 1862, Latta Letter.

[85] E. G. Drake to William Preston Johnston, August 13, 1876, Johnston Papers, Barret Collection.

[86] Munford, "Albert Sidney Johnston," *ibid.*

Polk's wagons and artillery. Johnston cleared the road and sent the tardy column forward. The time was now 4:00 P.M.[87]

Johnston has often been censured for requiring almost three days to move his army twenty miles for an attack. This assuredly was a slow and cumbrous march. Yet, taking into account the want of training of officers and men and the nature of roads and weather, perhaps it was remarkable that the Southern force moved and deployed as expeditiously as it did.[88]

Knowing that in the coming battle all depended on the spirit of his troops, Johnston sought to nerve them for a supreme effort. Aware of the power of rhetoric upon the Southern mind, he wrote in his own hand a brief but stirring address to be read to the men at intervals on the march and in bivouac. He appealed to them to expel from their soil the "agrarian mercenaries" who had been sent to despoil the South of liberty, property, and honor. He reminded them of the "precious stake involved," of the "fair, broad, abounding land, [and] the happy homes [that would] be desolated . . . by defeat." He said that the eyes of millions of Southerners rested upon the advancing army and that the Confederate warriors must show themselves "worthy of their race and lineage [and of] the women of the South." "With such incentive to brave deeds, and with the trust that God is with us your generals will lead you confidently to the combat, assured of success." [89]

Johnston rode from one organization to another along the line of march, and while the corps were being deployed he imparted to officers and men his own determination and confidence. To one regiment he said, "I am glad to find you in such good spirits. I think

[87] All accounts of the Shiloh campaign published by participants, including Beauregard, make it appear that the original intention was to attack on the fifth. But the language of the order seems unmistakably to mean that Hardee was to march on the third and deploy before daybreak of the fourth. That he was supposed to remain in attack formation for twenty-four hours within sight of the enemy outposts seems unreasonable. For a convincing discussion of this point, see Williams, *P. G. T. Beauregard,* p. 129 n. Beauregard later wrote that the attack was planned to occur "two or three days earlier than it did." Beauregard to William Preston Johnston, March 9, 1877, Johnston Papers, Barret Collection.

[88] The author has observed entanglements and delays in the movement and deployment of formations in World War II reminiscent of Johnston's march. Yet these modern organizations had every advantage over Johnston's army in training, transportation, communications, roads, and maps.

[89] Johnston to "Soldiers of the Army of the Mississippi," in Scrapbook, M. J. Solomons Papers.

we will beat the Yankees out today." [90] To another, "Well, boys, look down the muzzles of your guns, and aim low, today you will have warm work to do!" [91] With these and many other words and manners, Johnston stirred the enthusiasm of his men.[92] They burst into cheers upon his approach and marched toward the battle with an unsurpassed will to victory.

Beauregard's attack order was unique in its provision for a tandem formation of corps spread across the entire army front. This arrangement made inevitable the early intermingling of the troops of Hardee and Bragg, as well as those of the reserve units when they were committed to action. The Confederate generals have been justly criticized for this awkward plan, Beauregard for conceiving it and Johnston for approving it. In his message of April 3 to Davis, Johnston indicated a superior attack formation, in which the three corps would move abreast: Polk on the left, Hardee in the center, and Bragg on the right. Breckinridge was to be in reserve.[93] No satisfactory explanation can be given for the disparity between these two plans.

After the war, Johnston's supporters placed upon Beauregard all of the blame for the faulty attack formation. William Preston Johnston, Jefferson Davis, and General Bragg charged that Beauregard deliberately altered Johnston's plan in the written order that was circulated to the subordinate commanders on the fourth. "The general plan (Johnston's) was admirable," wrote Bragg; "the elaboration simply execrable." [94] Johnston did not see the written order until the troops were on the march; feeling that it was then too late to make a change, said his son, Johnston accepted the Beauregard plan and wired Davis the details.[95] Beauregard's most authoritative biographer feels that each of the two generals simply was unaware of what the other was doing.[96] It seems more reasonable to suppose that in the haste and tension of the hour, either Johnston told Beaure-

[90] J. W. Pownall, "Sick Report Book of Company F, 70th Regiment," Louisiana Historical Association Collection.

[91] Unidentified newspaper clipping, April 9, 1862, Scrapbook, Johnston Papers, Barret Collection.

[92] Latta to "My Dear Mary," April 10, 1862, Latta Letter.

[93] *Official Records*, Ser. I, Vol. X, Pt. II, p. 387.

[94] Bragg to William Preston Johnston, December 16, 1874, Johnston Papers, Barret Collection.

[95] William Preston Johnston, "The Lost Dispatch," *ibid.*

[96] Williams, *P. G. T. Beauregard*, p. 128.

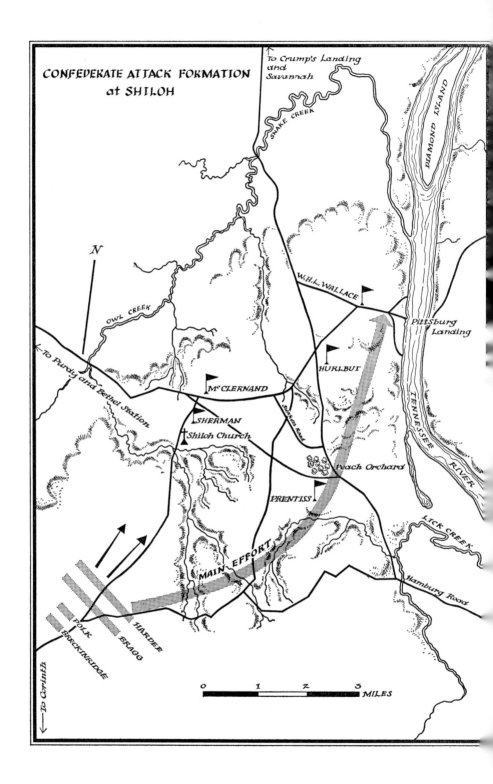

CONFEDERATE ATTACK FORMATION at SHILOH

N

To Crump's Landing and Savannah

SNAKE CREEK

DIAMOND ISLAND

W.H.L. WALLACE

Pittsburg Landing

OWL CREEK

To Purdy and Bethel Station

HURLBUT

McCLERNAND

Sunken Road

TENNESSEE RIVER

SHERMAN

Shiloh Church

Peach Orchard

PRENTISS

LICK CREEK

MAIN EFFORT

Hamburg Road

POLK

BRECKINRIDGE

HARDEE

BRAGG

To Corinth

0   1   2   3   MILES

gard how he wished the attack made and Beauregard forgot the details, or Johnston thought he had given them to his second-in-command when actually he had forgotten to do so. Regardless of how the plan was formulated, Johnston was acquainted with it before the battle began; as commander of the army he must bear the ultimate responsibility for accepting it.

Bragg's misplaced division moved into line shortly after 4:00 P.M. on April 5; Breckinridge's reserve arrived a short time later. The bedraggled but confident Confederate army was at last in position to attack.

Beauregard now lost his resolve. Approaching Bragg in the road just behind the Confederate line, Beauregard expressed his disappointment over the delay in the attack. Soon Polk joined the two. Beauregard said that the hope of surprising the enemy was now gone, that the Confederate army must be returned to Corinth. Bragg agreed with Beauregard.[97] Johnston rode up, attracted by loud voices. Beauregard then appealed to Johnston to withhold the attack, urging that the success of the plan depended upon surprise. "Now they will be entrenched to the eyes," Beauregard cried.[98]

Beauregard was overcome with a virulent case of command "buck fever." A great army, after weeks of travail in concentrating its forces, now stood poised for the assault, only to have the second-in-command decide that the entire offensive must be canceled. Beauregard later claimed that this was not his intention, that he recommended instead a reconnaissance in force to lure the Federal army out of its strong position at the river bank and enable the Confederates to strike it on the move. This explanation appears to have been an afterthought by Beauregard; those present at the famous conference in the road remembered no such suggestion being made at the time.[99] Beauregard's sudden loss of nerve is difficult to explain. It may have been the result of a physical illness which had afflicted him for some weeks; Johnston attributed Beauregard's unsteadiness to this cause. Or it may have been another manifestation of a certain instability in Beauregard's nature, the same that had caused him

[97] William Preston Diary, April 5, 1862, War Department Collection of Confederate Records.

[98] Roman, *Military Operations of General Beauregard*, I, 277–279.

[99] See Munford to William Preston Johnston, October 19, 1877; Preston to William Preston Johnston, April 18, 1862, both in Johnston Papers, Barret Collection; and Parks, *General Leonidas Polk, C.S.A.*, p. 230.

initially to throw up his hands in dismay when he learned of the disparity in the numbers of the opposing armies in Kentucky.

Whatever the cause, Beauregard's conduct obliged Johnston to make the supreme command decision of the western campaign. To ignore the earnest plea of an officer of Beauregard's stature—full general, hero of Fort Sumter and Manassas, coauthor of the present offensive, and second-in-command of the army—was no light matter.

Johnston now faced the moment of truth described by the philosopher on war, von Clausewitz:

As soon as difficulties arise—and that must always happen when great results are at stake—then things no longer move on of themselves. . . . The machine itself then begins to offer resistance, and to overcome this the Commander must have a great force of will. . . . As the forces in one individual after another become prostrated, and can no longer be excited and supported by an effort of his own will, the whole inertia of the mass gradually rests its weight on the will of the Commander: by the spark in his breast, by the light of his spirit, the spark of purpose, the light of hope, must be kindled afresh in others: in so far only as he is equal to this, he stands above the masses and continues to be their master. . . . In war more than anywhere else in the world things happen differently to what we had expected, and look differently when near, to what they did at a distance. The Commander finds himself in a constant whirlpool of false and true information, of mistakes committed through fear, through negligence, through precipitation, of contraventions of his authority, either from mistaken or correct motive, of accidents which no mortal could have foreseen. In short he is the victim of a hundred thousand impressions, of which the most have an intimidating, the fewest an encouraging tendency. . . . High courage and stability of character stand proof against them as the rock resists the beating of the waves. He who would yield to these impressions would never carry out an undertaking.[100]

Johnston listened courteously to Beauregard and the others, then said quietly that he yet hoped to find the enemy unprepared.[101] Finally, Johnston declared, "We shall attack at daylight tomorrow." [102]

That night Johnston pitched his headquarters just behind the Confederate line. His soldiers slept on their arms. Around a small

[100] Carl von Clausewitz, *On War*, I, 55, 192.

[101] Roman, *Military Operations of General Beauregard*, I, 278–279.

[102] Bragg, "General Albert Sidney Johnston and the Battle of Shiloh," Johnston Papers, Barret Collection.

campfire Johnston sat for a while with his staff and subordinate commanders. They talked of the coming battle. Johnston was confident of victory. To one staff officer he said, "I believe I will hammer 'em beyond doubt." [103] To another, "Tomorrow at twelve o'clock we will water our horses in the Tennessee River." [104] His associates retired to their tents. Johnston was left alone.

His heart must have been full as he looked into the dying embers. In many ways this army was more than an army to him; his son has aptly compared him to a Highland chief leading his clan into combat. Encamped about him were numerous friends of a lifetime and comrades from the old Army. General Polk was his roommate at West Point. Hardee was his subordinate in the Second Cavalry. Colonel William Preston of his staff was brother to his first wife. There were associates from days in the Republic of Texas, from the storming of Monterrey, from cavalry service on the Texas frontier, from the ill-starred Utah expedition, and from the burning march across the desert to join the Confederacy. Perhaps Johnston contemplated his own varied experiences that had led him ultimately to this moment; doubtless his thoughts went out to his wife and children in California. At last he lay down to rest; tomorrow would bring the climax of his career and of his life.

[103] Munford, "Albert Sidney Johnston," *ibid.*
[104] D. W. Yandell to William Preston Johnston, November 11, 1877, *ibid.*

Shiloh and Fulfillment

~~~~~~

JOHNSTON AROSE before daybreak of April 6 and awakened the members of his staff. The woods about him teemed with men eating hasty breakfast and readying themselves and their arms for battle. It was a tense and solemn moment; for hundreds of them this would be the final meal. Soon the Confederate ranks were moving forward through the cool, clear dawn. Beauregard now joined Johnston at his headquarters. Johnston was buoyant with the hope of victory; Union prisoners taken the evening before confirmed that his adversary expected no attack. Still Beauregard doubted the wisdom of an offensive, and renewed his argument that the army ought to return to Corinth. Before Johnston could reply, gunfire sounded from the front. "The battle has opened, gentlemen," Johnston said; "it is too late to change our dispositions now." [1]

Johnston told Beauregard that he planned to accompany the forward line; Beauregard was to remain in the rear and supervise

[1] Bragg, "General Albert Sidney Johnston and the Battle of Shiloh," Johnston Papers, Barret Collection.

the movement of troops and supplies to the front. Mounting his horse Fire-eater, Johnston beckoned to his staff and rode toward the sound of battle.[2]

As Johnston approached the front, all omens seemed to portend Confederate victory. Everywhere his appearance sharpened the ardor of his advancing troops. With words of greeting and encouragement he stirred them to their depths. Grasping the hand of a youthful colonel who was a distant kinsman and a warm friend of his son, Johnston cried, "I never see you but I think of William [Preston Johnston]. I hope you may get through safely today, but we must win a victory." Placing his hand upon the shoulder of a young officer who had served with him in Utah, he said, "My son, we must this day conquer or perish." To Brigadier General Thomas C. Hindman of Arkansas, he said, "You have earned your spurs as major-general. Let this day's work win them." To an Arkansas regiment, he exclaimed, "Men of Arkansas! they say you boast of your prowess with the bowie-knife. Today you wield a nobler weapon—the bayonet. Employ it well." [3] Even the elements appeared to smile upon Johnston and his army. The sun rose brilliant upon a country of fresh-leaved oaks, brightened throughout with the white blossoms of dogwood and here and there with the soft pink of farmhouse peach orchards.[4] The Confederate soldiers looked at the sky and spoke of the "sun of Austerlitz." [5]

Fighting began at about 5:00 A.M. as Hardee's advancing line met a Union reconnaissance party of three companies from General Benjamin M. Prentiss's division. Fiercely driving in the light Federal column, the Confederates swept into the Union camp with a crash of musketry and a Rebel yell. The battle of Shiloh was on—the greatest battle yet fought in the Civil War.[6]

Johnston's decision to attack was now justified; the Union army was taken unawares. Shiloh has been called "one of the most com-

[2] William Preston, "Memoranda of A. S. Johnston's Death"; and Munford, "Albert Sidney Johnston," both in *ibid.*

[3] Johnston, *Life of Johnston*, pp. 583–584.

[4] For descriptions of Shiloh before the battle opened, see S. R. Latta to "My Dear Mary," April 10, 1862, Latta Letter; E. L. Shepard to "Dear Wife," March 29, 1862; and E. Colby to "Dear Father," April 4, 1862 (typescripts), all in Miscellaneous Manuscripts Collection, Shiloh National Military Park Library.

[5] Johnston, *Life of Johnston*, p. 582.

[6] The Confederates called it Shiloh because it was fought near a small Methodist church named Shiloh. The Federals called it the Battle of Pittsburg Landing.

plete surprisals recorded in the history of this war." [7] Indeed, it was one of the greatest strategic surprises in all military history. Grant was not with his army but at his headquarters in the Cherry mansion at Savannah, nine miles downriver from Pittsburg Landing. Sherman, a division commander, was the ranking Union officer on the field. He expected no battle.[8] There was no entrenchment, no line of defense. The Union army was in no way arrayed for battle but was scattered about in division encampments of no tactical formation. General Lew Wallace's division was still at Crump's Landing four miles downriver from the rest of the army. Many of the Northern soldiers were eating breakfast when the Confederates struck. Grant himself was at breakfast. He is said to have been in the act of lifting his coffee cup to his mouth when he heard the first cannon fire from Shiloh. Setting down the cup untasted, he boarded a waiting vessel and steamed urgently to join his embattled army.

On his way to the battlefield, Grant stopped at Crump's Landing. Instead of ordering Wallace to march at once to Pittsburg Landing, as he ought to have done, Grant told him to stand by for further orders. Through an incredible series of circumstances, including taking the wrong road and losing his way in the woods, Wallace would not reach the nearby battlefield until the end of the day. Grant arrived at Pittsburg Landing shortly after 8:00 A.M.[9]

Johnston never had an opportunity to explain why he believed that his opponent would be unprepared. The tardiness and want of caution in the Confederate approach gave ground for Beauregard's fear that the Federals would be braced for an assault. But Johnston's intuition was keener than Beauregard's. Johnston's abandonment of the Kentucky line had created in the minds of the Union commanders a false concept of Southern morale and of Johnston's own qualities. Both Grant and Sherman were blinded by overconfidence; they were out of touch with the strategic realities of their situation. Grant later revealed that he thought the Southerners robbed of the will to fight by the loss of Fort Donelson.[10] Grant's complacency at Shiloh came also of a serious flaw in his character as a commander— his inability to anticipate enemy strategy. "[Grant] don't care a

[7] J. F. C. Fuller, *The Generalship of Ulysses S. Grant*, p. 102.
[8] William T. Sherman to "Dear Brother," May 7, 1862, W. T. Sherman Papers.
[9] Catton, *Grant Moves South*, pp. 214–217.
[10] Grant, *Personal Memoirs of U. S. Grant*, p. 191.

damn for what the enemy does out of his sight," Sherman said of him.[11]

The dispatches of Grant and Sherman on the eve of Shiloh make clear that they expected no attack there. On March 17 Grant wrote Halleck expressing surprise over the report of a spy that Johnston was in Corinth; apparently the possibility of a junction of the two wings of the Confederate army had not occurred to Grant.[12] Even after learning of the junction, the Federal commanders failed to grasp its significance. On April 5 Sherman wrote to Grant, "I do not apprehend anything like an attack on our position." [13] Grant wrote Halleck, "I have scarcely the faintest idea of an attack (general one) being made upon us." [14] When Buell's leading division reached Savannah on April 5, Grant neglected to hasten these reinforcements to Pittsburg Landing. Instead, he planned to send them by boat early the next week. To one of the brigade commanders, Grant said, "There will be no fight at Pittsburg Landing; we will have to go to Corinth where the rebels are fortifying." [15] To turn a retreat into a counteroffensive is considered to be one of the most difficult feats in warfare; neither Grant nor Sherman dreamed that Johnston could do it.[16]

Johnston must have sensed this fatal error in the thinking of his antagonists. A profound student of the science of war has said:

If in appearance great risks [are] run, it [is] with the full knowledge that the enemy's character or his apprehensions would prevent him from taking those simple precautions by which the critics point out that the whole enterprise might easily [be] ruined. "They [great generals] penetrate . . . their adversary's brain!" [17]

Johnston had penetrated Grant's brain.

Apologists for Grant seek to exculpate him from the military sin of being taken by surprise at Shiloh. They point out that Grant

---

[11] Quoted in T. Harry Williams, "The Military Leadership of North and South," in *Why the North Won the Civil War* (David Donald, ed.) , p. 42.

[12] *Official Records,* Ser. I, Vol. X, Pt. II, pp. 42–43.

[13] *Ibid.,* Pt. I, pp. 93–94.

[14] *Ibid.,* p. 89.

[15] *Ibid.,* p. 331.

[16] Frank Schaller, "A Review of the Life and Character of the Late General Albert Sidney Johnston," in *The Spirit of Military Institutions* (Marshal Auguste F. Marmont, ed.) , p. 255.

[17] G. F. R. Henderson, *The Science of War,* p. 175.

had recommended to Halleck a more aggressive strategy which, if adopted, would have made impossible the Battle of Shiloh. Halleck's original orders to Grant were to await the arrival of Buell's army at Pittsburg Landing, avoiding a general engagement until the Federal concentration was accomplished. Before Johnston's troops reached Corinth, Grant wrote Halleck indicating a desire to seize the rail junction while it was lightly held by Beauregard. Halleck rejected the plan. Grant was right in believing that Corinth could then be taken with ease; Beauregard had there at the time only about 15,000 men, against whom Grant could have thrown almost three times that number. Yet this does not relieve Grant of misjudging Confederate capabilities and intentions, or of the responsibility of protecting his command against surprise.

This reasoning in favor of Grant's strategy assumes more than it proves. It assumes that without a Battle of Shiloh there would have been no surprise of Grant. But Beauregard was not obliged to remain in Corinth to be destroyed by Grant's superior numbers. Since Beauregard later abandoned Corinth without giving battle, he obviously considered the salvation of his army to be of greater importance than a hopeless defense of the town. The mere seizure of Corinth would not have prevented the junction of the two wings of the Confederate army before the arrival of Buell; they could have been united south of Corinth. If necessary, Beauregard could have moved east along the Memphis and Charleston Railroad to meet Johnston, while Grant at Corinth would have been still another day's march away from Buell.

In his memoirs Grant indicated that the Confederate concentration ought to have been blocked by bold and intelligent moves on the part of the Federal high command. But at the time Grant made no mention of any such measures, other than the seizure of Corinth, for he was unaware of the Confederate attempt to concentrate. He cannot be credited with the foresight to prevent what he failed to foresee. Nor would Grant have been likely to exercise more precaution against attack at Corinth than at Pittsburg Landing. The easy capture of another objective would seem hardly to have altered his erroneous conception of Confederate capabilities, or to have abated his dangerous overconfidence. If Grant had moved against Corinth when he wished to do so, there would have been no Battle of Shiloh; but there might have been a Battle of Corinth just as full of surprises and imponderables to tease the historians of later generations.[18]

Johnston reached the front at sunrise to find Hardee's line in hot combat with the Federal troops of Prentiss's division. Though taken by surprise, the Federals had recovered quickly and were fighting for their lives. Observing Hindman's Confederate brigade stopped and disorganized, and suffering heavy casualties, Johnston quickly rallied the stragglers and sent them back into the fight. Animated by the General's presence, Hindman's ranks pressed forward with spirit, and the Federals yielded ground, but stubbornly.[19]

Seeing that Hardee advanced with difficulty and severe loss, Johnston now ordered Bragg to come up.[20] Already Bragg was on the move; by 7:00 A.M. his large corps was meshed into the line with Hardee's units. All moved forward through wood and across field in a roar of musketry and artillery such as no man there had ever before heard.

In the wake of the advancing line, Johnston rode forward to reconnoiter enemy positions and observe the progress of his attack. At two cabins located on the edge of a large open field, he stopped to watch Cleburne's Arkansas brigade go into action. Across the field went the troops, with loud cheers and confident strides; heavy volleys of musketry rang out; soon the Northern position was in Confederate hands.

Riding into the captured enemy camp, Johnston found the full evidence of soldiers taken by surprise. Breakfast still lay on makeshift tables; baggage was unpacked; knapsacks, arms, ammunition, colors, and stores were left untouched and abandoned. The abundance of such booty tempted men who were hungry, weary, and new to discipline, or who were by nature given to pilfering or thievery. Finding Confederate stragglers looting the rich camp, Johnston sent

[18] Johnston was aware of the possibility that Grant might seize Corinth before the Confederate army was concentrated. Johnston left no explicit statement of his plans if this should occur. He made clear, however, that he intended to attack Grant's army there if possible; if not, Johnston would withdraw farther south and await a more favorable opportunity. See Jeremy F. Gilmer to "My Dear Loulie," March 12, 1862, Gilmer Papers.

[19] William Preston Diary, April 6, 1862, War Department Collection of Confederate Records. See also Preston to William Preston Johnston, April 18, 1862; and Preston, "Memoranda of Albert Sidney Johnston's Death," both in Johnston Papers, Barret Collection.

[20] William Preston Diary, April, 6, 1862, War Department Collection of Confederate Records.

them forward to the fight.[21] To an officer among them, the General spoke in sharp rebuke; then, perhaps seeing the man contrite, he picked up a tin cup and said more softly, "Let this be my share of the spoils today." [22] A column of Federal prisoners was led into Johnston's presence. Many were of German descent and spoke English brokenly. Some threw themselves upon the ground at Johnston's feet, begging their lives. He spoke kindly to them. "Why men," he said, "you don't suppose we kill prisoners, do you? Go the rear & you will be safe there." [23] Johnston found General Hardee at this camp and conferred briefly with him over the course of the battle. Then he rode on.[24]

The time was now past 9:00 o'clock. Save for two reserve brigades under Breckinridge, the entire army was in action. All of the Union force at Pittsburg Landing was in the fight, for Sherman and Prentiss were quickly reinforced by McClernand, W. H. L. Wallace, and Hurlbut. Almost eighty thousand men were engaged in mortal combat.

Across a front of three miles, through wood and field, over hill and down ravine, the battle raged.[25] It rose and fell in fury as position after position was won and lost and won again. The one great battle broke into scores of miniature battles, each with its own front and its own objective; yet all remained components of the master engagement, and all strove toward the master objectives—to destroy the Union army or to save it. Never before had Americans waged such attack; never before had they manned such defense. Long a place of peace and worship, Shiloh was now a place of carnage. The ground was littered with the dead and dying and with the sundry debris of war; everywhere were broken guns and caissons, abandoned wagons, ambulances, ammunition, baggage, and fallen or riderless mounts. Rebel yells, shouted orders, cries of fear or anger, screams of the wounded, and neighing and trampling of

[21] *Ibid.*

[22] Johnston, *Life of Johnston,* p. 612.

[23] D. W. Yandell to William Preston Johnston, November 11, 1877, Johnston Papers, Barret Collection.

[24] D. W. Reed, *The Battle of Shiloh and the Organizations Engaged,* p. 403.

[25] For descriptions of the battle, see Otto Eisenschiml, *The Story of Shiloh,* pp. 40–41; Catton, *Grant Moves South,* p. 235; Fuller, *The Generalship of Ulysses S. Grant,* p. 108; Basil W. Duke, "The Battle of Shiloh," *Southern Bivouac,* II (January, 1884), 201–216.

horses all mingled with the crash of arms and bursting of shells in one great incessant din. Trees splintered and snapped before cannon balls, or were cut through with swarms of musket bullets. A pall of gunsmoke lay over the field.

Back from the holocaust of battle streamed lines of wounded, stunned, or terror-stricken men. Thousands of Northern soldiers broke before the Confederate assault and fled in panic to the river's edge under the bluff; by midmorning perhaps one fourth of Grant's army was there.[26] Entire Confederate regiments fell into disorganization, straggling, and looting. "Since [Shiloh] I have been in many pitched battles including Perryville, Murfreesboro, Chickamauga & Franklin," a veteran wrote after the war, "but none ever made the same impression upon me." [27] Both Grant and Sherman remembered Shiloh's first day as being equal in ferocity to any other engagement in the war.[28] Shiloh was the epitome of battle.

Once on the battlefield, General Grant commanded his army with the coolness and courage for which he is renowned. Yet his hasty message to Buell from Shiloh remains today the most convincing testimony to the fury of the Confederate assault.

The attack on my forces has been very spirited from early this morning [said Grant]. The appearance of fresh troops on the field now would have a powerful effect both by inspiring our men and disheartening the enemy. If you can get upon the field, leaving all your baggage on the east bank of the river, it will be a move to our advantage and possibly save the day to us. The rebel force is estimated at over 100,000 men.[29]

[26] Students of Shiloh have long disputed how many of Grant's soldiers abandoned the battle. Grant and his supporters have insisted that the number was grossly exaggerated in contemporary newspaper accounts and in the reports of General Buell and his subordinates. That the desertion rate was high, however, seems beyond question. "At Shiloh, a great many did run," writes Bruce Catton. "After the battle was a couple of hours old, probably a fourth of Grant's army was huddled under the shelter of the river bank in the rear, completely leaderless and useless." See Catton, "Union Discipline and Leadership in the Civil War," *Marine Corps Gazette* (January, 1956) , p. 24. Buell never wavered in his belief that Grant's army was beaten when Buell's reinforcements arrived. He estimated Grant's effective troops at no more than 5,000 by late afternoon. "The rest were either killed, captured, wounded, or scattered in inextricable and hopeless confusion for miles along the bank of the river." See Don Carlos Buell to William Preston Johnston, April 2, 1873, Johnston Papers, Barret Collection.

[27] R. F. Learned to D. W. Reed, March 22, 1904, Miscellaneous Manuscripts Collection, Shiloh National Military Park Library.

[28] Lloyd Lewis, *Sherman: Fighting Prophet*, p. 232; Sherman, *Memoirs of General Sherman*, I, 275.

[29] *Official Records*, Ser. I, Vol. LII, Pt. I, pp. 232–233.

A month after the battle, Grant still insisted that he had been attacked by 70,000 Confederates.[30] Such exaggeration of Johnston's numbers by so steady an opponent was unintended tribute of the highest order.

The Confederate left inexorably pressed back the Union right—the divisions of Sherman and McClernand. But the Confederate right, which was supposed to sweep faster and shear the enemy away from his base on the river, was halted by the desperate resistance of Prentiss, Hurlbut, and W. H. L. Wallace. From positions along a wooded wagon trail (later called a sunken road by veterans of Shiloh), and across the edge of a small peach orchard, the Union soldiers aimed a sheet of fire into the Confederate ranks. Repeatedly the Confederates charged against this Union strong point; again and again they recoiled from the slaughter. The spot was like a "hornets' nest," they said. There the Confederate main effort was stopped.[31]

During the first three hours of the battle, Johnston moved across the front from left to right, conferring with corps, division, and brigade commanders. From all parts of the field he received information through his staff and through messengers; he personally observed the terrain and enemy positions to his front. At about 9:30 Johnston was at another of the captured camps when he received from Captain S. H. Lockett of the Engineers a written message and penciled sketch showing the location of the enemy troops holding up the Confederate right. As shells began to fall about him, Johnston rode with his escort into a small ravine for cover. For a short while he studied Lockett's message and listened closely to the sound of the battle. He judged the situation accurately: his left still advanced, but his right faltered. The main effort on the right must be put in motion.[32]

At 10:20 Johnston sent a staff officer to order Breckinridge's reserve into the attack. Breckinridge was to feel his way to the river and turn the flank of the enemy.[33] At 11:00 o'clock Captain Lockett reported to Johnston, who then sat with his staff on the brow of a ridge overlooking the line. Since Breckinridge still had not ap-

---

[30] Catton, *Grant Moves South*, p. 263.

[31] Reed, *The Battle of Shiloh*, pp. 53, 59.

[32] William Preston Diary, April 6, 1862, War Department Collection of Confederate Records.

[33] *Ibid.*

peared, Johnston ordered Lockett to report to Breckinridge and to lead his column into position.[34]

Johnston now moved to the right to supervise and animate the assault at the critical point of the battle. As he and his staff rode through another captured encampment, he found himself surrounded with wounded men; some were Confederate, but most were Union prisoners. All were unattended. Johnston sent for Confederate medical officers. Then he turned to the surgeon of his own staff, Dr. D. W. Yandell, and said, "Look after these wounded people, the Yankees among the rest. They were our enemies a moment ago. They are prisoners now." Dr. Yandell remonstrated mildly; he ought to remain with Johnston, he said. The General ordered him to stay, promising to call him if he should leave.[35]

But Johnston promptly rode away; in the heat of the moment he likely forgot his surgeon. Soon Johnston was on the battle line. All Confederate commanders on the right of the field testified that from this time forward Johnston was busy placing them in position, giving direction to their advance, and inspiring them with his words and presence. He ordered General Withers of Bragg's Second Division to shift his troops to the far right in order to strike the enemy flank. The brigades of this division were all either ordered or personally placed in position by Johnston. Shortly after 12:00 noon, Breckinridge's reserve brigades joined the Confederate assault.[36] Johnston himself sent them into action near the right flank of Bragg's sector. "A few more charges and the day [is] ours," he assured one brigade commander.[37]

He promised amiss; Union resistance was too formidable to be overcome by a few more charges. For the next two hours the Confederates sought to dislodge Prentiss by striking at his front and flank. All attempts failed. Perhaps Johnston ought to have bypassed the Hornets' Nest. But this was easier said than done in the heavy woods and rugged draws that lay between the Federal position and the

[34] S. H. Lockett, "Surprise and Withdrawal at Shiloh," in *Battles and Leaders of the Civil War* (R. U. Johnson and C. C. Buel, eds.) , I, 604–606.

[35] Yandell to William Preston Johnston, November 11, 1877, Johnston Papers, Barret Collection.

[36] For reports of division and brigade commanders indicating Johnston's actions, see *Official Records*, Ser. I, Vol. X, Pt. I, pp. 404, 407, 532, 554, 547–549, 569, 621. See also Joseph W. Rich, *The Battle of Shiloh*, pp. 64–65.

[37] *Official Records*, Ser. I, Vol. X, Pt. I, p. 621.

Tennessee River. Moreover, the bypass was a tactical maneuver not developed until later wars. Johnston redoubled his efforts to smash the enemy stronghold.

At last the Confederate attack at the Hornets' Nest began to falter from severe casualties and physical exhaustion. At about 2:00 P.M., General Breckinridge approached Johnston to say that he could no longer prevail upon one of his regiments (a Tennessee organization) to advance. "Oh, yes, general," replied Johnston, "I think you can." He sent Tennessee Governor Isham G. Harris, of his staff, to address the regiment and place it on line for another charge. When Breckinridge still demurred, Johnston said, "Then, I will help you." [38]

He then proceeded with Breckinridge to the front of the reluctant regiment. Riding along the line, Johnston spoke to the men in calm and confident words. Touching their bayonets, he said, "These will do the work. . . . Men, they are stubborn; we must use the bayonet." Upon reaching the center of the line, he suddenly wheeled Fire-eater and called out, "I will lead you!" With spirits rekindled, the Confederate soldiers swept forward behind their general; the enemy to their immediate front gave way, and the objective of the charge was taken. Whether Johnston actually led the assault all the way is uncertain. Perhaps he got it started, then dropped back to the rear. Certainly, he was under hot fire for a time, for a musket ball ripped the sole of one boot, and Fire-eater was slightly wounded in two places. He was elated with the success of the charge. He pointed to his damaged boot and said, almost gaily, to Harris, "Governor, they came very near putting me hors de combat in that charge." [39]

A Federal battery opened fire from the woods to the left. Johnston quickly sent Harris to order Colonel Statham of Breckinridge's command to wheel his brigade to the left and silence the battery. Harris galloped to Statham and delivered the order, then returned to Johnston. As Harris approached, Johnston suddenly reeled in the saddle. Grasping Johnston's coat to steady him, Harris asked, "General, are you wounded?" Johnston replied slowly and emphatically, "Yes, and I fear seriously." They were on the crest of a small ridge, exposed to sporadic enemy fire. With his arm about the General, and assisted by a Captain Wickham, Harris guided their horses to a sheltered spot in a wooded ravine a short distance to the rear. There Harris and

[38] Johnston, *Life of Johnston*, pp. 613–615.
[39] *Ibid.*

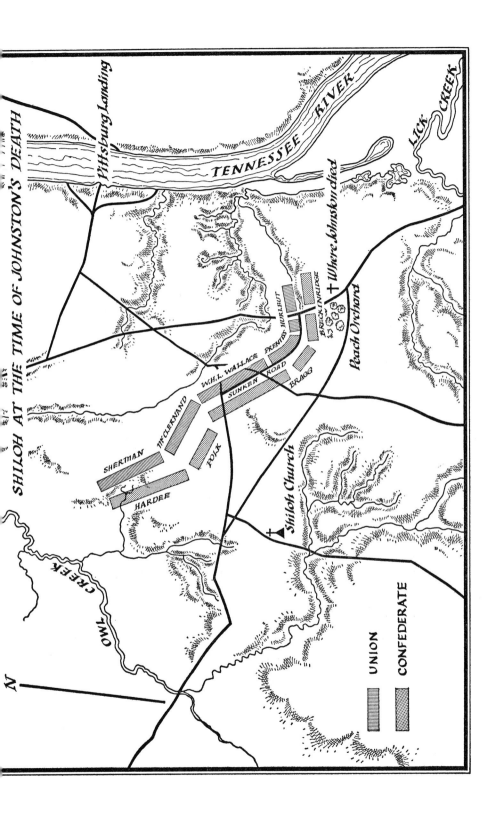

SHILOH AT THE TIME OF JOHNSTON'S DEATH

TENNESSEE RIVER

LICK CREEK

Pittsburg Landing

+ Where Johnston died

BRECKINRIDGE

Peach Orchard

W.H.L. WALLACE   PRENTISS   HURLBUT

SUNKEN   ROAD

BRAGG

McCLERNAND

SHERMAN

POLK

HARDEE

Shiloh Church

OWL   CREEK

N

UNION

CONFEDERATE

the Captain got Johnston off his horse and laid him on the ground.[40]

Ignoring a wound in Johnston's leg that was bleeding profusely, Harris tore open his clothing and searched for a body wound. He found none. He then lifted Johnston's head and gave him a swallow of brandy as a stimulant. Colonel William Preston and others of Johnston's staff now arrived. Preston dismounted and knelt beside his stricken kinsman. "Johnston, don't you know me?" Preston asked. There was no response. Preston called for whiskey. Captain Dudley M. Haydon attempted to pour a bit of it down Johnston's throat, but the General did not swallow it; the liquor ran down his chin. Haydon felt of Johnston's chest, then turned to Preston and said that the heart had ceased to beat. "My God," cried Preston as the truth came to him. "My God. Haydon, is it so?" Albert Sidney Johnston was dead.[41]

He died from loss of blood. An apparently stray and spent Minié ball had struck the back of his right leg, just below the knee. Penetrating half through his leg, its passage tore the popliteal artery. Through the rent in this vessel Johnston's lifeblood escaped.[42] He probably died within fifteen minutes, or less, after being wounded. In the flush of battle, he at first may not have realized that he was hit. Or, as some have speculated, he may have been insensible to the wound because of the impairment of a nerve in his leg by Felix Huston's old duel shot; through the years this limb had been given to occasional numbness.

Why Johnston's associates failed to care for this wound is puzzling. They may have been blinded by panic to the critical nature of it, or they may have been ignorant of the quick danger from bleeding. On Johnston's person was a tourniquet that could have stanched the flow of blood.[43] The physician who doubtless would have used the tourniquet was, by Johnston's order, attending wounded Confederates and Union prisoners in a nearby ravine. Johnston's earlier act of humanity toward friend and foe may have cost him his life.

The General's death stunned the members of his staff. Preston was his kin; Haydon was a personal friend of many years; and others of

[40] *Ibid.* See also Isham G. Harris to Preston, April 6, 1862, written in William Preston Diary, War Department Collection of Confederate Records.

[41] Dudley Haydon in unidentified newspaper clipping, Johnston Papers, Barret Collection. See also Preston, "Memoranda of A. S. Johnston's Death," *ibid.*

[42] Yandell to William Preston Johnston, November 11, 1877, *ibid.*

[43] *Ibid.*

briefer acquaintance had already come to look upon Johnston with near reverence. But they could not long give way to sorrow, for the battle still went on about them. Wrapping his body in a blanket, they bore it back to General Beauregard's headquarters at the Shiloh church. The General's identity was concealed; the curious were told that the corpse was that of a Colonel Jackson of Texas.[44] Beauregard's staff surgeon, Dr. Choppin, examined Johnston's body, located the fatal Minié ball, and noted also a slight wound on one of Johnston's thighs.[45]

Beauregard was shocked to learn of Johnston's death, but he gave orders at once that the attack be continued. Some of the exhausted and straggling Confederate units were re-formed and sent back into the line at the Hornets' Nest.[46] General Ruggles, a brigade commander, wisely collected and concentrated a great battery of sixty-two cannon against the Sunken Road. Exposed on both flanks as the remainder of the Union army withdrew toward Pittsburg Landing, General Prentiss still fought doggedly at this line. Grant earlier had ordered him to hold the position at all cost; Prentiss took him at his word. At last Prentiss was surrounded and trapped; at 5:00 o'clock he surrendered with the remnant of his brigade—about 2,200 men. The Confederates again pressed toward the coveted landing.[47]

But the delay at the Hornets' Nest was fatal to Confederate hopes. While Prentiss was being overcome, Colonel Webster of Grant's staff gathered an immense battery of artillery on the high ground above Pittsburg Landing. Around this position Grant's withdrawn and shaken army braced for the final blow. The stroke did not fall. Two Confederate brigades approached the Federal citadel, only to be repulsed by Webster's guns.[48] Shortly after 6:00 o'clock Beauregard ordered the Confederate forces to cease the attack and withdraw for the night. This decision was a grave mistake; Beauregard ought either to have risked all in a desperate assault on the last Federal position, or to have led his army back to Corinth during the night of the sixth. To await attack the next day by Grant's strengthened army was to invite disaster.

The battle opened again early on the morning of the seventh. The

[44] Haydon in unidentified newspaper clipping, *ibid.*
[45] Preston to William Preston Johnston, April 7, 1862, *ibid.*
[46] Roman, *Military Operations of General Beauregard,* I, 297–299.
[47] Horn, *The Army of Tennessee,* pp. 134–143.
[48] Catton, *Grant Moves South,* pp. 236–242.

tables were now turned. Reinforced the previous afternoon by Lew Wallace's division from Crump's Landing and one brigade of Buell's army, and during the night by Buell's 21,000 fresh troops, Grant attacked with overwhelming numbers. Throughout the morning the battle raged over the ground of the day before; slowly the Confederates yielded before Grant's relentless pressure. By midafternoon the Confederate resistance was spent. Beauregard broke off action and withdrew his disorganized and dispirited troops to Corinth. Grant made no determined pursuit, thus squandering perhaps the war's greatest opportunity to destroy or capture an opposing army.[49]

The Confederate counteroffensive at Shiloh had failed in its mission. The South had lost the most critical contest of the war for control of what Johnston called the "seat of vitality of the Confederacy"—the Mississippi Valley.

Would Johnston have won the Battle of Shiloh if he had lived? Would a final assault against Grant's position on the evening of the sixth have brought victory to the Confederates? Any answer to these questions is speculation. In their official reports, Bragg and Hardee attributed to Johnston's death the failure to destroy Grant's army on the sixth.[50]

No one cause probably contributed so greatly to our loss of time, which was the loss of success, as the fall of the commanding general [said Bragg]. For want of a common superior to the different commands on that part of the field, great delay occurred after this misfortune, and that delay prevented the consummation of the work so gallantly and successfully begun.[51]

---

[49] Fuller, *The Generalship of Ulysses S. Grant,* p. 112.

[50] Hardee's report is in *Official Records,* Ser. I, Vol. X, Pt. I, pp. 405–412.

[51] *Ibid.,* pp. 463–470. In their personal letters written immediately after the battle, none of the corps commanders mentioned Johnston's death as affecting the outcome of the contest. Bragg and Hardee were then writing primarily of their own exploits in battle; they had no interest in the roles of others. "The behavior of the troops from Pensacola & Mobile [Bragg's troops] is beyond praise," Bragg wrote his wife. "It is the theme of admiration." See Braxton Bragg to "My Dearest Wife," April 8, 1862, Bragg Papers (photostatic copies), Manuscript Division, Library of Congress. *"Entre nous,"* Hardee wrote to a friend, "don't regard me as vain, but tell me frankly the *on dit* respecting myself. I have had many compliments on my personal bearing, and would like to know what you have heard in Memphis." See William J. Hardee to Mrs. Stover, April 9, 1862, Hardee Papers. In writing to his wife two days after the battle, Polk said that the enemy army was badly whipped on the first day, that it ought to have been captured, and that another hour of daylight would have made this possible. Five

This was also the opinion of the rank and file of Confederate soldiers who fought at Shiloh.[52] Jefferson Davis firmly believed it. After the war this feeling among Southerners hardened into a conviction that Beauregard took command after the day was won and threw away the victory by halting the attack.

Students of the Civil War today generally feel that Johnston's death did not alter the outcome of the battle. Contrary to the belief of Jefferson Davis and many other Southerners, say these critics, Beauregard did not call off the engagement at the moment of victory. Instead, he continued the attack for almost four hours after Johnston's death, and pressed the Confederate line forward as long as it had the strength and organization to advance.[53]

The conclusion that Johnston could not have destroyed Grant's army is likely to endure; it is supported by impressive evidence. Yet it must remain conjecture. It rests upon the substitution of Beauregard for Johnston in the command equation. Since Beauregard put forth an earnest effort and failed, it argues, therefore Johnston also would have failed. This reasoning denies that Johnston could have done what Prentiss did in the Sunken Road, or Stonewall Jackson at Manassas and other engagements, or Sheridan after Cedar Creek. It denies that a great leader can in moments of crisis lift his troops, however exhausted, to superhuman effort. It insists that Beauregard's orders from far behind the line were as effective as Johnston's presence at the key point on the battlefield.[54]

The Confederate drive lost momentum when Johnston fell. Not that his death was a signal for the Southern army to halt and await an order from Beauregard to resume fighting; the general action against the enemy continued. But participants in the battle agreed that, for a period after Johnston's fall, the fury of the Confederate assault waned. In spite of all efforts to keep his death a secret, the

---

months later, in writing his official report, Polk eulogized Johnston's leadership and implied that Johnston would have gained a complete victory at Shiloh if he had lived through the battle. See Parks, *General Leonidas Polk, C.S.A.*, pp. 236–237.

[52] Lawson to "Dear Ma," April 18, 1862, Johnston Papers, Barret Collection.

[53] For discussions of this point, see Williams, *P. G. T. Beauregard*, pp. 141–142; Horn, *The Army of Tennessee*, p. 137; Parks, *General Leonidas Polk, C.S.A.*, pp. 235–236.

[54] McWhiney, "Braxton Bragg at Shiloh," *Tennessee Historical Quarterly* (March, 1962), pp. 27–29, questions Beauregard's wisdom in stopping the battle without consulting the corps commanders or without personally observing the condition at the front.

word spread quickly throughout both armies. Grant said it encouraged his own hard-pressed men.[55] Sherman said:

> The rebel army, commanded by General Albert Sidney Johnston . . . beyond all question fought skillfully from early morning till about 2 P.M., when their commander-in-chief was killed. . . . There was then a perceptible lull for a couple of hours, when the attack was renewed, but with much less vehemence, and continued up to dark.[56]

This was the time that Colonel Webster began collecting the guns for the final defense of the landing. "For one," said General Hurlbut, who late in the afternoon assembled the troops to support Webster's battery, "I was exceedingly grateful for the cause be it what it might, which gave us abundant time to take up a new position & prepare to hold it to the death."[57] Alive and animated with the prospect of victory, Johnston might not have granted the respite for which Hurlbut expressed a just gratitude.

Johnston's strategy that led to the Battle of Shiloh may be judged thus: If it had been perfectly executed, his plan of withdrawing south of the Tennessee River could have been proved sound by a great victory at Shiloh. The move drew enemy forces deep into the South, far from their bases of supply and communication. It baffled Johnston's opponents as to his intentions and capabilities. It ultimately enabled him to seize upon a flaw in their deployment and mood, and to strike one segment of the invading army before it was joined by the other.

But Johnston's retrograde movement also gave opportunity for serious mistakes on his part. The first and most grievous of these was the decision to concentrate a large body of troops in Fort Donelson, where they were lost. Had Johnston not sent these troops there, or had Floyd been of the courage and resourcefulness to extricate them and rejoin Johnston in Nashville, the result at Shiloh might have been quite different from what it was. An eminent student of Shiloh has said that an additional Confederate reserve of 5,000 men might have destroyed Grant's army there.[58] If this be true, the 12,000 to 15,000 Confederate troops lost in Fort Donelson surely would have accomplished Johnston's objective at Shiloh.

[55] Grant, *Memoirs of U. S. Grant*, p. 187.
[56] Sherman, *Memoirs of General William T. Sherman*, I, 245.
[57] S. A. Hurlbut to William Preston Johnston, November 22, 1877, Johnston Papers, Barret Collection.
[58] Williams, *Lincoln Finds a General*, III, 376.

The disaster of losing the troops in Fort Donelson might have been counteracted by Johnston if Van Dorn's force of 20,000 men in Arkansas had been ordered east of the Mississippi in time to join the Confederate offensive at Shiloh. Johnston awakened too late to this possibility.

With his advantage of surprise, Johnston might have destroyed Grant's army with the troops he had available, had they been deployed with maximum effect. The Confederate attack formation at Shiloh was ill-designed to cut the Union army away from its base on the river. Such an accomplishment would have called for a massing of Southern strength on the right, say Bragg's large corps followed by Polk and Breckinridge in reserve; just enough troops ought to have been committed on the left to occupy the Federal divisions there and keep them from being shifted to meet the main effort. Such an "unbalanced line to the right" might have thrust its way to the landing before the Union army could recover from its surprise and form a defense in depth. Johnston sought during the course of the battle to correct this error; he extended a part of Bragg's corps to the extreme right after it was on the line, and he sent Breckinridge's reserve to the support of the right. Johnston lost his life in attempting to direct his attack at this point; the corrective action possibly came too late, anyway.

Since Johnston's death, some have expressed the opinion that he was a suicide. Despondent over earlier reverses, they say, and despairing of victory in the present engagement, Johnston deliberately exposed himself to enemy fire at Shiloh. Years later, Gideon Pillow wrote that, on the night before the battle, Johnston confided to him his intention to win the coming fight or leave his body on the field.[59] One student of Johnston's career sees in the manner of his dying the culmination of a long death urge. From time to time throughout his life, says novelist and historian Shelby Foote, Johnston "behaved like a man in search of death." [60]

Yet these suggestions of suicide leave much unsaid. All who were with Johnston on the eve of Shiloh remembered that he was confident of success in the great offensive. Those who accompanied him in the battle, or who encountered him momentarily during the day, testified to his remarkable buoyancy of spirit on the

[59] Gideon J. Pillow to William Preston Johnston, June 2, 1876, Johnston Papers, Barret Collection.
[60] Shelby Foote, *Shiloh*, p. 17.

field. In spite of the long delay before the Hornets' Nest, Johnston still felt that victory was in his grasp. He may indeed have told Pillow that he would win or die in the effort, but this is a sentiment common to commanders when the fate of a nation hangs upon the battle. Johnston was killed while his army was still advancing; neither his mood nor the situation indicated suicide.

Johnston has been almost universally censured for exposing himself recklessly on the battle front. Certainly the true role of an army commander is not to lead regimental charges. But great captains, ancient and modern, have at critical moments in the combat inspired their troops with personal deeds of valor and hazard. Alexander, Caesar, and Napoleon did it in wars of old; Rommel and Patton did it in a war of our own day. "Above everything else . . . in battle the [Civil War] officer had to be absolutely fearless," says Bruce Catton. "From army commander on down, he had to show physical courage rather ostentatiously. If he could not do that, he could not do anything." [61] This was especially true in leading the green soldiers that Johnston commanded at Shiloh. "Under the circumstances," says Kenneth Williams, another renowned student of Civil War military leadership, "it was the best thing [Johnston] could do, for as an inspirer and leader of men he was outstanding." [62] There are times in battle when the situation requires that the army commander temporarily place himself at the head of a subordinate command. But for the fatal Minié ball that struck him down, Johnston was where he ought to have been at Shiloh.

Many have held that in remaining on the front line, Johnston was out of touch with the battle as a whole, that Beauregard was actually in command of the Confederate army at Shiloh. Beauregard later encouraged this belief. [63]

Johnston's role in the Shiloh offensive was this: Johnston decided, seconded by Beauregard, that Grant's army would be attacked at Pittsburg Landing; Johnston decided, with Beauregard's recommendation, when the attack would be made; Johnston delegated to Beauregard the writing of march and attack order, and accepted the plan when it was presented to him; and Johnston decided, over Beauregard's vehement protest, that the attack would be carried out.

[61] Catton, "Union Discipline and Leadership in the Civil War," *Marine Corps Gazette* (January, 1956), p. 24.
[62] Williams, *Lincoln Finds a General*, III, 363.
[63] Roman, *Military Operations of General Beauregard*, I, 347–351.

After the battle was opened by Hardee's corps, Johnston ordered Bragg's corps into action; Johnston later ordered a part of Polk's corps into action; Johnston personally located the point of decisive resistance in the battle, and directed the Confederate main effort against it; finally, Johnston ordered Breckinridge's reserve corps into action at the place and time of his own choosing. Notwithstanding Johnston's location during the battle, Johnston actually made every major Confederate command decision between his arrival in Corinth and his death on the field of Shiloh.

Considering the inexperience of officers and men, the nature of the terrain, and the faulty attack formation, the Confederate army at Shiloh was led with perhaps maximum effect. Critics speak of the loss of alignment of the assault forces, of a lack of close central control, and of the tendency of the battle to break into many local, loosely coordinated engagements. All this is true. But such was inevitable in a battle involving the number and condition of the troops and the rugged and heavily wooded area of Shiloh. It could not have been fought as a football game is conducted, according to a system of prearranged plays. In this respect, Shiloh has been called by Kenneth Williams a truly modern battle.[64] One may question whether in any other offensive of the Civil War an army the size of Johnston's struck with the impact or maintained throughout a day the relentless pressure exerted by the Confederates in this contest. Certainly it was not again done by a force of so little experience.

While Johnston made the primary decisions that committed the army and the various corps to action, and set the direction of the Confederate thrust, Beauregard energetically performed the duties of second-in-command. He exercised control over the rear, keeping informed on the situation through his staff, moving reserve units forward to positions where they might be readily employed by Johnston as the battle progressed, sending ammunition to the front, re-forming stragglers, and ordering idle or withdrawing formations back to points in the line where he judged they were most needed.[65] The corps commanders worked out among themselves a practical solution to the problem of the intermingling of their troops. They divided the front: Hardee took command of the left, Polk of the center, and Bragg of the right.

[64] Williams, *Lincoln Finds a General*, III, 363.
[65] Roman, *Military Operations of General Beauregard*, I, 286–297; also Williams, *P. G. T. Beauregard*, p. 139.

Johnston's most important function on the battlefield was inspiring his raw troops to fierce and sustained effort. In this role he was superb. Except for the one occasion, he did not inspire by leading charges against the enemy. He did it by his bearing and appearance on the field, "sitting on his horse where the bullets were flying like hail stones . . . cool, collected, self-possessed but . . . animated & in fine spirits." [66] Moving throughout the morning across much of the front, he imparted to his men by word and gesture a measure of his own determination and courage.

Subordinate commanders and staff officers alike attested to the electric effect on the entire army of Johnston's presence.

To those who saw [Johnston] that day, as the writer did [a young Confederate recalled], in all the glorious fever of that delirious success, mounted upon a magnificent steed, his massive figure seeming to enlarge to gigantic size with the ardor of battle, his noble face aflame with his indomitable spirit of fight, he was the ideal embodiment of the fiery essence of war.[67]

Doubtless this image of Johnston at Shiloh was embellished by time, imagination, and Confederate patriotism, but it rings true to all accounts of his activities on the field. Even Colonel Thomas Jordan, implacable critic of Johnston's strategy, acknowledged his remarkable combat leadership. "Johnston stimulated the onslaught by his personal presence on the right," wrote Jordan, "where the press was fiercest, the resistance the most effective." [68] General Beauregard also paid homage to Johnston's power of inspiration. In taking command after Johnston's death, Beauregard forbade his subordinates to spread word of the event. "Beauregard knew what effect it would produce upon the troops." [69] In his official report of the battle, written on April 11, Beauregard said, "General Johnston [showed] the highest qualities of the commander, and a personal intrepidity that inspired all around him, and gave resistless impulsion to his columns at critical moments." [70]

The ability of a general to fire his men with spirit and initiative is as important in deciding the outcome of a battle as are the orders

[66] Jacob Thompson to William Preston Johnston, November 18, 1877, Johnston Papers, Barret Collection.

[67] I. W. Avery in *Cincinnati Daily Enquirer*, n.d. (clipping) , in *ibid.*

[68] Jordan and Pryor, *Campaigns of Lieut. General N. B. Forrest*, p. 124.

[69] Roman, *Military Operations of General Beauregard*, I, 297.

[70] *Official Records*, Ser. I, Vol. X, Pt. I, p. 387.

given on the field, says a perceptive student of Grant's rise to fame. He concludes:

The cohesion and persistency [of the Confederate army at Shiloh] in its attack . . . were really marvelous, and an enduring tribute to its commander. . . . Lee and Jackson, with their insight into the soldier mind, more than overcame the disparity in numbers which was against them. . . . In the West, Grant possessed this insight; so did Albert Sidney Johnston; that was why Shiloh was one of the hardest-fought battles of all time.[71]

To evaluate Johnston as a general is difficult; he died too early in the Civil War to demonstrate his full capabilities. Death on the battlefield, after taking Grant by surprise, made Johnston a martyred genius in Southern eyes; it "placed a halo around his head," complained Beauregard.[72] "Those who a short time ago were clamoring against General Johnston would now snatch him from the grave," a soldier wrote from Corinth shortly after the Battle of Shiloh.[73] On the eve of Shiloh, Major Gilmer had written of the Confederate generals at Corinth, "Among them all there is not a Napoleon." [74] But after the battle, Gilmer said of Johnston, "He devoted talents of the highest order, energies unceasing, and earnestness never surpassed, and a singleness of purpose never equalled." [75]

Jefferson Davis called Johnston the "great pillar of the Confederacy," her outstanding general.[76] Richard Taylor, son of Zachary Taylor, and a brilliant general in the Confederate army, later wrote, "[Albert Sidney Johnston] was the foremost man of all the South; and had it been possible for one heart, one mind, and one arm, to save her cause, she lost them when [he] fell on the field of Shiloh." [77] Johnston's son, William Preston Johnston, eulogized his father in a biography published in 1878, portraying him as a strategist and commander without peer. The people of the South took these sayings to heart. If Albert Sidney Johnston had not fallen at Shiloh, they said, he would have destroyed Grant's army there; he would

---

[71] A. L. Conger, *The Rise of U. S. Grant*, pp. 252–268.

[72] Beauregard, "Extract of a Letter to Marrin," Beauregard Papers.

[73] Lawson to "Dear Ma," April 18, 1862, Johnston Papers, Barret Collection.

[74] Gilmer to "My Dear Loulie," March 29, 1862, Gilmer Papers.

[75] Gilmer to James D. McCabe, October 19, 1863, quoted in Nichols, *Confederate Engineers*, p. 49 n.

[76] Jefferson Davis, *A Short History of the Confederate States of America*, p. 147.

[77] Taylor, *Destruction and Reconstruction*, p. 285.

have saved the west for the Confederacy; and possibly he would have led the South to victory in the war.

Twenty years after the Civil War, the currents of opinion began to shift. In 1884 General Beauregard's account of the conflict was published, seriously questioning Johnston's competence as a general. Beauregard suggested that most of Johnston's wise moves were inspired by Beauregard, that most of Johnston's errors were made against Beauregard's advice. General Grant wrote in *Century Magazine* in 1885 that Johnston died too early either to prove or disprove the lofty estimate of his generalship widely held at the outbreak of the war.[78] But Grant later wrote in his memoirs that he was convinced that Johnston was weak and indecisive.[79] Many recent military historians support the views of Beauregard and Grant. General J. F. C. Fuller, a student of Grant's military operations, dismisses Johnston as a "brave but stupid" man.[80] Beauregard's definitive biographer says, "Nothing that Johnston did in his brief career justifies the belief that he had the elements of greatness. Many things that he did suggest that he was not qualified for high command." [81] Exaggerated praise of Johnston thus inspired exaggerated disparagement.

Johnston's reputation as a general suffers today from contrast with the inflated estimates of his prowess rendered both before and after the Civil War. In spite of long service in the army, Johnston came to the Confederacy with no experience in combat command. Yet he was hailed initially as a warrior beyond compare, and he was assigned the most difficult mission of the Civil War—to defend the broad, river-threaded Mississippi Valley against the vastly superior armies and navy of the North. Few generals in history have been as great as Johnston was then supposed to be; perhaps none have been as great as the people of the South later remembered him to have been.

Johnston's reputation today suffers also from contrast with records of other Civil War generals made in the maturity of their careers. These men grew immeasurably with experience as the war continued. Of Grant and Sherman at Shiloh, a Union veteran of the

---

[78] Ulysses S. Grant, "The Battle of Shiloh," *Century Magazine*, XXIX (February, 1885) , 608.
[79] Grant, *Memoirs of U. S. Grant*, pp. 153, 166.
[80] Fuller, *The Generalship of Ulysses S. Grant*, p. 82.
[81] Williams, *P. G. T. Beauregard*, p. 116.

battle aptly said, "They had to learn their art, and the country and their army had to pay the cost of their teaching." [82] A perceptive student of Grant's military growth believed it "deliberately planned by some guiding intelligence. . . . There is no question," he wrote, "that Shiloh afforded Grant the most important tactical lessons of his military career." [83] Grant revealed in his memoirs that he learned far more than tactics at Shiloh; he came out of that stern apprenticeship with an entirely new concept of the war.[84]

What would be the renown today of any other general in that campaign, if he had been struck down in the middle of the afternoon of April 6, 1862? Of Beauregard, voicing dismay at Bowling Green and hysterically advising retreat before a shot was fired at Shiloh? Of "Crazy" Sherman, fretting over the threat of Johnston's thin columns in Kentucky and shouting in rude surprise at the opening Confederate charge at Shiloh, "My God, we are attacked"? Or of Grant, expressing puzzlement over the presence of Johnston and his troops at Corinth, and saying to the commander of Buell's advance brigade, "There will be no fight at Pittsburg Landing; we will have to go to Corinth where the rebels are fortifying"? All these men were then novices in the waging of war. All made errors of the first magnitude, either of strategy or tactics, or of insight into the mind of their own troops or those of the enemy. All grew in stature with the war. Johnston was denied this opportunity.

To suppose that Johnston would have learned nothing from a campaign that taught others so much would be unjust. Johnston still had the capacity to grow. "War is a great game," he once wrote, "in which the choice of position makes the result." [85] His decisions regarding Shiloh and future Confederate strategy illustrated how far beyond this concept of positional warfare he had come. Fort Donelson must have taught him the danger of splitting his army; the failure to bring Van Dorn to Corinth in time for the battle must have impressed Johnston with the need to concentrate all available troops for decisive strokes; the intermingling of his troops at Shiloh must have shown him the error of spreading corps across the entire

---

[82] Warren Olney, "The Battle of Shiloh," clipping from *Overland Monthly* (June, 1883), Johnston Papers, Barret Collection.

[83] Conger, *The Rise of U. S. Grant*, p. 268.

[84] Grant, *Memoirs of U. S. Grant*, pp. 303–304.

[85] Johnston to William Preston Johnston, February 23, 1849, Johnston Papers, Barret Collection.

battle front, if it was he who needed such lesson. Delays and snarls such as those of the march from Corinth and the deployment of the army would have remedied themselves with increasing discipline and experience of troops and subordinate officers.

If Johnston's behavior in abandoning the Kentucky line indicated a want of boldness and ingenuity, his determination to strike Grant at Pittsburg Landing showed that this weakness was overcome. The attack at Shiloh was more than the blind lashing out of a cornered and desperate man. Johnston planned it as the initial stroke in a great counteroffensive to clear the western Confederacy of invaders. With an army swelled to 60,000 men by the addition of Van Dorn's troops, Johnston would destroy the forces first of Grant and then of Buell before they joined; then he would recover the states of Tennessee and Kentucky. Possibly he would carry the war across the Ohio. This was not the strategy of timidity.[86]

Had Johnston lived, he doubtless would have emerged from Shiloh with vastly enhanced prestige, regardless of the outcome of that contest, for he demonstrated there that he had the will and courage to fight, and that in moments of crisis his judgment and determination transcended that of fellow Confederates. He demonstrated also that he could anticipate and confound his adversary.

I am sustained by the definite conclusion and capable thought of thousands who were present and now survive [wrote a veteran of Sherman's division at Shiloh], [that] it was emphatically a soldier's fight, well put in the expression that the rebels out-generalled us, but that we out-coloneled them.[87]

Johnston's conduct on the battlefield secured him in the hearts of his own men. He showed unsurpassed steadiness and spirit of attack in as severe combat as Americans had ever experienced. Soldiers who saw him in the crucible of Shiloh knew that his was metal to withstand the hottest flame, that the humblest musketeer in the army would never be ordered to take a step that his commander would hesitate to take, if necessary. This was the leadership that fired the

[86] Earl Van Dorn to his wife, April 6, 1862, quoted in *A Soldier's Honor,* p. 71.

[87] Lucian B. Crooker, *A Section of a Battle: Observations upon the Conduct of the 55th Illinois Infantry in the First Day's Battle of Shiloh,* pp. 4–5.

souls of a hastily assembled, untrained, and ill-armed body of South-erners and transformed them into the most formidable striking force that America had then seen. Johnston's presence would have been an incalculable asset to the Confederacy in the trying years to come.

Epilogue

~~~~~~~~~~~~~~~~~~~~~~~~~~~~~~~~~~~~~~

AFTER JOHNSTON'S TRAGIC DEATH, Colonel Preston requested of General Beauregard that Johnston's staff be permitted to carry his body from the little church on the Shiloh battlefield to New Orleans for temporary burial until the family could choose a permanent resting place. Beauregard consented, and that night Dr. Choppin injected whiskey into Johnston's blood vessels to preserve the body during the long journey south.[1] The next morning Johnston's staff placed his body in a wagon and rode in somber cavalcade from Shiloh's field of death to Corinth, where the body was prepared for burial.[2] From there they went by train to New Orleans, arriving on April 9, to be met at the depot by Governor Thomas O. Moore of Louisiana and General Mansfield Lovell, commander of Confederate troops defending the city.[3] The General's

[1] D. W. Yandell to William Preston Johnston, November 11, 1877, Johnston Papers, Barret Collection.

[2] William Preston Diary, April 7, 1862, War Department Collection of Confederate Records.

[3] Unidentified newspaper clippings in Scrapbook, Johnston Papers, Barret Collection.

body was borne to the City Hall, where it lay in state for two days. On the afternoon of the eleventh, with his staff as pallbearers, Johnston was laid to rest in the St. Louis cemetery. At the invitation of Mayor John T. Monroe of New Orleans, he was buried in the Monroe family tomb.[4]

For almost five years Johnston's body remained in the cemetery in New Orleans. Admirers from time to time decorated the vault with garlands and flowers. One citizen wrote and fixed upon the tomb a poem eulogizing Johnston as "a great captain," mourned by a bereaved people and claimed by three commonwealths.[5] But Johnston's final resting place was not to be New Orleans. He was known to have preferred burial in Texas; to his brother-in-law, William Preston, he once said, "When I die, I want a handful of Texas earth on my breast." [6] In the fall of 1866, after obtaining the approval of Johnston's family, the Texas Legislature resolved to bring Johnston's body to Austin for interment. A committee of distinguished Texans was appointed escort for the solemn task.[7]

On January 23, 1867, Johnston's body was removed from the St. Louis cemetery. A brief religious service was held beside the tomb, in the presence of a throng of admirers and mourners. Pallbearers were former Confederate generals, including Beauregard, Bragg, Hood, Richard Taylor, and Longstreet.[8] From New Orleans, Johnston's body was taken to Galveston, then to Houston, and at last to Austin.

Bitterness and irony attended this movement. Fearing a demonstration of Confederate sympathy, or feigning to fear such, the military authorities in Galveston forbade a funeral procession planned there by Johnston's former comrades. The result was a great outpouring of indignation and Confederate sympathy; thousands of persons filed past the coffin as it lay on the wharf at Galveston. Other thousands paid homage to his memory when his body passed through Houston.[9]

Johnston's body, with its escort, arrived in Austin on February 1. Governor James W. Throckmorton received it with appropriate

[4] *Daily Delta,* April 12, 1862.
[5] *Daily Picayune,* November 4, 1862, and November 2, 1865.
[6] Johnston, *Life of Johnston,* p. 699.
[7] H. P. N. Gammel (ed.), *The Laws of Texas, 1822–1897,* V, 1179–1180.
[8] Unidentified newspaper clippings in Scrapbook, Johnston Papers, Barret Collection.
[9] *Ibid.*

oratory; for a day it lay in state in the Capitol. Again great numbers moved past the bier and covered it with laurel and flowers. On the afternoon of February 2, Johnston was buried in the Texas State Cemetery, to take his place among the honored dead of Texas.[10]

No spot could have been more fitting for Johnston's sepulchre. He had assisted in the founding of Austin; he had resided in Austin when it was a frontier capital of the Republic of Texas; later, he had lived happily in Austin with his family. Perhaps his own words of the past came back to him now: "Austin is in the . . . most beautiful & lovely country that the 'blazing eye' of the sun looks upon in his journey from the east to the west."[11] Albert Sidney Johnston had come home.

[10] *Weekly Texas State Gazette* (Austin), February 2, 1867, quoted in *Dallas Weekly Herald,* February 9, 1867.

[11] Johnston to George Hancock, October 24, 1839, Johnston Papers, Barret Collection.

BIBLIOGRAPHY

Manuscripts

Army Papers, Republic of Texas. Texas State Archives, Austin, Texas.

Atkinson, Henry, Letter Books (April 3–May 27, 1832; May 26–September 23, 1832). Black Hawk War Collection, Illinois State Historical Library, Springfield, Illinois. Microfilm copies in Manuscripts Division, Howard-Tilton Memorial Library, Tulane University, New Orleans, Louisiana.

Atkinson, Henry, Order Book (April 5–August 29, 1832). Black Hawk War Collection, Illinois State Historical Library, Springfield, Illinois. Microfilm copies in Manuscripts Division, Howard-Tilton Memorial Library, Tulane University, New Orleans, Louisiana.

Ballinger, Betty, Papers. Manuscripts Division, Rosenberg Library, Galveston, Texas.

Bancroft, Mrs. Hubert H. "Utah Notes." Bancroft Library, University of California, Berkeley, California.

Barret, Mrs. Mason, Collection of Albert Sidney and William Preston Johnston Papers. Manuscripts Division, Howard-Tilton Memorial Library, Tulane University, New Orleans, Louisiana.

Beauregard, P. G. T., Papers. Manuscript Division, Library of Congress, Washington, D.C. Microfilm copies of selected items in Manuscripts Division, Howard-Tilton Memorial Library, Tulane University, New Orleans, Louisiana.

Becker, Charles. "History of the Expedition against the Mormons in 1857." Church Historian's Office, Church of Jesus Christ of Latter-Day Saints, Salt Lake City, Utah.

Bigler, Henry W., Journal. In Mormon File, uncatalogued. Huntington Library, San Marino, California.

Black Hawk War Collection. Illinois State Historical Library, Springfield, Illinois. Microfilm copies of selected items in Manuscripts Division, Howard-Tilton Memorial Library, Tulane University, New Orleans, Louisiana.

Boswell, R. P., Letters. In possession of E. D. Brigance, Henderson, Tennessee. Photostatic copies in Manuscripts Division, Howard-Tilton Memorial Library, Tulane University, New Orleans, Louisiana.

Bragg, Braxton, Papers. Manuscripts Division, Duke University Library, Durham, North Carolina. Copies of selected items in Manuscripts Division, Howard-Tilton Memorial Library, Tulane University, New Orleans, Louisiana.

Bragg, Braxton, Papers. Western Reserve Historical Society, Cleveland, Ohio. Photostatic copies in Manuscript Division, Library of Congress, Washington, D.C. Copies of selected items in Manuscripts Division, Howard-Tilton Memorial Library, Tulane University, New Orleans, Louisiana.

Brown, Lorenzo, Diary (typescript). Manuscripts Division, Brigham Young University Library, Provo, Utah.

Candland, David, Diary (typescript). Manuscripts Division, Brigham Young University Library, Provo, Utah.

Civil Service File, Republic of Texas. Texas State Archives, Austin, Texas.

Cox, Orvill S., Diary (microfilm copy). HM FAC 521. Huntington Library, San Marino, California.

Crosby, Jesse W., Diary (typescript). Manuscripts Division, Brigham Young University Library, Provo, Utah.

Cumming, Alfred, Papers. Manuscripts Division, Duke University Library, Durham, North Carolina. Microfilm copies of selected items in Manuscripts Division, Howard-Tilton Memorial Library, Tulane University, New Orleans, Louisiana.

Deed Books B, F, and J. Office of the Clerk of Court, Brazoria County, Angleton, Texas.

Dowdle, John Clark, Diary (typescript). Manuscripts Division, Brigham Young University Library, Provo, Utah.

Edwards, Esaias, Diary (typescript). Manuscripts Division, Brigham Young University Library, Provo, Utah.

Egan, William M., Journal. Collection of Western Americana, Yale University Library, New Haven, Connecticut. Microfilm copy in Manuscripts Division, Howard-Tilton Memorial Library, Tulane University, New Orleans, Louisiana.

Farr, Winslow, Diary (typescript). Manuscripts Division, Brigham Young University Library, Provo, Utah.

Gilmer, Jeremy F., Papers. Southern Historical Collection, University of North Carolina Library, Chapel Hill, North Carolina. Microfilm copies of selected items in Manuscripts Division, Howard-Tilton Memorial Library, Tulane University, New Orleans, Louisiana.

Ginn, John L. "Mormon and Indian Wars." Collection of Western Americana, Yale University Library, New Haven, Connecticut. Microfilm copy in Manuscripts Division, Tulane University Library, New Orleans, Louisiana.

Hardee, William J., Papers. Manuscript Division, Library of Congress, Washington, D.C. Microfilm copies of selected items in Manuscripts Division, Howard-Tilton Memorial Library, Tulane University, New Orleans, Louisiana.

Haris, Silas. "A Sketch of Silas Haris' Life" (microfilm copy). HM MS. Film 132. Huntington Library, San Marino, California.

Harley, Edwin, Diary. In Mormon File, uncatalogued. Huntington Library, San Marino, California.

Harris, Isham G., Letter Book (microfilm copy). Tennessee State Library and Archives, Nashville, Tennessee; and Manuscripts Division, Howard-Tilton Memorial Library, Tulane University, New Orleans, Louisiana.

"Headquarters Book of Albert Sidney Johnston" (copy). Louisiana Historical Association Collection, Manuscripts Division, Howard-Tilton Memorial Library, Tulane University, New Orleans, Louisiana.

Horne, Mary. "Migration and Settlement of the Latter-Day Saints." Bancroft Library, University of California, Berkeley, California.

Huntington, Oliver B., Diary (typescript). Manuscripts Division, Brigham Young University Library, Provo, Utah.

Illinois Militia Documents, 1833. Illinois State Historical Library, Springfield, Illinois.

"In the Court of Claims." 1886. Fitz John Porter Papers, Manuscript Division, Library of Congress, Washington, D.C.

Johnston, Albert Sidney. "Headquarters Book of Albert Sidney Johnston" (copy). Louisiana Historical Association Collection, Manuscripts Division, Howard-Tilton Memorial Library, Tulane University, New Orleans, Louisiana.

Johnston, Albert Sidney, Papers. Manuscripts Division, Kentucky Historical Society, Louisville, Kentucky. Photostatic copies of selected items in Manuscripts Division, Howard-Tilton Memorial Library, Tulane University, New Orleans, Louisiana.

Johnston, Albert Sidney, Papers. Manuscript Division, Library of Congress, Washington, D.C. Microfilm copies of selected items in Manuscripts Division, Howard-Tilton Memorial Library, Tulane University, New Orleans, Louisiana.

Johnston, Albert Sidney. "Partial Report of Operations around Bowling Green, 1861." War Department Collection of Confederate Records, National Archives, Washington, D.C.

Johnston, Albert Sidney, Paymaster Records. Louisiana Historical Association

Collection, Manuscripts Division, Howard-Tilton Memorial Library, Tulane University, New Orleans, Louisiana.

Johnston, Albert Sidney, and William Preston Johnston, Papers. Mrs. Mason Barret Collection, Manuscripts Division, Howard-Tilton Memorial Library, Tulane University, New Orleans, Louisiana.

Johnston, Josiah Stoddard, Papers. Manuscripts Division, Historical Society of Pennsylvania, Philadelphia, Pennsylvania. Microfilm copies of selected items in Manuscripts Division, Howard-Tilton Memorial Library, Tulane University, New Orleans, Louisiana.

"Journal History" (microfilm copy). Church Historian's Office, Church of Jesus Christ of Latter-Day Saints, Salt Lake City, Utah.

Langston, John. "History of John Langston" (microfilm copy). HM MS. Film 124. Huntington Library, San Marino, California.

Latta, S. R., Letter. In possession of R. F. Little, Metairie, Louisiana.

McAllister, J. D. T., Diary (typescript). Manuscripts Division, Brigham Young University Library, Provo, Utah.

McLean, Ephraim. "My Connexion with the Mexican War." Manuscripts Division, Rosenberg Library, Galveston, Texas.

Mace, Wandle, Journal (typescript). Manuscripts Division, Brigham Young University Library, Provo, Utah.

"Minutes of Examination of Indian Prisoners." Secretary of War Files, National Archives, Washington, D.C. Typescript copy in Black Hawk War Collection, Illinois State Historical Library, Springfield, Illinois.

Miscellaneous Documents Collection. Texas State Archives, Austin, Texas.

Miscellaneous Manuscripts Collection. Jefferson Davis Shrine [Beauvoir], Biloxi, Mississippi.

Miscellaneous Manuscripts Collection. Shiloh National Military Park Library, Shiloh, Tennessee.

Miscellaneous Orders and Letters, Provo Military District Record (typescript). Manuscripts Division, Brigham Young University Library, Provo, Utah.

Morris, George. "Autobiography" (typescript). Manuscripts Division, Brigham Young University Library, Provo, Utah.

Phelps, J. W., Papers. Manuscripts Division, New York Public Library, New York, New York. Microfilm copies of selected items in Manuscripts Division, Howard-Tilton Memorial Library, Tulane University, New Orleans, Louisiana.

Polk, Leonidas, Papers. Department of Archives, University of the South Library, Sewanee, Tennessee. Microfilm copies in Southern Historical Collection, University of North Carolina Library, Chapel Hill, North Carolina.

Polk Leonidas, Papers. Manuscript Division, Library of Congress, Washington, D.C. Microfilm copies of selected items in Manuscripts Division, Howard-Tilton Memorial Library, Tulane University, New Orleans, Louisiana.

Porter, Fitz John, Papers. Manuscript Division, Library of Congress, Washington, D.C. Microfilm copies of selected items in Manuscripts Division, Howard-Tilton Memorial Library, Tulane University, New Orleans, Louisiana.

Post Orders, United States Military Academy, 1822–1826. Department of Archives, United States Military Academy, West Point, New York.

Pownall, J. W. "Sick Report Book of Company F, 70th Regiment." Louisiana Historical Association Collection, Howard-Tilton Memorial Library, Tulane University, New Orleans, Louisiana.

Preston, William, Diary. War Department Collection of Confederate Records, National Archives, Washington, D.C.

Provo Military District Record. Manuscripts Division, Brigham Young University Library, Provo, Utah.

"Questions Propounded to Genl. A. S. Johnston by the Special Committee of the House of Representatives, and Answers." War Department Collection of Confederate Records, National Archives, Washington, D. C.

Record of Orders, Returns and Courts-Martial of 2nd Brigade, 1st Division, Nauvoo Legion (typescript). Manuscripts Division, Brigham Young University Library, Provo, Utah.

Records of the Clerk of Court, Brazoria County, Angleton, Texas. Deed Books B, F, and J.

Records of the Town Clerk, Salisbury, Connecticut. Copies of selected items in Manuscripts Division, Howard-Tilton Memorial Library, Tulane University, New Orleans, Louisiana.

Records of the War Department. National Archives, Washington, D.C.

Reynolds, John, Order and Letter Book (April 13–May 5, 1832). Black Hawk War Collection, Illinois State Historical Library, Springfield, Illinois. Microfilm copy in Manuscripts Division, Howard-Tilton Memorial Library, Tulane University, New Orleans, Louisiana.

Richards, Franklin D. "Narrative." Bancroft Library, University of California. Berkeley, California.

Richards, Jane. "Reminiscences." Bancroft Library, University of California, Berkeley, California.

Roman, Alfred, Papers. Manuscript Division, Library of Congress, Washington, D.C. Microfilm copies of selected items in Manuscripts Division, Howard-Tilton Memorial Library, Tulane University, New Orleans, Louisiana.

Romney, Hannah Hood Hill. "Autobiography" (microfilm copy). HM MS. Film 147. Huntington Library, San Marino, California.

Rusk, Thomas J., Papers. Archives, University of Texas Library, Austin, Texas. Microfilm copies of selected items in Manuscripts Division, Howard-Tilton Memorial Library, Tulane University, New Orleans, Louisiana.

Sherman, W. T., Papers. Manuscript Division, Library of Congress, Washington, D.C. Microfilm copy in Manuscripts Division, Howard-Tilton Memorial Library, Tulane University, New Orleans, Louisiana.

Smith, Ashbel, Papers. Archives, University of Texas Library, Austin, Texas. Microfilm copies of selected items in Manuscripts Division, Howard-Tilton Memorial Library, Tulane University, New Orleans, Louisiana.

Smith, Azariah, Journal (microfilm copy). HM MS. Film 314. Huntington Library, San Marino, California.

Smith, Elias, Journal. HM MS. Film 245. Huntington Library, San Marino, California.

Solomons, M. J., Papers. Manuscripts Division, Duke University Library, Durham, North Carolina.

Stout, Allen Joseph, Journal (microfilm copy). HM FAC 560. Huntington Library, San Marino, California.

Stout, Hosea, Diary (typescript). Manuscripts Division, Brigham Young University Library, Provo, Utah.

Texas Historical Society Papers. Manuscripts Division, Rosenberg Library, Galveston, Texas.

Tracy, Nancy. "Narrative." Bancroft Library, University of California, Berkeley, California.

Ulmer, I. B., Jr., Papers. Southern Historical Collection, University of North Carolina Library, Chapel Hill, North Carolina. Microfilm copies of selected items in Manuscripts Division, Howard-Tilton Memorial Library, Tulane University, New Orleans, Louisiana.

Walker, Charles L., Diary (typescript). Manuscripts Division, Brigham Young University Library, Provo, Utah.

War Department Collection of Confederate Records. National Archives, Washington, D.C.

Whitney, Mrs. Ellen. "Chronology of the Black Hawk War," in Black Hawk War Collection, Illinois State Historical Library, Springfield, Illinois.

Wells, Daniel. "Narrative." Bancroft Library, University of California, Berkeley, California.

Young, Brigham, Papers. Collection of Western Americana, Yale University Library, New Haven, Connecticut. Microfilm copies of selected items in Howard-Tilton Memorial Library, Tulane University, New Orleans, Louisiana.

Public Documents

House Executive Document 71, 35th Congress, 1st Session. Vol. X. Washington, D.C.: Government Printing Office, 1858.

House Executive Document 2, 35th Congress, 2nd Session. Vol. II, Pt. II. Washington, D.C.: Government Printing Office, 1859.

House Executive Document No. 2, 35th Congress, 2nd Session. Vol. II, Pt. III. Washington, D.C.: Government Printing Office, 1859.

Senate Executive Document No. 11, 35th Congress, 1st Session. Vol. III. Washington, D.C.: Government Printing Office, 1858.

Senate Executive Document No. 1, 35th Congress, 2nd Session. Vol. I. Washington, D.C.: Government Printing Office, 1859.

Senate Executive Document 2, 36th Congress, 1st Session. Vol. II. Washington, D.C.: Government Printing Office, 1860.

The War of the Rebellion: A Compilation of the Official Records of the Union and Confederate Armies. 127 vols. and index. Washington, D.C.: Government Printing Office, 1880–1901.

Newspapers

American Flag (Matamoros, Mexico), 1846. In Library of Congress, Washington, D.C.

Cincinnati Daily Enquirer. Clipping, n.d., in Johnston Papers, Barret Collection.

Dallas Weekly Herald, 1867. In Texas State Library, Austin, Texas.

Daily Delta (New Orleans), 1861. In Public Library, New Orleans, Louisiana.

Daily Picayune (New Orleans), 1846, 1862, 1865. In Public Library, New Orleans, Louisiana.

Daily True Delta (New Orleans), 1861. In Public Library, New Orleans, Louisiana.

Deseret News (Salt Lake City), 1858–1859. In Brigham Young University Library, Provo, Utah.

Galveston Weekly News, 1855. In Rosenberg Library, Galveston, Texas.

New York Daily Tribune, 1858–1859. In Library of Congress, Washington, D.C.

New York Times, 1858. In Library of Congress, Washington, D.C.

Oakland Tribune, 1935. In Bancroft Library, University of California, Berkeley, California.

San Francisco Daily Herald. Clipping, n.d., in Johnston Papers, Barret Collection.

San Francisco Evening Bulletin, 1861. In Bancroft Library, University of California, Berkeley, California.

St. Louis Globe-Democrat. Clipping, n.d., in Scrapbook, Johnston Papers, Barret Collection.

Valley Tan (Salt Lake City), 1858–1859. In Public Library, Salt Lake City, Utah.

Books and Pamphlets

A Soldier's Honor: With Reminiscences of Major-General Earl Van Dorn. By his comrades. New York: Abbey Press, 1902.

Alter, J. Cecil (ed.) . *The Utah War: Journal of Albert Tracy.* Salt Lake City: Utah State Historical Society, 1945.

Anderson, Nels. *Desert Saints: The Mormon Frontier in Utah.* Chicago: University of Chicago Press, 1942.

Arrington, Leonard J. *Great Basin Kingdom: An Economic History of the Latter-Day Saints, 1830–1900.* Cambridge: Harvard University Press, 1958.

Barker, Eugene C. (ed.) . *The Austin Papers.* 3 vols. Washington, D.C.: American Historical Association, Vols. I, II, 1924, 1928. Austin: University of Texas, Vol. III, 1927.

Barker, Eugene C. *The Life of Stephen F. Austin: Founder of Texas, 1793–1836.* Dallas: Cokesbury Press, 1926.

Bean, George W. *Autobiography of George Washington Bean.* Salt Lake City: Utah Printing Company, 1945.

Before the Indian Claims Commission. Chicago, n.d. In Black Hawk War Collection, Illinois State Historical Library, Springfield, Illinois.

Best, Edna H. *The Historic Past of Washington, Mason County, Kentucky.* Cynthiana, Kentucky: Hobson Book Press, 1944.

Billon, Frederic L. *Annals of St. Louis in Its Territorial Days.* St. Louis: Privately printed for the author, 1888.

Binkley, William C. *The Expansionist Movement in Texas, 1836–1850.* Berkeley: University of California Press, 1925.

Binkley, William C. *The Texas Revolution.* Baton Rouge: Louisiana State University Press, 1952.

Boynton, Edward C. *History of West Point and of the United States Military Academy.* New York: D. Van Nostrand Company, Inc., 1863.

Brown, John Mason. *Memoranda of the Preston Family.* Frankfort, Kentucky: S. I. M. Major, 1870.

Butler, Mann. *A History of the Commonwealth of Kentucky.* N.p., n.d.

Cable, George Washington. "New Orleans before the Capture," in *Battles and Leaders of the Civil War,* II, 14–21. Edited by R. U. Johnson and C. C. Buel. New York: Century Company, 1884–1888.

Catton, Bruce. *Grant Moves South.* Boston: Little, Brown & Company, 1960.

Christian, Asa K. *Mirabeau Buonaparte Lamar.* Austin: Von Boeckman–Jones Company, 1922.

Cist, Henry M. *The Army of the Cumberland.* New York: Charles Scribner's Sons, 1882.

Clift, G. Glenn. *History of Maysville and Mason County.* 2 vols. Lexington: Transylvania Printing Company, 1936.

Cole, Cyrenus. *I am a Man: The Indian Black Hawk.* Iowa City: State Historical Society of Iowa, 1938.

Conger, Arthur L. *The Rise of U. S. Grant.* New York: Century Company, 1931.

Cox, James. *Old and New St. Louis.* St. Louis: Central Biographical Publishing Company, 1894.

Crooker, Lucian B. *A Section of a Battle: Observations upon the Conduct of the 55th Illinois Infantry in the First Day's Battle of Shiloh.* N.p., n.d.

Darby, John F. *Personal Recollections.* St. Louis: G. I. Jones and Company, 1880.

Davis, Jefferson. *A Short History of the Confederate States of America.* New York: Belford Company, 1890.

Donald, David (ed.). *Why the North Won the Civil War.* Baton Rouge: Louisiana State University Press, 1960.

Drake, Benjamin. *The Life and Adventures of Black Hawk.* Cincinnati: G. Conclin, 1844.

Duke, Basil W. *History of Morgan's Cavalry.* Cincinnati: Miami Printing and Publishing Company, 1867.

Eisenschiml, Otto. *The Story of Shiloh.* Chicago: Chicago Civil War Round Table, 1946.

Floyd, John B. *Report of the Secretary of War.* Washington: Government Printing Office, 1858.

Foote, Shelby. *Shiloh.* New York: New American Library, 1961.

Friend, Llerena. *Sam Houston: The Great Designer.* Austin: University of Texas Press, 1954.

Fuller, J. F. C. *The Generalship of Ulysses S. Grant.* New York: Dodd, Mead & Company, 1929.

Furniss, Norman F. *The Mormon Conflict, 1850–1859.* New Haven: Yale University Press, 1960.

Gammel, H. P. N. (ed.). *The Laws of Texas, 1822–1897.* 10 vols. Austin, 1866–1898.

Grant, Ulysses S. *Personal Memoirs of U. S. Grant.* Edited by E. B. Long. New York: World Publishing Company, 1952.

Green, Rena Maverick (ed.). *Samuel Maverick, Texan, 1803–1870.* San Antonio: Privately printed, 1952.

Gulick, Charles A., Jr., and Katherine Elliott (eds.). *The Papers of Mirabeau Buonaparte Lamar.* 6 vols. Austin: A. C. Baldwin & Sons, Printers, 1920–1927.

Hafen, Leroy R., and Ann W. (eds.). *The Utah Expedition, 1857–1858.* Glendale, California: A. H. Clark Company, 1958.

Herr, John K., and Edward S. Wallace. *The Story of the U.S. Cavalry, 1775–1942.* Boston: Little, Brown & Company, 1953.

Historical Addresses Delivered at the Centennial Celebration in Salisbury, Connecticut. Pittsfield, Massachusetts: n.p., 1876.

Hogan, William R. *The Texas Republic: A Social and Economic History.* Norman: University of Oklahoma Press, 1947.

Hollon, W. Eugene. *Beyond the Cross Timbers: The Travels of Randolph B. Marcy, 1812–1887.* Norman: University of Oklahoma Press, 1955.

Horn, Stanley F. *The Army of Tennessee.* New York: Bobbs-Merrill Company, Inc., 1941.

Jackson, Donald (ed.). *Black Hawk: An Autobiography.* Urbana: University of Illinois Press, 1955.

Johnson, R. U., and C. C. Buel (eds.). *Battles and Leaders of the Civil War.* 4 vols. New York: Century Company, 1884–1888.

Johnson, Richard W. *A Soldier's Reminiscences in Peace and War.* Philadelphia: J. B. Lippincott Company, 1886.

Johnston, William Preston. *The Johnstons of Salisbury.* New Orleans: Press of L. Graham & Son, 1897.

Johnston, William Preston. *The Life of General Albert Sidney Johnston.* New York: D. Appleton & Company, Inc., 1878.

Jordan, Thomas. "Notes of a Confederate Staff Officer at Shiloh," in *Battles and Leaders of the Civil War*, I, 594–595. Edited by R. U. Johnson and C. C. Buel. New York: Century Company, 1884–1888.

Jordan, Thomas, and Roger Pryor. *The Campaigns of Lieut. General N. B. Forrest and of Forrest's Cavalry*. New York: Blelack & Company, 1868.

Kennedy, Elijah R. *The Contest for California in 1861*. Boston: Houghton Mifflin Company, 1912.

Keyes, Erasmus D. *Fifty Years' Observations of Men and Events, Civil and Military*. New York: Charles Scribner's Sons, 1884.

Lewis, Lloyd. *Sherman: Fighting Prophet*. New York: Harcourt, Brace and Company, Inc., 1932.

Lockett, S. H. "Surprise and Withdrawal at Shiloh," in *Battles and Leaders of the Civil War*, I, 604–606. Edited by R. U. Johnson and C. C. Buel. New York: Century Company, 1884–1888.

Marmont, Marshal Auguste F. *The Spirit of Military Institutions*. Translated by Frank Schaller. Columbia, South Carolina: Evans and Cogswell, 1864.

Nichols, James L. *Confederate Engineers*. (No. 5 in Confederate Centennial Studies Series.) Tuscaloosa: Confederate Publishing Company, 1957.

O'Dea, Thomas F. *The Mormons*. Chicago: University of Chicago Press, 1957.

Olmsted, Frederick Law. *A Journey through Texas*. 2 vols. New York: Dix, Edwards & Company, 1857.

Parks, Joseph H. *General Leonidas Polk, C.S.A.* Baton Rouge: Louisiana State University Press, 1962.

Price, George F. *Across the Continent with the Fifth Cavalry*. New York: D. Van Nostrand Company, Inc., 1883.

Rawle, William. *A View of the Constitution of the United States of America*. Philadelphia: P. H. Nicklin, 1829.

Reed, D. W. *The Battle of Shiloh and the Organizations Engaged*. Washington: Government Printing Office, 1903.

Reynolds, John. *My Own Times*. Belleville, Illinois: B. H. Perryman, Printer, 1855.

Rhodes, James Ford. *History of the United States from the Compromise of 1850*. 9 vols. New York: Macmillan Company, 1900–1928.

Rich, Joseph W. *The Battle of Shiloh*. Iowa City: State Historical Society of Iowa, 1911.

Richardson, Rupert Norval. *The Comanche Barrier to South Plains Settlement*. Glendale, California: Arthur H. Clark Company, 1933.

Rodenbough, Theophilus F. (ed.). *From Everglade to Cañon with the Second Dragoons*. New York: D. Van Nostrand Company, Inc., 1875.

Roman, Alfred. *The Military Operations of General Beauregard in the War between the States, 1861 to 1865*. 2 vols. New York: Harper & Brothers, 1884.

Rowland, Dunbar (ed.). *Jefferson Davis, Constitutionalist: His Letters, Papers and Speeches*. 10 vols. Jackson: Mississippi Department of Archives and History, 1923.

Sacramento City and Its Resources: A Souvenir of the Bee. Sacramento: H. S. Crocker Company, 1894.

Schaller, Frank. "A Review of the Life and Character of the Late General Albert Sidney Johnston, C.S.A.," in *The Spirit of Military Institutions*, by Marshal Auguste F. Marmont. Columbia, South Carolina: Evans and Cogswell, 1864.

Shaw, Arthur Marvin. *William Preston Johnston: A Transitional Figure of the Confederacy*. Baton Rouge: Louisiana State University Press, 1943.

Shepard, Elihu H. *The Early History of St. Louis and Missouri.* St. Louis: Southwestern Book and Publishing Company, 1870.

Sherman, William T. *Memoirs of General William T. Sherman.* 2 vols. New York: D. Appleton & Company, Inc., 1875.

Simpson, James H. *Report of Explorations across the Great Basin of the Territory of Utah.* Washington: Government Printing Office, 1876.

Singletary, Otis A. *The Mexican War.* Chicago: University of Chicago Press, 1960.

Smith, Justin H. *The Annexation of Texas.* New York: Baker & Taylor Company, 1919.

Smith, Justin H. *The War with Mexico.* 2 vols. New York: Macmillan Company, 1919.

Stenhouse, Thomas B. H. *The Rocky Mountain Saints.* New York: D. Appleton & Company, Inc., 1873.

Stevens, Frank E. (ed.) . *Wakefield's History of the Black Hawk War.* Chicago: The Caxton Club, 1908.

Stevens, Frank E. *The Black Hawk War.* Chicago: F. E. Stevens, 1903.

Strode, Hudson. *Jefferson Davis: Confederate President.* New York: Harcourt, Brace and Company, Inc., 1959.

Taylor, Jesse. "The Defense of Fort Henry," in *Battles and Leaders of the Civil War,* I, 368–372. Edited by R. U. Johnson and C. C. Buel. New York: Century Company, 1884–1888.

Taylor, Richard. *Destruction and Reconstruction: Personal Experiences of the Late War.* Edited by Richard B. Harwell. New York: Longmans, Green & Company, Inc., 1955.

Thompson, Edwin Porter. *History of the First Kentucky Brigade.* Cincinnati: Caxton Publishing House, 1868.

Thwaites, Reuben Gold. *How George Rogers Clark Won the Northwest and Other Essays in Western History.* Chicago: A. C. McClurg & Company, 1903.

United States War Department. *The War of the Rebellion: A Compilation of the Official Records of the Union and Confederate Armies.* 127 vols. and index. Washington, D.C.: Government Printing Office, 1880–1901.

von Clausewitz, Karl. *On War.* Translated by J. J. Graham. 3 vols. New York: E. P. Dutton & Company, Inc., 1940.

Williams, Amelia W., and Eugene C. Barker (eds.) . *The Writings of Sam Houston, 1813–1863.* 8 vols. Austin: University of Texas Press, 1938–1943.

Williams, Kenneth P. *Lincoln Finds a General.* 5 vols. New York: Macmillan Company, 1949–1959.

Williams, T. Harry. *P. G. T. Beauregard: Napoleon in Gray.* Baton Rouge: Louisiana State University Press, 1954.

Williams, T. Harry. "The Military Leadership of North and South," in *Why the North Won the Civil War.* Edited by David Donald. Baton Rouge: Louisiana State University Press, 1960.

Winfrey, Dorman H., *et al.* (eds.) . *Texas Indian Papers, 1825–1843.* 4 vols. Austin: Texas State Library, 1959–1961.

Wood, Oliver E., (ed.) . *The West Point Scrap Book.* New York: D. Van Nostrand Company, Inc., 1874.

Wortham, Louis J. *A History of Texas: From Wilderness to Commonwealth.* 5 vols. Fort Worth: Wortham-Molyneaux Company, 1924.

Wyeth, John Allan. *Life of General Nathan Bedford Forrest.* New York: Harper & Brothers, 1899.

Yoakum, Henderson K. *History of Texas.* 2 vols. New York: Redfield, 1855.
Younger, Edward (ed.). *Inside the Confederate Government: The Diary of Robert Garlic Hill Kean.* New York: Oxford University Press, 1957.

Articles

Anderson, Robert. "Reminiscences of the Black Hawk War," *Report and Collections of the State Historical Society of Wisconsin,* X (1888), 167–176.
Buell, Don C. "Shiloh Reviewed," *Century Magazine,* XXXI (February, 1886), 749–781.
Catton, Bruce. "Union Discipline and Leadership in the Civil War," *Marine Corps Gazette* (January, 1956), pp. 18–25.
Denis, Alberta Johnston. "Mrs. Albert Sidney Johnston," *Texas Magazine,* I (May 1897), 427–430.
Duke, Basil W. "The Battle of Shiloh," *Southern Bivouac,* II (January, 1884), 201–216.
Dustin, Charles M. "The Knights of the Golden Circle," *Pacific Monthly,* XXVI (November, 1911), 495–504.
Editorial, *Harper's Weekly,* II (January 30, 1858), 72–74.
Editorial, *Pony Express Courier,* XIV (March, 1948), 2.
Gilbert, Benjamin F. "The Confederate Minority in California," *California Historical Society Quarterly,* XX (June, 1941), 154–170.
Gilbert, Benjamin F. "The Mythical Johnston Conspiracy," *California Historical Society Quarterly,* XXVIII (June, 1949), 165–173.
Grant, Ulysses S. "The Battle of Shiloh," *Century Magazine,* XXIX (February, 1885), 593–613.
Hall, Eliza Calvert. "Bowling Green and the Civil War," *The Filson Club History Quarterly,* XI (October, 1937), 241–251.
Hall, Martin H. "Albert Sidney Johnston's First Confederate Command," *The McNeese Review,* XIII (1962), 3–12.
Hamilton, Holman. "Zachary Taylor and the Black Hawk War," *Wisconsin Magazine of History,* XXIV (March, 1941), 305–315.
Hopkins, Casper T. "The California Recollections of Casper T. Hopkins," *California Historical Society Quarterly,* XXVI (September, 1947), 253–266.
Liddell, St. John R. "Liddell's Record of the Civil War," *Southern Bivouac,* I NS (December, 1885), 411–420; (February, 1886), 529–535.
McWhiney, Grady. "Braxton Bragg at Shiloh," *Tennessee Historical Quarterly* (March, 1962), pp. 19–30.
Morgan, James M. "Extracts from the Reminiscences of General George W. Morgan," *Southwestern Historical Quarterly,* XXX (January, 1927), 178–205.
Muckleroy, Anna. "The Indian Policy of the Republic of Texas," *Southwestern Historical Quarterly,* XXV (April, 1922), 229–260; XXVI (July, 1922–April, 1923), 1–29, 128–148, 184–206.
Olney, Warren. "The Battle of Shiloh," *Overland Monthly,* V (June, 1883), 577–589.
Roland, Charles P. "Albert Sidney Johnston and the Loss of Forts Henry and Donelson," *Journal of Southern History,* XXIII (February, 1957), 45–69.
Roland, Charles P. "Albert Sidney Johnston and the Shiloh Campaign," *Civil War History,* IV (December, 1958), 355–382.
Roland, Charles P., and Richard C. Robbins (eds.). "The Diary of Eliza (Mrs. Albert Sidney) Johnston: The Second Cavalry Comes to Texas," *Southwestern Historical Quarterly,* LX (April, 1957), 463–500.

Scammell, J. M. "Military Units in Southern California, 1853–1862," *California Historical Society Quarterly*, XXIX (September, 1950) , 229–240.

Smith, Henry, "The Indian Campaign of 1832," *Report and Collections of the State Historical Society of Wisconsin*, X (1888) , 150–166.

Stowers, Robert E., and John M. Ellis (eds.) . "Charles A. Scott's Diary of the Utah Expedition, 1857–1861," *Utah Historical Quarterly*, XVIII (April, 1960) , 389–402.

Unpublished Studies

Allen, Lorna Bagley. "A Study of the Alleged Mormon Rebellion." Master's thesis, Brigham Young University, Provo, Utah, 1931.

Cannon, M. Hamlin. "The Mormon War: A Study in Territorial Rebellion." Master's thesis, George Washington University, Washington, D.C., 1938.

Gardner, Hamilton. "The Utah Territorial Militia." Utah Historical Society Library, Salt Lake City, Utah.

Hansen, Ralph. "The Nauvoo Legion in Utah." Master's thesis, Brigham Young University, Provo, Utah, 1954.

Mathis, Don Richard. "Camp Floyd in Retrospect." Master's thesis, University of Utah, Salt Lake City, Utah, 1959.

Whitney, Ellen. "Chronology of the Black Hawk War." Illinois State Historical Library, Springfield, Illinois.

Zobell, Alfred L. "Thomas L. Kane: Ambassador to the Mormons." Master's thesis, University of Utah, Salt Lake City, Utah, 1944.

INDEX

DATE DUE			
			PRINTED IN U.S.A.
GAYLORD			